Atlas of European Architecture

Atlas
of
European
Architecture

Brian Sachar

 VAN NOSTRAND REINHOLD COMPANY

Copyright © 1984 by Research Publishing Corporation
Library of Congress Catalog Card Number 83–1171
ISBN 0–442–28149–8

Printed in the United States of America

Published by Van Nostrand Reinhold Company Inc.
135 West 50th Street
New York, New York 10020

Van Nostrand Reinhold Company Limited
Molly Millars Lane
Wokingham, Berkshire RG11 2PY, England

Van Nostrand Reinhold
480 La Trobe Street
Melbourne, Victoria 3000, Australia

Macmillan of Canada
Division of Gage Publishing Limited
164 Commander Boulevard
Agincourt, Ontario M1S 3C7, Canada

16 15 14 13 12 11 10 9 8 7 6 5 4 3 2 1

Library of Congress Cataloging in Publication Data
Sachar, Brian.
  Atlas of European architecture.
  Includes indexes.
  1. Architecture—Europe. I. Title.
NA950.S2 1984   720′.94   83–1171
ISBN 0–442–28149–8

Contents

List of Maps

Preface and Acknowledgments

This atlas is designed to be of use to the architect, traveler, historian, artist, and interested layman. It succinctly categorizes, describes, and locates buildings and urban spaces of architectural merit in Western Europe. The entries described range from 4700 B.C. to the present.

In the course of writing this book, I have worked with many people and would now like to thank them for their assistance:

Mary Luka, Hazel Dick, Jet Hofstee, Linda Venator, and Beth Tondreau;

Paulien Houwink for her valuable advice on the Netherlands chapter;

the New York tourist offices and embassies of the relevant countries, especially Charles Ocheltree of the Spanish National Tourist Office;

Barbara Heitel, Clark Kellogg, Christopher Landis, Christina Hutchings, Ellen Sokolow-Molinari, and Janice Slivko for their assistance with the maps;

Jeff Bianco, Revel Fox, John Rennie, and Henry Villet for supplying photographs, as well as the many architects who generously sent me pictures of their own work;

in particular, Franziska Porges of Architectural Color Slides for allowing me to use many of the slides in her professional collection; these slides may be obtained directly from Architectural Color Slides, 197 Grant Street, Lexington, MA 02173;

and finally, Gage Cogswell for doing a marvelous job typing this manuscript.

Introduction

How to Use This Book

This book is divided into twelve chapters; each chapter encompasses a single country. The buildings listed in each country are arranged in an alphabetical sequence derived from their geographic location (town or city name). The buildings listed under a town name are then arranged in a chronological sequence in accordance with the date of construction of each building. Smaller towns that are generally associated with a larger city or town are listed under the respective city's heading. These out-of-sequence place names can still be found alphabetically, by using the Index of Towns. All town names are spelled in the language of the country. The English equivalent, when applicable, is given in parentheses, sometimes with a third alternative if the country has two official languages. All prefixes are ignored; towns such as Bad Hersfeld, Den Haag, Le Havre are listed under their proper (second) name: Hersfeld, Haag, Havre.

Every entry listed in this book is numbered. A typical entry with explanation is shown here. The entry number relates to a map in the relevant chapter (each chapter has its own series of numbers, beginning with 1). There are two series of maps in this book: country maps and city maps. Every location listed in the text with a coordinate in roman type (for example, A2) is indicated on the country map. Every site in a major city with a coordinate in italic type (for example, *A3*) is indicated on a city map. Use the grid coordinates on the borders of each map to find the precise location of an entry.

A photograph illustrating a particular entry always appears beneath the address or architect's name for that entry.

The symbol • indicates another structure close to the entry that is worth seeing. The symbol c is used as an abbreviation for century throughout the book.

Use the Index of Architects at the back of this book to find buildings by particular architects.

For the sake of consistency and clarity, architects' last names throughout the book are preceded by their first initials only.

Useful Information

The central and overseas tourist offices of each country can supply a list of the local tourist offices throughout the country. A telephone call to the local tourist office in advance can save the disappointment of a wasted trip.

Many of the buildings in this book are privately owned and are not open to the public. Ask permission to visit by writing in advance. Certain buildings are open to specialist tours; inquire about this at the tourist office. Even those buildings open to the public may have certain restricted areas or may require that you be guided around the building.

A flashlight and binoculars are very useful in dimly lit churches and cathedrals. Some churches in Europe have coin-operated lighting for certain paintings—take enough change. Many of the smaller churches are only open at certain hours. If closed, inquire in the neighborhood if the custodian is available. Certain triptychs are kept closed for security reasons but are opened on request.

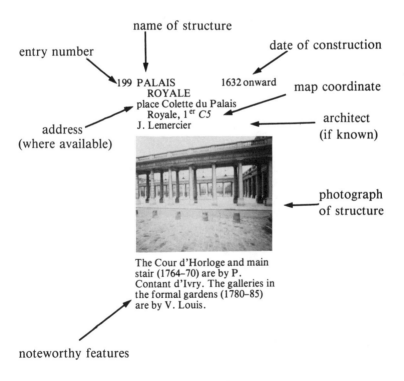

name of structure

entry number

date of construction

199 PALAIS ROYALE
1632 onward

map coordinate

place Colette du Palais Royale, 1er *C5*
J. Lemercier

architect (if known)

address (where available)

photograph of structure

The Cour d'Horloge and main stair (1764–70) are by P. Contant d'Ivry. The galleries in the formal gardens (1780–85) are by V. Louis.

noteworthy features

To my mother and the
memory of my father

Austria

Pacher Altarpiece; *see entry 62*

Austria

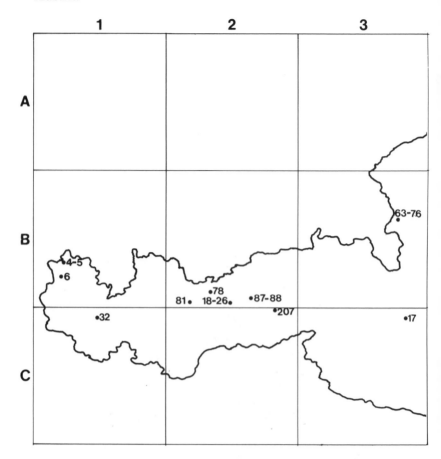

ADMONT B4

1 STIFT   18th c
(Benedictine abbey)

Rebuilt after a fire in 1865. The
original rococo library (1774)
survived.

ALTENBURG A5
6 km (4 mi) SW of Horn

2 STIFT   1650–1742
(Benedictine abbey)

Fine grouping of baroque
buildings. The library (1730–33)
and grand stair are by J.
Munggenast.

BAD (prefix)
See proper (second) name

BAD–HALL B4
19 km (12 mi) W of Steyr

3 LANDESVILLA   1912–14
(forestry station)
Parkstrasse
M. Balzarek

•1 km (0.6 mi) away, to the
southwest, is Pfarrkirchen, a
church with a delightful rococo
interior (1744).

BREGENZ B1

4 HAUPTSCHULE   1914
(high school)
Belruptstrasse 37
E. Braun

5 SIEDLUNG AN   1971–76
    DER ACH
(housing)
Achsiedlungsstrasse
J. Albrecht, E. Schulze-
Fielitz, and G. Wratzfeld

CHRISTKINDL
See Steyr

DORNBIRN B1

6 ORF STUDIO   1969–72
(television station)
Höchsterstrasse
G. Peichl

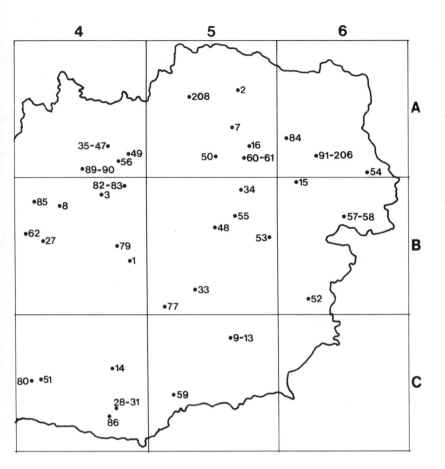

4	5	6

•208 •2

•7

35-47• •84
•49 50• •16 •91-206
•89-90 •56 •60-61 •54

82-83• •34 •15
•3
•85 •8 •55
•48 •57-58
•62 53•
•27 •79
•1

•33 •52
•77

•9-13

•14
80• •51 •59
28-31
86

A B C

DÜRNSTEIN A5

7 PFARRKIRCHE   1720–26
(parish church)
J. Munggenast

Baroque church on the Danube.

GMUNDEN B4

8 STRANDBAD   1927
(beach facilities)
F. Gessner

GRAZ C5

Museum: Joanneum
Landesmuseum (Alte Galerie),
Raubergasse 10. 12th- to 16th-c
Styrian altarpieces and stained
glass works.

9 LANDHAUS   1557–65
(provincial council)
Landhausgasse
D. d'Allio

Arcaded courtyard.

10 VERWALTUNGS-   1932
      GEBÄUDE DER GRAZER
      STADTWERKE

(office building)
Andreas Hoferplatz 15
R. Steinbochl

11 SEELSORGE-   1969–71
      ZENTRUM
(parish center)
Eisteichsiedlung
F. Schuster

12 DR. FREY HOUSE   1970–72
Bunsengasse
E. A. Plischke

Outskirts of Graz

13 KATHOLISCHE   1963–69
      PÄDAGOGISCHE
      AKADEMIE
(Catholic academy)
Georgigasse 85–89,
   Graz-Eggenburg
G. Domenig and E. Huth

GURK C4

14 DOM   1140–1200
(Gurk Cathedral)

The finest Romanesque
building in Austria. Gothic
front porch and modifications

to the roof vaulting. Well-preserved interiors with 13th-c wall paintings (especially in the Bishop's Chapel). Baroque high altar (1626–32) and pulpit (1740). Fine crypt (1174).

HEILIGENKREUZ B6
30 km (19 mi) SW of Wien

15 STIFT   1135–87
(Abbey of the Holy Cross)

Romanesque nave. Gothic choir added later (1288–95).

HERZOGENBURG A5
12 km (7 mi) N of St-Pölten

16 KLOSTER   18th c
(monastery)

Founded in the 12th c; rebuilt in the baroque style. Great hall and stair (1716–18) by J. B. Fischer von Erlach. Great hall frescoes by B. Altomonte.

HOFGASTEIN (Bad) C3

17 KURZENTRUM   1970–74
(spa)
R. Stelzer and W. Hutter

INNSBRUCK B2

Museum: Tiroler Landesmuseum Ferdinandeum, Museumstrasse 15. Mainly Tyrolean paintings. Some works by Baldung, Breu, and Amberger; 17-c Dutch masters.

18 HOFKIRCHE   1553–63
(church)
Hofgasse

The Grabmal Kaiser Maximilians I (Mausoleum of Maximilian, 1584) inside is an outstanding Renaissance work. Also see the separate Silberne (silver) chapel; tomb of Philippine Welser (first bay, left).

19 DOM-ZU ST. JAKOB 1717–22
(cathedral)
Domplatz

Interiors by C. and E. Asam.

20 HOFBURG   1770
(palace)
Rennweg

Tyrolean baroque. Riesensaal (giant's hall) within.

21 APARTMENT   1930–31
    BUILDING
Erzherzog Eugenstrasse 7
W. Stigler

22 SIGMUND-KRIPP-   1964
    HAUS
(youth center)
Sillgasse 8a
J. Lackner

23 ORF STUDIO   1969–72
(television station)
Rennweg
G. Peichl

One of a series of similar buildings around the country, all by Peichl.

Outskirts of Innsbruck

24 HAUPTSCHULE   1930–31
(high school)
Fürstenweg 13, Innsbruck-Hötting
F. Baumann and T. Prachensky

25 PFARRKIRCHE   1958–60
    PIUS X
(church)
Innsbruck-Neu Arzl
J. Lackner

26 PFARRKIRCHE   1965–67
(church)
Völs
J. Lackner

ISCHL (Bad) B4

27 KURMITTELHAUS   1930
(thermal bathhouse)
Bahnhofstrasse
C. Holzmeister

KLAGENFURT C4

28 KÜNSTLERHAUS   1913–14
(museum)
Goethepark 1
F. Baumgartner

29 DR. HERBST VILLA 1930–33
Getreidegasse 17
S. Schiffler

30 HOCHSCHULE FÜR 1970–71
    BILDUNGSWISSEN-
    SCHAFTEN
(technical high school)
Hochschulstrasse 67
R. Rainer

31 STRANDBAD MARIA   1973
    LORETTO
(swimming baths)
K. Hack and F. Orsini-Rosenberg

KLOSTERNEUBURG

See Wien (entry 206)

LANGEN AM ARLBERG C1

12 km (7 mi) W of St. Anton

32 KIRCHE   1928–29
(church)
H. Fessler

LEOBEN B5

33 FORSCHUNGS-   1969–73
    ZENTRUM ALPINE
    MONTANGESELL-
    SCHAFT
(research institute)
G. Domenig and E. Huth

LILIENFELD B5

34 STIFT   1202–30
(abbey)
Gothic. Early hall choir.

LINZ A4

Museum: Neue Galerie der
Stadt Linz/Wolfgang-Gurlitt-
Museum, Blütenstrasse 15.
19th- and 20th-c German and
Austrian painters: Schiele,
Kokoschka, etc.

35 PRIESTERSEMINAR- 1717–25
    KIRCHE
(church)
Dametzstrasse
J. L. von Hildebrandt

36 SIEDLUNG   1921
    SCHARLINZ
(housing)
Haydnstrasse
K. Kuhne

37 TABAKFABRIK   1929–35
(tobacco factory)
Untere Donaulände 74
P. Behrens and A. Popp

38 ROSENBAUER   1930
    HOUSE
Pöstlingberg 116
L. Welzenbacher

39 KOLPINGHAUS   1930–31
    CENTER
Langgasse 13
H. Steineder

40 KIRCHE   1958–61
    ST. THERESIA
(church)
Losensteinerstrasse 6
R. Schwarz

41 BRUCKNERHAUS   1962–73
(concert hall)
Untere Donaulände
K. and H. Siren

42 SYNAGOGUE   1966–68
Bethlehemstrasse 26
F. Goffitzer

43 ORF STUDIO   1969–73
(television studio)
Blumauerstrasse/Franckstrasse
G. Peichl

44 AMTSGEBÄUDE   1970–73
    DER LANDES-
    REGIERUNG
(regional administration offices)
Kärntnerstrasse
Werkgruppe Linz (Frohnwieser,
Pammer, Telesco, and
Werthgarner)

45 KATHOLISCHE   1970–75
    PÄDAGOGISCHE
    AKADEMIE
(Catholic academy)
Salesianumweg
O. Sackmauer and F. Riepl

Outskirts of Linz

46 SIEDLUNG   1965–69
(housing)
Puchenau
R. Rainer

47 SIEDLUNG   1966–76
    VOGLER
(housing)
Hörsching
G. Feuerstein

MARIAZELL B5

48 KIRCHE   1644–1704
(church)
D. Sciassia

Interesting Gothic structure
enlarged by complex baroque
extensions on three sides. The
original Gothic porch is flanked
by towers added by Sciassia.
Baldachin by J. E. Fischer von
Erlach. High altar (1704) by
J. B. Fischer von Erlach.

MAUTHAUSEN A4

26 km (16 mi) E of Linz

49 LAGER DENKMAL   1949
(concentration camp memorial)

Rock quarry that became an
extermination camp (1939–45).
Staircase of Death.

MELK A5

50 STIFT   1702 onward
(Benedictine abbey)
J. Prandtauer

Completed by J. Munggenast after Prandtauer's death. This spectacular baroque church is magnificently sited above the Danube River. The superb church interiors are by J. M. Rottmayr, Fanti, and Troger. The other abbey buildings are only slightly less elaborate.

MILLSTATT C4

51 STIFT   11th c onward
   (abbey)

   Fine Romanesque doorway (on the church portal) and cloisters (Gothic vaulting added later).

OBERWART B6

52 SEELSORGE-   1966–68
   ANLAGE
   (parochial center)
   Maria Himmelfahrt Kirche
   G. Domenig and E. Huth

PAYERBACH B5

53 KHUNER HOUSE   1930
   Kreuzberg
   A. Loos

   Now Pension Alpenhof.

ROHRAU A6
6 km (4 mi) S of Petronell

54 SCHLOSS   16th c onward
   ROHRAU

   Private painting collection of Graf Harrach; Spanish, Dutch, French, and Italian 17th- and 18th-c paintings. Limited access.

ST. ÄGYD AM NEUWALD B5
31 km (19 mi) E of Mariazell

55 EVANGELISCHE   1902–3
   LANDKIRCHE
   (church)
   J. Hoffmann

ST. FLORIAN A4
18 km (11 mi) SE of Linz

56 STIFT   1686–1724
   (abbey)
   C. Carlone

Completed by J. Prandtauer. Fine open stair (1708–14) by Prandtauer. Marmorsaal and library ceiling frescoes by B. Altomonte. In the Altdorfer Galerie are fourteen paintings by A. Altdorfer.

ST. MARGARETHEN B6 (Steinbruch)
14 km (9 mi) E of Eisenstadt

57 ARCHITECT'S HOUSE 1960
   R. Rainer

58 BILDHAUER-   1967
   UNTERKÜNFTE
   (artists' houses)
   J. G. Gsteu

ST. PAUL IN LAVANTTAL C5
50 km (30 mi) E of Klagenfurt

59 STIFTSKIRCHE   1260
   (abbey church)

   Excellent Romanesque church. Gothic roof vault.

ST. PÖLTEN A5

60 STIFTSKIRCHE   1266
   (abbey church)

   Romanesque. Restored.

61 DR. STOHR HOUSE   1900
   Kremsergasse
   J. M. Olbrich

ST. WOLFGANG B4

62 KIRCHE   15th c
   (church)

   The extraordinary altarpiece (1481) by Michael Pacher is a Gothic masterpiece.

SALZBURG B3

63 FRANZISKANER-   1200
    KIRCHE   onward
    (Franciscan church)
    Franziskanergasse (just off
      the Domplatz)

Romanesque nave. Gothic
chancel (1408) by H.
Stethaimer.

64 DOM   1614–55
    (Salzburg Cathedral)
    Domplatz
    S. Solari

Italian Renaissance with
baroque elements. •A passage
off the SW corner of the
adjacent Kapitelplatz leads to
St. Peterskirche (Romanesque,
remodeled in the 17th C).

65 KAJETANER-   1685–1700
    KIRCHE
    (church)
    Kajetanerplatz
    G. Zuccalli

66 DREIFALTIG-   1694–1701
    KEITSKIRCHE
    (church)
    Makartplatz, off
      Dreifaltigkeitsgasse
    J. B. Fischer von Erlach

Frescoes by J. M. Rottmayr.

67 KOLLEGIENKIRCHE
    (church)   1694–1707
    Max-Reinhardt-Platz
    J. B. Fischer von Erlach

68 URSULINENKIRCHE
    (church, now   1699–1705
    Markuskirche)
    Gstättengasse
    J. B. Fischer von Erlach

69 MIRABELL GARTEN 1721–26
    (gardens)
    Mirabell Platz

J. L. von Hildebrandt
remodeled the mansion; only
the grand staircase remains
after a fire in 1818. The
gardens (1690) are by J. B.
Fischer von Erlach.

70 VERLAGSHAUS   1926
    KIESEL
    (publishing house)
    Rainerstrasse 19–21
    W. Deininger

71 ORF STUDIO   1969–73
    (television studio)

Nonntaler Hauptstrasse
G. Peichl

Outskirts of Salzburg

72 PFARRKIRCHE   1955–56
    ZUM KOSTBAREN BLUT
    (church)
    Geissmayerstrasse,
      Salzburg-Parsch
    Arbeitsgruppe 4 (Holzbauer,
    Kurrent, Spalt)

73 MIERKA HOUSE   1956
    Salzburg-Mönchstein
    O. Haerdtl

74 KOLLEG ST. JOSEF   1961–64
    (seminary)
    Traunstrasse, Salzburg-Aigen
    Arbeitsgruppe 4 (Holzbauer,
    Kurrent, Spalt)

75 BILDUNGSHAUS   1965–75
    (cultural center)
    Ernst Greinstrasse,
      Salzburg-Aigen
    W. Holzbauer

76 ST. VITALIS   1967–72
    SEELSORGEZENTRUM
    (parish center)
    Salzburg-Kendlersiedlung
    W. Holzbauer

SECKAU B5
11 km (7 mi) N of Knittelfeld

77 STIFT   12th C onward
    (abbey)

Altered in the 15th and 19th C.
The Mausoleum of Karl II
(1587–1612, end north aisle)
is an early example of Austrian
baroque design.

SEEFELD B2

78 HOTEL BERGHOF   1929–30
    S. Mazagg

SPITAL AM PYHRN B4

79 STIFTSKIRCHE   1714–30
    (abbey church)

Baroque. Altarpiece by Kremser
Schmidt (1780). Fine trompe
l'oeil by B. Altomonte in the
chancel.

SPITTAL AN DER DRAU C4

80 PALAIS PORCIA   1527–40
    (palace)

Italian Renaissance. Elegant courtyard.

STAMS B2
35 km (22 mi) W of Innsbruck

81 STIFTSKIRCHE   1732
    (abbey church)

Baroque remodeling of a Romanesque church. The abbey buildings were also remodeled at this time. Notable Fürstensaal (prince's hall) and grand stair.

STEYR B4

82 KIRCHE   1706–12
    (church)
    Christkindl (3 km/2 mi W of Steyr)
    C. Carlone

Completed by G. Prandtauer.

83 SEELSORGE-   1958–71
    ZENTRUM
    (parochial center)
    Ennsleiten
    Arbeitsgruppe 4
    (Holzbauer, Kurrent, Spalt)

TULLN A6

84 KARNER   1250
    (funerary chapel)

Polygonal plan. Original carvings on facades in good condition.

UNTERBUCHBERG AM ATTERSEE B4

85 GAMERITH HOUSE 1933–34
    E. A. Plischke

VIENNA
See Wien

VIKTRING C4
3 km (2 mi) SW of Klagenfurt

86 STIFT   1142–1202
    (abbey)

Modeled after Fontenay, France. Stained glass installed after 1390.

VOLDERS B2
5 km (3 mi) E of Hall

87 SERVITENKIRCHE 1620–54
    (church)

Complex centralized plan with fine rococo decoration.

88 THURNER HOUSE 1969–72
    P. Thurner

WELS A4

89 DR. SAMITZ VILLA 1909–11
    Pollheimerstrasse 4
    H. Muthesius

90 SCHOOL OF   1929–30
    ECONOMICS
    Vogelweiderstrasse 2–4
    H. Steineder

WIEN A6 (Vienna)

Tourist Information:
Fremdenverkehrsverband für Wien, Kinderspitalgasse 5 (tel. 43–1608).

Architect's Institute:
Österreichischer Architekten- und Ingenieur Verein, Eschenbachgasse 9 (tel. 57–0522).

Architectural Bookstore:
Freytag-Berndt und Artaria, Kohlmarkt 9.

Museums: Akademie der Bildenden Künste, Schillerplatz 3. Paintings by Cranach, Bosch (*Last Judgment*). 17th-c Flemish and Dutch schools.
    Albertina, Augustinerstrasse 1. Outstanding collection of engravings, old master's drawings, and prints. Limited selections shown in rotation.
    Kunsthistorisches Museum, Maria-Theresien-Platz. A major collection of all European schools; paintings by van Eyck, van der Weyden, Brueghel, Vandyke, Rembrandt, Vermeer, Dürer, Holbein, Giorgione, Titian, Tintoretto, Valásquez. Salt-cellar by Cellini.
    Museum Moderner Kunst, Palais Liechtenstein, Fürstengasse 1. 20th-c paintings and sculpture: Klimt, Munch, Mondrian, and others.
    Museum des 20 Jahrhunderts. See entry 189.
    Neue Galerie in der Stallburg, Stallburg 2. 19th- and 20th-c French and German paintings.
    Österreichische Galerie, Schloss Belvedere. See entry 109. In the Unteres (lower) Belvedere: Gothic art (in the Orangerie) and baroque paintings. In the Oberes (upper) Belvedere: 19th- and 20th-c paintings (Klimt) and sculpture.

91 STEPHANSDOM 1258 onward
    (cathedral)
    Stephansplatz *B2*

Gothic. Built over 12th-c sanctuary. Rebuilt in the Romanesque style after severe fire in 1258. Replaced by Gothic structure (1304–1491). Fine South tower (1359–1433). Damaged by Turks (1683), destroyed in 1945, and completely rebuilt since then.

92 MARIA AM   13th–14th c
    GESTADE
    (church)
    Salvatorgasse *A2*

Flamboyant Gothic western facade. Interesting seven-sided tower with pierced dome above.

93 AUGUSTINER-   14th c
    KIRCHE   onward
    (church)
    Augustinerstrasse *C2*

Restored to the original Gothic style in 1784.

Wien

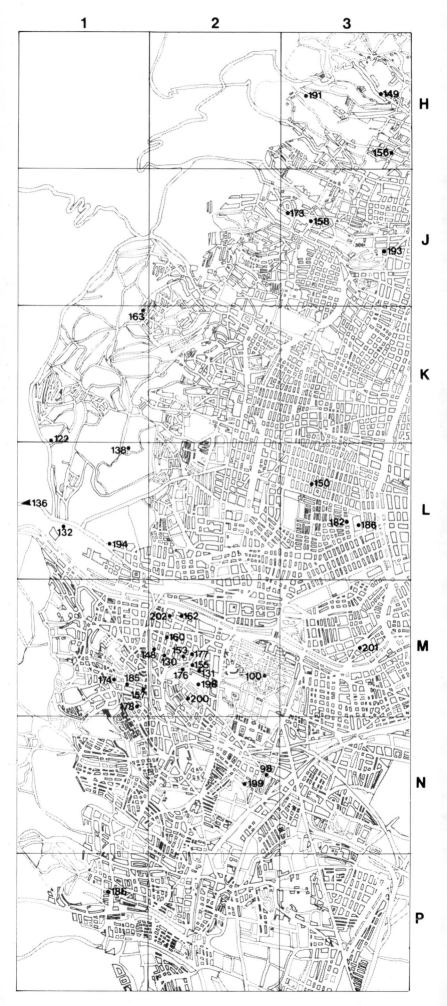

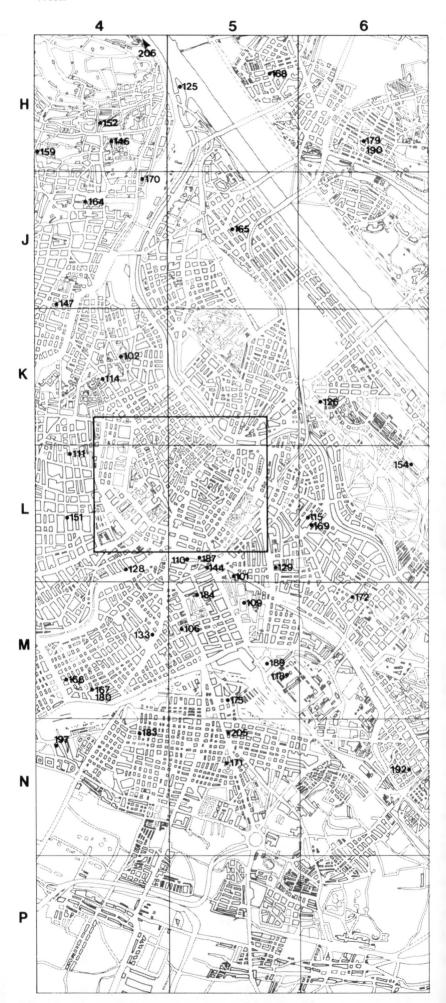

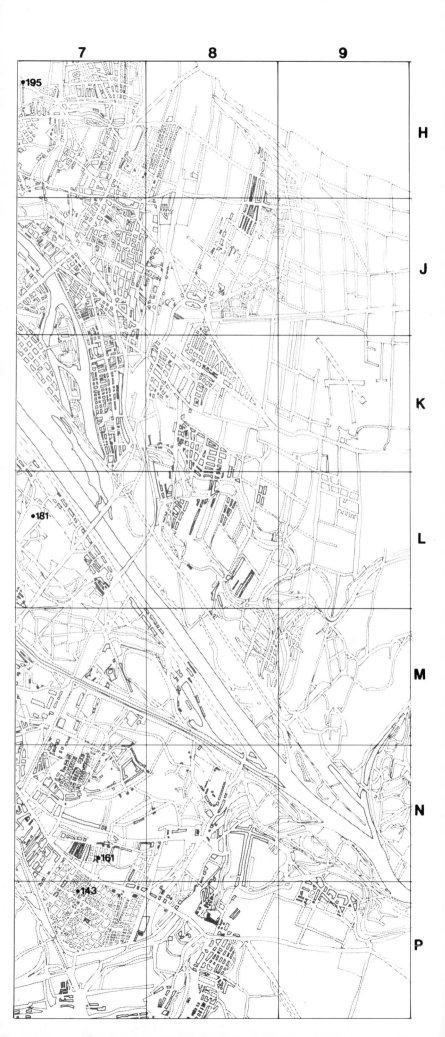

Wien detail

```
              1                    2                    3
        ┌──────────────┬──────────────────┬──────────────┐
        │              │            •140  │              │
        │              │  •119N           │              │
   A    │  •119A       │                  │              │
        │              │                  │              │
        │  •119K       │                  │              │
        │              │        •92       │              │
        │ •119H   99•  │•108 •104    •116 │              │
        │      •119M   │         137• •120│     •139     │
   B    │      135•196••105•134│   •95    │              │
        │•119L 141 203••96     │    112   │              │
        │         124 91•      │          │   •119F      │
        │         145 •142     │  119C•   │              │
        │    •94  •113         │          │              │
   C    │•107 93• •97  103•    │ 119G•    │              │
        │  •119J               │  •119E •117          │
        │        •119B         │          │              │
        │      204• •121       │  •119D   │              │
        │  •119I               │          │              │
        │  •127    •123        │          │              │
        └──────────────┴──────────────────┴──────────────┘
```

94 HOFBURG 1547–1913
(palace) *B2*

A large complex of buildings
built over five centuries:
Schweizerhof (1547–52);
Stallburg (1558–65);
Amalienburg (1575–1600 by
P. Ferabosco and N. Pacassi);
Leopoldinischer Trakt (1660–66
by P. Luchesi, D. and M.
Carlone, and L. von Montoyer);

Nationalbibliothek (national
library; 1723–30 by J. B. and
J. E. Fischer von Erlach;
altered by N. Pacassi, 1763–69);
Reichskanzlereitrakt (imperial
chancellery; 1723–30 by J. L.

von Hildebrandt and J. E.
Fischer von Erlach); Spanische
Hofreitschule (Spanish riding
school; 1729–35 by J. E.
Fischer von Erlach); Burgtor
(1821–24 by L. Cagnola and R.
von Nobile); Neue Hofburg
(1881–1913 by G. Semper, K.
von Hasenauer, E. Forster, F.
Ohmann, and L. Baumann).

95 ALTE 1627–31
JESUITENKIRCH
(Church of the Jesuits)
Dr. Ignaz Seipel-Platz *B3*

Trompe l'oeil paintings
(1703–5) by A. Pozzo.

96 PESTSÄULE 1683
(plague column)
Graben *B2*
L. Burnacini and J. B. Fischer
von Erlach

97 PALAIS 1685–87
LOBKOWITZ
(palace)
Lobkowitz Platz *C2*
G. P. Tencala

98 PALAIS 1694
HETZENDORF
(palace)
Hetzendorfer Strasse 79 *N2*

Rebuilt in 1743 by N. Pacassi.

99 STADTPALAIS 1694–1705
LIECHTENSTEIN
(palace)
Bankgasse 9 *B1*
D. Martinelli and others

100 SCHÖNBRUNN   1696–1713
(imperial palace)
Schönbrunner Schloss-
strasse *M2*
J. B. Fischer von Erlach and
N. Pacassi

The garden is by A. von
Stekhoven and F. Hohenburg
von Hetzendorf; baroque zoo
(1752) by J. N. Jadot de Ville-
Issey; Gloriette and artificial
Roman ruin (1775) by F.
Hohenburg von Hetzendorf;
greenhouse (1882) by F.
Segenschmid.

101 PALAIS   1697–1704
       SCHWARZENBERG
(palace)
Rennweg *L5*
J. L. von Hildebrandt

Interiors (1720–23) by J. B.
Fischer von Erlach; garden
by J. E. Fischer von Erlach.

102 GARTENPALAIS 1697–1711
       LIECHTENSTEIN
(palace)
Liechtensteinstrasse 48 *K4*
D. Martinelli

103 WINTER PALACE OF   1698
       PRINCE EUGEN
Himmelpfortgasse 8 *C2*
J. B. Fischer von Erlach and
J. L. von Hildebrandt

104 PALAIS SCHÖNBORN- 1699
       BATTHYÁNY
(palace)
Renngasse 4 *B2*
J. B. Fischer von Erlach

105 PETERSKIRCHE   1703–8
(St. Peter's Church)
Petersplatz *B2*
G. Montani and J. L. von
Hildebrandt

106 PALAIS SCHÖNBURG 1706
(palace)
Starhemberggasse 11 *M5*
J. L. von Hildebrandt

107 PALAIS TRAUTSON   1710
(palace)
Museumstrasse 7 *C1*
J. B. Fischer von Erlach

108 PALAIS KINSKY   1713–16
(palace)
Freyung 4 *B2*
J. L. von Hildebrandt

Remarkable staircase.

109 THE BELVEDERE   1714–23
Obere (Upper)—Prince Eugen-
Strasse *M5*
Unteres (Lower)—Rennweg 6
J. L. von Hildebrandt

The Lower Belvedere (1714–15)
is joined to the Upper
Belvedere (1720–23) by a series
of terraced baroque gardens.

110 KARLSKIRCHE   1716–37
(St. Charles's Church)
Karlsplatz *L5*
J. B. Fischer von Erlach

This is von Erlach's
masterpiece, completed after
his death in 1723. The facade
uses antique Greek, Roman,
and baroque elements. The twin
columns are modeled after
Trajan's column in Rome. The
dome is decorated with
frescoes by J. M. Rottmayr.

111 PIARISTENKIRCHE 1716–53
(church)
Jodok Fink-Platz *L4*
J. L. von Hildebrandt

Octagonal plan; altered by
K. I. Dientzenhofer.

112 ALTE   1753–55
       UNIVERSITÄT
(old university)
Dr. Ignaz Seipel-Platz 2 *B3*
J. N. Jadot de Ville-Issey

113 PALAIS   1782–84
       PALLAVICINI
(palace)
Josefsplatz *B2*
F. Hohenburg von Hetzendorf

114 JOSEPHINUM   1783–85
Währinger Strasse 25/
       Van Swieten Gasse *K4*
I. Canevale

115 PALAIS   1806
       RASUMOFSKY
(palace)
Rasumofskygasse 23 *L6*
L. von Montoyer

116 SYNAGOGUE   1826
Seitenstettengasse 2–4 *B3*
J. Kornhäusel

117 MÜNZAMT   1835–38
(Austrian Mint)
Am Heumarkt 1 *C3*
P. Sprenger

118 ARSENAL   1849–56
Arsenalstrasse *M5*
L. Förster and T. Hansen

119 THE RINGSTRASSE

The fortifications destroyed by Napoleon were removed in 1857 when Emperor Franz-Joseph ordered the construction of a boulevard in their place to unite the inner Old City and the new suburbs that had grown beyond. The buildings listed below were part of this master plan.

a Votivkirche   1856–79
     (votive church)
     Rooseveltplatz *A1*
     H. Ferstel

b Staatsoper   1861–69
     (state opera house)
     Opernring *C2*
     E. Van der Nüll and
     A. Sicard von Sicardsburg

c Palace of   1864–68
     Archduke Wilhelm
     Parkring 8 *B3*
     T. Hansen

d Palace of   1864–69
     Archduke Ludwig Viktor
     Schwarzenbergplatz 1 *C3*
     H. Ferstel

e Palais Moennich–   1867
     Larisch
     (palace)
     Johannesgasse 26 *C3*
     E. Van der Nüll and
     A. Sicard von Sicardsburg

f Museum für   1868–71
     Angewandte Kunst
     (museum of arts and
     crafts)
     Stubenring 5 *B3*
     H. Ferstel

g Palais Henckel–   1870
     Donnersmarck
     (palace)
     Parkring 14 *C3*
     J. Romano and
     A. Schwendenwein

h Neue Rathaus   1872–73
     (new town hall)
     Rathausplatz *B1*
     F. von Schmidt

i Akademie der   1872–76
     Bildenden Künste
     (academy of fine arts)
     Schillerplatz 3 *C2*
     T. Hansen

j Natur und   1872–81
     Kunsthistorisches
     Museum
     (natural and art history
     museum)
     Burgring *C1*

     G. Semper and K. von
     Hasenauer

k Neue Universität   1873–83
     (new university)
     Dr Karl Lueger-Ring *A1*
     H. Ferstel

l Parlament   1873–83
     (parliament)
     Dr Karl Renner-Ring *B1*
     T. Hansen

m Burgtheater   1874–88
     (theater)
     Dr Karl Lueger-Ring *B1*
     G. Semper and K. von
     Hasenauer

n Palais Sturany   1887
     (palace)
     Schottenring 21 *A2*
     F. Fellner and H. Helmer

120 GRIECHENKIRCHE   1858
     (Greek church)
     Fleischmarkt 13 *B3*
     T. Hansen

121 MUSIKVEREIN   1868–69
     (concert hall)
     Bösendorferstrasse 12 *C2*
     T. Hansen

122 WAGNER HOUSE I   1886–88
     Hüttelbergstrasse 36 *K1*
     O. Wagner

Built for himself. • Wagner built a second house for himself next door at no. 38 in 1913.

123 KARLSPLATZ   1894–98
     STADTBAHN–PAVILLON
     (subway station)
     Karlsplatz *C2*
     O. Wagner

Wagner designed the Vienna underground stations and buildings.

124 ANKER HOUSE 1895
Graben 10 *B2*
O. Wagner

125 NADELWEHR 1897
NUSSDORF
(canal lock)
near Nussdorfer Platz *H5*
O. Wagner

126 RIESENRAD 1897
(ferris wheel)
Prater *K6*
W. Basset

The wheel dominates the city
skyline.

127 SECESSION 1898
BUILDING
Friedrichstrasse 12 *C2*
J. M. Olbrich

Olbrich was influenced by
Klimt in this design. The
Vienna Secession (sezessionstil)
was founded by G. Klimt,
Olbrich, J. Hoffmann, and
K. Moser in 1897. O. Wagner
joined this group in 1897.

128 MAJOLIKAHAUS 1898–99
Linke Wienzeile 38–40 *L4*
O. Wagner

Six-story apartment building
faced with majolica tile
decorated in the Jugendstil
manner.

129 PORTOIS & FIX 1900
BUILDING
Ungargasse 59–61 *L5*
M. Fabiani

130 HOUSE 1900–1901
Beckgasse 30 *M2*
J. Plecnik

131 VILLA SCHOPP 1900–1902
Gloriettegasse 21 *M2*
F. Ohmann and J. Hackhofer

132 VOJCSIK HOUSE 1901
Linzerstrasse 375 *L1*
O. Schönthal

133 FLORA-HOF 1901
HOUSING
Wiedner Hauptstrasse 88 *M4*
O. Laske

134 HOUSE AND STORE 1901–2
Bognergasse 10 *B2*
O. Laske

135 ARTARIAHAUS 1902
(apartments)
Kohlmarkt 9 *B2*
M. Fabiani

136 PURKERSDORF 1903–5
SANATORIUM
Wiener Strasse 72–80,
Purkersdorf *L1*
J. Hoffmann

137 ZACHERLHAUS 1903–5
Bauernmarkt-Brandstätte 6 *B2*
J. Plecnik

138 STEINHOFKIRCHE 1903–7
(church)
Baumgartner Hohe 1 *L1*
O. Wagner

Cruciform plan with tiled
interiors. Jugendstil decoration
in excellent condition. One of
Wagner's finest buildings.

139 ÖSTERREICHISCHE 1904–6
POSTSPARKASSE
(savings bank)
Georg Cochplatz 2 *B3*
O. Wagner

Architectural decoration
reduced to the minimum.
The revolutionary interiors
rival any of A. Loos's work in
their severity and discipline.

140 SCHÜTZENHAUS 1904–8
(lock gate building)
Obere Donaustrasse, at the
canal *A2*
O. Wagner

141 ELISABETH- 1904–8
DENKMAL
(monument)
Volksgarten *B1*
F. Ohmann

142 KÄRNTNERBAR 1907
Kärntner Durchgang, off
Kärntnerstrasse *B2*
A. Loos

A tiny bar. Brilliant interior,
in perfect condition.

143 ZENTRAL- 1907–10
FRIEDHOF
(cemetery)
Simmeringer Hauptstrasse *P7*
M. Hegele

144 FRENCH EMBASSY 1909
Technikerstrasse *L5*
G. Chedanne

145 KNIZE MEN'S 1909–13
STORE
Graben 13 *B2*
A. Loos

146 AST HOUSE 1910
Steinfeldgasse 2 *H4*
J. Hoffmann

147 LOOSHAUS 1910
(own house)
Michaeler Platz 3 *J4*
A. Loos

148 STEINER HOUSE 1910
St. Veit-Gasse 10 *M2*
A. Loos

Slightly altered, this is the first
of a series of houses by Loos
in which he developed his
concept of Raumplan (space-
plan).

149 VILLA 1910
Cobenzlgasse *H3*
O. Strnad, J. Frank, and
O. Wlach

150 KIRCHE 1911
(church)
Herbststrasse 82 *L3*
J. Plecnik

Very early exposed-concrete
structure.

151 APARTMENT 1911
BUILDINGS
Neustiftgasse 40 and
Doblergasse 4 *L4*
O. Wagner

152 VILLA BERNATZKI 1911–14
Springsiedelgasse 28 *H4*
J. Hoffmann

153 SCHEU HOUSE 1912
La Roche-Gasse 3 *M2*
A. Loos

154 RACETRACK 1912
GRANDSTAND
Prater *L6*
O. Schönthal

155 PRIMAVESI HOUSE 1913
Gloriettegasse 14–16 *M2*
J. Hoffmann

Forerunner of the Palais
Stoclet, Brussel.

156 PRIVATE VILLAS 1913
Kaasgrabengasse 12–18,
30–38 *H3*
J. Hoffmann

157 HOUSE 1913
Nothartgasse/Sauraugasse *M1*
A. Loos

158 VILLA 1914
Wilbrandtgasse 3 *J3*
J. Frank, O. Strnad and
O. Wlach
• No. 37 (1935–36) is by H. Glas.

159 VILLA LEMBERGER 1914
Grinzinger Allee 50 *H4*
J. Kotera

160 STRASSER HOUSE 1919
(remodeling)
Kupelwiesergasse 28 *M2*
A. Loos

161 KREMATORIUM 1922
Simmeringer Hauptstrasse
337 *N7*
C. Holzmeister

162 RUFER HOUSE 1922
Schliessmanngasse 11 *M2*
A. Loos

163 SIEDLUNG HEUBERG 1922
(public housing)
Pointengasse Am Heuberg *K1*
A. Loos and H. Mayer

Brilliant use of greenhouse
elevations (for vegetable
cultivation) on low-cost
row-housing scheme.

164 KNIPS HOUSE 1924
Nusswaldgasse 20 *J4*
J. Hoffmann

165 WINARSKYHOF 1924
(public housing)
Stromstrasse 36–38 *J5*
P. Behrens, J. Frank,
J. Hoffmann, O. Strnad, and
O. Wlach

166 REUMAN-HOF 1924
(public housing)
Margaretengürtel 100–112 *M4*
H. and F. Gessner

167 MATTEOTTI-HOF 1925–27
(public housing)
Siebenbrunnenfeldgasse
26–30 *M4*
H. Schmid and H. Aichinger

168 KARL SEITZ-HOF 1926
(public housing)
Jedleseerstrasse 86–94 *H5*
H. and F. Gessner

169 VILLA 1926–28
WITTGENSTEIN
Kundmanngasse 19 *L6*
L. Wittgenstein and
P. Engelmann

Currently overrated.

170 KARL MARX-HOF 1927
(housing)
Heiligenstädter Strasse
82–92 *J4*
K. Ehn

Powerful massing in a
well-planned, if rather
grandiose, scheme.

171 AMALIENBAD 1927
(public baths)
Reumannplatz *N5*
Schmalhofer and O. Nadel

172 RABENHOF 1927–29
(housing)
Baumgasse 29–41 *M6*
H. Schmid and H. Aichinger

173 MÖLLER HOUSE 1928
Starkfriedgasse 19 *J3*
A. Loos

Symmetrical cubic massing
similar to Loos's Tzara house
in Paris.

174 WERKBUND- 1928–30
SIEDLUNG
(experimental housing) *M1*

Modeled after the Werkbund
Exhibition at Stuttgart (1927)
Veitingergasse—
71, 73: H. Haring (Berlin)
75, 77: R. Bauer
79–85: J. Hoffmann
87–93: A. Lurçat (Paris)
95, 97: W. Sobotka
99, 101: O. Wlach
103, 105: J. Jirasek
107, 109: E. A. Plischke
111, 113: J. Wenzel
115, 117: O. Haerdtl
Jagdschlossgasse—
68, 70: Wagner-Freynsheim

72, 74: O. Breuer
76, 78: J. F. Dex
80, 82: A. Grünberger
88, 90: E. Lichtblau
Woinovichgasse—
1, 3: H. Gorge
5, 7: J. Groag (Paris)
9: R. Neutra (Los Angeles)
11: H. A. Vetter
13–19: A. Loos
2, 4: M. Schutte-Lihotzky
(Moscow)
6, 8: M. Fellerer
10, 12: G. Guevrekian
(Paris)
14–20: G. Rietveld
(Utrecht)
22: E. Wachberger
24, 26: W. Loos
28, 30: A. Bieber and
O. Niedermoser
32: J. Frank
34: H. Haring (Berlin)
Jagićgasse—
8, 10: C. Holzmeister
12: E. Wachberger
Engelbrechtweg—
4, 6: H. Haring (Berlin)
5, 7: O. Strnad
9, 11: A. Brenner

175 UMSPANNWERK   1929–31
FAVORITEN
(transformer)
Humboldtgasse 1–5 *M5*
E. Kastner and F. Waage

176 MALFATTI-   1930–32
SIEDLUNG
(housing)
Franz Schalk-Platz 3–7 *M2*
C. S. Drach

177 VILLA   1931
Wenzgasse 12 *M2*
J. Frank and O. Wlach

178 LOCKERWIESE   1928–32
(public housing)
Faistauergasse 1 *M1*
Schartelmüller

179 SPEISER–HOF   1929
(housing)
Franklinstrasse 20 *H6*
E. Lichtblau

180 ARBEITSAMT   1929–30
(labor exchange)
Siebenbrunnenfeldgasse/
Amtshausgasse *M4*
H. Steigholzer and H. Kastinger

181 STADIUM   1931
Prater *L7*
O. E. Schweizer

182 SEIPEL-   1933–34
DOLLFUSS KIRCHE
(church)
Vogelweidplatz 7 *L3*
C. Holzmeister

183 FRIEDENSKIRCHE   1936
(church)
Quellenstrasse 197 *N4*
R. Kramreiter

184 FUNKHAUS   1936–38
(radio station)
Argentinierstrasse 30 *M5*
C. Holzmeister, H. Schmid,
and H. Aichinger

185 PREFABRICATED   1954
HOUSING
Veitingergasse *M1*
C. Auböck and R. Rainer

186 STADTHALLE   1954–58
(cultural center)
Vogelweidplatz *L3*
R. Rainer

The swimming baths (1960–70)
are also by Rainer.

187 HISTORISCHES   1954–59
MUSEUM DER STADT
WIEN
(Museum of the City of Vienna)
Karlsplatz *L5*
O. Haerdtl

188 SIEDLUNG   1956–64
MAUERBERG
(housing)
Mauerberggasse *P1*
R. Rainer

189 MUSEUM DES   1958, 1962
20 JAHRHUNDERTS
(museum of the twentieth
century)
Schweizer Garten *M5*
K. Schwanzer

Originally Austrian Pavilion
at EXPO 58, Brussels. Rebuilt
on present site in 1962.
Temporary exhibitions of
20th-c paintings and
sculpture.

190 SCHOOL FOR   1961
HANDICAPPED
CHILDREN
Franklinstrasse 27 *H6*
W. Schutte

191 BELLEVUE   1961–63
RESTAURANT
Himmelstrasse 150 *H3*
W. and T. Windbrechtinger

192 GLAUBENSKIRCHE 1962–63
(church)
Braunhubergasse 20 *N6*
R. Rainer

193 KIRCHE   1963
(students' chapel)
Peter-Jordan-Strasse 29 *J3*
O. Uhl

194 BAUMGARTEN   1964
KIRCHE
(church)
Hütteldorfer Strasse 280 *L1*
J. G. Gsteu

195 KIRCHE   1964–67
(prefabricated church)
Siemensstrasse 26 *H7*
O. Uhl

196 RETTI CANDLESHOP   1965
Kohlmarkt 10 *B2*
H. Hollein

A very sophisticated and
slick design.

197 MEIDLING   1966–68
     REHABILITATION
     CENTER
Koglergasse *N4*
G. Peichl

198 ARCHITECT'S HOUSE   1967
Weidlichgasse 17 *M2*
R. Rainer

199 SEELSORGE-   1968–71
     ZENTRUM
(parish center)
Marschallplatz 6 *N2*
J. G. Gsteu

200 ORF–ZENTRUM   1968–74
(radio and television center)
Küniglberg *M2*
R. Rainer

201 SPARKASSE   1970–72
(savings bank)
Sparkasseplatz 4 *M3*
J. G. Gsteu

202 GROTHUSEN   1970–72
     OFFICE BUILDING
Auhofstrasse 41a *M2*
H. Puchhammer and G. Wawrik

203 JUWELIER-   1972–74
     GESCHÄFT SCHULLIN
(jewelry store)
Graben 26 *B2*
H. Hollein

Sensual play of forms and
luxurious materials, perfectly
suited to the objects displayed.

204 ÖSTERREICHS   1978
     VERKEHRSBURO
(Austrian Travel Agency)
Opernring 3–5 (opposite the
     opera house) *C2*
H. Hollein

Historic references (Wagner's
savings bank, see entry 139)
used in a good renovation.
• A similar interior by Hollein
is the nearby Israeli tourist
office.

205 ZENTRALSPARKASSE   1979
(bank)
Favoritenstrasse 188 *N5*
G. Domenig

Grotesque.

Outskirts of Wien

206 STIFT   1114–33 onward
     KLOSTERNEUBURG
(abbey)
North of Wien, on the Donau
     (Danube) *H4*

Rebuilt in the baroque style by
D. d'Allio. Superb altarpiece
(1181) by Nicholas of Verdun.

ZELL AM ZILLER C2

207 KIRCHE   1782
(church)

ZWETTL A5

208 STIFT   1138 onward
(abbey)
3 km (2 mi) NE of Zwettl

Gothic church (1343–83)
reworked in the baroque style.

Belgium

St.-Cyr House; *see entry 41*

Belgium

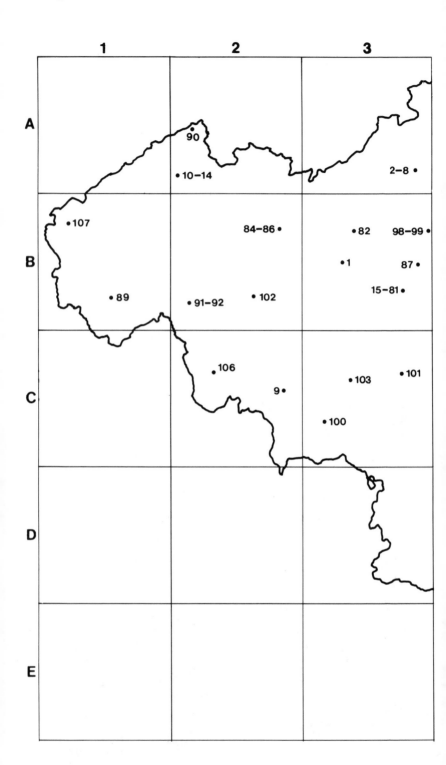

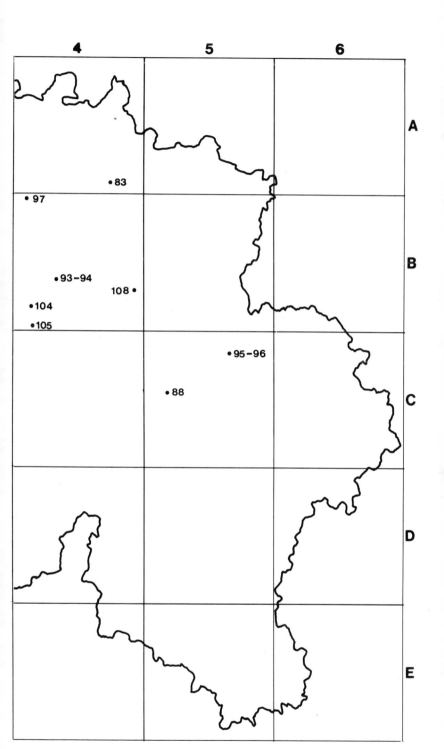

AALST B3
(Alost)
23 km (14 mi) W of Brussel

1 ST. MARTIN   1480–1566
(church)
Grote Markt
J. van der Wouwe, H. and D.
Waghemakere

Gothic. Baroque facade built in
1730. Rubens's *St. Roch* in the
south transept.

ANTWERPEN A3
(Antwerp/Anvers)

Tourist Information: Suikerrui
19 (tel. 322284)

Architect's Institute: Orde van
Architecten, 104 RUCA Plain,
2610 Wilrijk (tel. 397858).

Museums: Koninklijk Museum
voor Schone Kunsten, Leopold
de Waelplaats. 15th- to 20th-c
Flemish paintings. Rubens's
(*Madonna and Child with
Saints*), Vandyke, van Eyck
(*Madonna of the Fountain*),
Brueghel, Ensor, and others.
Small Dutch and Italian
collection.
   Museum Mayer van den
Bergh, Lange Gasthuisstraat
19. Flemish 15th- to 17th-c
paintings in a modern
reconstruction of a 16th-c
home. Period furniture and
sculpture.
   Middelheim Openlucht-
museum voor Beeldhouwkunst
(open-air museum of sculpture),
Middelheimlaan 61. Sculpture
by Rodin, Maillol, Moore, etc.
   Plantin-Moretus Museum,
Heilige Geeststraat. Printing
museum. Some Rubens
paintings.
   Rubens Huis (Rubens's
house), Rubensstraat 9. Built by
Rubens from 1610–17. Much
restored. Some paintings by
Rubens and contemporary
furnishings.

2 ONZE LIEVE-   1352–1584
   VROUWE KATHEDRAAL
(Cathedral of Our Lady)
Groenplaats 21

Continuously rebuilt. Fine
north tower (1431–1525). The
largest cathedral in Belgium
(triple aisles). Three Rubens
masterpieces inside: *The
Raising of the Cross* (north
transept), *The Descent from
the Cross* (south transept) and
The Assumption (high altar).

3 ST. JACOBUS-   1491–1656
   KERK
(church)
Lange Nieuwstraat 73

Late Gothic. Rubens chapel
(paintings temporarily in the
Museum voor Schone Kunsten).

4 ST. PAULUS   1533–1621
(church)
St. Paulusstraat

Late Gothic remodeled in the
baroque style ca. 1670. Many

important paintings by Rubens,
Vandyke, Jordaens, and others.

5 STADHUIS   1561–65
(town hall)
Grote Markt
C. de Vriendt (Floris)

The first Renaissance-style
building in Northern Europe by
a non-Italian architect. Rebuilt
in 1575. •16th- to 17th-c guild
houses surround the square.

6 KAREL   1614–21
   BORROMEUS KERK
(Church of St. Charles
Borromeo)
Hendrik Conscienceplein
P. Huyssens and F. Aguilon

Rebuilt after 1718. The design
of the mannerist facade is
traditionally ascribed to
Rubens.

7 HOUSES   ca. 1900
Cogels Osylei and
   Transvaalstraat

A street of art nouveau
mansions.

8 CENTRAAL STATION   1905
(railway station)
Koningin Astridplein
L. Delacenserie

CHÂTEAU DE
BELOEIL C2
22 km (14 mi) NW of Mons

9 CHÂTEAU DE   1682–1770
   BELOEIL

Rebuilt in 1900. Rich interiors
with period furnishings. Fine
park in the French manner.

BRUGGE A2
(Bruges)

A medieval town with
hundreds of original
buildings that have been
carefully maintained and
restored.

Museums: Groeninge Museum,
Dijver. Flemish primitives;

van Eyck, van der Goes, Memling, etc.

Memling Museum, St.-Jans Hospitaal, Mariastraat. Works by Memling (*Reliquary of St. Ursula, Marriage of St. Catherine*, etc.).

10 ST. SALVATORS   1200
   (cathedral)   onward
   Heilige Geeststraat

Gothic. Flamboyant ambulatory (1480–1530). Upper section of west tower built 1844–71.

11 BELFRY   1282–96
   Grote Markt

The belfry dominates the square, which is lined with medieval market halls. The upper octagonal section was added from 1482–87.

12 STADHUIS   1376
   (town hall)
   Burgplein
   L. de Male

Gothic, oak vaulted hall. Restored in 1871.

13 HEILIG   1134 onward
   BLOEDBAZILIEK
   (Basilica of the Holy Blood)
   Burgplein

Romanesque lower chapel. Gothic upper chapel built in the 15th c.

14 ONZE LIEVE-   13th–15th c
   VROUWE
   (church)
   St. Katelijnestraat

Madonna and Child by Michelangelo on right of altar.

BRUSSEL B3
(Brussels/Bruxelles)

Tourist Information: 61 rue du Marché aux Herbes (tel. 5139090).

Architect's Institutes: Ordre des Architectes, Conseil National, 160, rue de Livourne (tel. 6470669).

Archives d'Architecture Moderne (Archive of Modern Architecture), 4, rue Paul Spaak (tel. 491502).

Museums: Musée des Beaux-Arts (Ixelles), 71, rue J. van Volsem. 19th- and 20th-c Belgian and French paintings.

Horta Museum. See entry 44.

Musées Royaux des Beaux-Arts: *Musée d'Art Ancien,* 3, rue de la Régence. (See entry 26.) 14th- to 19th-c paintings by Bouts, Memling, van der Weyden, Brueghel, Rubens, Vandyke, Hals, Gauguin, etc. *Musée d'Art Moderne,* Place Royale. 20th-c paintings.

15 CATHÉDRALE   1226 onward
   ST.-MICHEL
   place Ste.-Gudule *D5*

West facade and towers built from 1525–75.

16 ÉGLISE DES   1615
   AUGUSTINS
   (church)
   Formerly at the place de Brouckère, now rebuilt at the Église de la Ste.-Trinité, rue du Bailli. *D7*
   J. Franckaert

Demolished in 1893. The facade was preserved and moved to its present site.

17 ÉGLISE DU   1657–76
   BÉGUINAGE
   (church)
   place du Béguinage *E4*
   L. Fayd'herbe

Baroque.

18 NOTRE DAME   1664–94
   DU BON SECOURS
   (church)
   rue du Marché au Charbon *E5*
   J. Cortvrindt and P. P. Merckx

Hexagonal plan.

19 BELLONE HOUSE   1697
   46, rue de Flandre *E4*
   J. Cosyn

20 GRAND'   1697 onward
   PLACE *E5*

Only the Town Hall (1402–55) survived the French bombardment in 1695. The houses on the square were rebuilt immediately afterwards, mostly in the Flemish baroque style.

21 PLACE ROYALE *D5*   1773–80
   N. Barré and B. G. Guimard

22 PLACE DES   1775
   MARTYRS *D4*
   C. A. Fisco

The monument to Mérode (1898) is by H. van de Velde.

23 STE. MARIE   1845–53
   (church)
   place de la Reine *D4*
   L. Van Overstraeten

Brussel

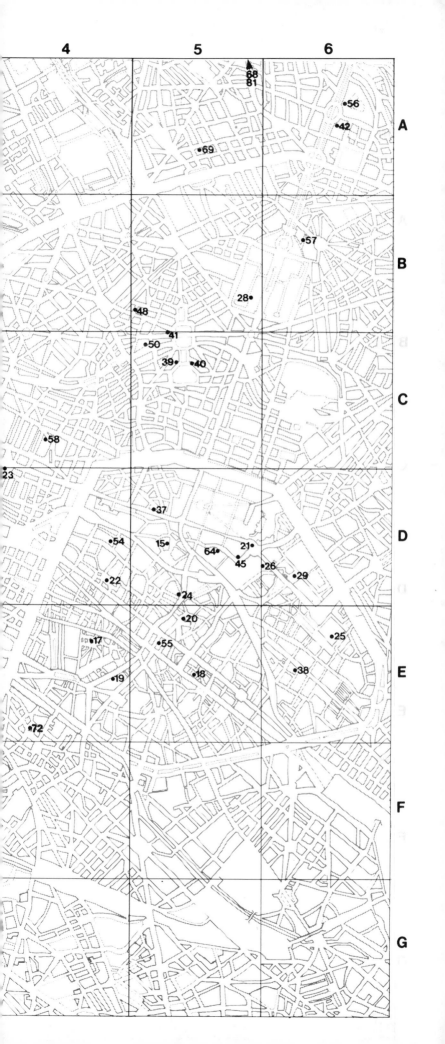

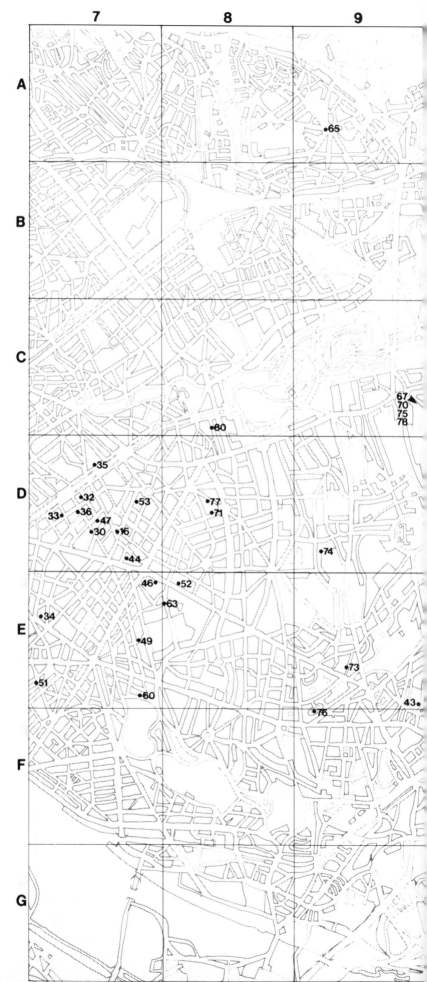

Brussel

24 GALERIES   1846
     ST. HUBERT
   rue du Marché aux Herbes *D5*
   J. P. Cluysenaer

   The first glass-covered shopping
   arcade in Europe.

25 PALAIS DE JUSTICE 1866–83
   (Palace of Justice)
   place Poelaert *E6*
   J. Poelaert

   A monstrous building
   dominating the city skyline.

26 MUSÉE D'ART   1875–81
     ANCIEN
   3, rue de la Régence *D6*
   A. Balat

27 CONSERVATOIRE   1879
     ROYAL
   (Royal Conservatories)
   avenue du Parc-Royal *D1*
   A. Balat

28 PARC DU   1880
     CINQUANTENAIRE *B5*
   G. Bordiau

   The arch (1905) is by C. Girault.
   The Lambeaux Pavilion (1889)
   is by V. Horta.

29 PLACE DU   1890
     PETIT SABLON *D6*
   H. Beyaert

30 MAISON HANKAR   1893
   (own house)
   71, rue Defacqz *D7*
   P. Hankar

   •Nos. 48 (Maison Ciamberlani,
   1897) and 50 (Janssens, 1898)
   are also by Hankar.

31 AUTRIQUE HOUSE   1893
   242, chaussée de Haecht,
     opposite rue Vanderweyer *C3*
   V. Horta

32 TASSEL HOUSE   1893
   6, rue Paul-Emile Janson *D7*
   V. Horta

   Interior slightly altered.

33 OTLET MANSION   1894
   48, rue de Livourne/rue de
     Florence *D7*
   O. Van Rijsselberghe

   Interiors by H. van de Velde.

34 WINSSINGER HOUSE   1894
   66, rue Hôtel des Monnaies *E7*
   V. Horta

   Altered.

35 SOLVAY MANSION   1894
   224, avenue Louise *D7*
   V. Horta

The stables on the rue Lens are
worth visiting. •No. 344 avenue
Louise (Hallait house, 1903) is
also by Horta.

36 HOUSE   1894
   83, rue de Livourne *D7*
   O. Van Rijsselberghe

   The architect's own house.

37 FLOWER SHOP   ca. 1895
   13, rue Royale *D5*
   P. Hankar

   Art nouveau storefront.

38 SCHOOL   1895
   40, rue St.-Ghislain *E6*
   V. Horta

39 VAN EETVELDE   1895
     MANSION
   4, avenue Palmerston *C5*
   V. Horta

40 DEPREZ–VAN DE   1896
     VELDE MANSION
   avenue Palmerston/3, rue
     Bodougnat *C5*
   V. Horta

41 ST.-CYR HOUSE   1896
   11, Square Ambiorix *C5*
   G. Strauven

   Exuberant facade squeezed onto
   a minute site.

42 HOUSE   1896
   249, avenue de Tervueren,
     WSP *A6*
   P. Hankar

43 'BLOEMENWERF'   1896
     VILLA
   102, avenue Vanderaey *E9*
   H. van de Velde

   •No. 118 is also by van de
   Velde.

44 HORTA HOUSE AND   1898
     STUDIO
   23–25, rue Americaine *D7*
   V. Horta

Now the Horta Museum.
Virtuoso performance of design
and workmanship.

45 OLD ENGLAND STORE 1899
   80, rue Montagne de la Cour *D5*
   P. Saintenoy

46 'LES HIBOUX' HOUSE 1899
   55, avenue Brugmann *E7*
   E. Pelseneer

47 HOUSE   1900
   83, rue Faider *D7*
   A. Rosenboom

48 HOUSE 1900
4, rue de l'Abdication *B5*
G. Strauven

•No. 31, Maison Braecke
(1901), is by V. Horta.

49 PEEREBOOM HOUSE 1900
12, rue Jef Lambeaux *E7*
G. A. Peereboom

50 HOUSE ca. 1900
85, boulevard Clovis *C5*
G. Strauven

51 HOUSES ca. 1900–1903
1–25, rue Vanderschrick *E7*
E. Blérot

52 DUBOIS MANSION 1901
80, avenue Brugmann *E8*
V. Horta

The interiors have been altered.

53 PIERRON HOUSE 1903
157, rue de l'Aqueduc *D7*
V. Horta

54 GROS WAUCQUEZ 1903
STORE
20, rue des Sables *D4*
V. Horta

55 CAFÉ FALSTAFF 1903
17–19, rue Henri-Maus *E5*
E. Houbion

Art nouveau café with
original interiors.

56 PALAIS STOCLET 1904–11
(mansion)
297, avenue de Tervueren *A6*
J. Hoffmann

Admission very difficult. Try to
see the murals by Klimt in the
dining room.

57 CAUCHIE HOUSE 1905
5, rue des Francs *B6*
P. Cauchie

The fine art nouveau street
mural is by Cauchie.

58 SCHOOL ca. 1905
229 and 243, rue Josaphat *C4*
H. Jacobs

Good interiors.

59 THREE HOUSES ca. 1905
7, 9, 11, avenue Maréchal
Foch *C3*
H. Jacobs

60 NELISSEN HOUSE 1905
5, avenue du Mont Kemmel *E7*
A. Nelissen

61 HOUSE ca. 1905
43, avenue Louis Bertrand *C3*
G. Strauven

62 HOUSING 1910
rue Henri Jacobs/rue Dr. Elie
Lambotte *B2*
H. Jacobs

63 ORTHOPEDIC CLINIC 1910
53, rue Henri Wafelaerts *E8*
A. Pompe

Altered almost beyond
recognition, the massing of the
facade is still recognizable.

64 PALAIS DES 1920
BEAUX-ARTS
23, rue Ravenstein *D5*
V. Horta

65 CITÉ-JARDIN 1920–25
FLORÉAL
avenue van der Swaelmen *A9*
J. Eggericx, L. François,
and R. Moenart.

Landscaping by L. van der
Swaelmen. The rural qualities of
this garden-city scheme should
be compared to the Cité
Moderne (entry 66).

66 CITÉ MODERNE 1922–25
place de Coopérateurs *G3*
V. Bourgeois

Landscaping by L. van der
Swaelmen. Important town
planning scheme. The influence
of F. L. Wright and T. Garnier
is apparent.

67 DE KONINCK HOUSE 1924
105, avenue Fond 'Roy *C9*
L. H. De Koninck

The architect's own house. In
1968 he built apartments
above it.
•The Langlet house (1926), next
door at No. 103, also by De
Koninck, has also been radically
altered by him.

68 KAPELLENVELD 1924–26
GARDEN SUBURB
avenue Emile Vandervelde *A5*
H. Hoste, A. Pompe, J. F.
Hoeben and P. Rubbers

Layout and landscaping by L.
van der Swaelmen.

69 JESPERS STUDIO 1928
HOUSE
149, avenue du Prince
Héritier *A5*
V. Bourgeois

70 VILLA 1929
28, avenue Marie-Jeanne *C9*
M. Leborgne

71 PUTTEMANS HOUSE 1929
112, rue Camille Lemonnier *D8*
R. Puttemans

72 ST.-JEAN-BAPTISTE   1930
(church)
parvis du St.-Jean-Baptiste *E4*
J. Diongre

73 DOTREMONT   1931–32
HOUSE
3, avenue de l'Echevinage *E9*
L. H. De Koninck

74 HOUSES   1932–33
28–32 avenue Roberts Jones *D9*
C. Colassin

75 LEY HOUSE   1934
200, avenue du Prince
d'Orange *C9*
L. H. De Koninck

76 HOUSING   1934–36
75–87, square Coghen *F9*
L. H. De Koninck

77 'MAISON DE VERRE'   1935
(house)
69, rue Jules Lejeune *D8*
P. A. Michel

Altered.

78 BERTEAUX HOUSE   1937
59, avenue du Fort Jaco *C9*
L. H. De Koninck

79 APARTMENTS   1954
avenue Ciceron *A3*
W. Vandermeeren

80 APARTMENTS AND   1968
OFFICES
6, rue Emile Claus *C8*
C. Emery and D. Limbosch

81 MEDICAL   1969–74
FACULTY BUILDING
avenue de l'Assomption,
Woluwe-Saint-Lambert *A5*
L. Kroll

The adjacent subway station
(1978) is also by Kroll.

DENDERMONDE B3
(Termonde)

82 ONZE LIEVE   14th–15th c
VROUWE
(church)
Kerkstraat

Two paintings by Vandyke;
Crucifixion (baptistry) and
Adoration of the Shepherds
(north aisle).

GEEL A4

83 ST. DYMPNA   1344–1492
(church)

Mausoleum of Jean III (1554)
by C. de Vriendt. •Nine km (5
mi) south on the N20 is
Tongerlo Abbey, which has a
copy of *The Last Supper* (1507)
by Leonardo's pupil Andrea
del Solario, in good condition.
11 km (7 mi) further south on
the N2O is Averbode Abbey
(founded in 1134, mostly
rebuilt after a fire in 1942).
The baroque church (1672, by
D. van der Ende) has a rich yet
austere interior.

GENT B2
(Ghent/Gand)

The old section of the city has
many medieval buildings in
fine condition.

Museum: Museum voor Schone
Kunsten, Citadel Park. Flemish
and Dutch primitives (Bosch),
some old masters, and a
pleasant collection of modern
art.

84 'S-GRAVENSTEEN   ca. 900
(castle)   onward
Geldmuntstraat

Good example of a feudal
castle. Well restored in
1913.

85 ST. BAAF'S   1290 onward
KATHEDRAAL
(cathedral)

*The Adoration of the Mystical
Lamb,* a masterpiece by the
van Eyck brothers (1426), is in
the sixth chapel, off the
ambulatory. Many other works
of art (Rubens, tenth
ambulatory chapel).

86 STADHUIS   1518 onward
(town hall)
Botermarkt/Hoogpoort

Flamboyant Gothic facade on
the Hoogpoort. •The cloth hall
(1425–44) and belfry (1321–
80) are on the south side
of the town hall. Opposite, to
the west, is the church of
St. Niklaas (1230–1432).

GRIMBERGEN B3
8 km (5 mi) N of Brussel

87 ST. SERVAAS   1660 onward
(abbey church)
G. van Zinnik

A large baroque church. Rococo
sacristy (1763).

HUY C5

88 NOTRE-DAME   1311–1536
(collegiate church)

Gothic. Fine rose window.

IEPER B1
(Ypres)

89 LAKENHALLE   1200–1304
(cloth hall)
Grote Markt

One of the largest Gothic structures in Europe. Destroyed in 1914; completely rebuilt in 1934.

KNOKKE A2

90 NELLENS HOUSE   1972
N. de Saint Phalle

A curiosity; the habitable woman/Guadi/graffiti "synthesis".

KORTRIJK B2 (Courtrai)

91 STADHUIS   14th c
(town hall)
Grote Markt

Flamboyant Gothic. Restored in 1962.

92 ST. MAARTENS KERK 15th c
(St. Martin's church)
Grote Markt (SE corner)

• An interesting beguinage of forty baroque houses surrounds a private courtyard, just north of St. Maartens. Past the beguinage is the church of Ons Lieve Vrouwe with Vandyke's *Raising of the Cross* in the north transept.

LEUVEN B4 (Louvain)

93 STADHUIS   1448–63
(town hall)
Grote Markt

Richly decorated flamboyant Gothic. Built by M. de Layens.

94 ST. PIETER   1425–97
(church)
Grote Markt

Brabant Gothic. Noteworthy rood screen and cross (1500). Restored after 1945. Triptychs by Bouts in the fifth and tenth ambulatory bays (clockwise).

LIÈGE C5 (Luik)

Museum: Musée des Beaux-Arts, 34, rue de l'Académie. 19th- and 20th-c Belgian and French paintings.

95 ÉGLISE   10th c onward
ST. BARTHOLOMÉE
(church)
place Paul Janson

Romanesque church with a baroque interior. Baptismal font (1107–18) by Renier de Huy.

96 ÉGLISE   11th–16th c
ST. JACQUES
(church)
place St.-Jacques

Flamboyant Gothic.

LIER B4

97 ST. GOMMAIRE   1425–1510
(church)
Rechtestraat

Flamboyant Gothic. Good stained glass.

MECHELEN B3 (Mechlin/Malines)

98 ST. ROMBOUT   1217 onward
(cathedral)
Grote Markt

Gothic exterior, baroque interior. Superb tower (1452–1546, restored 1975). *Crucifixion* by Vandyke (south transept). •*The Adoration of the Magi,* a tryptych by Rubens, is in St. Jan's Church, nearby.

99 ONZE LIEVE   15th–17th c
VROUWE OVER DE DIJLE
(church)
Onze Lieve Vrouwestraat

Rubens's *Miraculous Draught of Fishes* (south transept).

MONS C3

100 ST. WAUNDRU   1450–1590
(church)
square Franklin Roosevelt

Brabant Gothic. •The belfry nearby is one of the few baroque belfries still remaining in Belgium.

NIVELLES C3
(Nijvel)

101 COLLÉGIALE   11th–13th c
    ST. GERTRUDE   onward
    (church)

Rebuilt many times. Fine Romanesque crypt.

OUDENAARDE B2
(Audenarde)

102 STADHUIS   1525–36
    (town hall)
    Grote Markt
    H. van Pede

Flamboyant Gothic. Superb door carvings inside.

SOIGNIES C3
(Zinnik)

103 ST. VINCENT   960 onward
    MADELGAR
    (collegiate church)

Romanesque choir. Renaissance choir stalls (1576).

TERVUREN B4
13 km (8 mi) E of Brussel

104 LA NOUVELLE   1927
    MAISON
    (house)
    1, avenue Albert 1
    H. van de Velde

TOMBEEK B4
3 km (2 mi) SE of Overijse

105 SANATORIUM   1933–36
    JOSEPH LEMAIRE
    M. Brunfaut

A good early modern-movement building.

TOURNAI C2
(Doornik)

106 NOTRE-DAME   1140–1200
    (cathedral)
    rue de l'Hôpital Notre Dame

Monumental grouping of five towers around the crossing. This cathedral significantly influenced early Gothic cathedrals in France.

VEURNE B1
(Furnes)

107 ST. WALBURGA 1230 onward
    (church)

Choir rebuilt in 1385. Transepts completed in 1903.

ZOUTLEEUW B4
(Léau)

108 ST. LEONARDUS 13th–16th c
    (church)

The interior decoration is intact. Tabernacle (1552) by C. de Vriendt off the north transept.

Denmark

Vor Frelsers Kirke; *see entry 31*

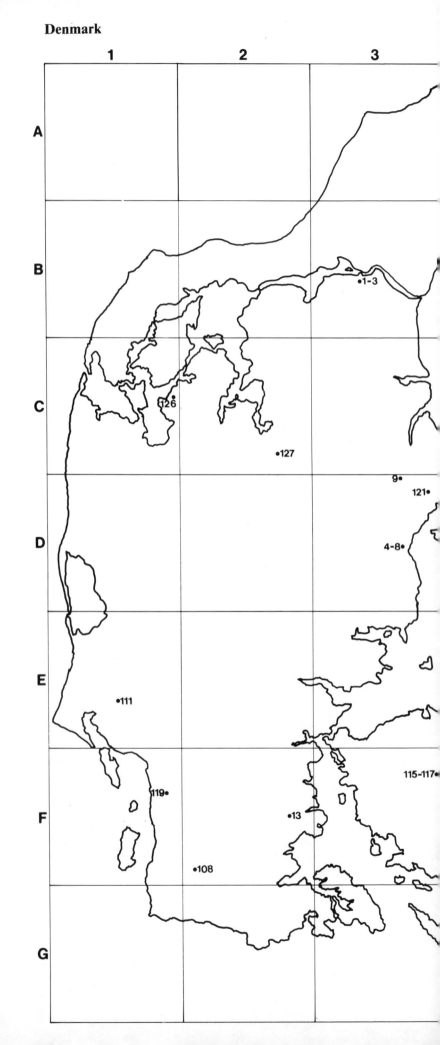

Denmark

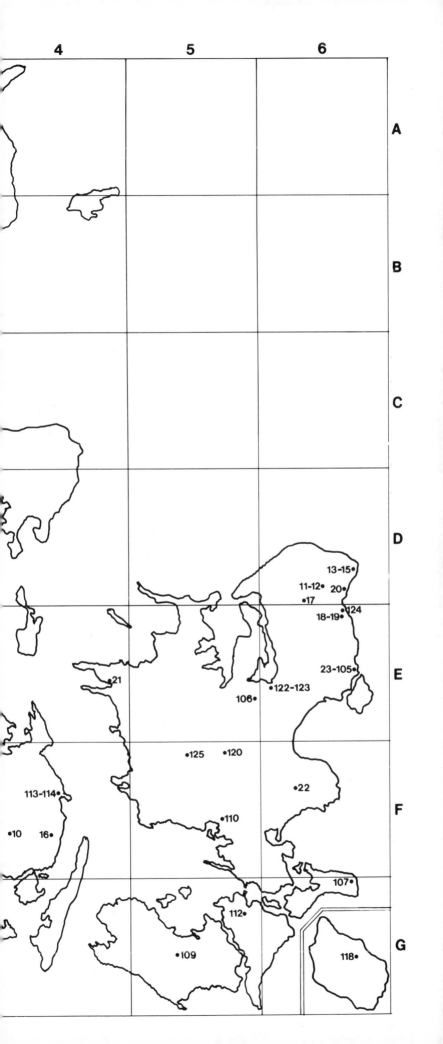

ÅLBORG B3

1 SCT. BUDOLFI   1438–1663
   KIRKE
   (church)
   Algade

   Rebuilt in 1778–80. Restored in
   1900 and 1941.

2 CARL CHRISTENSEN   1957
   FACTORY
   Riihimäkivej
   A. Jacobsen

3 NORDJYLLANDS   1963–72
   KUNSTMUSEUM
   (North Jutland Museum of Art)
   Kong Christians Alle 50
   A. and E. Aalto with J. Baruël

   The skylit gallery is a typical
   example of Aalto's mastery of
   this genre. Danish paintings
   from 1890 on.

ÅRHUS D3

4 VOR FRUE KIRKE   ca. 1100
   (Our Lady's Church and
   Monastery)
   Vestergade

   Medieval frescoes in chapter
   hall.

5 ÅRHUS   1201 onward
   CATHEDRAL
   Bispetorvet

   Romanesque. Rebuilt in the
   15th c and revaulted in the
   Gothic style. Restored in 1921.

6 DEN GAMLE BY   18th–19th c
   Viborgvej

   Museum of sixty reconstructed
   Danish houses.

7 ÅRHUS   1933–69
   UNIVERSITY
   Nordre Ringgade
   C. F. Møller

   K. Fisker and P. Stegmann were
   involved in the initial planning.
   Brick buildings integrated into
   the landscape.

8 RÅDHUS   1941
   (town hall)
   Rådhuspladsen
   E. Møller and A. Jacobsen

CLAUSHOLM D3
28 km (17 mi) N of Århus

9 MANOR HOUSE   1693–1701
   N. Tessin the Younger

COPENHAGEN
See København

EGESKOV F4
E of Kvaerndrup

10 EGESKOV SLOT   1550–54
   (castle)

   Restored in 1885. French garden
   laid out in 1730.

FREDENSBORG D6
15 km (9 mi) SE of Helsingør

11 FREDENSBORG   1719–26
   SLOT
   (castle)
   J. C. Krieger

   Extended from 1774–76. The
   park was laid out in 1760. The
   palace is open to the public in
   July; the park, year-round.

12 TERRASSERNE   1963
   (terrace houses)
   Helsingørvejen/Slotsgade
   J. Utzon

   Each house has a courtyard
   opening onto a communal green
   space.

HELSINGØR D6
(Elsinore)

13 SCT. OLAI   ca. 1200–1559
   KIRKE
   (cathedral)
   Sct. Olai Gade

14 KRONBORG SLOT   1574–85
   (castle)
   Kronborgvej, north of town
   center
   A. van Opbergen

   Outstanding Renaissance castle.
   Extended in 1700. Fine
   Renaissance chapel.

15 KINGO TERRACE   1958–60
   HOUSES
   Gurrevej, Kingosvej
   J. Utzon

HESSELAGERGÅRD F4
14 km (9 mi) N of Svendborg

16 MANOR HOUSE   1538

   Restored from 1951–61.
   •Another manor house, with
   fine grounds, is Glorup, 7 km
   (4 mi) further north.

HILLERØD D6

17 FREDERIKSBORG   1602–20
   SLOT
   (castle)

   Rich, heavy interiors.
   Noteworthy chapel. Restored
   in 1860. French garden.

HØRSHOLM E6

18 PALACE SQUARE   1734–44
   AND CHURCH
   L. de Thurah

19 EMPIRE CHURCH   1822
   Folehavevej
   C. F. Hansen

   •A terrace housing scheme
   (1966) in Kristineparken by J.
   Bo and V. Wohlert is close by.

HUMLEBAEK D6
10 km (6 mi) S of Helsingør

20 LOUISIANA   1958
   (gallery of modern art)
   Gl Strandvej 13
   J. Bo and V. Wohlert

A beautiful series of spaces integrated into the surrounding landscape. The collection of 20th-c art and sculpture is outstanding. Sculpture garden by O. Nørgård.

KALUNDBORG E4

21 VOR FRUE KIRKE   1170–90
(cathedral)

Greek cross plan with an octagonal tower at the end of each arm and over the crossing. Rebuilt in the late 19th c. Restored in 1921.

KARISE F6

22 MOLTKE CHAPEL   1761–66
C. F. Harsdorff

Refined classic revival building.

KØBENHAVN E6
(Copenhagen)

Tourist Information: Danmarks Turistråd, H. C. Andersens Boulevard 22 (tel. 111415).

Architect's Institute: Dansk Arkitektforening, Bredgade 66 (tel. 131290).

Bookstore: Busch Arnold International Boghandel, Købmagergade 49.

Museums: Ny Carlsberg Glyptothek, Dantes Plads 5. Mainly sculpture. An excellent collection of ancient (Egyptian, Greek, Etruscan, and Roman) and 19th-c French pieces (Rodin). Thorvaldsen, Henning, Nielsen, and other Danish works. Also 19th-c Danish and French impressionist paintings.
   Kunstindustrimuseet, Bredgade 68. European and oriental decorative arts.
   Statens Museum for Kunst, Sølvgade. Danish national collection. Also Flemish, French (N. Poussin), Italian (Titian, Mantegna), and other schools. See entry 52.
   Thorvaldsens Museum, Porthusgade 2. A complete collection of all the works (most are copies) of Bertel Thorvaldsen, as well as his own collection of antique art. See entry 48.

23 FRILANDS-   1600–1900
   MUSEET
   Kongevejen 100, Sorgenfri *M2*

National museum of rural houses.

24 ROSENBORG SLOT   1606–17
   (castle)
   Øster Voldgade 4 *B1*

Royal summer palace, now museum and barracks. Impressive Knights' Hall.

25 BØRSEN   1619–25
   (stock exchange)
   Børsgade *A3*
   L. and H. Steenwinkel the Younger

26 NYBODER TERRACE   1631
   HOUSES
   Sct. Paulsgade 21–40 *A1*
   H. Steenwinkel the Younger

Most houses date from the 18th c.

27 RUNDETÅRN   1637–56
   AND TRINITATIS KIRKE
   (observatory and church)
   Købmagergade *B2*
   H. Steenwinkel the Younger

28 HOLMENS KIRKE   1642
   (church)
   Holmens Kanal *A3*
   L. Blasius

29 KASTELLET   1663 onward
   (castle)
   Forbindelsevej *A1*

Planned by H. Ruse.

30 CHARLOTTEN-   1672–83
   BORG
   Kongens Nytorv 1 *A2*
   E. Janssen

Royal castle, now the Royal Academy.

31 VOR FRELSERS KIRKE 1696
   (Our Savior's Church)
   Sankt Annaegade *A3*
   L. van Haven

The spire (1750) is by L. de Thurah.

København

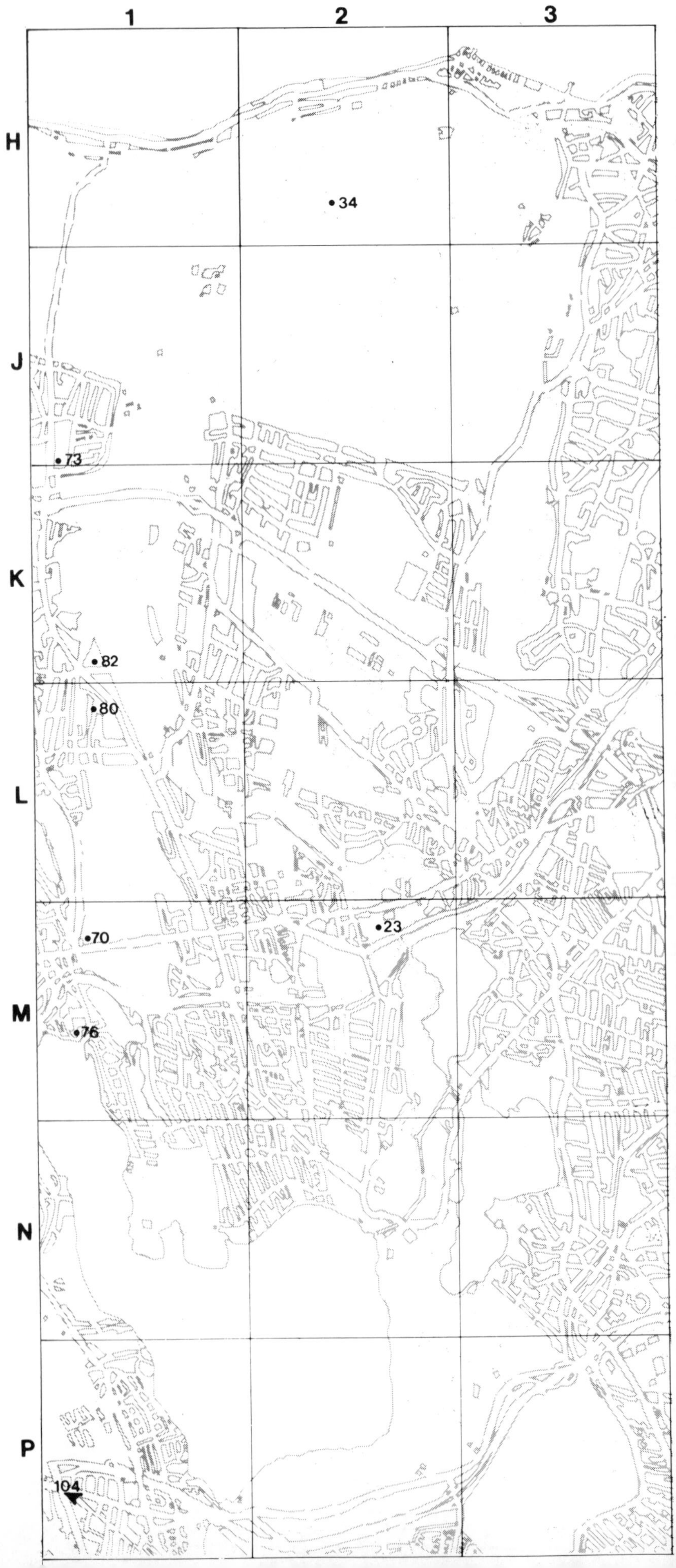

1 2 3

H

• 34

J

• 73

K

• 82

• 80

L

• 70

• 23

M

• 76

N

P

104

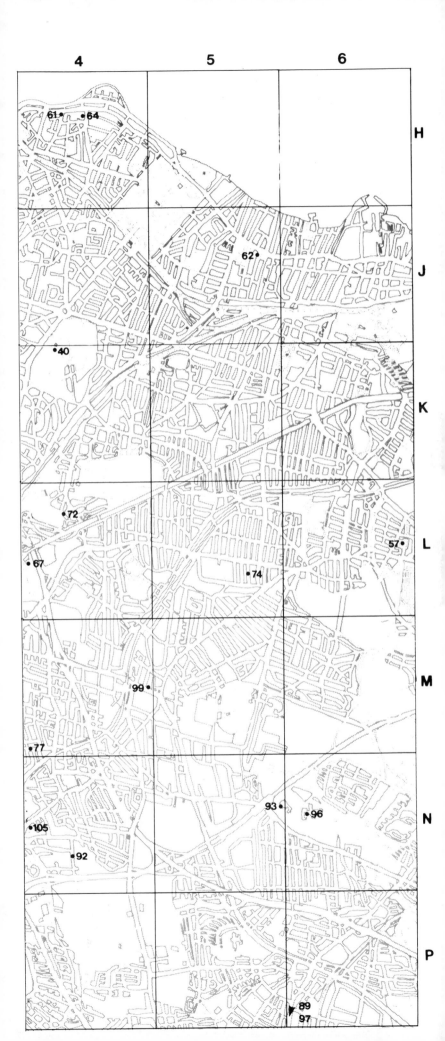

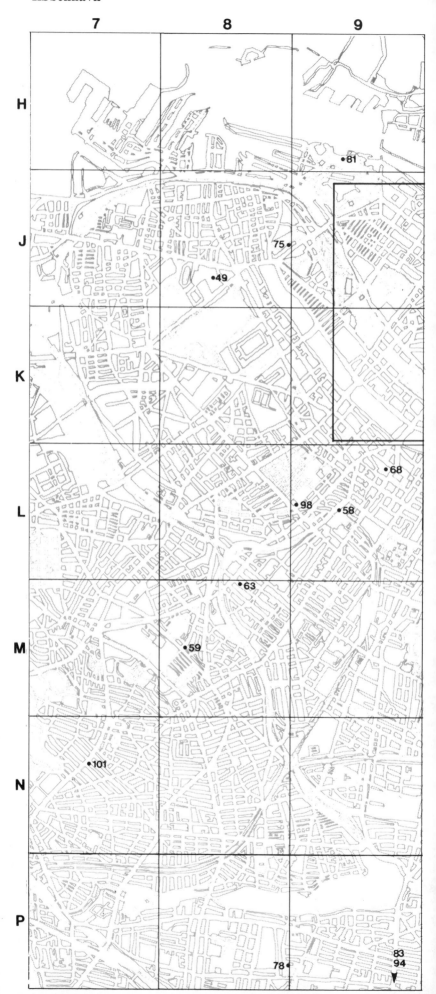

København

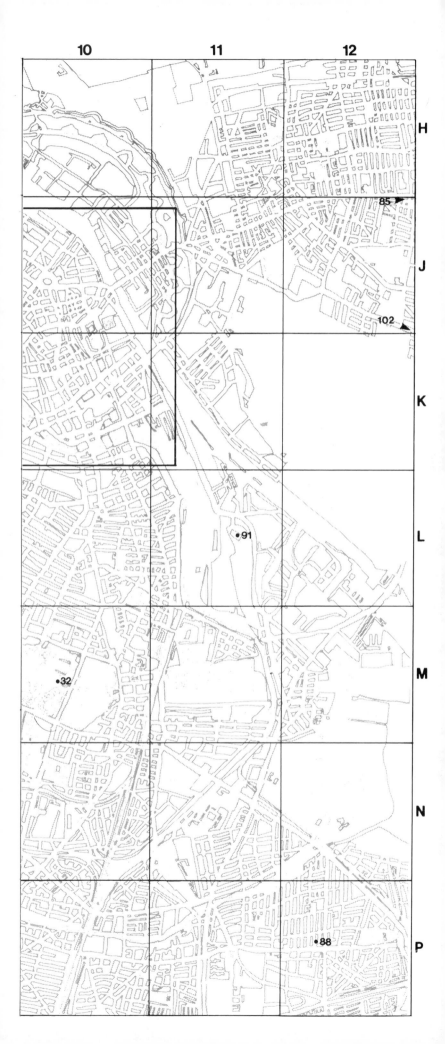

København detail

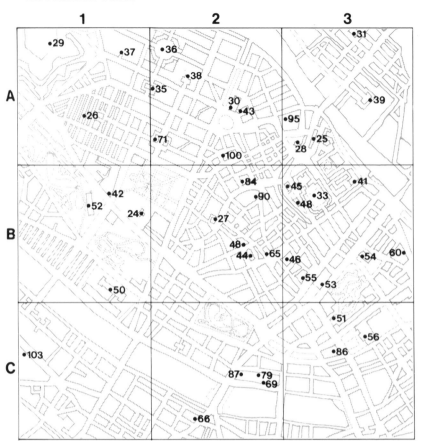

The palace was largely rebuilt
under Haüsser's direction in
the baroque style. The riding
school was the only section that
survived a fire in 1794. The
palace was rebuilt, burned down
again in 1884, and was again
rebuilt.

Magnificent baroque royal
hunting lodge with original
interiors.

On axis with the Amalienborg
Palace.

Eigtved traveled in Italy. The
facades show the influence of
F. Iuvara's Palazzo Madama in
Torino.

39 CHRISTIANS KIRKE 1755–59
(church)
Strandgade *A3*
N. Eigtved

Rococo.

40 BERNSTORFF'S 1765
PALACE
(now a school)
Jaegersborg Alle,
Charlottenlund *K3*
N. H. Jardin

41 CHRISTIAN IV'S 1767
BRYGHUS
Frederiksholms Kanal 29 *B3*
C. F. Harsdorff

Brewery converted to a naval
store.

42 SØLVGADE KASERNE 1771
(former barracks)
Sølvgade 40 *B1*
N. H. Jardin

43 HARSDORFF'S HUS 1780
Kongens Nytorv 3–5 *A2*
C. F. Harsdorff

The architect's own house.

44 VOR FRUE KIRKE 1810–29
(Church of Our Lady)
Nørregade *B2*
C. F. Hansen

Doric portico outside, coffered
Roman barrel vault inside.

45 CHRISTIANSBORG 1810–26
SLOTSKIRKE
(church)
Christiansborg slotsplads *B3*
C. F. Hansen

46 DOMHUSET 1815
(town hall and law courts)
Nytorv 21 *B3*
C. F. Hansen

47 THORVALDSEN 1838–48
MUSEUM
Porthusgade 2 *B3*
G. Bindesbøll

Polychromatic Etruscan style.
Frieze by J. Sonne.

48 UNIVERSITY LIBRARY 1851
Fiolstraede *B2*
J. D. Herholdt

49 LAEGEFORENINGENS 1853
BOLIGER
(medical association's housing
estate)
Østerbrogade 57, Østerbro *J8*
G. Bindesbøll

Planned low-density housing to
avoid congestion (and the
spread of disease).

50 MUNICIPAL HOSPITAL 1860
Øster Farimagsgade 5 *B1*
C. F. Hansen

51 PANTOMIMETEATRET 1874
(Royal Theater)
Tivoli, Vesterbrogade 3 *C3*
V. Dahlerup

52 STATENS MUSEUM 1888–95
FOR KUNST
(Royal Museum of Fine Arts)
Sølvgade *B1*
V. Dahlerup

Renovated by E. and N. Koppel,
Edstrand and Thyrring in 1970.

53 KØBENHAVNS 1892–1905
RÅDHUS
(town hall)
Rådhuspladsen *B3*
M. Nyrop

Won commission for this
building in an open design
competition. Successful
synthesis of several diverse
styles.

54 GLYPTOTEKET 1892–1906
(museum)
Dantes Plads 32 *B3*
V. Dahlerup

Completed by H. Kampmann.

55 PALACE HOTEL 1910
Rådhuspladsen 57 *B3*
A. Rosen

56 CENTRAL RAILWAY 1911
STATION
Banegaardsplad *C3*
H. Wenck

57 GRUNDTVIGS 1921–40
KIRKE
(church)
På Bjerget, Bispebjerg *L6*
P. V. Jensen Klint and K. Klint

A Danish village church
enlarged to a monumental scale.
See entry 117.

58 HORNBAEKHUS 1922
APARTMENTS
Ågade 126–34 *L9*
K. Fisker

59 BAKKEHUSENE 1923
(terrace houses)
Hulgaardsvej/Hvidkildevej *M8*
I. Bentsen and T. Henningsen

These houses became the model
for many terrace housing
schemes.

60 POLICE 1919–24
HEADQUARTERS
Hambrosgade *B3*
H. Kampmann and A. Rafn

61 KLAMPENBORG 1933–61
H4
Bellavista housing 1933
Strandvejen 419–433

Bellevue theater 1937
(now cinema)
Strandvejen

Terrace housing 1950–55
Strandvejen 413

Bellevue housing 1961
Strandvejen 417

All by A. Jacobsen.

62 BLIDAHPARK 1934
HOUSING ESTATE
Strandvejen, Hellerup *J5*
I. Bentsen and others

63 NOVO MEDICAL 1934–35
FACTORY
Fuglebakkevej *M8*
A. Jacobsen

64 FIVE HOUSES 1935–59
AND A STUDIO

Solystvej 5, 7, 9; Hvidorevej 24,
28; Klampenborg *H4*
M. Lassen

65 STELLING'S HUS   1937
(shop and offices)
Gammeltorv 6 *B2*
A. Jacobsen

66 BETHLEHEMS KIRKE   1937
(church)
Åboulevarden 8 *C2*
K. Klint

67 MARIEBJERG   1937
   CREMATORIUM
Mariebjergvej, Gentofte *L4*
F. Schegel

Landscaping by G. Brandt.

68 RADIOHUSET   1937–45
(national broadcasting house)
Rosenørns Alle 22 *L9*
V. Lauritzen

69 VESTERSØHUS   1939
   APARTMENTS
Vester Søgade 44–78 *C2*
K. Fisker and C. F. Møller

70 SØLLERØD RÅDHUS   1942
(town hall)
Øverødvej 2, Holte *M1*
A. Jacobsen and F. Lassen

71 DRONNINGEGARDEN
   APARTMENTS   1943–58
Dronningens Tvaergade 23–45
   A2
K. Fisker and S. E. Kristensen

72 UNGDOMSHUSENE   1949
   APARTMENTS
Niels Steensensvej 22–60 *L4*
A. Jacobsen

73 NAERUMVAENGE   1950–59
(housing estate and shopping
center)
Skodsborgvej, Naerum *J1*
P. Suenson

74 MUNKEGÅRDSSKOLEN
(primary school)   1952–56
Vangedevej 178, Søborg *L5*
A. Jacobsen

A very influential design. Every
classroom opens onto a private
open-air courtyard.

75 UNITED STATES OF   1954
   AMERICA EMBASSY

Dag Hammarskjølds Alle 24,
Østerbro *J8*
R. Rapson and J. van der
Muelen

76 PRIVATE HOUSE   1954
Ved Furesen, Dronninggård-
salle, Holte *M1*
J. Utzon

77 SKOLEPARKEN I   1955
(terrace houses)
Triumfvej, Gladsaxe *M4*
J. Bo and K. Hallberg

78 RØDOVRE RÅDHUS   1955
(town hall)
Rødovre Parkvej 150 *P8*
A. Jacobsen

•The adjacent library (no. 140)
is also by Jacobsen (1969).

79 JESPERSEN OFFICE   1955
   BUILDING
Nyropsgade 18 *C2*
A. Jacobsen

80 SØLLERØD   1955
(housing estate)
Vangebovej, Holte *L1*
E. and N. Koppel

81 LANGELINIE   1957
   RESTAURANT
Langelinie *H9*
E. and N. Koppel

82 VANGEBO   1957–60
   PRIMARY SCHOOL
Vangeboled 9, Holte *K1*
G. Bornebusch, M. Bruel, H.
Larsen, and J. Selchau

83 GLOSTRUP RÅDHUS   1958
(town hall)
Hovedvejen, Glostrup *P9*
A. Jacobsen

84 BIKUBEN   1958
(savings bank)
Silkegade 8 *B2*
P. Kjaergaard

85 TÅRNBY RÅDHUS   1959
(town hall)
Amager Landevej 74/
   Tårnbyvej, Tårnby *J12*
H. Gunnlogsson and J. Nielsen

86 SAS, ROYAL HOTEL   1960
Hammerichsgade 1–5 *C3*
A. Jacobsen

87 BYGGECENTRUM 1960
(building center)
Gyldenløvesgade 19 *C2*
E. and N. Koppel

88 SANKT NICOLAJ 1960
KIRKE
(church)
Strøbyvej 2, Hvidovre *P12*
J. O. von Spreckelsen

89 TOMS FABRIKKER 1961
(chocolate factory)
Ringvej B4/Ballerup Byvej,
Ballerup *P5*
A. Jacobsen

90 ILLUM'S BOLIGHUS 1961
(department store)
Amagertorv 10 *B2*
K. Kørbing

91 JERNBANETOLDKAMMER
(railway customs office) 1962
Vasbygade, Vesterbro *L11*
E. and N. Koppel

92 NOVO MEDICAL 1962–67
FACTORY
Smørmosevej, Bagsvaerd *N4*
A. Jacobsen

93 TELEVISION 1962–72
STUDIOS AND OFFICES
Mørkhøjvej 170, Gladsaxe *N5*
V. Lauritzen

94 ALBERTSLUND 1963–68
(new town), *P9*
P. Bredsdorff, O. Nørgård,
V. Møller-Jensen, T. Arnfred,
M. J. Petersen, and J. O.
Sørensen

One- to three-story units. Heavy
precast concrete construction.

95 DANMARKS 1965–75
NATIONALBANK
Holmens Kanal 17 *A3*
A. Jacobsen

96 BLÅGARD 1966
SEMINARY
Mørkhøjvej *N6*
J. Bo, K. and E. Clemmensen

97 VINFIRMAET 1966
GEORG BESTLE
(office and warehouse)
Meterbruen 24–28, Skovlunde
P6
H. Gunnlogsson and J. Nielsen

98 DET SJAELLANDSKE 1966
LANDSARKIV
(Zealand archives)
Jagtvej 10, Norrebro *L9*
E. and N. Koppel

99 BUDDINGE KIRKE 1970
(church)
Buddingevej, Søborg *M4*
I. and J. Rasmussen

Monopitch roofs on brick walls
strung along a well-scaled entry.

100 PISTOLSTRAEDE *A2* 1971
E. Møller

Street of renovated houses
(1730).

101 ST. ANTONI CHURCH 1972
AND NURSING HOME
Frederikssundsvej 225,
Brønshøj *N7*
V. Wohlert

102 BELLA 1972–75
EXHIBITION CENTER
Sjaellandsbroen/Faelleddiget,
Vestamager *J12*
O. Meyer

103 PANUM 1972–82
UNIVERSITY
Blegdamsvej *C1*
E. and N. Koppel, Edstrand
and Thyrring

104 FARUM 1974
MIDTPUNKT
(housing estate)
Bregnerødvej, Farum *P1*
J. O. Sørensen, V. Møller-
Jensen, and T. Arnfred

105 BAGSVAERD 1974–76
KIRKE
(church)
Bagsvaerd Hovedgade 189–191,
Bagsvaerd *N4*
J. Utzon

A sophisticated design (and
congregation for accepting it).

LEDREBORG
MANOR E5
10 km (6 mi) SW of Roskilde

106 LEDREBORG 1744–55
MANOR
J. C. Krieger, L. de Thurah,
and N. Eigtved

LISELUND
MANOR G6
5 km (3 mi) NE of Møn

107 LISELUND MANOR   1792
A. de la Calmette

Miniature neoclassic gem. The
charming English gardens have
suffered from land erosion but
a Swiss cottage and Chinese
pavilion survive.

LØGUMKLOSTER F2

108 KIRKE   1173–1300
(abbey church)

The church is original; the
cloisters (1961, by R. Grane,
R. Aas, C. T. Sørensen, J. P.
Tunggren Have), modern.

MARIBO G5
on Lolland Island

109 DOMKIRKE   1413–70
(cathedral)
•Alholm Castle (1350 onward),
24 km (15 mi) SE of Maribo, on
the sea, is a moated castle built
around a medieval fortress.
Restored in 1889.

NAESTVED F5

110 SCT. PETER'S KIRKE   1375
(church)

The largest Gothic church in
Denmark.

NØRHOLM E1
near Varde

111 MANOR HOUSE   1780
A fine, small baroque building.

NØRRE ALSLEV G5
on Falster Island

112 KIRKE   1325 onward
(church)

NYBORG F4

113 SLOT   1170
(castle)

Restored from 1919–23.

114 NYBORG KIRKE   1388–1428
(church)

ODENSE F3

115 SCT. KNUDS   1286–ca. 1480
KIRKE
(church)
Vestergade

Gothic. Good crypt.

116 SCT. HANS   13th–15th c
KIRKE
(church)
Nørregade

The adjoining monastery was
converted into a palace (ca.
1700) and then remodeled in
1841 in the neoclassic style.

117 FREDENSKIRKE   1916–20
(church)
Skibshusvej
P. V. Jensen Klint

Prototype for the Gruntvig
church (see entry 57).

ØSTELARS G6
on Bornholm Island
(*Note:* Bornholm Island is
approximately 140 km/87 mi
further east than is shown on the
map. Access from Finland and
Germany.)

118 ØSTELAR KIRKE   12th c
(church)

Circular plan. Elongated west
and east apses. Similar round
churches on Bornholm Island
at Ny, Nylar, and Sct. Olof.

RIBE F1

119 DOMKIRKE   ca. 1130 onward
(cathedral)

Transitional Romanesque and
Gothic structure. Unusual
Romanesque dome. Nave
revaulted in the 13th c. •Many
half-timbered houses in the old
section of the town.

RINGSTED F5

120 SCT. BENDTS   1170 onward
KIRKE
(church)

Romanesque. Gothic vaulting
(after a fire in 1241). Royal
tombs. •The town hall close by
is by S. E. Rasmussen.

ROSENHOLM D3
15 km (9 mi) N of Århus

121 ROSENHOLM   1567 onward
SLOT
(mansion)
H. Rosenkrantz

16th-c mansion in the French
style.

ROSKILDE E6

122 DOMKIRKE   ca. 1160 onward
(Cathedral of St. Luke)

Transitional Romanesque
Gothic. Twin spires added in
1635. The mausoleum for
Danish royalty. Fine neoclassic
revival sepulchral chapel (1774,
enter through sixth bay, right
aisle) for Frederik V by
C. F. Harsdorff. •The palace
(1733) adjacent to the cathedral
is by L. de Thurah.

123 VIKINGES-   1968
     KIBSHALLEN
(Museum of Viking ships)
at the harbor
E. C. Sørensen

RUNGSTED E6
20 km (12 mi) N of København

124 TERRACE HOUSES   1962
    Rungsted Strandvej/Rungsted
     Kyst
J. Bo and V. Wohlert

SORØ F5

125 KIRKE   1160 onward
    (abbey church)

SPOTTRUP SLOT C1
castle 20 km (12 mi) W of Skive

126 SPOTTRUP   1450 onward
    SLOT
    (castle)

Double moat. Some baroque
interiors. Restored in 1937.

VIBORG C2

127 DOMKIRKE   ca. 1140 onward
    (cathedral)

Modeled after Speyer cathedral
in Germany. Totally rebuilt,
1862–76. Only the original
crypt has survived.

Finland

Cemetery Chapel; *see entry 150*

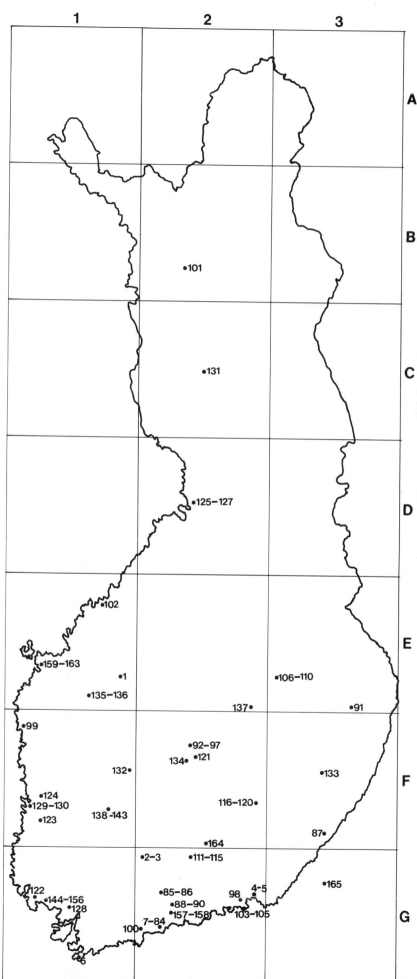

Finland

Helsinki

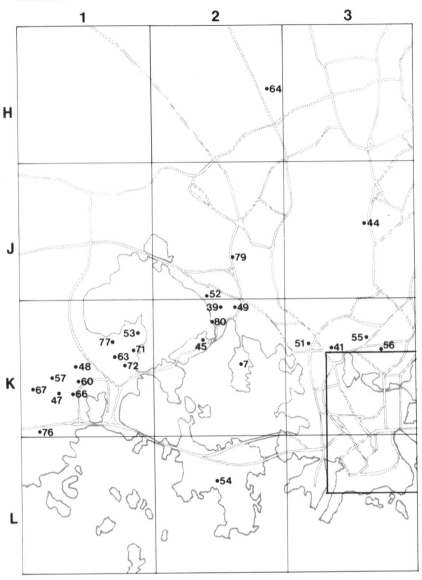

ALAJÄRVI E1

1 KAUPUNGINTALO   1969
(town hall)
A. Aalto

HÄMEENLINNA G2
(Tavastehus)

2 KIRKKO   1798
(Lutheran church)
Kauppatori
L. J. Désprez

Restored (1965) by A.
Ruusuvuori.

3 HOTEL AULANKO   1938
P. E. Blomstedt

Completed by M. Blomstedt
and M. Lampen. Later
extended.

HAMINA G2
(Fredrikshamn)

4 KAUPUNGINTALO   1798
(town hall)
Brockman

Restored by C. L. Engel in 1840.
This is the centerpiece of an

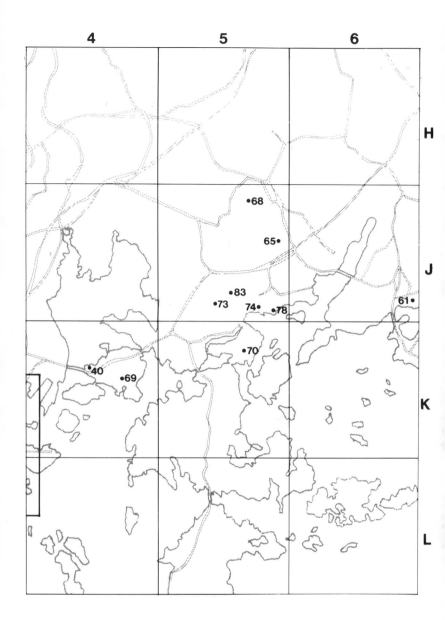

octagonal town plan dating
from 1772.

5 KOULU   1962
(secondary school)
Vesikatu 7
K. and H. Siren

HANKO G1
(Hangö)

6 HYVON–KUDENEULE 1955
  TEXTILE FACTORY
Hopearanta
V. Revell

HELSINKI G2
(Helsingfors)

Tourist Information: Helsinki
City Tourist Office,
Pohjoisesplanadi 19 (tel.
169–3757).

Architect's Institute: Suomen
Arkkitehtiliitto, Eteläesplanadi
22A, (tel. 640–801).

Museums: Amos Andersonin
Taidemuseo, Yrjönkatu 27.
20th-c Finnish art.
    Museum of Architecture,
Puistokatu 4. Architectural
exhibitions and information.
    Ateneum Taidemuseo,
Kaivokatu 2. 18th- to 20th-c
Finnish artists. Some
French impressionists
(Gauguin) and contemporary
European works.
    Didrichsenin Taidemuseo,
Kuusilahdenkuja 3. Private
collection of modern art.
Restricted admission; check
first with tourist office.

Helsinki detail

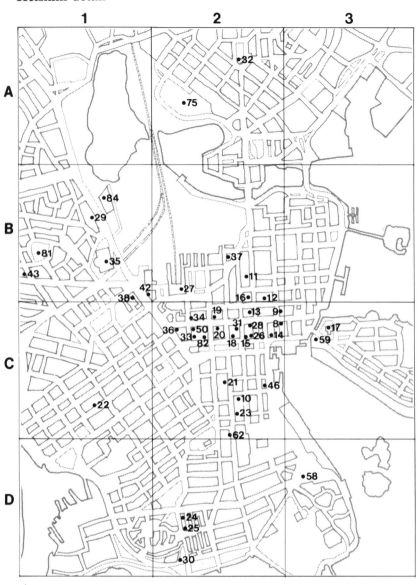

14 KAUPUNGINTALO 1833
(town hall)
Pohjoisesplanadi 11–13 *C2*
C. L. Engel

Renovation (1967–73) by A. Ruusuvuori.

15 SAS/SYP 1837
BANKING OFFICE
Pohjoisesplanadi 23 *C2*
A. F. Granstedt

Renovation by K. Gullichsen in 1962.

16 YLIOPISTON KIRJASTO 1844
(university library)
Unioninkatu 36 *B2*
C. L. Engel

17 USPENSKI 1868
TUOMIOKIRKKO
(Greek Orthodox cathedral)
Katajanokka *C3*
A. M. Gornostajeff

18 GRÖNQVIST HOUSE 1882
Pohjoisesplanadi 25–27 *C2*
C. Höijer

•No. 29, the KOP Bank (1887, former Hotel Kämp), is also by Höijer.

19 LUNDQVIST HOUSE 1900
(office building)
Aleksanterinkatu 13 *C2*
S. A. Lindqvist

20 POHJOLA INSURANCE 1901
COMPANY BUILDING
Aleksanterinkatu 44 *C2*
H. Gesellius, A. Lindgren, and E. Saarinen

21 STUDENTS' UNION 1901
Kasarmikatu 40 *C2*
K. Hard

22 STUDENTS' HOUSE 1903
Lönnrotinkatu 29 *C1*
W. Thome and K. Lindahl

23 OFFICE BUILDING 1905
Korkeavuorenkatu 35 *C2*
L. Sonck

24 EIRA SAIRAALA 1905
(hospital)
Laivurinkatu 29 *D2*
L. Sonck

25 VILLA JOHANNA 1906
Laivurinkatu 25 *D2*
S. A. Lindqvist

26 BANK 1906
Pohjoisesplanadi 19 *C2*
L. Sonck and V. Jung

Renovation (1968) by A. Ruusuvuori.

27 RAUTATIEASEMA 1906–14
(central railway station)
Rautatientori *B2*
E. Saarinen

Saarinen's first major building.

28 OFFICE BUILDING 1908
Unioninkatu 30 *C2*
H. Gesellius

29 KANSALLISMUSEO 1910
(National Museum)
Mannerheimintie 34 *B1*
H. Gesellius, A. Lindgren, and E. Saarinen

30 VILLA ENSI 1911
Merikatu 23 *D2*
S. A. Lindqvist

31 STOCK EXCHANGE 1911
Fabianinkatu 14 *C2*
L. Sonck

32 KALLIO KIRKKO 1912
(church)
Itäinen Papinkatu 2 *A2*
L. Sonck

33 KÄSITEOLLISU- 1921
USPANKKI
(bank)
Keskuskatu 1 *C2*
E. Saarinen

34 HELSINGIN 1929
OSAKEPANKKI
(bank)
Aleksanterinkatu 17 *C2*
P. E. Blomstedt

35 EDUSKUNTATALO 1930
(House of Parliament)
Mannerheimintie 30 *B1*
J. S. Siren

36 STOCKMANN 1930
DEPARTMENT STORE
Keskuskatu 2 *C2*
S. Frosterus

Frosterus won the design competition to build this in 1916.

37 POHJA INSURANCE 1930
COMPANY BUILDING
Kaisaniemenkatu 6 *B2*
O. Kallio

First horizontal strip windows
in Helsinki.

38 GLASS PALACE 1935
(office building)
Mannerheimintie 22 *B1*
V. Revell, N. Kokko, and
H. Riihimäki

39 VILLA AALTO 1937
Riihitie 20, Munkkiniemi *K2*
A. Aalto

Own house.

40 HOUSE 1939
Lautturikuja, Kulosaari *K4*
J. Jaatinen

41 OLYMPIC STADIUM 1940–52
Eteläinen Stadiontie *K3*
Y. Lindegren and T. Jäntti

Later extended.

42 OFFICE BUILDING 1949
Mannerheimintie 9 *B1*
E. Huttunen

43 FINNISH SCHOOL 1950
OF ECONOMICS
Runeberginkatu 14 *B1*
H. Harmia and W. Baeckman

44 APARTMENT 1951
BUILDING
Mäkelänkatu 86 *J3*
Y. Lindegren

45 HOUSE AND 1951–61
STUDIO
Kuusisaari, Munkkiniemi *K2*
A. Ervi

46 INDUSTRIAL CENTER 1952
AND PALACE HOTEL
Eteläranta 10 *C2*
V. Revell and K. Petäjä

47 TAPIOLA CENTER 1952–69
(shopping center, swimming
baths, and department store)
Heikintori, Tapiola *K1*
A. Ervi

Ervi won the commission for
the community center in an
open design competition.
Loosely based on the English
garden city concept, these
buildings are well integrated
into the landscape.

48 TERRACE HOUSES 1954
Menninkäisentie 8–10, Tapiola
K1
V. Revell

The nursery and kindergarten
(1954) at No. 7 are also by
Revell.

49 APARTMENT 1954
BUILDINGS
Riihitie 12–14, Munkkiniemi *K2*
A. Aalto

50 RAUTATALO 1954
OFFICE BUILDING
Keskuskatu 3 *C2*
A. Aalto

Elegant courtyard.

51 NATIONAL 1956
PENSIONS INSTITUTE
(office building)
Minna Canthinkatu 15 *K3*
A. Aalto

52 STUDIO 1956
Tiilimäki 20, Munkkiniemi *J2*
A. Aalto

53 KIRKKO 1957
(student chapel)
Otaniemi *K1*
K. and H. Siren

Burned in 1976, an identical
replica was built in 1978. A
masterpiece, created by the
simplest means possible.

54 LAUTTASAARI 1958
   KIRKKO
   (church)   .
   Myllykallio, Lauttasaari *L2*
   K. Petäjä

55 KULTUURITALO 1958
   (House of Culture)
   Sturenkatu 4 *K3*
   A. Aalto

Auditorium and offices for
Finnish trade unions.

56 WORKERS' 1959
   INSTITUTE ANNEX
   Helsinginkatu 26 *K3*
   A. Blomstedt

57 APARTMENTS 1961
   Riistapolku, Tapiola *K1*
   A. Blomstedt

58 HOUSE 1961
   Myllytie 5 *D3*
   A. Ervi

59 ENSO GUTZEIT 1962
   HEAD OFFICE
   Kanavaranta 1 *C3*
   A. Aalto

60 ATRIUM HOUSES 1962–64
   Hakalehto, Tapiola *K1*
   P. Ahola

61 SYP BANKING 1963
   INSTITUTE
   Vuosaari *J6*
   M. and R. Ypyä

62 OFFICE BUILDING 1964
   Kasarmikatu 22 *C2*
   T. Korhonen

63 OTANIEMI 1964
   YLIOPISTO
   (technical university)
   Otaniemi *K1*
   A. Aalto

•The library (also by Aalto) was
built in 1970.

64 FINNISH- 1964
   RUSSIAN SCHOOL
   Kirjokalliontie 2, Etelä-
   Kaarela *H2*
   O. Sipari

65 PUOTINHARJU 1965
   SHOPPING CENTER
   Puotinharju *J5*
   E. Karvinen

66 TAPIOLA KIRKKO 1965
   (church)
   Tapion Raitti, Tapiola *K1*
   A. Ruusuvuori

67 WEILIN & GÖÖS 1965
   PRINTING WORKS
   Ahertajantie 5, Tapiola *K1*
   A. Ruusuvuori

The roof is hung from four
monumental air ducts.

68 MYLLYPURO 1966
   SHOPPING CENTER *J5*
   E. Karvinen

69 KULOSAARI KOULU 1966
   (primary school)
   Kyösti Kalliontie 1, Kulosaari
   K4
   O. Lappo

70 APARTMENT 1966
   BUILDING
   Pellonperäntie 9, Tammisalo *K5*
   T. Penttilä

71 URDSGJALLAR 1966
   STUDENT HOUSE
   Otaniemi *K1*
   K. Moberg

72 DIPOLI 1966
   (students' clubhouse)
   Otaniemi *K1*
   R. Pietilä and R. Paatelainen

73 ROIHUVUORI KOULU 1967
   (primary school)
   Vuorenpeikontie 7,
   Roihuvuori *J5*
   A. Ruusuvuori

74 HOUSE 1967
   Puolaharju 41, Marjaniemi *J5*
   R. Kauria

75 HELSINKI TEATTERI 1967
   (municipal theater)
   Eläintarhantie 5 *A2*
   T. Pentillä

76 SUVIKUMPU 1967–69
   RESIDENTIAL AREA
   Suvikumpu, Tapiola *K1*
   R. Pietilä and R. Paatelainen

77 DISTRICT HEATING 1968
   AND POWER PLANT
   Otaniemi *K1*
   A. Aalto

78 HOUSE 1968
   Puolaharju 18, Marjaniemi *J5*
   P. Saiminen

79 POHJOLA INSURANCE 1969
   COMPANY BUILDING
   Lapinmäentie 1 *J2*
   V. Revell and H. Castren

80 HOTEL 1969
   KALASTAJATORPPA
   Kalastajatorpantie 1,
   Munkkiniemi *K2*
   M. Tavio

81 TEMPPELIAUKIO 1969
   KIRKKO
   ("rock" church)
   Lutherinkatu 3 *B1*
   T. and T. Suomalainen

82 ACADEMIC BOOK 1969
   SHOP
   Pohjoisesplanadi 39 *C2*
   A. Aalto

83 ROIHUVUORI KIRKKO 1970
   (church)
   Tulisuontie, Roihuvuori *J5*
   L. Silvennoinen

84 FINLANDIA HALL 1971–75
   Karamsininkatu 4 *B1*
   A. Aalto

Concert hall and congress
center. A superb building.

HYVINKÄÄ G2
(Hyvinge)

85 HYVINKÄÄ KIRKKO 1961
   (parish church and center)
   A. Ruusuvuori

Pyramidal form.

86 RAUHANNUMMI 1972
   CHAPEL AND
   CEMETERY
   A. Ruusuvuori

IMATRA F3

87 VUOKSENNISKA 1958
   KIRKKO
   (church)
   A. Aalto

An asymmetrical design. The
very complex interior can be
divided into three separate
meeting halls by enormous
sliding partitions made of
solid concrete.

JÄRVENPÄÄ G2

88 AINOLA 1904
L. Sonck

Jean Sibelius's home.

89 ARTISTS' HOUSE 1967
Riihitie
K. Mikkola

90 JÄRVENPÄÄ KIRKKO 1968
(church)
Kirkkotie 6
E. Elomaa

Off shutter concrete inside and
out. The building owes
something to La Tourette in
France but makes its own
statement with conviction.

JOENSUU E3

91 KAUPUNGINTALO 1914
(town hall)
E. Saarinen

JYVÄSKYLÄ F2

92 TEATTERI 1923–25
(city theater)
Kauppakatu 30
A. Aalto

93 VOCATIONAL 1951–57
SCHOOL OF CENTRAL
FINLAND
Sepänkatu/Rajakatu
M. and K. Petäjä

94 JYVÄSKYLÄ 1952–72
COLLEGE OF
EDUCATION
Keskussairaalantie
A. Aalto

Grouped around an open
courtyard.

95 MUSEUM OF 1961
CENTRAL FINLAND
Keskussairaalantie/Haarakatu
A. Aalto

•The Alvar Aalto Museum
(1973, by Aalto) is adjacent.

96 TRADE SCHOOL AND 1963
TECHNICAL INSTITUTE
Viitaniementie
M. and K. Petäjä

97 POLICE STATION 1968
Hannikaisenkatu/Kilpisenkatu
A. Aalto

This is part of the town center
designed by Aalto in 1964.

KARHULA G2
10 km (6 mi) N of Kotka

98 SUNILA 1936–39
CELLULOSE FACTORY
AND RESIDENTIAL AREA
A. Aalto

Second stage built 1951–54.

KASKINEN F1
(Kaskö)

99 KIRKKO 1965
(new church)
E. Kråkström

KIRKKONUMMI G2
20 km (12 mi) SW of Helsinki

100 HVITTRÄSK 1902
(architects' houses and studio)
Luoma
H. Gesellius, A. Lindgren, and
E. Saarinen

KITTILÄ B2

101 SÄRESTÖ GALLERY 1971
R. Pietilä, R. Paatelainen, and
R. Särestöniemi

A luxurious sauna, swimming
pool, and art gallery built from
pine logs.

KOKKOLA E1
(Gamlakarleby)

102 KAUPUNGINTALO 1845
(town hall)
Mannerheiminaukio
C. L. Engel

KOTKA G2

103 BANK BUILDING 1935
Kirkkokatu 6
P. E. Blomstedt

Outstanding functionalist
design.

104 KOULU 1971
(secondary school)
Langinkoski, Keisarimajantie
O. Sipari

105 BANK BUILDING AND 1971
APARTMENT HOUSE
Kotkankatu 16
K. and H. Siren

KUOPIO E3

106 TUOMIOKIRKKO 1795–1812
(cathedral)
J. Rijf, then P. Granstedt

Restored (1961) by Ström and
Tuomisto.

107 KAUPUNGINTALO 1884
(town hall)
Tulliportinkatu
F. A. Sjöström

108 TEATTERI 1963
(city theater)
H. Stenros and R. V.
Luukkonen

109 KIRJASTO 1966–67
(municipal library)
Maaherrankatu 12
M. Hakala

110 ALAVA KIRKKO 1969
(church)
Keihäskatu 5
A. Schütz

LAHTI G2

111 KAUPUNGINTALO 1912
(town hall)
Puistokatu
E. Saarinen

112 CONCERT HALL 1954
Sibeliuskenkatu 8
K. and H. Siren

113 KOP BANK ANNEX 1964
Aleksanterinkatu 10
V. Revell

114 KIRKKO 1970
(church)
Kirkkokatu 4
A. Aalto

115 SALPAUSSELKÄ 1972
KIRKKO
(church)
on the road to Tampere
H. Löfström

MIKKELI F2
(Skt. Michel)

116 KIRKKO 1817
(wooden church)
Otavankatu 9
C. Bassi

117 PROVINCIAL 1824
GOVERNMENT OFFICES
Maaherrankatu 16
C. L. Engel

118 KAUPUNGINTALO 1911
(town hall)
S. A. Lindqvist

119 WATER TOWER 1912
Naisvuori
S. A. Lindqvist

120 POLICE STATION 1968
Maaherrankatu 10
A. Ruusuvuori

MUURATSALO F2
island close to Säynätsalo

121 ARCHITECT'S 1953
SUMMER VILLA
A. Aalto

Courtyard house with adjacent
experimental structures.

NAANTALI G1
(Nådendal)
20 km (12 mi) W of Turku

122 KULTARANTA 1916
(summer residence of the
president)
Luonnonmaa
L. Sonck

NAKKILA F1

123 NAKKILA KIRKKO 1937
(church)
E. Huttunen

NOORMARKKU F1

124 VILLA MAIREA 1938
A. Aalto

An extraordinary synthesis of
man and nature is achieved
in this country house.

OULU D2
(Uleåborg)

125 TUOMIOKIRKKO 1770–77
(cathedral)
Kirkkokatu
D. Högman

Rebuilt by C. L. Engel
(1827–32). Restored in 1932.

126 SOK OFFICES 1940
AND STORE
Kansankatu 47
E. Huttunen

127 TEATTERI 1972
(city theater)
M. and M. Jaatinen

PAIMIO G1
25 km (16 mi) E of Turku

128 TUBERCULOSIS 1929–33
SANATORIUM
A. Aalto

A superbly confident design.
Every detail, including the
sanitary ware, was custom-
designed by Aalto. Now
Paimio Hospital.

PORI F1
(Björneborg)

129 KAUPUNGINTALO 1831-41
(old town hall)
Hallituskatu 12
C. L. Engel

130 KIRKKO 1863
(church)
off Pohjoispuisto
G. T. Chiewitz and J. von
Heideken

ROVANIEMI C2

131 KIRJASTO 1965
(municipal library)
A. Aalto

Part of the town center master
plan designed by Aalto in 1963.

RUOVESI F1

132 KALELA 1894
(artist's studio)
A. Gallèn-Kallela

SAVONLINNA F3

133 SAVONLINNA 1475
CASTLE onward
E. A. Tott

SÄYNÄTSALO

134 KAUPUNGINTALO 1952
(town hall)
A. Aalto

Arranged around an elevated
courtyard. Red brick, copper
roof.

SEINÄJOKI E1

135 CIVIC CENTER 1958-66
A. Aalto

Church (1958-60), town hall
and library (1965), and parish
hall (1966). Aalto won the

commission for this center
in two separate design
competitions.

136 RAUTATIEASEMA 1972
(railway station)
H. Castren

SUONENJOKI E2

137 KAUPUNGINTALO 1968-71
(town hall)
P. Heino, E. Hyvämäki, and
R. Parkkinen

TAMPERE F1
(Tammerfors)

138 TUOMIOKIRKKO 1902-7
(cathedral)
off Rautatienkatu
L. Sonck

139 YLIOPISTO 1960-67
(university)
Viinikankatu
T. Korhonen

140 VATIALA 1961
CEMETERY CHAPEL
Kangasalantie
V. Revell

141 SAMPOLA 1962
EDUCATIONAL
INSTITUTE
Sammonkatu
T. Penttilä and K. Virta

142 RATINA STADIUM 1966
Tampereenvaltatie
T. Penttilä

143 KALEVA KIRKKO 1966
(church)
Liisanpuisto
R. Pietilä and R. Paatelainen

Irregular plan pulled straight
up without any vertical
articulation. Slip-cast
concrete interior, tiled
exterior.

TURKU G1
(Åbo)

Museum: Turku Taidemuseo,
Puolalanpuisto. 19th- and
20th-c Finnish artists (Gallèn-
Kallela).

144 TUOMIKIRKKO 1230-90
(cathedral) onward
off Uudenmaankatu

145 TURKU LINNA 1280-1588
(castle)
Aurakatu, off Linnankatu
(by the harbor)

146 KIRKKO 1846
(orthodox church)
Kauppatori
C. L. Engel

147 LOUNAIS-SUOMEN 1928
MAALAISTENTALO
(agricultural house)
Humalistonkatu 7
A. Aalto

148 TURUN SANOMAT 1929
NEWSPAPER BUILDING
Kauppiaskatu 5
A. Aalto

Early functionalist building.
First round skylights used by
Aalto.

149 ÅBO AKADEMI 1935
KIRJASTO
(book tower library)
Tuomiokirkkokatu 2–4
E. Bryggman

Annex (1957) by W. Baeckman.

150 CEMETERY 1940–41
CHAPEL
Turku Cemetery
E. Bryggman

The Chapel of the Holy Cross
(1967) is by P. Pitkänen.

151 YLIOPISTO 1954 onward
(Turku university)
Vesilinnanmäki
A. Ervi

152 TEATTERI 1962
(municipal theater)
Östra Strandgaten
R. V. Luukkonen and
H. Stenros

153 KOP BANK BUILDING 1964
Aurakatu 8
V. Revell

154 WÄINÖ AALTONEN 1967
MUSEUM
It. Rantakatu 38
I. and M. Aaltonen

155 SIBELIUS MUSEUM 1967
Piispankatu 17
W. Baeckman

156 INSTITUTE BUILDING 1969
OF ÅBO AKADEMI
Porthaninkatu 3
W. Baeckman and H. Löfström

TUUSULA G2
16 km (10 mi) N of Helsinki

157 ARTIST'S 1899–1902
STUDIO
Halosenniemi
P. Halonen

158 HYRYLÄ KIRKKO 1968
(parish center)
K. Mikkola and J. Pallasmaa

VAASA E1
(Vasa)

159 COURT OF 1857–62
APPEALS
Rantapuisto
C. A. Setterberg

160 KIRKKO 1867
(Trinity church)
SW of Kauppatori (market
square)
C. A. Setterberg

161 COMMERCIAL 1958–62
CENTER
V. Revell

162 HUUTONIEMI 1964
KIRKKO
(church and parish center)
A. Ruusuvuori

Off shutter concrete exterior,
face-brick interior. The church
plan distorts the rectangular
geometry to form an irregular
cube with a warped planar
ceiling.

163 ÖSTERBOTTENS 1968
MUSEUM
(annex)
Koulukatu 2
E. Kråkström

VIERUMÄKI F2

164 SPORTS INSTITUTE 1933–36
E. Bryggman

VIIPURI
now Vyborg, USSR

165 MUNICIPAL 1930–35
LIBRARY
A. Aalto

Aalto won the design
competition to build this in
1927. Badly damaged during the
Russo-Finnish war, now
restored. Undulating internal
roof used here by Aalto for the
first time.

France

Château De Blois; *see entry 43*

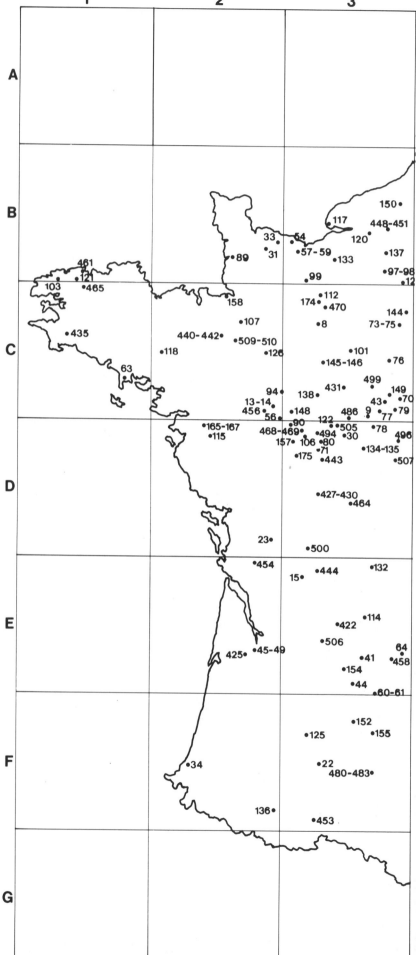

France

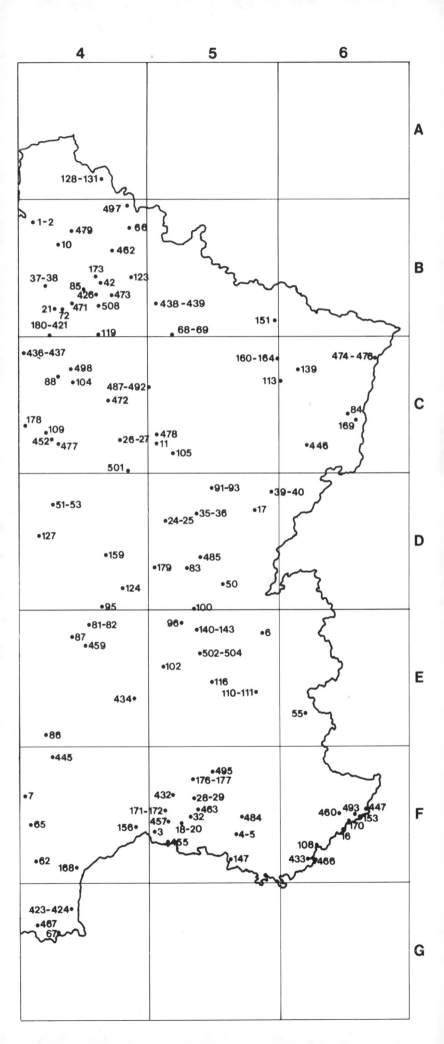

ABBEVILLE B4

1 ST.-VULFRAN   1488 onward
(church)
rue St.-Vulfran

Flamboyant Gothic. Badly
damaged in WWII. •The church
at St.-Riquier (13 km/8 mi NE)
has a fine interior; the Gothic
exterior has weathered badly.

2 CHÂTEAU DE   1645
   LA BAGATELLE

Built for Abraham van Robais.
Rococo decoration in the style
of Huet and Boucher. Louis
XV and XVI furniture.

AIGUES–MORTES F5

3 FORTIFIED   ca. 1272
   RAMPARTS

Built by S. Boccanegra of
Genoa. The Tower of
Constance, originally moated,
was connected to the ramparts
in the 16th C.

AIX–EN–PROVENCE F5

Museum: Musée Granet, place
St.-Jean de Malte. Greek and
Roman sculpture. Paintings
by Clouet, Rubens (*Beheading
of St. Paul*), Rembrandt,
Granet, Ingres (*Jupiter and
Thetis*), Cézanne, etc.
Cézanne's studio on avenue
Paul-Cézanne is just north
of the town.

4 CATHÉDRALE   ca. 1175
   ST.-SAUVEUR
rue J. De-la-Roque

14th-C tower. Flamboyant
Gothic facade built ca. 1525
with notable carved walnut
doors (1505-8) on the west.
Inside is N. Froment's *Triptych
of the Burning Bush* (1476).
5th-C baptistry. Romanesque
cloisters.

5 STE.-MARIE-   17th C
   MADELAINE
(church)
rue Portalis

Triptych of the Annunciation
(1445) by Jean Chapus. One
wing is in the Musée d'Art
Ancien in Brussel, the other in
the Netherlands (one section in

the Rijksmuseum, Amster-
dam, the other in the Museum
Boymans-van Beuningen,
Rotterdam).

AIX–LES–BAINS E5

Museum: Musée du Docteur
Faure, boulevard des Côtes.
19th-C paintings. Sculpture
by Rodin.

6 HÔTEL DE VILLE   16th C
(town hall)

Former château d'Aix. •On the
opposite side of Lac du Bourget
is Hautecombe Abbey (ca. 16th
C) with a richly decorated
church (restored in 1824).

ALBI F4

Museum: Musée Toulouse-
Lautrec, place de l'Archevêque.
Housed in the fortified Palais de
la Berbie. Extensive collection
of paintings by Toulouse-
Lautrec. Also works by Degas,
Matisse, Rodin, and other
contemporaries of Toulouse-
Lautrec.

7 CATHÉDRALE   1282–1512
   STE.-CECILE
place Ste.-Cecile

Fortress church in brick. Rood
screen (ca. 1500) with
flamboyant carving.
Flamboyant south porch added
in 16th C.

ALENÇON C3

8 NOTRE-DAME   14th C–1444
(church)
Grand Rue

Flamboyant Gothic. Porch
(1490–1506) by J. Lemoine.
Stained glass windows (1530).
Tower, transept, and chancel
reconstructed in the 18th C.

AMBOISE C3

9 CHÂTEAU   15th–16th C
   D'AMBOISE
rue Victor Hugo

Most of the fortifications were
demolished (1631, ca. 1800, and
1940). The Chapelle St.-Hubert
(1490), a flamboyant Gothic
structure, is incorporated in the
ramparts. Modern stained glass.
•Da Vinci lived from 1516–19
in the Clos-Luce château
nearby, where exhibits and
models of his work are on
display.

AMIENS B4

Museum: Musée de Picardie, 48 rue de la République. Primitive paintings from northern France; 18th-c French works by Q. de la Tour (*Self-Portrait*), Fragonard, Boucher, and others; also works by Ribera and El Greco (*Portrait of a Man*). Greek and Roman antiquities.

10 CATHÉDRALE 1220–88
   NOTRE-DAME
place de Notre-Dame

Modeled after Reims. Nave (1220–76) by R. de Luzarches. Succeeded by T. de Cormont, then R. de Cormant (son). The magnificent west front has three doorways (ca. 1240) surmounted by a gallery of twenty-two statues (French kings) and a rose window. The wooden spire was built in 1529. 13th-c tombs in the nave. Superb choir stalls (1508–19).

ANCY-LE-FRANC C5

11 CHÂTEAU 1546
   D'ANCY-LE-FRANC
S. Serlio

One of the first classical Renaissance buildings in France. Interiors by F. Primaticcio and his school (see Fontainebleau). Frescoes by N. dell'Abbate in the Pharsale gallery. Restored in the 19th c.

ANET B3

12 CHÂTEAU D'ANET 1548
P. de l'Orme

The original courtyard scheme was largely destroyed during the French Revolution. The entrance screen, de l'Orme's finest surviving work, originally incorporated Cellini's *Nymph of Fontainebleau* (now in the Louvre). The fountain and chapel (sculpture by J. Goujon) have also survived.

ANGERS C2

Museum: Musée des Beaux-Arts (Logis Barrault), 10, rue de Musée. Most works of the sculptor P. David d'Angers. Paintings: Italian primitives, Dutch and Flemish 17th-c paintings, Ingres, Watteau, etc. An interesting Romanesque screen of archways is in the Préfecture next door.

13 CATHÉDRALE 1149–1274
   ST.-MAURICE
place Freppel

12th- to 16th-c stained glass windows. *St. Cecilia* (carved by P. David d'Angers) in the apse.

14 CHÂTEAU 1228–38 onward
   D'ANGERS
promenade du Bout-du-Monde

15th-c buildings inside the ramparts. Unique tapestry collection: *Apocalypse Tapestry* (1375–80) woven by N. Bataille, *Passion Tapestry,* and others.

ANGOULÊME E3

15 CATHÉDRALE 1105–28
   ST.-PIERRE onward
boulevard Desaix

Rebuilt ca. 1875. Latin cross plan roofed by a series of domes supported on pendentives. Fine west front. •The old city is encircled by well-preserved medieval ramparts.

ANTIBES F6

16 CHÂTEAU GRIMALDI 16th c
place de Château

Inside is the Musée Grimaldi, containing the rather staggering results of a short stay in this château by Picasso—paintings, drawings, ceramics. Some works by Léger, Calder, etc. •At Biot, 7 km (4.5 mi) N of Antibes, is the Musée National de Fernand Léger, with a comprehensive collection of his works from 1950–55.

ARC-ET-SENANS D5

32 km (20 mi) SW of Besançon

17 ROYAL SALT 1775–79
   MINES OF CHAUX
C. N. Ledoux

A very interesting utopian scheme.

ARLES F5

Museums: Museum of Christian Art, rue Balze. Various sarcophagi. Ancient gallery below (part of forum). Similar artifacts in the Museum of Pagan Art, place de la République. Some remains of a Roman necropolis can be seen along the allée des Sarcophages.

18 ARÈNES ca. 45 B.C.
   (Roman amphitheater)
Rond-Point des Arènes

Once used as housing. Restored
after 1828. In very good
condition.

19 THÉÂTRE   ca. 10 B.C.
      ANTIQUE
   (Roman theater)
   rue de la Calade (adjacent to
      the amphitheater)

20 ÉGLISE   11th–15th C
      ST.-TROPHIME
   (church)
   place de la République

   12th-C Romanesque doorway.
   The cloisters (good carvings)
   are entered through the adjacent
   building.

ASNIÈRES-SUR-OISE B4

36 km (22 m) N of Paris

21 ABBAYE   1228 onward
      DE ROYAUMONT

   Cistercian abbey, mostly
   destroyed during the French
   Revolution. Gothic refectory,
   cloister, and kitchens remain.
   The château (1785–89) is by
   L. Lemasson.

AUCH F3

22 CATHÉDRALE   15th–17th C
      ST.-PIERRE
   rue de la République

   Gothic. Superb choir stalls and
   good stained glass.

AULNAY D2

23 ST.-PIERRE   12th C
   (church)

   Romanesque. In outstanding
   condition.

AUTUN D5

Museum: Musée Rolin, 3 rue des
Bancs. Prehistoric artifacts and
Romanesque sculpture. *Nativity*
by the Master of Moulins.

24 PORTE ST.-ANDRÉ   30 B.C.
   (Roman gateway)
   rue de la Croix Blanche

   •Remains of a Roman theater
   are on rue Théâtre Romain.

25 CATHÉDRALE   1121–46
      ST.-LAZARE   onward
   Champs de Mars

   Fine Romanesque portal (*Last
   Judgment*) by Gislebertus in
   west front. Gothic nave.
   Museum of Romanesque
   sculpture in the sacristy.

AUXERRE C4

26 ÉGLISE   9th C onward
      ST.-GERMAIN
   (abbey church)
   place St.-Germain

   Carolingian crypt (841–59).
   9th-C frescoes depicting the
   life of St. Stephen.

27 CATHÉDRALE   13th–16th C
      ST.-ÉTIENNE
   place St.-Étienne

   Gothic. Romanesque crypt
   (1030).

AVIGNON F5

Museums: Musée du Petit
Palais, place du Palais. 14th-c
palace housing a unique
collection of 13th- to 16th-c
Italian paintings and 13th- to
15th-c paintings and sculpture
from the Avignon schools.
   Municipal Museum, rue de
l'Hôpital (across the river
in Villeneuve-lès-Avignon).
Coronation of the Virgin
(1453) by Charouton.
   Musée Calvet, rue Joseph-
Vernet. French paintings by
Vernet, Robert, Soutine, and
others.

28 PONT ST.-BÉNÉZET 1179–90
      AND CHAPEL
   (bridge)

   Four arches and the chapel
   of St. Nicolas remain.

29 PALAIS DES PAPES   1334–52
   (papal palace)
   place du Palais

   Huge fortress with bare
   interiors. Some frescoes by S.
   Martini in the banquet hall,
   (taken from Notre-Dame-des-
   Doms next door, which still
   retains two frescoes on the
   porch). •The 14th-c ramparts
   surrounding the old quarter
   were restored in the 19th c.

AZAY-LE-RIDEAU D3

30 CHÂTEAU   1518–29
      D'AZAY-LE-RIDEAU

Beautifully sited by G. Berthelot on an island in the Indre River. Heavy medieval machiolated cornice. Renaissance museum inside. • 11th-c church of St.-Symphorien on the right of the approach to the château.

BALLEROY B2
15 km (9 mi) SW of Bayeux

31 CHÂTEAU DE   1616–36
    BALLEROY
    F. Mansart

The first mature work by Mansart. Interior decorated with paintings by J. Lemoine.

LES BAUX–DE–PROVENCE F5

32 FORTIFIED   13th c onward
    VILLAGE

The older part ("dead village") with remains dating from the 13th c was destroyed in 1632. The more recent section has its charm.

BAYEUX B2

33 CATHÉDRALE   12th c
    NOTRE DAME   onward
    rue Bienvenu

Built over an earlier church (1077). Romanesque crypt and west tower. The remainder is rather cold Norman Gothic. •The Bayeux Tapestry is in the Musée de la Reine Mathilde opposite the cathedral.

BAYONNE F2

Museum: Musée Bonnat, 5, rue Jacques Lafitte. The collection was assembled by Leon Bonnat and includes many of his own works. Important Rubens, also works by El Greco, Goya, Rembrandt, Ingres, and others.

34 CATHÉDRALE   13th–14th c
    STE.-MARIE
    rue des Gouverneurs

14th-c cloisters. Stained glass windows (1531). •The citadel (1680) above the town is by S. Vauban.

BEAUNE D5

35 NOTRE DAME   1120 onward
    (collegiate church)
    off rue de la République

14th-c Gothic porch. Fine 15th-c tapestries.

36 HÔTEL-DIEU   1443–51
    (former hospital)
    rue de l'Hôtel-Dieu
    N. Rolin

Now an old-age home. Flemish Gothic. In the museum is a polyptych *The Last Judgment* by R. van der Weyden.

BEAUVAIS B4

37 CATHÉDRALE   1227–1568
    DE ST.-PIERRE
    rue St.-Pierre

The tallest Gothic cathedral ever built. Choir built 1247–72, collapsed in 1284, rebuilt 1337–47. Construction stopped just west of the transepts. The 150-m-high (500-foot) spire over the crossing collapsed in 1573 and was not rebuilt. Flamboyant chapel (1501–48) by M. Chambiges. The south transept facade has remarkably sculpted wooden doors (1535).

38 ST.-ÉTIENNE   12th–16th c
    (church)
    place St.-Étienne

Romanesque nave in strong contrast to the flamboyant Gothic choir. Stained glass windows (1518–54).

BESANÇON D5

Museum: Musée des Beaux-Arts, place de la Révolution. 16th- to 19th-c paintings. Some archeological exhibits.

39 CITADELLE   17th c
    (fortress)
    rue des Fusilles-de-la-Resistance
    S. Vauban

40 CATHÉDRALE   12th c
    ST. JEAN   onward
    Grande Rue

•The Porte Noire (Roman gateway) adjacent dates from ca. A.D. 167.

BEYNAC E3
7 km (4 mi) SW of Sarlat-la-Canéda

41 CHÂTEAU   13th c
    DE BEYNAC

Romantic site dominating the Dordogne River below.

BLÉRANCOURT B4
14 km (8.5 mi) SE of Noyon

42 CHÂTEAU DE   1618
    BLÉRANCOURT
    S. de Brosse

BLOIS C3

43 CHÂTEAU   13th–17th c
    DE BLOIS
    place du Château

Magnificent courtyard and interiors. A history of French architecture in one building: Salles des Etats—13th-c feudal hall; Charles d'Orléans Gallery, Louis XII Wing, and St.-Calais Chapel (ca. 1498–1503)—still medieval; François I Wing and staircase (1515–24)—early Renaissance; Gaston d'Orléans Wing (1635–38) by F. Mansart—fully classical. •6 km (4 mi) SE of Blois is Francois I's hunting lodge, the Château de Beauregard (16th- to 17th c, later extended by J. du Thier).

BONAGUIL E3
10 km (6 mi) NE of Fumel

44 CHÂTEAU   1485–1525
    B. de Roquefeuil

Designed to withstand artillery fire.

BORDEAUX E2

Museum: Musée des Beaux-Arts, 20 cours d'Albert. Paintings by Chardin, Delacroix, Redon, Veronese, Rubens, da Cortona, Roualt, and others. Sculpture by Lemoine, Rodin, Carpeaux, etc.

45 ST.-SUERIN   11th c
    (church)
    rue Capdeville

Facade rebuilt in the 19th c.

46 CATHÉDRALE   12th–17th c
    ST.-ANDRÉ
    cours d'Alsace et Lorraine

47 ST.-MICHÈLE   13th–16th c
    (church)
    place Canteloup

Gothic. Separate belfry.

48 PLACE ROYALE   1728–60
    J. J. Gabriel

49 GRAND THÉÂTRE   1772–88
    place de la Comédie
    V. Louis

Concert hall and theater. Monumental stairway. This provided the model for theaters for the next hundred years (Opéra, Paris, by C. Garnier).

BOURG–EN–BRESSE D5

50 BROU MONASTERY 1506–32
    boulevard de Brou

Church (1515–32) by van Boghem. Flamboyant Gothic with Renaissance details. The nave has a fine rood screen. Carved choir stalls and the tombs of Margaret of Austria and Philibert of Savoy in the choir. The stained glass was made locally.

BOURGES D4

51 CATHÉDRALE   1190–1260
    ST.-ÉTIENNE
    rue Porte Jaune

Double aisle. Enormous 12th-c crypt. Magnificent stained glass windows, ca. 1220 in choir, 15th- and 16th-c in chapels. Superb west front. •On the south side of the cathedral is the 15th-c Hôtel de Ville.

52 HÔTEL   1440–50
    JACQUES COEUR
    place Jacques Coeur

Palatial home for Charles VII's treasurer. In perfect condition.

53 HÔTEL   1487–1518
    LALLEMANT
    rue Hôtel Lallemant

Large Renaissance mansion. Now a museum of furniture.

BRÉCY B3
9 km (5.5 mi) E of Bayeux

54 CHÂTEAU   ca. 1650
    DE BRÉCY
    F. Mansart

BRIANÇON E6

55 CITADELLE   17th c
    (fortress)
    S. Vauban

•Vauban is also responsible for the church of Notre-Dame, avenue Vauban, in the picturesque Ville Haut (upper town).

BRISSAC C2
15 km (9 mi) SE of Angers

56 CHÂTEAU   1610–20
    DE BRISSAC

Rebuilt by C. de Cosse-Brissac. Original furniture and tapestries.

CAEN B3

Museum: Musée des Beaux-Arts, esplanade du Château. Paintings by Perugino, Veronese, Rubens, Vandyke, van der Weyden (*Virgin and Child*), N. Poussin, etc. Dürer and Rembrandt engravings.

57 LA TRINITÉ   1062–1110
    (Church of the Abbaye-aux-Dames)
    place de la Reine Mathilde

Founded by Matilda (wife of William the Conqueror). Romanesque. 11th-c nave revaulted in the 13th c. Much restored in the 19th c.

58 ST.-ÉTIENNE 1068–1115
(Church of the Abbaye-aux-Hommes)
place Monseigneur-des-Hameaux

Founded by William the Conqueror. Romanesque basilica plan with later additions. Apse extended to form chevet (1166). The west facade was the prototype of Gothic cathedrals throughout France. The facade towers were heightened in the 13th c.

59 ÉGLISE 1308–1545
ST.-PIERRE
(church)
place St.-Pierre

Flamboyant porch. Early Renaissance apse by H. Sohier (1518–45). The spire was rebuilt after 1945.

CAHORS E3

60 CATHÉDRALE 11th c
ST.-ÉTIENNE onward
rue du Maréchal Joffre

Choir rebuilt 1285–93. Chapels added in the 15th c. Fine 12th-c north door (originally on west front). 14th-c west front. Flamboyant 16th-c cloisters.

61 PONT VALENTRÉ 1308
(medieval bridge)
at the end of rue du President-Wilson

Three defensive towers. Gothic. Well restored in the 19th c.

CARCASSONNE F4

62 TOWN WALLS 6th–13th c
(old city)

Well-preserved fortified medieval town. Complete double row of ramparts (restored by E. E. Viollet-le-Duc, 1855–75). Cathédrale St.-Nazarre, within the walls; Romanesque nave (1095), Gothic transepts and choir (1300–1320). 13th- and 14th-c stained glass.

CARNAC C1

63 MEGALITHIC ca. 4700 B.C.–
MONUMENTS 2000 B.C.

Thousands of megaliths are in this area, some in alignments that extend over vast distances. Seven major sites in the immediate vicinity of Carnac are: Le Menec, Le Moustoir

(tumulus), Kercado, Kerlescan, Locmariaquer (Le Grand Menhir Brise, the largest menhir known, was 18.5 m/60 ft high; now broken into four pieces), Kermario, and St.-Michel (tumulus). The Miln and Le Rouzic Prehistorical Museum in Carnac has exhibits from all these sites.

CASTELNAU E3
32 km (20 mi) E of Souillac

64 CHÂTEAU 11th c onward
DE CASTELNAU

Triangular castle. 11th-c keep. Restored 1896–1932.

CASTRES F4

65 HÔTEL DE VILLE 1666
(town hall)
rue de l'Hôtel-de-Ville

Contains the Musée Goya: Spanish works, especially Goya's *Sitting of the Royal Philippine Company*.

LE CATEAU B4

Museum: Musée Henri Matisse, Hôtel de Ville (town hall). Works by Matisse, who was born in this town.

66 ÉGLISE 18th c
(church)

CÉRET G4

Museum: Musée d'Art Moderne, boulevard Maréchal Joffre. Fauvist paintings by Picasso, Matisse, Dufy, and others.

67 PONT DU DIABLE 14th c
(bridge)
Tech River

A single arch spans 45 m (150 ft).

CHALONS–SUR–MARNE B5

68 NOTRE-
DAME-EN-VAUX 12th c
(church)
quai Notre-Dame

Four spires. Fine south doorway (porch added in 1469). Good 16th-c stained glass.

69 CATHÉDRALE 13th c
DE ST.-ÉTIENNE
place St.-Étienne

12th-c Romanesque north tower.

CHAMBORD C3
15 km (9 mi) NE of Blois

70 CHÂTEAU 1519 onward
DE CHAMBORD
D. da Cortona (attributed)

Built for François I, who wished to divert the Loire to fill the moat. The architects compromised by diverting the Cosson. Military plan—central keep inside a square court. The remarkable double spiral staircase, originally open, was later enclosed. The roof terrace is a complete (fantasy) world all its own.

CHAMPIGNY–SUR–VEUDE D3
10 km (6 mi) SE of Chinon

71 STE. CHAPELLE   1508–43
(chapel)

Only the chapel remains. The château was destroyed on Richelieu's orders. Magnificent stained glass (1560–97) by R. Pinaigrier.

CHANTILLY B4
50 km (30 mi) N of Paris

72 CHÂTEAU   1560 onward
DE CHANTILLY

The Petit Château (1560) by J. Bullant remains intact; the Grand Château is a 19th-c reconstruction. The Musée Condé inside has an excellent painting collection: Poussin, Watteau, Ingres, Raphael, etc.; the library includes the illuminated manuscript *Très Riches Heures du Duc de Berry*, a masterpiece from the Limbourg workshop, begun in 1410. The stables (1721–36) by J. Aubert, a superbly confident design, housed the Prince de Condé's horses, dogs, and huntsmen.

CHARTRES C3

73 CATHÉDRALE   1194–1260
DE NOTRE DAME

Only the west front (1140–60, south tower 1145–70, north tower added 1507–14) and crypt survived a fire in 1194. Rebuilt immediately. Chartres was the first cathedral to fully utilize the structural support of flying buttresses to enlarge the clerestory windows to a maximum size. Unique (complete) 13th-c stained glass windows. Transept: south porch (1224–50) describes the New Testament (in sculpture); north porch (ca. 1230), the Old Testament and coming of the Messiah.

74 ST.-PIERRE   11th–13th c
(church)
rue St.-Pierre

In poor condition.

75 MAISON   1920 onward
PICASSIETTE
(house and chapel)
rue du Repos 22
R. Isidore

Naive ceramic decoration. May be visited on weekends.

CHÂTEAUDUN C3

76 CHÂTEAU   12th–16th c
DE CHÂTEAUDUN
promenade St.–Lubin

Spectacular site above the Loire. Fine 15th-c statues in the chapel.

CHAUMONT–SUR–LOIRE C3
18 km (11 mi) NE of Amboise

77 CHÂTEAU DE   1465–1510
CHAUMONT-SUR-LOIRE

Rebuilt by C. d'Amboise. Medieval, with Renaissance detail. Elaborate stables.

CHENONCEAUX D3
6 km (4 mi) E of Blére

78 CHÂTEAU   1513–21
DE CHENONCEAUX

Built on the foundations of a watermill in the river Cher by Thomas Bohier (mostly supervised by his wife, Catherine). Earlier château demolished (only the keep was kept and redecorated by Bohier). Bridge over the Cher (1555–59) by P. de l'Orme for Diane de Poitiers. Two-story gallery (ca. 1576) above the bridge added by J. Bullant.

CHEVERNY C3
14 km (9 mi) SE of Blois

79 CHÂTEAU DE   1634
CHEVERNY
H. de Cheverny

Neoclassical. Fine original interiors.

CHINON D3

80 CHÂTEAU   11th C onward
     DE CHINON
rue du Puy des Bancs

Three medieval castles (one has
since been demolished) were
connected to form the château.
Fortified site since Roman
times.

CLERMONT-FERRAND E4

81 NOTRE-DAME-   11th–12th C
     DU-PORT
rue du Port

Replaced an earlier 6th-C
church. Barrel-vaulted nave
carried on engaged columns
with fine carved capitals.

82 CATHÉDRALE   1248–95
     DE NOTRE DAME
place de la Victoire
J. Deschamps

West front and towers completed by E. E. Viollet-le-Duc
in the 19th C.

CLUNY D5

83 (THIRD) ABBEY   1089–1121
     CHURCH OF SAINT
     HUGH
rue Kenneth J. Connant

This extraordinary building
was wantonly destroyed in
1798. Only the south transept
(Chapelle St.-Etienne) and two
towers (Les Barabans) have
survived. Some column capitals
are in the *farinier* (granary).
•Other monastic buildings have
survived: Palais de Jacques
d'Amboise (now the town
hall), the abbey complex, and
the Palais de Jean de Bourbon.
The decoration of Cluny
probably resembled the
frescoes that remain at Berzé la
Ville nearby.

COLMAR C6

Museum: Musée Unterlinden,
place des Unterlinden. M.
Grünewald's Isenheim Altar
(ca. 1515), an altarpiece with
painted, movable wings, is a
work of searing intensity. The
statues are by N. de Haguenau.
Paintings by Schongauer,
Isenmann, and others.
Schongauer's *Madonna of the
Rose Garden* (1473) is
temporarily in the Dominican
church, rue des Serruriers.

84 ST.-MARTIN   1234–1366
     (church)
place de la Cathédrale

Much restored. 15th-C stained
glass windows.

COMPIÈGNE B4

85 CHÂTEAU   1738–85
     DE COMPIÈGNE
place du Général de Gaulle
J. A. Gabriel

Restored Napoleon III interiors
by C. Percier and P. F. L.
Fontaine. Original furniture.

CONQUES E4
11 km (7 mi) E of Decazeville

86 ST.-FOY   11th–12th C
     (abbey church)

Romanesque pilgrimage church.
Superb *Last Judgment* on the
west doorway tympanum. The
rich treasury has two medieval
masterpieces: the *Reliquary of
Pepin d'Aquitaine* and the
Statue of St. Foy.

CORDÈS-ORCIVAL E4
11 km (7 mi) N of Le Mont-Dore

87 CHÂTEAU   13th–15th C
     DE CORDÈS

Picturesque. Restored in the
17th C. The park is by A. Le
Nôtre. •The Romanesque
church at Orcival is well
preserved.

COURANCES C4
3 km (2 mi) N of Milly

88 CHÂTEAU DE   17th C
     COURANCES
C. Gaillard

Restored ca. 1870. The park, by
A. Le Nôtre, has splendid
ornamental water fountains,
pools, cascades, and other
effects.

COUTANCES B2

89 CATHÉDRALE   1218–74
     DE NOTRE-DAME
place du Parvis

The present Gothic structure
replaced an earlier church begun
in 1056. Some portions of the
older church are still visible.
Fine octagonal lantern tower
above the crossing. Some 13th-
and 14th-C glass.

CUNAULT D3
12 km (8 mi) NW of Saumur

90 NOTRE-DAME   12th C
     (church)

Fortified west front. Excellent
sculpture (column capitals).

DIJON D5

Museum: Musée des Beaux-
Arts, place de la St.-Chapelle.
In the east wing of the Palais
des Ducs de Bourgogne (14th
to 18th C). Sculptures from
the Chartreuse Champmol
(founded in 1380 by Philip the
Bold): tomb of Philip the Bold
by C. Sluter, altarpiece by J.
de Baerze (wings by M.
Broederlam). Also European
paintings of all schools. •The
Well of Moses (ca. 1404) and
an entrance portal, both
notable works by Sluter, are on
the grounds of the Chartreuse
de Champmol (now a
hospital).

91 CATHÉDRALE   1271-88
   ST.-BÉNIGNE   onward
   place St.-Bénigne

92 NOTRE-DAME   13th C
   (church)
   rue Musette/rue de la Préfecture

93 ST.-MICHEL   16th C
   (church)
   place St.-Michel

   Flamboyant Gothic

ÉCUILLÉ C2
20 km (12 mi) N of Angers

94 CHÂTEAU DU   1468-73
   PLESSIS-BOURRÉ
   J. Bourré

   Essentially unchanged
   (including furnishings) since
   being built. Painted ceiling in
   Guard Room.

EFFIAT D4
17 km (10 mi) SW of Vichy

95 CHÂTEAU D'EFFIAT   1627

   Built by Marshal d'Effiat.
   Neoclassic entry. Park by A. Le
   Nôtre.

EVEUX-SUR-
L'ARBRESLE E5
26 km (16 mi) W of Lyon

96 LE COUVENT   1957-59
   STE.-MARIE-DE-LA-
   TOURETTE
   2 km (1 mi) SE of l'Arbresle
   Le Corbusier

Dominican monastery. The
perfect opportunity for Le
Corbusier to build his vision
of an ideal community. Austere,
with interiors of great power.

EVREUX B3

97 CATHÉDRALE   1120-1530
   NOTRE-DAME
   rue de Verdun

   Rebuilt after 1200. Flamboyant
   north facade (16th C) by J.
   Cossart. Spire destroyed in
   1940.

98 ÉGLISE ST.-TAURIN   14th C
   (church)
   place St.-Taurin

   Noted 13th-C shrine. Good
   stained glass.

FALAISE B3
30 km (19 mi) SE of Caen

99 CHÂTEAU   12th-13th C
   DE FALAISE

   Powerful fortress, parts of
   which were demolished in the
   18th C. Massive keep.

FAREINS D5
25 km (15 mi) N of Lyon

100 CHÂTEAU DE   1606-10
    FLÉCHÈRES
    A. du Cerceau

    Henry IV style. Central block
    with flanking wings.

LA FERTÉ-
BERNARD C3
45 km (28 mi) NE of Le Mans

101 ÉGLISE NOTRE-   1450-1600
    DAME-DES- MARAIS
    place de la République

    Transitional flamboyant
    Gothic/Renaissance church.

FIRMINY E5
10 km (6 mi) SW of St.-Etienne

102 YOUTH CENTER,   1961-68
    STADIUM, AND UNITE
    D'HABITATION
    Le Corbusier

    Badly maintained. The church
    of St. Pierre, by Le Corbusier,
    has been left unfinished since
    1974.

LE FOLGOËT B1
2 km (1 mi) W of Lesneven

103 NOTRE-DAME   1366-1423
    (church)

    Notable belfry. 15th-C rood
    screen.

FONTAINEBLEAU
C4

104 CHÂTEAU   16th-19th C
    DE FONTAINEBLEAU
    rue Denecourt

Irregular plan built around five
courtyards. The Cour Ovale
(Renaissance courtyard) is
entered by way of the Porte
Dorée (1528-40, by G. le
Breton). Important interiors:
Galerie François Premier
(1533-40) by R. Fiorentino
and F. Primaticcio. This is the
first major work of the
Fontainebleau school.
Primaticcio was also responsible
for the Chambre de la Duchesse
d'Etampes (1541-43), the Salle
de Bal, and Galerie d'Ulysse
(1541). Garden: Jardin Anglais,
Labyrinth, etc. The Parterre
is by A. Le Nôtre.

FONTENAY C5
5 km (3 mi) NE of Montbard

105 CISTERCIAN   1130–47
    ABBEY

Unadorned, in accordance with the rules of the order. In excellent condition.

FONTEVRAULT–L'ABBAYE D3
16 km (10 mi) SE of Saumur

106 FONTEVRAULT   12th c
    ABBEY   onward
    place des Plantagenets

Used as a prison until 1963. Now being restored. Abbey church (ca. 1099–1119): single nave roofed by four domes (rebuilt 1910) on pendentives (as in Perigeux). Ste.-Marie Cloisters: Gothic, then Renaissance. The refectory (reroofed in 1515) adjoins the kitchen, an octagonal tower originally surrounded by eight chapels. 16th-c chapter house.

FOUGÈRES C2

107 CHÂTEAU   13th–15th c
    DE FOUGÈRES
    rue de la Pinterie

Hilltop fortress. Machiolated curtain walls and towers in good condition. •Below is the flamboyant Gothic church of St.-Sulpice (15th to 18th c).

FRÉJUS F6

Extensive Roman remains (ca. 1st c b.c.) in poor condition: amphitheater, theater, aqueduct, extensive port buildings, etc.

108 CITÉ   4th c onward
    ÉPISCOPALE
    place Formigé

Fortified complex of a baptistry (ca. 4th c), cathedral (10th c onward) and 13th-c cloisters.

GERMIGNY–DES–PRÉS C4
30 km (19 mi) E of Orléans

109 ÉGLISE   ca. 800
    (church)

Built by Theodulf, Bishop of Orléans. Only one apse and its mosaic (*The Ark of the Covenant*) have survived. The rest of the church is a reconstruction (1839–76).

GRENOBLE E5

Museums: Musée de Peinture et Sculpture, place de Verdun. Excellent collection of modern art. Also many major works by Claude, G. de la Tour, Delacroix (*St. George*), Canaletto, Zurbarán, Fantin-Latour, Rubens (*St. Gregory and Domitilla*), Matisse, etc. The Fantin-Latour museum is across the rue Gémond.

110 CATHÉDRALE   12th–13th c
    DE NOTRE-DAME
    place de Notre-Dame

15th-c tabernacle.

111 ST.-ANDRÉ   13th c
    (church)
    place St.-André

•Just to north, on the quai Stéphane Jay, is the 15th-c Palais de Justice.

HARAS–DU–PIN C3
13 km (8 mi) E of Argentan

112 LE PIN   1714–28
    (stud farm)
    J. Hardouin-Mansart

Unchanged. The courtyard is enclosed by a handsome iron screen.

HAROUÉ C5
3 km (2 mi) E of Tantonville

113 CHÂTEAU DE   1720–31
    CRAON
    G. Boffrand

Entrance gates by J. Lamour (also responsible for the wrought-iron work of the place Stanislas, Nancy). Tapestries designed by C. Le Brun.

HAUTEFORT E3
32 km (20 mi) S of St.-Yrieix-la-Perche

114 CHÂTEAU DE   17th c
    HAUTEFORT
    N. Rambourg

Built over an earlier castle.

HAUTE–GOULAINE D2
15 km (9 mi) E of Nantes

115 CHÂTEAU   15th and 17th c
    DE HAUTE-GOULAINE

The flamboyant Gothic central building is flanked by two 17th-c wings. Moated on three sides.

HAUTERIVES E5
27 km (16.5 mi) N of Romans-sur-Isère

116 PALAIS IDÉAL   1879–1912
    F. Cheval

Cheval, a postman, picked up stones on his delivery routes every day for thirty years. He built this remarkable house out of these stones with glass and mosaic chips, intending it to be his monument and tomb. Upon completion he discovered that French law would not allow him to be buried in his shrine. He then built an equally remarkable tomb (1912–22) in the public cemetery.

LE HAVRE B3

117 ÉGLISE   1951–57
    ST.-JOSEPH
    (church)
    boulevard François Premier
    A. Perret

•The reconstructed town of Le Havre (after 1946) was planned by Perret, who also designed the town hall.

JOSSELIN C2

118 CHÂTEAU DE   16th c
      JOSSELIN
rue de Trente

The flamboyant Gothic facade contrasts with the fortified south facade. The moat is now a flower garden. Only the residential part of this fortress remained after the defenses were destroyed in 1629.

JOUARRE B4
3 km (2 mi) S of La Ferté-sous-Jouarre

119 CRYPT OF   ca. 650
      NOTRE DAME
in the Benedictine Abbey

Merovingian. The tombs of Abbess Theodochilde (d. 662) and her brother Angilbert are in the crypt.

JUMIÈGES B3
25 km (15.5 mi) W of Rouen

120 ABBEY CHURCH   1040–67
      OF NOTRE DAME (ruined)

The west front, flanked by two octagonal towers, is the oldest in France. Attached to the abbey is the ruined church of St.-Pierre, the triforium of which dates from Carolingian times (ca. 940).

KERJEAN B1
5 km (3 mi) S of Plouzévede

121 CHÂTEAU DE   16th c
      KERJEAN

Fortified Renaissance castle.

LANGEAIS D3

122 CHÂTEAU DE   1465–69
      LANGEAIS

Exceptionally well-preserved fortress. Excellent period furniture and tapestries. The ruined stone keep in the garden is one of the first built in France (ca. 1000 by Foulques Nerra).

LAON B4

123 CATHÉDRALE DE   1160
      NOTRE DAME   onward
place du Parvis

Influential building (Reims, etc.). The strikingly modeled west front (1160–1225) rises to form two open octagonal towers decorated with carved oxen (to commemorate their help in building the cathedral).

LAPALISSE D4

124 CHÂTEAU DE   15th c
      LAPALISSE

Feudal castle remodeled in the Renaissance style. 15th-c Gothic chapel. Some Flemish tapestries.

LARRESINGLE F3
7 km (4 mi) SW of Condom

125 FORTIFIED VILLAGE 13th c

Castle in the center. Recently restored.

LAVAL C2

126 CHÂTEAU   12th c onward
      DE LAVAL
place de la Trémoille

Impressive keep.

LIGNIÈRES D4

127 CHÂTEAU DE   1645
      LIGNIÈRES
L. Le Vau

LILLE A4

Museum: Musée des Beaux-Arts, place de la République. A major collection of paintings: Flemish, Dutch (Rubens's *Descent from the Cross,* Vandyke's *Christ on the Cross*); French (Delacroix, Courbet, and others); Spanish (Goya's *Majas Walking*). Italian (Michelangelo) and French drawings. Rubens's *Martyrdom of St. Catherine* is in the church of Ste.-Catherine.

128 ST.-MAURICE   14th–15th c
      (church)
rue de Paris

Gothic. Remodeled in 1872.

129 CITADELLE   1666–74
      (fortress)
avenue du 43e-Régiment-
      d'Infantry
S. Vauban

•The Porte de Paris, a huge triumphal arch on rue de Paris, is also by Vauban.

130 CATHÉDRALE   1856
      NOTRE-DAME-   onward
      DE-LA-TREILLE
rue de la Monnaie
H. Clutton and W. Burges

Clutton and Burges won the commission for this building in an open design competition.

131 HOUSE   1898
14, rue de Fleurs
H. Guimard

LIMOGES E3

132 CATHÉDRALE   1273
      ST.-ÉTIENNE   onward
rue de la Cathédrale

Begun by J. Deschamps.

LISIEUX B3

133 CATHÉDRALE   1170
      ST.-PIERRE   onward
place Thiers

LOCHES D3

134 ST.-OURS   11th and 12th c
    (church)
    rue Pactius (inside the Cité
      Mediévale)

Unique pyramidal vaulting (by
T. Pactius, ca. 1168). 11th-c
frescoes in the crypt.

135 CHÂTEAU   14th c onward
    DE LOCHES
    N of St.-Ours

Tour Agnès Sorel (tower) and
tomb of Agnès Sorel. •The
donjon (keep) is at the south
end of the Cité Mediévale and is
part of the powerful ramparts
surrounding the Cité.

LOURDES F2

136 BASILICA OF   1958
    ST. PIUS X
    esplanade des Processions
    (underground)
    P. Vago and E. Freyssinet

LOUVIERS B3

137 CATHÉDRALE DE   13th c
    NOTRE-DAME   onward
    rue de la Poste/rue du Quai

Reworked in the flamboyant
Gothic style in the 15th c.

LE LUDE C3

138 CHÂTEAU   1457 onward
    DU LUDE

Rectangular courtyard. Gothic
north facade and later
(Renaissance) garden facade.

LUNÉVILLE C6

139 CHÂTEAU DE   1703–6
    LUNÉVILLE
    place de la 2ᵉ-Div.-de-Cavalerie
    G. Boffrand

Park by E. Héré de Corny.

LYON E5

Museum: Musée des Beaux-
Arts, place des Terreaux.
Excellent collection: Delacroix,
Tintoretto, El Greco, Rubens,
Gauguin (*Nave Nave Mahana*),
and many more important
works from all schools.

140 CATHÉDRALE   12th–15th c
    ST.-JEAN
    rue St.-Jean

13th-c stained glass.

141 HÔTEL-DIEU   1741–48
    (hospital)
    quai Jules Courmont/rue de
      la Barre
    J. G. Soufflot

142 GALLO-ROMAN   1975
    MUSEUM
    Fourvière hill
    B. Zehrfuss

Built underground on the
actual Roman site. A theater,
temple, odeum, and other
remains have been excavated.

143 PALAIS DES   1913–18
    SPORTS
    (stadium)
    18, rue Président Edouard
      Herriot
    T. Garnier

•Other works by Garnier in
Lyon are the La Mouche
Abattoir (1908–13); Edouard
Herriot Hospital; and urban
design and housing: Grange
Blanche (1911–25); and Etats-
Unis District (1920–35).

MAINTENON C3
19 km (12 mi) N of Chartres

144 CHÂTEAU   16th c onward
    DE MAINTENON

Park by A. Le Nôtre. The
unfinished aqueduct is by
S. Vauban.

LE MANS C3

145 CATHÉDRALE   11th–15th c
    ST.-JULIEN
    place St.-Michel

Romanesque nave, 11th c,
reinforced with pointed arches
in the 12th c. Windows restored
in the 19th c. Superb 12th-c
doorway (compare with
Chartres) in south porch. Choir;
double ambulatory of unequal
height, completed in 1254,
original glass. North transept
completed ca. 1440, rose
window in 1430. On the right is
the Renaissance tomb (1473) of
Charles d'Anjou by F. Laurana.

146 NOTRE-DAME-   12th–16th c
    DE-LA-COUTURE
    (church)
    place A. Briand

Virgin (1571) by G. Pilon
opposite the pulpit.

MARSEILLE F5

147 UNITÉ   1946–52
    D'HABITATION
    (apartments)
    280, boulevard Michelet
    Le Corbusier

Brilliant use of off shutter concrete. Remarkable roof garden.

MAZÉ C3
24 km (15 mi) E of Angers

148 CHÂTEAU DE   1775
    MONTGEOFFROY

Built by Barré. The interiors are unique in that every piece and painting has been preserved in its original setting.

MENARS C3
6 km (4 mi) N of Blois

149 CHÂTEAU   17th–18th c
    DE MENARS

Completed by J. A. Gabriel, then J. G. Soufflot. Temple of Love and other follies by Soufflot on the grounds.

MESNIÈRES–EN–BRAY B3
6 km (4 mi) NE of Neufchâtel-en-Bray

150 CHÂTEAU   1540–46 onward
    DE MESNIÈRES

Renaissance. Now a school.

METZ B5

151 CATHÉDRALE   1250
    ST.-ÉTIENNE   onward
    En Fournirue

Incorporates earlier Romanesque church (now a chapel on the south aisle). West front rebuilt in 1903 after being radically altered in the 18th c. Excellent stained glass: rose window at west end and in the choir. Modern glass in the choir ambulatory. Altar (1865) by E. E. Viollet-le-Duc.
•The town hall (1766–81) across the square is by G. F. Blondel.

MOISSAC F3

152 ST.-PIERRE   12th and 15th c
    (abbey church)
    rue de la République

Magnificent 12th-c south portal (originally on west front). Exquisite carved capitals (1085–1115) in the cloister.

MONACO F6
(principality)

MONTE CARLO

153 CASINO   1878
    place Casino
    C. Garnier

As opulent as his Opéra in Paris. •Between the casino and the sea is the hexagonally planned Les Spéluges (congress center, hotel, and apartments by J. Ginsberg).

MONPAZIER E3

154 CHÂTEAU   10th c
    DE BIRON   onward

Assorted buildings dating from medieval times until the 17th c. 15th-c chapel.

MONTAUBAN F3

Museum: Musée Ingres, 19, rue de la Mairie. Thirty paintings and many drawings by Ingres. His *Vow of Louis XIII* is in the cathedral on rue de Notre Dame.

155 PLACE NATIONALE   1616

Early design of a public square modeled after the place des Vosges, Paris (entry 194).

MONTPELLIER F4

Museums: Musée Fabre, rue Montpellieret. A very good collection. Paintings by Veronese, Rubens, Houdon, Greuze, Courbet (*Bonjour, Monsieur Corbet*), Delacroix (*Les Femmes d'Alger*), and others. The Musée Atger nearby has a good collection of old master drawings (some paintings).

156 AQUEDUCT   1753–67
    (ST.-CLEMENT) AND
    WATER TOWER
    promenade du Peyrou
    A. Giral

MONTREUIL–BELLAY D3
16 km (10 mi) S of Saumur

157 CHÂTEAU   13th–15th c
    DE MONTREUIL
    place des Ormeaux

Gatehouse (13th to 15th c); Petit Château (kitchen modeled after Fontevrault) and Château Neuf (both 15th c). The church of Notre Dame, a flamboyant Gothic structure, is within the château's defenses.

MONT-ST.-MICHEL C2

158 FORTIFIED   8th–16th c
    ABBEY AND ISLAND

Incomparable. The abbey is a complex of many discrete parts built into and around the granite peak of the island. Some of these are:

Church: Romanesque nave (1017–1144, built over an earlier Carolingian church—Notre-Dames-sous-Terre), Gothic apse (1446–1521, rebuilt after a structural failure). The three western bays were demolished in 1780 to avoid further damage to the remaining structure.

The Merveille: Built 1211–28. Various spaces of astounding magnificence, especially the cloister, refectory, and Knights' Hall. Noteworthy crypts.

MOULINS D4

159 CATHÉDRALE   15th c
    NOTRE-DAME
rue François Péron

Flamboyant Gothic. Good stained glass. *The Madonna and Child* triptych (ca. 1498) by the Master of Moulins is in the sacristy.

NANCY C5

Museums: Musée des Beaux-Arts, 3, place Stanislas. Paintings by Rubens, Perugino, da Cortona, and 16th- to 20th-c French artists.
Musée Historique Lorraine, Palais Ducal, Grande Rue. French paintings.

160 ÉGLISE   1480–87
    DES CORDELIERS
(Franciscan church)
Grande Rue/rue Jacquot

Notable tombs, especially that of Phillipa de Gueldre (ca. 1548) by L. Richier.

161 PLACE STANISLAS   1750–57
E. Héré de Corny

Ironwork by J. Lamour. Héré's scheme linked this square with the place de la Carriere, where he skillfully incorporated the existing Palais du Gouvernement and two hotels by G. Boffrand in a monumental design.

162 VILLA   1899–1902
    MAJORELLE
1, rue Louis Majorelle
H. Sauvage with L. Majorelle, A. Charpentier, and F. Jourdain

163 VILLAS LES ROCHES 1902–4
    AND LES GLYCINES
67–71, avenue Foch
E. Andre

"Nancy School" art nouveau.
•Other houses in Nancy by Andre are 92–92 bis, quai Claude-le-Lorrain (1903) and a studio house at 30, avenue du Sergent-Blandan (1903), as well as the entrance to the Parc de Saurupt.

164 APARTMENT   1903–4
    BUILDING
24, rue Lionnois
L. Weissenburger

•Weissenburger (with Mienville) built the Hôtel-Brasserie Excelsior (1910), where some fine art nouveau interiors survive.

NANTES D2

Museum: Musée des Beaux-Arts, 10, rue Georges-Clémenceau. Paintings by Rubens, Ingres, Courbet (*Winnowers*), Delacroix, Géricault, G. de la Tour (*Dream of St. Joseph*), Guardi, Rouault, Dufy, etc.

165 CATHÉDRALE   1434–1893
    ST.-PIERRE-ET-
    ST.-PAUL
place St.-Pierre

The plain facade was restored in 1930. Inside (south transept) is the tomb of Francis II and Margaret de Foix (1503–7), a Renaissance masterpiece by M. Colombe.

166 CHÂTEAU   1466 onward
    DE NANTES
rue du Château

The fortified exterior contrasts with the transitional Gothic/Renaissance residential palace within.

167 UNITÉ   1952–55
    D'HABITATION
(apartments)
Rézé-les-Nantes, off route D258
Le Corbusier

NARBONNE F4

168 CATHÉDRALE   13th–14th c
    ST.-JUST
place R. Salengro

Gothic. Only the extremely tall choir was built. Towers and Chapelle de l'Annonciade added in the 15th c. •Adjacent is the fortified Archbishops' Palace (10th to 17th c) now housing two museums (archeology, ceramics, and painting).

NEUF–BRISACH C6

169 NEW TOWN   1697–1708
    AND DEFENSES   onward
S. Vauban

Vauban museum.

NICE F6

Museums: Musée Marc Chagall, avenue Docteur-Ménard, Cimiez. Works by Chagall.
Musée Jules Cheret, 33, avenue des Baumettes. Boudin, Dufy, Monet, Renoir, and 18th-c French paintings.
Musée Matisse, 164, avenue Arènes. Works by Matisse.

170 ÉGLISE ST.-JACQUES 17th c
(church)
off place P. Gautier (toward the château)

A replica of Il Gesù, Roma (entry I–373).

NÎMES F5

Museum: Musée des Antiques, Maison Carrée, place de la Comédie.

This museum of Roman remains is housed in the best-preserved Roman temple extant. Built in 16 B.C.

171 ARÈNES 1st C A.D.
(Roman amphitheater)
places des Arènes

In excellent condition. Dry stone construction.

172 TEMPLE ca. A.D. 130
DE DIANE
off the jardin de la Fontaine

Probably a nymphaeum. •The Tour Magne (ca. 10 B.C.) is on the peak of Mont Cavalier (overlooking the gardens). The gardens date from 1750.

NOYON B4

173 CATHÉDRALE 1150–13th c
DE NOTRE-DAME
rue St.-Eloi

Earliest use of a triforium. Alternate round and compound piers originally supported sexpartite vaulting. After collapsing in 1293, they were replaced with quadripartite vaulting.

CHÂTEAU D'O C3
N of Mortrée

174 CHÂTEAU D'O 15th–18th c
Fine Renaissance château.

OIRON D3
11 km (7 mi) E of Thouars

175 CHÂTEAU 1518 onward
D'OIRON

Gothic/Renaissance. Luxurious decoration by the Fontainebleau school.

ORANGE F5

176 ARC DE ca. 30 B.C.
TRIOMPHE
(Triumphal Arch of Tiberius)
N of Orange on the N7

In excellent condition. The west face has been restored.

177 THÉÂTRE ca. 10 B.C.
ANTIQUE
(Roman theater)
place des Frères-Mounet

The best-preserved theater extant. The stage wall is original. The statue of Augustus and the seats are restored. The remains of a Roman gymnasium and capitol are adjacent.

ORLÉANS C4

178 CATHÉDRALE 1601–1829
STE.-CROIX
place Ste.-Croix

Earlier cathedral destroyed in 1568. Rebuilt in the Gothic style. 18th-c woodwork in the choir by J. Degoullons from designs by J. Hardouin-Mansart, J. A. Gabriel and C. Le Brun.

PARAY-LE-MONIAL D5

179 SACRÉ-COEUR 1109
(church)
rue des Écoles
Closely modeled after Cluny.

PARIS B4

Tourist Information: Accueil de France, 127 avenue des Champs-Elysées (tel. 720 0496).

Architects' Institutes: Conseil National de l'Ordre des Architectes, 78, avenue Raymond Poincaré (tel. 723 7211).

Academie d'Architecture, 9, Place des Vosges (tel. 887 8310).

Architectural Bookstore: La Hune, 170 boulevard St.-Germain.

Châteaux and Gardens: La Demeure Historique, Association des propriétaires de monuments historiques privés, 57, quai de la Tournelle (tel. 329 0286). Information on châteaux open to the public throughout France.

Guided Tours (of sites usually closed to the public): Paris et son histoire, 82, rue Taitbout (tel. 526–2677).

Caisse Nationale des Monuments Historiques, 62, rue St.-Antoine (tel. 272–4569).

In foreign languages: Trois Mil, 35 rue le Boetie (tel. 256–0011).

Pariscope lists the program of guided tours every week.

Maps: *Paris par Arrondissement* (at any newsstand) is the best street guide available.

Museums: Musée National d'Art Moderne, Centre Georges Pompidou, Plateau Beaubourg. 20th-c paintings. Research library and related facilities. See entry 368.

Musée d'Art Moderne de la Ville de Paris, 11, avenue du President Wilson. 20th-c paintings.

Musée de Cluny, 6, place Paul-Painlevé. Medieval and Renaissance decorative and fine arts. See entry 188.

Musée Cognaq-Jay, 25, boulevard des Capucines. Reconstruction of an 18th-c townhouse. 18th-c woodwork, decorative arts, and paintings.

Musée Guimet, 6, place d'Iéna. Oriental works of art.

Musée Jacquemart-André, 158, boulevard Haussmann. Excellent collection of works by Rembrandt, Vandyke, Fragonard, Boucher, Tiepolo, Titian, Uccello (*St. George and the Dragon*), and others.

Musée du Jeu de Paume, place de la Concorde. The finest collection of French impressionist works in existence.

Musée du Louvre, place du Carrousel. One of the greatest art museums in the world.

Musée Marmottan, 2, rue Louis-Boilly. Mainly for the later works of Monet.

Musée de Monuments Français, Palais de Chaillot (1937, by Carlu, Boileau, and Azéma), place du Trocadéro. Monumental and architectural sculpture from all parts of France arranged by geographical regions and period. Also reproductions of mural paintings.

Musée Gustave Moreau, 14, rue de la Rochefoucauld. Works by Moreau displayed in his studio.

Musée du Petit Palais, avenue Winston-Churchill. 17th- to 19th-c paintings and decorative arts.

Musée Picasso, Hôtel du Juigne, place de Thorigny. Works by Picasso, as well as his own collection.

Musée Rodin, Hôtel Biron, 77, rue de Varenne. Works and drawings by Rodin.

Orangerie des Tuileries, place de la Concorde. Monet's *Nymphéas* are displayed in the basement.

180 ST.-   11th c onward
GERMAIN-DES-PRÉS
(church)
boulevard St.-Germain-des-Prés, 6e *D5*

Continuously rebuilt since 542. The oldest sections to survive date from the 11th and 12th c. The marble columns in the ambulatory are from the original Childebert church (542). Pulpit (1827) by A. C. Quatremère-de-Quincy. Major restoration in the 19th-c.

181 ST.-MARTIN-   1130 onward
DES-CHAMPS
(church)
rue Réaumur/rue St.-Martin (N side), 3e *C6*

Romanesque chancel. Gothic refectory by P. de Montreuil.

182 CATHÉDRALE   1163–1345
DE NOTRE-DAME
(cathedral)
place du Parvis Notre Dame, 4e *D6*

Begun by Bishop Maurice de Sully. Transepts by P. de Montreuil. North transept facade (1250) by Jean of Chelles. St. Stephen's portal (south transept) built in 1258. Restored (1841–64) by E. E. Viollet-le-Duc (who included a statue of himself among the apostles on the reconstructed spire). •The Keeper's house and treasury (1866), place du Parvis Notre Dame, are also by Viollet-le-Duc.

183 CHAPELLE   12th c
ST.-AIGNAN
(church)
19, rue des Ursins, 4e *D6*

The only medieval church in the Cité. Restricted admission times; check with Tourist Office first.

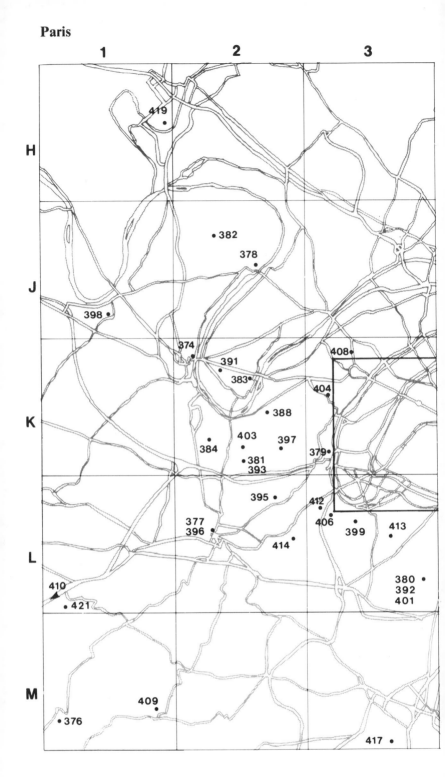

184 STE.-CHAPELLE   1245–48
   (chapel)
   boulevard du Palais, (inside the
      Palais de Justice, 1er *D5*
   P. de Montreuil

   A Gothic masterpiece. No solid
   walls—the 13th-c stained glass
   windows extend from floor to
   ceiling on all sides. Crypt below.

185 ST.-SÉVERIN   ca. 1250–1681
   (church)
   rue St.-Séverin/rue St.-Jacques,
      5e *E5*

   Flamboyant double
   ambulatory. 15th- and 16th-c
   stained glass.

186 CHÂTEAU   14th c onward
      DE VINCENNES
   avenue de Paris *E9*

   Magnificent keep. The chapel
   (14th to 16th c) has fine
   16th-c stained glass.

187 HÔTEL DE SENS   1475–1507
   rue de l'Hôtel de Ville, 4e *D6*

   Medieval residence.

188 HÔTEL DE   1485–1500
      CLUNY
   place Paul Painlevé/boulevard
      St.-Michel, 5e *E5*

   Built over the ruins of a 3rd-c
   Roman bathhouse, some parts

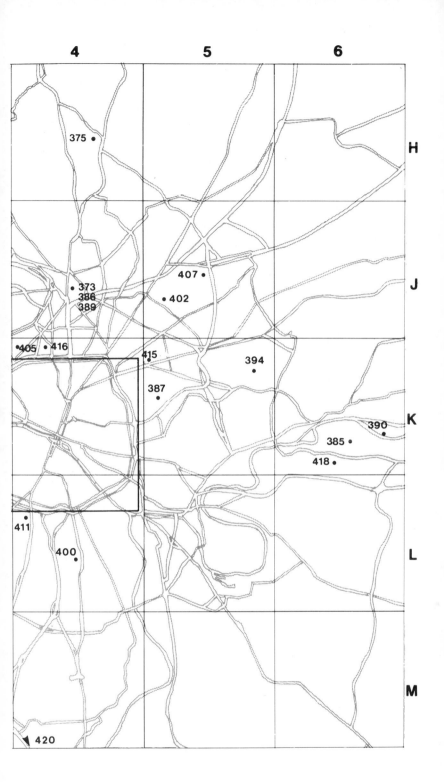

of which have survived. Now a
museum of the Middle Ages:
decorative arts, tapestries
(*The Lady and the Unicorn*
series), etc.

189 ST.-ÉTIENNE-   1492–1626
    DU-MONT
(church)
place Ste.-Geneviève, 5ᵉ *E5*

Triple-pedimented facade
(1610–26). The very fine
roodscreen (1545) is by P. de
l'Orme (extended over aisles
in 1606).

190 ST.-GERVAIS-   1492–1657
    ST.-PROTAIS

(church)
place St.-Gervais, 4ᵉ *D6*

Flamboyant Gothic. Classical
facade (1616–23) of
superimposed orders added by
S. de Brosse.

191 ST.-EUSTACHE   1532–1637
(church)
rue Rambuteau/rue du Jour,
    1ᵉʳ *C5*

Renaissance building with a
medieval plan. The original
west facade was later replaced
by a classical design, 1772–87.

Paris detail

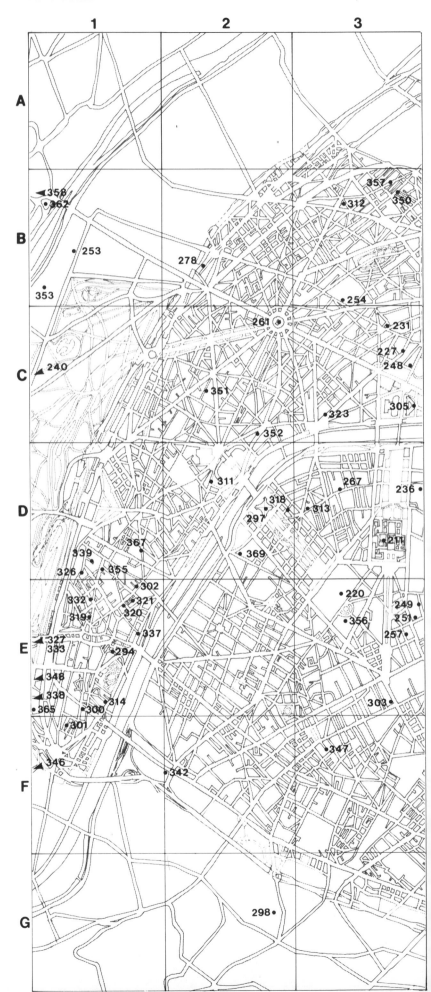

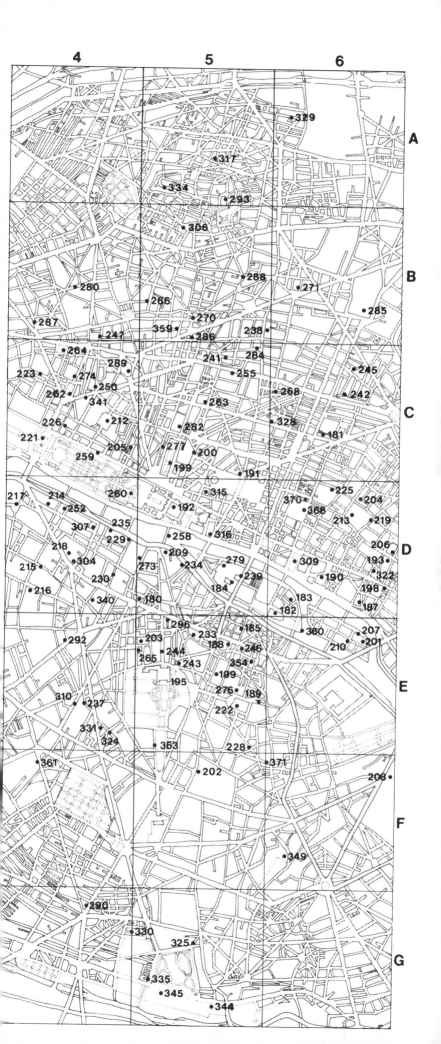

Paris detail

192 THE LOUVRE 1546–1878
place du Carrousel, 1ᵉʳ *D5*
P. Lescot, J. Lemercier, L. Le
Vau, C. Perrault, C. Percier and
P. F. L. Fontaine, L. T. J.
Visconti, etc.

193 HÔTEL DE 1585
LAMOIGNON
(now the Historic Library of
Paris)
24, rue Pavée, 4ᵉ *D6*
J. B. du Cerceau

First example in Paris of
Corinthian pilasters used in
a colossal order.

194 PLACE DES 1605–12
VOSGES, 4ᵉ *D7*
C. Chastillon

The oldest square in Paris.

195 PALAIS 1615 onward
DU LUXEMBOURG
(Luxembourg Palace, now the
Senate)
rue de Vaugirard, 6ᵉ *E5*
S. de Brosse

Enlarged in 1790. Interiors
(1795) by J. F. T. Chalgrin,
of which only the main stair
survives. Murals by Delacroix
in the library. Garden facade
(1836–44) by A. de Gisors.

196 THE SORBONNE 1624–42
place de la Sorbonne, 5ᵉ *E5*
J. Lemercier

The church (1635–42) is an
example of the "Jesuit style" of
the counter-Reformation. See
the second facade facing the
main courtyard of the
Sorbonne. Tomb of Richelieu
(1694) by C. Le Brun (sculptor:
F. Girardon) in the chancel.

197 HÔTEL DE SULLY 1625–69
62, rue St.-Antoine, 4ᵉ *D7*
J. A. du Cerceau

198 ST.-PAUL- 1625–34
ST.-LOUIS
(church)
rue St.-Antoine (opposite rue de
Sévigné), 4ᵉ *D6*
F. Derand

Modeled after Il Gesù, Roma.
The first domed church in
Paris.

199 PALAIS 1632 onward
ROYALE
place Colette du Palais
Royale, 1ᵉʳ *C5*
J. Lemercier

The Cour d'Horloge and main
stair (1764–70) are by P.
Contant d'Ivry. The galleries in
the formal gardens (1780–85)
are by V. Louis.

200 BANQUE DE 1635–1719
FRANCE
(Bank of France)
rue de la Vrillière/rue Croix
des Petits Champs, 1ᵉʳ *C5*
F. Mansart

Former Hôtel de la Vrillière.
Remodeled (1719) by R. de
Cotte, who executed the rococo
gallery.

201 HÔTEL ca. 1640–50
LAMBERT
2, rue St.-Louis-en-l'Ille, 4ᵉ *E6*
L. Le Vau with C. Le Brun and
E. Le Sueur

The Hercules gallery is the finest
example of Le Brun's surviving
works.

202 VAL-DE-GRÂCE 1645–67
(church)
rue du Val de Grâce/place Alph.
Laveran, 5ᵉ *F5*
F. Mansart

Completed by J. Lemercier and
G. Le Duc. The dome, after St.
Peter's, Roma, in turn
influenced Sir Christopher
Wren's design for St. Paul's in
London.

203 ST.-SULPICE 1646–1780
(church)
place St.-Sulpice, 6ᵉ *E5*
Gamard, then L. Le Vau and
others

Facade (1732–37) by G. N.
Servandoni. North tower (1777)
and organ loft by J. F. T.
Chalgrin. Chapelle de la Vierge
(1774) by C. De Wailly.

204 HÔTEL   1648–51
      GUÉNÉGAUD
    60, rue des Archives/rue des
      Haudriettes, 3ᵉ *D6*
    F. Mansart

    Now a museum.

205 ST.-ROCH   1653–1736
    (church)
    rue St.-Honoré/rue St.-Roch,
      1ᵉʳ *C4*
    J. Lemercier

    Lady Chapel by J. Hardouin-
    Mansart. Facade (1736) by
    R. de Cotte.

206 HÔTEL CARNAVALET   1655
    23, rue de Sévigné/rue des
      Francs Bourgeois, 3ᵉ *D6*
    F. Mansart

    Remodeling of the mansion
    built in 1544 by P. Lescot. Now
    a museum.

207 HÔTEL DE   1656–57
      LAUZUN
    17, quai d'Anjou, 4ᵉ *E6*
    L. Le Vau

    Splendid interiors.

208 THE SALTPÊTRIÈRE 1656–67
      HOSPITAL
    boulevard St.-Marcel/square
      Marie-Curie, 13ᵉ *Fo*
    L. Le Vau and P. Le Muet

    The Chapel of St. Louis (1670)
    in the formal garden is by
    L. Bruant.

209 INSTITUT DE   1661–87
      FRANCE
    quai de Conti, 6ᵉ (opposite the
      Pont des Arts) *D5*
    L. Le Vau

210 ST.-LOUIS-   1664–1726
      EN-L'ILLE
    (church)
    21, rue St.-Louis-en-l'Ille/rue
      Poulletier, 4ᵉ *E6*
    L. Le Vau

211 HÔTEL DES   1671–76
      INVALIDES
    place des Invalides, 7ᵉ *D3*
    L. Bruant

The Esplanade des Invalides is
by R. de Cotte (1704–20). The
Église du Dôme (church,
1677–1735), place Vauban, by
J. Hardouin-Mansart, is the
outstanding monument of the
French classical style. Greek
cross plan. Napoleon's Tomb

(1842) by L. T. J. Visconti is in
an open crypt under the dome.

212 PLACE   1685–1720
      VENDÔME, 1ᵉʳ *C4*

The facades (1685–88) are by
J. Hardouin-Mansart. The
houses behind the facades were
built between 1702 and 1720.
The column (1805 by J.
Gondoin and J. B. Lepère),
destroyed 1871, reerected soon
afterwards, has a replica of the
original statue of Napoleon as
Caesar upon it. No. 19 (Hôtel
d'Évreux, 1710) is by J.
Lassurance.

213 HÔTEL DE SOUBISE   1700
    60, rue des Francs-Bourgeois/
      rue des Archives, 3ᵉ *D6*
    P. A. Delamair

    Rococo salons (1732–37) by G.
    Boffrand, paintings by C. J.
    Natoire, reliefs by J. B.
    Lemoyne. Now the National
    Archives. Visits allowed upon
    written application.

214 HÔTEL DE   1714
      BEAUHARNAIS
    78, rue de Lille, 7ᵉ *D4*
    G. Boffrand

    Interiors (1803–6) by N.
    Bataille.

215 RUE DE GRENELLE, 7ᵉ *D4*

    Most of the mansions lining the
    street are now either
    government offices or
    embassies. Entry is difficult,
    if not impossible.

    No. 15   Hôtel de   1775
               Bérulle
             P. C. Convers

    No. 73   Hôtel de   1775–92
               Gallifet
             A. F. Legrand

             Most of the interiors
             have been
             preserved.

    No. 79   Hôtel   1713
               d'Estrées
             R. de Cotte

             Now the Russian
             Embassy.

    No. 106 Temple de   1747–56
               Panthémont
             P. Contant d'Ivry

    No. 110 Hôtel de   1776
               Rochechouart
             M. Cherpitel

             Ministry of
             Education

No. 118 Hôtel de 1733
Villars
Leroux and N.
Pineau

No. 127 Hôtel du 1770
Châtelet
M. Cherpitel

Nos. 138–140 Hôtel du 1720
Noir–Moutiers
J. Courtonne

Now the French
National
Geographic
Institute.

No. 151 Apartment 1898
Building
J. Lavirotte

The Fountain of the
Four Seasons
(1739–45), off
boulevard Raspail,
is by E.
Bouchardon.

216 HÔTEL DE 1720
MATIGNON
54, rue de Varenne, 7e *D4*
J. Courtonne

Now the residence of the Prime
Minister. Ingenious plan. The
antechamber (1731) by N.
Pineau is a rococo masterpiece.

217 ASSEMBLÉE 1720 onward
NATIONALE
(National Assembly)
place du Palais Bourbon, 7e *D4*
Giardini, then J. Lassurance,
then J. A. Gabriel, then
J. Aubert

Former Palais Bourbon. The
portico (1803–8) on the quai
d'Orsay was designed by B.
Poyet to complement the
facade of the Madelaine across
the place de la Concorde. The
chamber remodeling, vestibule,
Salon du Roi, and library are
by J. de Joly (1828–36). The
Hôtel de Lassay (now the Petit
Bourbon) was incorporated into
this complex in 1785.

218 HÔTEL DE 1732
ROQUELAURE
(Ministry of Works)
246, boulevard St.-Germain,
7e *D4*
Leroux and N. Pineau

Grand Salon and Salon Rouge.

219 HÔTEL DE ROHAN 1740
87, rue Vielle-du-Temple,
3e *D6*

Former Hôtel de Strasbourg.
The *Horses of Apollo* relief by
R. Le Lorrain is above the
stables in the entrance
courtyard.

220 ÉCOLE 1751–88
MILITAIRE
avenue de la Motte Piquet,
7e *E3*
J. A. Gabriel

The chapel is open to the public.

221 PLACE DE 1753–90
LA CONCORDE, 8e *C4*
J. A. Gabriel

Gabriel won the design
competition held for this
project. The symmetrical Hôtel
de Crillon and Ministère de la
Marine (1757–75) are by him.
The fountains and obelisk
(from Luxor) were added by
J. I. Hittorff (1836–40). The
Pont de la Concorde bridge
(1787–90) is by J. R. Perronet
(widened in 1932). The view of
the Arc de Triomphe is framed
by G. Coustou's superbly
sculpted *Marly Horses*
(1740–45). •The entrance to the
Paris sewer system (tours
available) is near the Lille
statue (opposite the Jeu de
Paume).

222 STE.-GENÉVIÈVE 1756–90
(the Pantheon)
place du Panthéon, 5e *E5*
J. G. Soufflot

Completed by J. B. Rondelet
(1780–90). Altered afterwards
by A. C. Quatremère-de-
Quincy. Greek cross plan.
Elegant interiors with very
slender piers and Corinthian
columns. Complex triple dome
with clerestory lighting. Pediment sculptures (1837) on
facade by P. David d'Angers.
•The École de Droit (law
school, 1763), on the north side
of Ste.-Geneviève, is also by
Soufflot.

223 HÔTEL 1763–68
ALEXANDRE
16, rue de la Ville-l'Evêque,
8e *C4*
E. L. Boullée

224 CHAPELLE DES 1765
AMES DU PURGATOIRE
(chapel)
in the church of Ste.-Marguerite
de Charonne, rue de
Charron, 11e, *D8*
V. Louis

Early coffered barrel-vault
roof. Decoration by Brunet.

225 HÔTEL DE HALLWYL 1766
28, rue Michel le Comte, 3e *D6*
C. N. Ledoux

Of the original interiors, only
the stair remains.

226 HÔTEL DE 1767
ST.-FLORENTIN
2, rue St.-Florentin, 1er *C4*
J. A. Gabriel and J. F. T.
Chalgrin

Only the exterior facade remains
unchanged.

227 HÔTEL DE LA 1768
VAUPALIÈRE
25, avenue Matignon, 8e *C3*
L. M. Colignon

228 CHAPELLE DU 1768
ST.-ESPRIT
(church)
30, rue Lhomond, 5e *E5*
J. F. T. Chalgrin

The convent is by J. G. Soufflot.

229 HÔTELS DE TESSE 1768
1, quai Voltaire/rue des Saints-
Pères, 7e *D4*
P. N. Rousset

230 ÉCOLE DES 1768–74
PONTS ET CHAUSSÉES
(school)
28, rue des Saints-Pères 7e *D4*
J. D. Antoine

Extended (1868–79) by R. de
Fleury.

231 ST.-PHILIPE 1768–84
DU ROULE
(church)
rue la Boetie/rue du Faubourg,
8e *C3*
J. F. T. Chalgrin

Chapelle de la Vièrge (1846)
by E. H. Godde. Chapelle des
Catéchismes (1853) by L.
Baltard.

232 PAVILLON CARRÉ 1770
DE BEAUDOUIN
121, rue de Menilmontant,
11e *C8*
P. L. Moreau-Desproux

233 ÉCOLE DE 1771–75
CHIRURGIE
(school of medicine)
rue de l'Ecole de Médecine,
6e *E5*
J. Gondoin

Only the exterior remains
unchanged.

234 HÔTEL DES 1771–77
MONNAIES
(the mint)
quai de Conti, 6e *D5*
J. D. Antoine

235 HÔTEL DE VILLETTE 1773
1, rue de Beaune/27, quai
Voltaire, 7e *D4*
C. De Wailly

236 HÔTEL DE 1774–77
MONACO
(Polish embassy)
57, rue St.-Dominique, 7e *D3*
A. T. Brongniart

Interiors badly altered.

237 HÔTEL DE LA COSTE 1776
22, rue Notre-Dame-des-
Champs, 7e *E4*
P. Dorléans

238 HÔTELS GIOX 1776–83
ET TITON
58–60, rue du Faubourg
Poissonnière, 10e *B5*
J. C. Delafosse

239 COUR DE MAI 1776–86
(May Court)
Palais de Justice
boulevard du Palais, 1er *D5*
P. L. Moreau-Desproux

Grand stair by J. D. Antoine.

240 PAVILLON DE 1777
BAGATELLE
Parc de Bagatelle, Bois de
Boulogne, 16e *C1*
F. J. Bélanger

Built in sixty-four days. Dome
added in the 19th c. Garden
(1778–80) in the English style.

241 HÔTEL DE 1778
MERCY-ARGENTEAU
16, boulevard Montmartre,
9e *C5*
F. Perlin

242 MAISON 1778–82
GIAMBONNE
62, rue René Boulanger, 10e *C6*
N. C. Girardin

243 THÉÂTRE 1778–85
FRANÇAIS
(Odéon)
place de l'Odéon, 6e *E5*
C. De Wailly and M. J. Peyre

The interior has been completely
altered.

244 HÔTEL DE 1779
NIVERNAIS
10, rue de Tournon, 6e *E5*
M. J. Peyre

245 HÔTEL GOUTHIÈRE 1780
6, rue Pierre Bullet, 10e *C6*
J. Métivier

246 COLLÈGE DE FRANCE 1780
place Marcelin Berthelot, 5e *E5*
J. F. T. Chalgrin

Extended by P. M. Letarouilly

247 LYCÉE 1780–83
CONDORCET
63, rue de Caumartin, 9e *B4*
A. T. Brongniart

School, former convent. Facade
rebuilt in 1864.

248 HÔTEL 1780–87
D'ARGENSON
38, avenue Gabriel, 8ᵉ *C3*
J. P. Lemoine de Couzon

249 HÔTEL DE M'LLE 1781
DE BOURBON-CONDÉ
12, rue Monsieur, 7ᵉ *E3*
A. T. Brongniart

The ground-floor salon is in
good condition. •No. 20 (Hôtel
de Montesquiou, 1781) is also
by Brongniart. No. 8 (Hôtel de
Jarnac, 1784) is by A. F.
Legrand.

250 HÔTEL D'AUMONT 1781
2, rue Caumartin 9ᵉ *C4*
A. Aubert

•No. 1 (Hôtel Deshays, 1781) is
also by Aubert.

251 MAISON 1781
BRONGNIART
49, boulevard des Invalides/
rue Oudinot, 7ᵉ *E3*
A. T. Brongniart

An upper floor was added later.

252 HÔTEL DE SALM 1783
(Légion d'Honneur)
6, rue de Lille, 7ᵉ *D4*
P. Rousseau

Rebuilt in 1878.

253 FOLIE ST.-JAMES 1784
(garden pavilion)
34, avenue de Madrid, Neuilly
B1
F. J. Bélanger

254 HÔPITAL BEAUJON 1784
208, rue du Faubourg-
St.-Honoré, 8ᵉ*B3*
N. C. Girardin

255 HÔTEL DE 1785
MONTHOLON
23, boulevard Poissonnière,
2ᵉ *C5*
F. Soufflot-le-Romain

256 ROTONDE DE 1785–89
LA VILLETTE
(tollhouse)
place de Stalingrad, 19ᵉ *B7*
C. N. Ledoux

Of the original forty-five
tollhouses that encircled Paris,
four survive. •Two others are
Rotonde de Monceau, place de
la République Dominicaine, 8ᵉ,
and Barrière d'Enfer, place
Denfert-Rochereau, 14ᵉ.

257 HÔTEL MASSERANO 1787
11, rue Masseran, 7ᵉ *E3*
A. T. Brongniart

•Nos. 3–5 (Maison Chamblin,
1789) are also by Brongniart.

258 PONT DES ARTS 1800–1803
(pedestrian bridge)
quai du Louvre/quai
Malaquais, 1ᵉʳ *D5*
L. A. de Cessart

Built by Delon.

259 RUE DE RIVOLI *C4* 1801–4
(urban design)
P. F. L. Fontaine and C. Percier

Extended by J. I. Hittorff in
1835.

260 ARC DU CARROUSEL 1806
place du Carrousel, 1ᵉʳ *D4*
P. F. L. Fontaine and C. Percier

Modeled after the Arch of
Septimus Severus, Roma.

261 ARC DE TRIOMPHE 1806–36
place de l'Étoile, 8ᵉ *C2*
J. F. T. Chalgrin

Completed by L. Goust, then
J. N. Huyot, then A. Bouet.
G. E. Haussmann added seven
radiating avenues to the circle
in 1854. The facades on the
circle are by J. I. Hittorff.

262 LA MADELEINE 1807–45
(church)
place de la Madeleine, 8ᵉ *C4*
P. Vignon

Interiors by J. J. M. Huvé. In
1814 this almost became Paris's
first railway station.

263 BOURSE 1809–15
(exchange)
place de la Bourse, 2ᵉ *C5*
A. T. Brongniart

Enlarged (1895–1902) by E. G.
Coquart.

264 CHAPELLE 1816
    EXPIATOIRE
    (Expiatory Chapel)
    square Louis XVI/rue
    Pasquier, 8ᵉ *C4*
    P. F. L. Fontaine and C. Percier

265 SÉMINAIRE DE 1820–38
    STE.-SULPICE
    place Ste.-Sulpice, 6ᵉ *E5*
    E. H. Godde

266 MAISON DE 1821
    MADEMOISELLE MARS
    rue de la Tour des Dames/
    rue de la Rochefoucauld,
    9ᵉ *B5*
    L. T. J. Visconti

267 ST.-PIERRE- 1822–32
    DU–GROS-CAILLOU
    (church)
    92, rue St.-Dominique, 7ᵉ *D3*
    E. H. Godde

268 NOTRE-DAME- 1823–30
    DE-BONNE-NOUVELLE
    (church)
    25 bis, rue de la Lune, 2ᵉ *C6*
    E. H. Godde

269 ST.-DENIS-DU- 1823–35
    ST.-SACREMENT
    (church)
    68 bis, rue du Turenne, 3ᵉ *D7*
    E. H. Godde

270 NOTRE-DAME- 1823–36
    DE-LORETTE
    (church)
    18, rue de Châteaudun/rue
    Fléchier, 9ᵉ *B5*
    H. Lebas

271 ST.-VINCENT- 1824–44
    DE-PAUL
    (church)
    place Franz-Liszt, 10ᵉ *B6*
    J. I. Hittorff

272 COLONNE DE 1831–40
    JUILLET
    (July Column)
    place de la Bastille, 4ᵉ *D7*
    J. L. Duc and J. A. Alavoine

273 ÉCOLE DES 1832
    BEAUX–ARTS
    (school of fine art)
    14, rue Bonaparte, 6ᵉ *D5*
    F. L. J. Duban

    •Parts of Anet (1550) by P. de
    l'Orme are in the entrance
    courtyard.

274 HÔTEL POURTALÈS 1836
    7, rue Tronchet, 8ᵉ *C4*
    F. L. J. Duban

275 ASILE D'ALIÉNÉS 1838–45
    DE CHARENTON
    (Charenton Asylum)
    Charenton-le-Pont (right bank
    of the Seine) *G9*
    E. J. Gilbert

276 BIBLIOTHÈQUE 1839–50
    STE.-GENÉVIÈVE
    (library)
    place du Panthéon, 5ᵉ *E5*
    H. Labrouste

    Important iron-framed building
    with neo-Renaissance facade.
    The interior's twin barrel-vaults

are of exposed iron. •The
librarian's house (1847) by
Labrouste is on place du
Panthéon/rue Valette. The
adjacent Collège Ste.-Barbe
(1840–52) is by H. and T.
Labrouste. Now the library of
the law faculty; only the facade
remains.

277 FONTAINE 1841–44
    MOLIÈRE
    (fountain)
    rue Molière/rue Richelieu,
    1ᵉʳ *C5*
    L. T. J. Visconti

278 CHAPELLE 1842–43
    ST.-FERDINAND
    boulevard Pershing, Neuilly-
    sur-Seine *B2*
    P. F. L. Fontaine

    The stained glass windows are
    by J. A. D. Ingres.

279 PALAIS DE JUSTICE 1842–70
    (law courts)
    rue de Harlay, 1ᵉʳ *D5*
    L. J. Duc and E. T. Dommey

280 HÔTEL COURMONT 1846–49
    28, rue de Liège, 8ᵉ *B4*
    E. E. Viollet-le-Duc

281 CIRQUE NAPOLÉON 1852
    (Cirque d'Hiver)
    boulevard des Filles du
    Calvaire, 11ᵉ *C7*
    J. I. Hittorff

282 BIBLIOTHÈQUE 1853–69
    NATIONALE
    (library)
    58, rue Richelieu, 2ᵉ *C5*
    H. Labrouste

Labrouste was responsible for
the main reading room (twelve
terra-cotta domes on iron
columns, each with an oculus)
and book stacks. The Mazarin
Gallery is by F. Mansart. The
facades on rue Richelieu are
by L. T. J. Visconti.

283 ST.-JEAN-BAPTISTE- 1854
    DE-BELLEVILLE
    (church)
    139, rue de Belleville/rue de
    Palestine, 19ᵉ *B8*
    J. B. A. Lassus

284 ST.-EUGÈNE 1854–55
    (church)
    rue Ste.-Cécile/rue du
    Conservatoire, 9ᵉ *C5*
    L. A. Boileau

285 GARE DU NORD 1859–65
(railway station)
place de Roubaix, 10ᵉ *B6*
J. I. Hittorff

286 APARTMENT 1860
BUILDING
23, rue Chauchat/rue
Lafayette, 9ᵉ *B5*
E. E. Viollet-le-Duc and A. de
Baudot

287 ST.-AUGUSTIN 1860–71
(church)
place St.-Augustin, 8ᵉ *B4*
V. Baltard

Exposed-iron structure.

288 MAISON 1861–62
VIOLLET-LE-DUC
(own house)
68, rue Condorcet, 9ᵉ *B5*
E. E. Viollet-le-Duc

289 OPÉRA 1862–75
place de l'Opéra, 9ᵉ *C4*
C. Garnier

Opulent entry stair; ceiling
painted by M. Chagall in
1964.

290 ST.-PIERRE-DE- 1864–72
MONTROUGE
(church)
place Victor Basch/88 avenue
du Général Leclerc, 14ᵉ *G4*
J. A. E. Vaudremer

291 PARC DES 1866–67
BUTTES-CHAUMONTS
(park)
place Armande Carrel, 19ᵉ *B8*
J. C. A. Alphand

292 MAGASIN DU 1873–76
BON MARCHÉ
(department store)
22, rue de Sèvres, 7ᵉ *E4*
L. A. Boileau and G. Eiffel

Iron and glass. Now hidden
behind masonry facades.

293 SACRÉ-COEUR 1874–1910
(church)
37, rue Chevalier-de-la-Barre,
18ᵉ *A5*
P. Abadie, L. Magne, and
others

Modeled after Abadie's
restoration of St. Front in
Périgueux.

294 NOTRE-DAME- 1876
D'AUTEUIL
(church)
2, place d'Auteuil, 16ᵉ *E1*
J. A. E. Vaudremer

295 TEMPLE 1877–80
PROTESTANT DE
BELLEVILLE
(church)
97, rue Julien Lacroix, 20ᵉ *C8*
J. A. E. Vaudremer

296 CERCLE DE 1878–79
LA LIBRAIRIE
117, boulevard St.-Germain,
6ᵉ *E5*
C. Garnier

•Maison Hachette (1882), also
by Garnier, is at 195, boulevard
St.-Germain.

297 TOUR EIFFEL 1887–89
(Eiffel Tower)
avenue Gustave Eiffel, 7ᵉ *D2*
G. Eiffel

298 MAISON JASSEDÉ 1893
63, avenue du Général de
Gaulle, Vanves *G2*
H. Guimard

299 LYCÉE 1894
VICTOR-HUGO
27, rue de Sévigné, 3ᵉ *D7*
A. de Baudot

Now a girls' school. The
pavilion in the rear courtyard
is an early example of
reinforced-concrete
construction.

300 HÔTEL CARPEAUX 1895
39, boulevard Exelmans, 16ᵉ *E1*
H. Guimard

301 ÉCOLE DU 1895
SACRÉ-COEUR
(school)
9, avenue de la Frillière, off rue
Parent de Rosan, 16ᵉ *F1*
H. Guimard

302 CASTEL 1895–98
BÉRANGER
14–16, rue La Fontaine, 16ᵉ *E1*
H. Guimard

•No. 65 rue La Fontaine is by
H. Sauvage (1927).

303 LYCÉE BUFFON 1895–99
(school)
boulevard Pasteur/rue de
Vaugirard, 15ᵉ *E3*
J. A. E. Vaudremer

304 MAISON GUADET 1896
(own house)
240 bis, boulevard St.-Germain,
7ᵉ *D4*
J. Guadet

305 PETIT PALAIS 1897–1900
(exhibition hall)
avenue Winston-Churchill,
8ᵉ *C3*
C. Girault

•The contemporary Grand Palais opposite (shown above) is by H. Deglane, L. Louvet, and A. Thomas.

306 ST.-JEAN-   1897–1905
        DE-MONTMARTRE
    (church)
    2, place des Abbesses, 18ᵉ *B5*
    A. de Baudot

    First French building of major importance built in exposed reinforced concrete.

307 GARE D'ORSAY   1898–1901
    (railway station)
    7–9, quai Anatole-France, 7ᵉ *D4*
    V. Laloux and L. Magne

308 GARE DE LYON   1899–1900
    (railway station)
    20, boulevard Diderot, 12ᵉ *E7*
    Tondoire and Denis

309 METRO   1899–1902
        ENTRANCE PAVILION
    place l'Hôtel de Ville, 4ᵉ *D6*
    H. Guimard

    Few pavilions have survived. Remaining open entries are now scattered throughout Paris.

310 GRAND BAZAR   1900
    (Magasins Réunis)
    134–36, rue de Rennes, 6ᵉ *E4*
    H. B. Gutton

    •No. 140 (Magasin Félix Potin, 1904) is by Auscher.

311 APARTMENT   1903
        BUILDING
    25 bis, rue Franklin, 16ᵉ *D2*
    A. Perret

312 HÔTEL MERCEDES   1903–4
    128, avenue de Wagram, 17ᵉ *B3*
    G. Chedanne

313 APARTMENT   1904
        BUILDING
    29, avenue Rapp, 7ᵉ *D3*
    J. Lavirotte

314 APARTMENT   1905
        BUILDING
    142, avenue de Versailles,
        16ᵉ *E1*
    H. Guimard

315 OFFICE BUILDING 1905
    16, rue du Louvre, 1ᵉʳ *D5*
    F. Jourdain

316 LA SAMARITAINE   1905
    (department store—older section)
    2, rue du Pont-Neuf, 1ᵉʳ *D5*
    F. Jourdain

    Extended in 1926 by Jourdain with H. Sauvage.

317 APARTMENT   1907
        BUILDING
    7, rue Tretaigne, 18ᵉ*A5*
    H. Sauvage

318 APARTMENT   1908
        BUILDING
    10, avenue Elisée-Reclus, 7ᵉ *D2*
    J. Guadet

319 HÔTEL GUIMARD   1909–10
    (own house)
    122, avenue Mozart, 16ᵉ *E1*
    H. Guimard

    •No. 120 (1926) is also by Guimard.

320 APARTMENT   1909–10
        BUILDING
    11, rue François-Millet, 16ᵉ *E1*
    H. Guimard

321 APARTMENT   1909–12
        BUILDINGS
    17–21, rue La Fontaine; 43, rue Greuze; 8–10 rue Agar;
        16ᵉ *E1*
    H. Guimard

    •No. 60, rue La Fontaine (the Mezzara House, 1911) is also by Guimard.

322 SYNAGOGUE   1911–13
    10, rue Pavée, 4ᵉ *D6*
    H. Guimard

323 THÉÂTRE   1911–13
        CHAMPS-ELYSÉES
    15, avenue Montaigne, 8ᵉ *C3*
    A. Perret

324 APARTMENTS   1912
    26, rue Vavin, 6ᵉ *E4*
    H. Sauvage

325 ATELIER   1922–23
        OZENFANT
    (house and studio)
    53, avenue Reille, 14ᵉ *G5*
    Le Corbusier and P. Jeanneret

    Slightly altered.

326 LA ROCHE-   1923
        JEANNERET HOUSES
    8–10, square du Docteur-Blanche, 16ᵉ *D1*
    Le Corbusier and P. Jeanneret

    Double house. Now the Fondation Le Corbusier.

327 LIPSCHITZ AND   1924
        MIESTSCHANINOFF
        HOUSE
    9, allée des Pins, Boulogne-Billancourt *E1*
    Le Corbusier and P. Jeanneret

    •No. 5 (Ternisien house, 1926) is by Le Corbusier.

328 FRANCE-SOIR   1924
        OFFICES
    100, rue Réamur, 2ᵉ *C6*
    P. Sardou

    •No. 124 (1903, probably by G. Chedanne) has a dramatic metal and glass facade.

329 APARTMENT   1924–26
        BUILDING
    13, rue des Amiraux, 18ᵉ *A6*
    H. Sauvage

Dramatic stepped facade clad in white tile.

330 HOUSES   1924–26
Villa Seurat, 14e *G5*
No. 1, Townsend; 3, Georg and Grommaire; 4, A. Lurçat; and 5, Bertrand.

331 APARTMENT   1925
    BUILDING
137, boulevard Raspail, 6^e *E4*
H. Sauvage

332 APARTMENT   1925–26
    BUILDING
18, rue Henri-Heine, 16^e *E1*
H. Guimard

Art deco influence now apparent.

333 COOK HOUSE   1926
6, rue Denfert-Rochereau, Boulogne-Billancourt *E1*
Le Corbusier and P. Jeanneret

•No. 8 (Hôtel Collinet, 1925) is by R. Mallet-Stevens. No. 5 (1933–36) is by G. H. Pingusson.

334 TZARA HOUSE   1926
15, avenue Junot, 18e *A5*
A. Loos

Slightly altered.

335 GUGGENBUHL HOUSE 1926
2, rue du Douanier/rue Nansouty, 14e *G5*
A. Lurçat

•No. 4, the Braque house, is by A. Perret (1927).

336 PLAINEX HOUSE   1927
24 bis, boulevard Masséna, 13e *G7*
Le Corbusier and P. Jeanneret

337 APARTMENT   1927
    BUILDING
25, avenue de Versailles, 16e *E1*
J. Ginsberg and B. Lubetkin

•No. 42 is by Ginsberg (1934). Flat facade with strong horizontal emphasis.

338 MAISON DE SALIS   1927
(house)
9, rue du Belvédère, 92 Boulogne-Billancourt *E1*
A. Lurçat

339 APARTMENT   1927
    BUILDING
5, rue Mallet-Stevens, 16e *D1*
R. Mallet-Stevens

340 DALSACE HOUSE   1928–31
    AND SURGERY
(Maison du Verre—house of glass)

31, rue St.-Guillaume, 7^e *D4*
P. Chareau and B. Bijvoet

A work of genius, in perfect condition. (All the original interiors and furnishings are intact.) The epitome of the machine age.

341 BALLY STORE   1928
(facade)
11, boulevard de la Madeleine, 9e *C4*
R. Mallet-Stevens

342 MARINE   1929–32
    NATIONALE
(office building)
8, boulevard Victor, 15e *F2*
A. Perret

343 CITÉ-REFUGE   1929–33
    DE L'ARMÉE DU SALUT
(Salvation Army refuge)
12, rue Cantagrel, 13e *G7*
Le Corbusier and P. Jeanneret

Altered later by Jeanneret and then disowned by Le Corbusier. Restored (with limited success) in 1980.

344 SWISS STUDENTS'   1930–32
    HOSTEL
7, boulevard Jourdan, Cité Universitaire, 14e *G5*
Le Corbusier and P. Jeanneret

The dormitory block is supported by heavy central pilotis. •The Brazilian hostel on avenue de la Porte Gentilly (1956–59), by Le Corbusier and L. Costa, is close by.

345 NETHERLANDS   1931
    PAVILION
63, boulevard Jourdan, Cité Universitaire, 14e *G5*
W. Dudok

346 HÔTEL DE VILLE   1931–34
(town hall)
avenue André Morizet,
    92 Boulogne-Billancourt *F1*
T. Garnier

347 APARTMENTS   1932
square de Vergennes, 15ᵉ *F3*
R. Mallet-Stevens

348 APARTMENT   1933
    BUILDING
24, rue Nungesser-et-Coli, 16ᵉ
    E1
Le Corbusier and P. Jeanneret

Le Corbusier's apartment and
studio were on the seventh and
eighth floors.

349 MOBILIER   1934
    NATIONAL OFFICES
1, rue Berbier du Mets, 13ᵉ *F6*
A. Perret

350 ÉCOLE NORMALE   1934
    DE MUSIQUE
(school of music)
76, rue Cardinet, 17ᵉ *B3*
A. Perret

351 PASSY FIRE STATION   1935
8, rue Mesnil, 16ᵉ *C2*
R. Mallet-Stevens

352 PUBLIC WORKS   1937
    MUSEUM
5, avenue d'Iéna, 16ᵉ *C2*
A. Perret

353 MAISONS JAOUL   1952–54
(two houses)
81, rue de Longchamp,
    Neuilly-sur-Seine *B1*
Le Corbusier

Two separate houses on a tight
site. Off shutter concrete frame
with brick infill.

354 APARTMENT   1953
    BUILDING
29, rue Jean-de-Beauvais,
    5ᵉ *E5*
P. Herbé, J. Le Couteur, and
J. Prouvé

355 APARTMENT   1954
    BUILDING
5, square Mozart, 16ᵉ *D1*
L. Mirabaud

The finely detailed curtain
wall is by J. Prouvé.

356 UNESCO   1954–58
    HEADQUARTERS
place de Fontenoy, 7ᵉ *E3*
M. Breuer, P. L. Nervi, and
B. Zehrfuss

Too many good intentions and
architects.

357 OFFICE BUILDING   1955
85, rue Jouffroy, 17ᵉ *B3*
E. Albert

Completely glazed facade
braced with an exposed
steel-tube frame.

358 CNIT EXHIBITION   1958
    HALL
Rond Point de la Défense,
    Courbevoie *B1*
R. Camelot, J. de Mailly, and
B. Zehrfuss

Huge triangular vaulted hall.

359 OFFICE BUILDING   1959
37, rue de la Victoire, 9ᵉ *B5*
J. Balladur

Skillful use of a very restricted
site.

360 DEPORTES DE   1962
    LA RESISTANCE
(memorial to the Resistance
deportations)
square de l'Ille-de-France, 4ᵉ *E6*
G. H. Pingusson

Remarkable monument,
making full use of a unique site
on the Seine.

361 GARE DU   1964
    MONTPARNASSE
    COMPLEX
(railway station)
rue de l'Arrivée/boulevard de
    Montparnasse, 15ᵉ *F4*
E. Beaudoin, R. Lopez,
de Hoyn, Arretche, and
Dubuisson

Appalling. An urban and
architectural disaster. The
high-rise tower Tour Maine-
Montparnasse (1972–73), by
Beaudoin, Cassan, de Marien,
and Saubotis, is similar.

362 NOBEL OFFICE   1966
    BUILDING
La Défense, Puteaux *B1*
J. de Mailly, Depussé, and
J. Prouvé

Thirty stories; curtain wall by
Prouvé.

363 FACULTY OF 1966
PHARMACY EXTENSION
4, avenue de l'Observatoire,
6e *E5*
P. Sirvin and C. Clouzeau

Successful juxtaposition. The
new extension completes and
reinterprets the historical
context in which it is sited.

364 PISCINE CARNOT 1968
(swimming baths)
36, boulevard Carnot, 12e *E9*
R. Taillibert

Swimming pool covered by a
retractable tensile membrane
roof.

365 STADIUM 1970
avenue du Parc des Princes,
16^e *E1*
R. Taillibert

366 FRENCH COMMUNIST 1971
PARTY HEADQUARTERS
2, place du Colonel Fabien,
19^e *B7*
O. Niemeyer, with P. Chemetov
and Deroche

367 APARTMENTS 1973
30, rue de Boulainvilliers, 16^e
D1
B. Hamburger

368 CENTRE 1974–77
GEORGES–POMPIDOU
rue du Renard/rue St.-Martin,
4e *D6*
R. Piano and R. Rogers

Cultural center for the arts.
The building is weathering
badly. The facades are of
interest.

369 AUSTRALIAN 1976
EMBASSY
rue J.-Rey/rue de la Fédération,
15e *D2*
H. Seidler with M. Breuer and
P. L. Nervi

A successful "prestige"
building. Skillfully planned.

370 HOUSING 1976–78
rue Rambuteau/rue St.-Martin,
4e *D6*
J. C. Bernard

371 APARTMENT 1978
BUILDINGS
rue Mouffetard/rue Jean-
Calvin, 5e *F6*
Groupe Cerise (Druenne,
Leblois, Moreau, and Steinz)

372 HOUSING 1978–79
rue des Hautes-Formes, 13e *G7*
C. de Portzamparc and
G. Benamo

Outskirts of Paris

373 CATHÉDRALE 1136–1281
DE ST.-DENIS
St.-Denis (12 km/7.5 mi N of
Paris) *J4*

The ambulatory (1140–44) built
by Abbot Suger marks the
beginning of the Gothic style:
for the first time, the pointed
arch, rib vault, and flying
buttress were used as one
unified construction system.
Suger built the west facade and
first two bays of the nave
(1136–40), the chancel, and
crypt (1140–44). P. de
Montreuil completed the nave
and transept (1247–81).
Restored (very badly) by Debret
(1813–46). This was corrected
by E. E. Viollet-le-Duc's
restoration (1858–79).
The mausoleums inside are
remarkable: François I by
P. de l'Orme and P. Bontemps;
Henry II and Catherine de
Médici by F. Primaticcio and
G. Pilon; Louis XII and Anne
de Bretagne by A. and G.
Giusti.

374 CHÂTEAU 12th c onward
DE ST.-GERMAIN
St.-Germain-en-Laye *K2*

The superb chapel (1230, by P.
de Montreuil) and keep (1368)
were retained when P. Chambiges rebuilt the château in
1539–49 for François I.
Restored in 1862. Now the
Museum of National An-
tiquities. The Grand Terrace, a
mile and a half long, is by A.
Le Nôtre.

375 CHÂTEAU 15th c onward
D'ECOUEN
Ecouen (18 km/11 mi N of
Paris) *H4*

Extended (1540) by J. Bullant.

376 CHÂTEAU 16th c onward
DE DAMPIERRE
Dampierre (30 km/18.5 mi W of
Paris) *M1*

Restored (1675–83) by
J. Hardouin-Mansart. Salon de
la Minerve by F. Duban (1839),
with murals by J. A. D. Ingres
(*l'Age d'Or*). Park by A.
Le Nôtre.

377 CHÂTEAU 17th–19th c
DE VERSAILLES
(palace)
Versailles *L2*
Le Roy, then L. Le Vau,
J. Hardouin-Mansart, J. A.
Gabriel, etc.

Unimaginably huge. See one
building or area per visit, or
join an official tour.
Interiors
Grand Apartment (1668).
L. Le Vau. Decoration by
C. Le Brun, who executed the
painted ceiling in the Hall of
Mirrors. Bernini's bust of
Louis XIV is in the Diana
Saloon.
Royal Apartments (1684–
1701). J. Hardouin-Mansart.

Chapelle (1699–1710).
J. Hardouin-Mansart. Completed by R. de Cotte.
Salon d'Hercule (1712).
Ceiling fresco (1733–36) by F. Lemoyne.
Petits Apartments (1738).
J. A. Gabriel.
Royal Opera (1768–70).
J. A. Gabriel. Built in wood, painted to resemble marble.
Museum of French History. 17th to 19th c French paintings and decorative arts.

Gardens   17th–18th c
and fountains

L. Le Vau, then C. Le Brun, A. Le Nôtre, J. Hardouin-Mansart, etc. Designed as an architectural extension of the palace. To the north are the two Trianons, an architecturally separate concept.

Grand Trianon   1687–88
J. Hardouin-Mansart
The French Pavilion (1750) between the Grand and Petit Trianons is a small masterpiece by J. A. Gabriel.

Petit Trianon   1761–68
J. A. Gabriel

In the gardens are the Grotto, Théâtre de la Reine (Queen's Theater), Belvédère, Temple d'Amour (Temple of Love—on a tiny island), and Hameau (an 'Austrian'

hamlet), all by R. Mique, built from 1777–85.

Close to the palace are the following 18th-c buildings.
Église   1765–70
St.-Symphorien
(church)
place St.-Symphorien
L. F. Trouard
Early barrel vaulted ceiling.

The St.-Louis Chapel, place St.-Louis, Versailles (1764–70), is also by Trouard.

Convent des   1767–72
Ursulines
(now Lycée Hoche)
73, avenue de St.-Cloud
R. Mique

Ecuries du   ca. 1772
Madame Du Barry
(stables)
19, avenue de Paris
C. N. Ledoux

Pavillon   1781–84
Comtesse de Provence
111, avenue de Paris
J. F. T. Chalgrin

378 CHÂTEAU DE   1642–46
    MAISONS
Maisons-Lafitte *J2*
F. Mansart

Mansart's masterpiece is the culmination of the neoclassic movement in France. Designed to entertain the king, the still-intact interiors are as refined and complete as the exterior decoration. The dining and games rooms (1772–87) are by Bellanger.

379 PARK   17th c
St.-Cloud *K3*
A. Le Nôtre

Waterfall by Lepautre and J. Hardouin-Mansart. Water cascades and fountains (only at certain times of the year).

380 CHÂTEAU   destroyed, 1798
    DE SCEAUX
Sceaux *L3*

The present château was built in the 19th c. Original buildings that survived are: Pavillon de l'Aurore (dome by C. Le Brun) and Petite Château and Orangery (1684) by J. Hardouin-Mansart. The park by A. Le Nôtre was recently restored.

381 PAVILLON DU   1750
    BUTARD
route des Puits, near
  Vaucresson (20 km/12.5 mi
  W of Paris) *K2*
J. A. Gabriel

382 PAVILLON DE   1753–54
    LA MUETTE
Forêt de St.-Germain (20 km/
  12.5 mi NW of Paris) *J2*
J. A. Gabriel

383 NYMPHAEUM   1762
2, avenue du Château, Chatou
  (16 km/10 mi W of Paris) *K2*
J. G. Soufflot

384 PAVILLON DE   1771–73
    MADAME DU BARRY
Louveciennes (21 km/13 mi W
  of Paris) *K2*
C. N. Ledoux

Important neoclassical building. Completely rebuilt and enlarged.

385 CHÂTEAU DE 18th c
 CHAMPS-SUR-MARNE
Champs-sur-Marne *K6*
J. B. Bullet

Interiors by J. B. Oudry, Huet,
and A. F. Desportes. Fine
ornamental garden.

386 CARMELITE CHURCH 1775
(now Justice de Paix)
22 bis rue Gabriel Péri,
 St.-Denis *J4*
R. Mique

Ionic portico and dome.

387 ST.-GERMAIN- 1785–87
 L'AUXERROIS
(church)
Romainville *K5*
A. T. Brongniart

388 CHÂTEAU DE 1800–1802
 MALMAISON
Rueil-Malmaison (15 km/9.5 mi
 W of Paris) *K2*
P. F. L. Fontaine and C. Percier

Now a museum. Lush original
interiors and furnishings.

389 ST.-DENYS- 1860–67
 DE-L'ESTRÉE
(church)
boulevard Jules Guesde,
 Saint-Denis *J4*
E. E. Viollet-le-Duc

390 USINE MÉNIER 1869–74
(factory)
Noisiel-sur-Marne (24 km/15 mi
 E of Paris) *K6*
J. Saulnier

Iron-framed building built over
the river. A facsimile of a
medieval timber-framed mill.

391 CHURCH 1877–82
rue du Maréchal Foch, Le
 Vésinet, Yvelines *K2*
L. A. Boileau

392 LYCÉE LAKANAL 1886–88
(school)
rue de Lycée-Lakanal,
 Sceaux *L3*
A. de Baudot

393 HOUSE 1922
85, boulevard de la République,
 Vaucresson *K2*
Le Corbusier and P. Jeanneret

Altered beyond recognition.

394 NOTRE-DAME 1923
(church)
avenue de la Résistance,
 Le Raincy *K5*
A. Perret

Confident and elegant use of
reinforced concrete. The stained
glass walls by M. Denis are
non-load bearing.

395 AUGER–PROUVOST 1925
 HOUSE
rue Balzac, Ville d'Avray *L2*
R. Mallet-Stevens

396 CASSANDRE HOUSE 1926
1, rue A.-Jay, Versailles *L2*
A. Perret

397 "LES TERRACES" 1926–27
(Stein house)
17, rue de Professor Victor-
 Pauchet, Garches *K2*
Le Corbusier and P. Jeanneret

Luxurious country house
designed around a complex
double-volume outdoor terrace.
Interiors altered.

398 VILLA SAVOYE 1928–31
("Les Heures claires")
82 chemin de Villiers, Poissy
 (24 km/15 mi NW of Paris)
 J1
Le Corbusier and P. Jeanneret

This classic example of 20th-c
functionalist architecture was
the culmination of Le
Corbusier's use of the elements
in his "five points of a new
architecture": pilotis, roof
garden, free plan, horizontal
window bands, and a free
facade.

399 MAISON VAN 1929
 DOESBURG
(own house)
29, rue Charles Infroit,
 Meudon-Val-Fleury *L3*
T. van Doesburg

400 GROUPE 1931–33
 SCOLAIRE KARL–MARX
(school)
avenue Karl Marx, Villejuif *L4*
A. Lurçat

401 TRAPPENARD 1932
 HOUSE
avenue Le Nôtre, Sceaux *L3*
R. Mallet-Stevens

402 CITÉ DE LA MUETTE 1934
(public housing)
avenue Jean Jaures, Drancy *J5*
M. Lods, E. Beaudoin and
V. Bodiansky

Prefabricated low- and high-rise
apartment blocks.
Revolutionary in its time,
this project became the
archetype of the bleak housing
projects of the 1940s and 1950s.

403 WEEKEND HOUSE 1934–35
85, boulevard de la République,
 La Celle St.-Cloud *K2*
Le Corbusier and P. Jeanneret

Small holiday house with a glass-covered, shallow, barrel-vaulted roof.

404 ÉCOLE DE   1935–36
    PLEIN AIR
(open-air school)
rue de la Procession, Suresnes
K3
M. Lods and E. Beaudoin

405 MAISON DU   1938–39
    PEUPLE AND MARKET
39–41 boulevard du General-Leclerc, Clichy *K4*
M. Lods, E. Beaudoin,
J. Prouvé and V. Bodiansky

A remarkable building. The auditorium may be altered with the flexible wall-and-ceiling system. Prouvé's metal-panel curtain wall has weathered badly because of poor maintenance.

406 PREFABRICATED   1953
    HOUSES
route des Gardes, Meudon *L3*
A. Sive and J. Prouvé

Beautifully detailed, modest one-family houses.

407 EMMAÜS   1954–58
    HOUSING
route des Petits-Ponts, le Blanc-Mesnil *J5*
G. Candilis, A. Josic, and S. Woods

Well-conceived low-budget housing.

408 VELOSOLEX   1956
    FACTORY
15, rue Laterale, Courbevoie *K3*
P. Devinoy

409 WOGENSCKY HOUSE 1956
70, avenue du Général-Leclerc, St.-Rémy-les-Chevreuse *M1*
A. Wogenscky

410 MAISON CARRÉ   1956–59
(private house)
Bazoches-sur-Guyonne
  (1.5 km/1 mi E of le Tremblay-sur-Mauldre)*L1*
A. Aalto

A little stiff, but still the work of the master. All fittings, lighting, furniture, etc., designed by Aalto.

411 CRÈCHE   1960–64
19, rue Hippolyte Mulin, Montrouge *L4*
J. Renaudie

412 WORKSHOP   1963
    CENTER FOR ARTISANS
5, rue Carle-Vernet, Sévres *L3*
G. Candilis, A. Josic, and S. Woods

Now A. Josic's office.

413 CHILDREN'S   1966
    LIBRARY
rue de Champagne, Clamart *L3*
J. Renaudie and others

Interesting formal solution. Wrightian plan of intersecting circles built in off shutter concrete.

414 HOUSING   1966
78, boulevard de la
  Libération, Chaville *L2*
Atelier d'Urbanisme et d'Architecture

415 MAISON DES JEUNES 1968
(youth center)
Les Courtillères, Pantin *K5*
J. Prouvé

Two barrel vaults linked by a common entry. This prototype was designed so that the users could erect and dismantle the structure by themselves.

416 QUARTIER   1975
    ROBESPIERRE
(housing)
St.-Ouen *K4*
P. Chemetov

417 HOUSING   1976
Saulx les Chartreux *M3*
P. Chemetov, H. Martin, and G. Gilbert

Low-cost housing laid out along a covered spine.

New towns
Check with the tourist office before you go.

418 MARNE LA VALLÉE *K6*
19 km (12 mi) E of Paris

Tourist Information: Paris tourist office or Lagny-sur-Marne tourist office, Cours Abbaye (tel. 430–6877).

  Ferme de Buisson area
    Housing: G. Granval, with M. Calka and B. Lassus
    Watertower: C. de Portzamparc
  Pyramides area
    Housing megastructure: M. Andrault and P. Parat
  L'Arche-Guédon area
    Housing ("Torcy terraces"): Ducharme, Larras, and others

419 CERGY–POINTOISE *H1*
30 km (18.5 mi) NW of Paris

Tourist Information: Parvis de la Préfecture (tel. (3)–032–1515)

  Administration center: Vasconi and Pencreach
  Cerclades housing: Deslandes

420 EVRY *M4*
25 km (15.5 mi) S of Paris

Tourist Information: place de l'Hôtel de Ville (tel. (6)–901–7011)

  "Pyramides" housing: Autran, Gruber, Macary, and others
  "Agora": Leconteur and Richard.

421 ST.-QUENTIN EN
YVELINES *L1*
30 km (18.5 mi) W of Paris

Tourist Information: Chapelle
Villedieu (tel. (3)-050-5170)

Les Arcades du Lac and Le
Viaduc (housing), Trappes:
Taller de Arquitectura/
Bofill (1975–77).

PÉRIGUEUX E3

422 CATHÉDRALE   12th c
ST.-FRONT
rue Taillefer

The plan is almost identical to
that of San Marco, Venezia;
Greek cross with five domes.
Romanesque bell tower. The
exterior turrets were added by
P. Abadie when he drastically
restored the church in 1858.
Romanesque cloisters. •The
church of St.- Étienne nearby
was badly damaged in 1577. The
remains house an enormous
17th-c oak reredos.

PERPIGNAN G4

423 PALAIS   1284 onward
DES ROIS DE MAJORQUE
(palace of the kings of majorca)
avenue G. Brutus

Fortified. Arcaded courtyard.
•An interesting comparison
is the Château de Salses, 15 km
(9 mi) north of Perpignan.
Originally a Spanish fortress,
later restored by S. Vauban.

424 CATHÉDRALE   1324–1509
ST.-JEAN
place Gambetta

"Devot Christ" crucifix (1307)
in the Chapelle du Christ. Altar
(1620) by B. Soler.

PESSAC E2
8 km (5 mi) SW of Bordeaux

425 CITÉ FRUGÈS   1926
(housing estate)
rue Henri Frugès/rue
Le Corbusier
Le Corbusier and P. Jeanneret

Many houses altered beyond
recognition. •Further down
the N650 near d'Archachon is
Lège. Le Corbusier designed
ten houses there (built in 1924)
that have also been radically
altered.

PIERREFONDS B4
14 km (8.5 mi) SE of Compiègne

426 CHÂTEAU   1390–1400
DE PIERREFONDS

Colossal. Destroyed under
Richelieu's orders. Totally
reconstructed by E. E. Viollet-
le-Duc from 1858–70. •Nearby,
Maison Sabatier (1860–63, now
an agricultural school) is also
by Viollet-le-Duc. 8 km (5 mi)
south is Morienval, which has
a fine Romanesque church

(1050–1122) with very early
Gothic rib vaulting.

POITIERS D3

427 BAPTISTÈRE   4th c onward
ST.-JEAN
(baptistry)
rue Jean Jaurès

The oldest Christian building
in France. 7th-c apse. Porch
added in the 11th c.
Merovingian sarcophagi,
Romanesque frescoes.

428 NOTRE-DAME-   11th c
LA-GRANDE
(church)
Grande Rue

Romanesque. Remodeled in the
15th c. Superb west facade.
Richly decorated interior.

429 CATHÉDRALE   1162 onward
ST.-PIERRE
rue de la Cathédrale

Largely Gothic. 14th-c west
front restored in the 19th c.
Towers incomplete. 12th- and
13th-c stained glass. •Behind
the cathedral is the church of
Ste-Radegonde, with a
Romanesque apse, Gothic
nave, and original 13th-c
windows.

430 ST.-HILAIRE-   1130–68
LE-GRAND
(church)
off rue de la Tranchée

Restored in the 19th c.

PONCÉ–SUR–LE–LOIRE C3
46 km (29 mi) SE of Le Mans

431 CHÂTEAU   17th c onward
Remarkable Renaissance
staircase.

PONT–DU–GARD F5
3 km (1.75 mi) NW of
Remoulins

432 ROMAN AQUEDUCT A.D. 14

In superb condition. Dry stone
construction.

PORT GRIMAUD F6
8 km (5 mi) from Ste.-Maxime
(on the sea)

433 TOURIST VILLAGE   1965–69
F. Spoerny

A very successful pastiche of a
Provençal fishing village.
Compares interestingly with
the Frugès housing at Pessac
by Le Corbusier.

LE PUY E4

434 CATHÉDRALE   12th C
NOTRE-DAME-DU-PUY
at the base of the Rocher
Corneille

Romanesque, with Arabic
influence. The cloister is
decorated with lava (local
building stone) mosaics.
• Above the cathedral is a
huge statue of the Virgin
(on the peak of the mountain).
The Chapel of St.-Michel
d'Aiguilhe (ca. 10th C), on
the adjacent peak, displays
some Mozarabic decoration.

QUIMPER C1

435 CATHÉDRALE   13th–15th C
rue Kéréon

15th-C stained glass windows.

RAMBOUILLET C4
52 km (32 mi) SW of Paris

436 CHÂTEAU   13th C onward
DE RAMBOUILLET
place de la Libération

Laiterie de la Reine (Queen's
Dairy, 1788) by J. J.
Thévenin on the grounds.

437 CHURCH   1872
rue de la République
A. de Baudot

REIMS B5
(Rheims)

438 PORTE DE MARS   2nd C A.D.
(Roman city gate)
place République

439 CATHÉDRALE   1211–94
DE NOTRE-DAME
place du Cardinal-Lucon/
rue Libergier
J. d'Orbais, then J. le Loup,
G. de Reims, B. de Soissons and
R. de Courcy

West tower completed in 1430.
Magnificent west facade and
rose window. Badly damaged
in WWI (crossing tower
destroyed). Very little stained
glass has survived.

RENNES C2

Museum: Musée des Beaux-
Arts, 20 quai Emile-Zola.
Paintings by Rubens (*Tiger
Hunt*), Jordaens (*Christ on the
Cross*), Veronese, G. de la
Tour (*Nativity*), and other
schools.

440 CATHÉDRALE   1787–1844
ST.-PIERRE
rue de la Monnaie

Rebuilt (for the third time).
15th-C Flemish altarpiece. Rich
interior.

441 PALAIS   1618–55
DE JUSTICE
(law courts)
place du Palais
S. de Brosse

Sumptuous decoration in the
Grand'Chambre (former
debating hall). Facade altered
in the 18th C.

442 HÔTEL DE VILLE   1734–43
(town hall)
place de la Mairie
J. A. Gabriel

RICHELIEU D3

443 CHÂTEAU DE   1631 onward
RICHELIEU AND TOWN
J. Lemercier

Commissioned by Richelieu.
Rectangular walled town; plan
resembles a Roman army
camp. The château was
destroyed. Only the park, some
garden pavilions, and the
orangery remain.

ROCHEFOUCAULD
(LA) E3
22 km (14 mi) NE of Angoulême

444 CHÂTEAU DE   12th C onward
LA ROCHEFOUCAULD

12th-C keep. Renaissance
wings added 1528–38. Noted
spiral staircase.

RODEZ F4

445 CATHÉDRALE   1277–1535
DE NOTRE-DAME
place d'Armes

Begun by J. Deschamps. Severe
facade. Richly decorated
tower (1510–26) north of the
apse.

RONCHAMP C6
23 km (14 mi) W of Belfort

446 NOTRE-DAME-   1950–54
DU-HAUT
(chapel)
Le Corbusier

Le Corbusier's genius appears here in its most lyrical form.

ROQUEBRUNE F6

447 EILEEN GREY HOUSE   1927–29
E. Grey with J. Badovici

This house, with its amazingly complete interiors (in good condition), was the first of two houses built by E. Grey. The house plans, published in 1929, may have provided some inspiration for P. Chareau and B. Bijvoet's Dalsace house, Paris (entry 340). Frescoes by Le Corbusier (who built his holiday cabin next door).
•A second house (1932–34, also by E. Grey) at Castellar nearby (on the D24 north of Menton) has a freer plan, but the interiors have suffered.

ROUEN B3

Museum: Musée des Beaux-Arts et de la Céramique, rue Thiers. Paintings by Rubens, Velásquez, G. David (*Virgin and Saints*), Monet, Perugino, Veronese, Géricault; good impressionist works. 16th- and 17th-c Rouen faience.

448 CATHÉDRALE DE NOTRE DAME   1201–1530
place de la Cathédrale

Earlier building destroyed in 1200. Rebuilding begun under J. d'Andelay was substantially complete in 1260. Flamboyant west front (1509–30) flanked by towers; south tower (Tour de Beurre—Butter Tower—paid for by Lent indulgences) built from 1485–1507. The cast-iron spire over the crossing replaced the earlier one of stone destroyed in 1822. Restored after 1945. Tomb of Louis de Brézé (1540), Diane de Poitiers's husband, by J. Goujon.

449 ÉGLISE ST.-OUEN   1318–1515
(church)
place Général de Gaulle

Splendid interior. West facade (poorly) rebuilt from 1845–51.

450 ST.-MACLOU   1432–1517
(church)
place Barthélemy, off rue de la République

Superbly confident flamboyant Gothic. Pentagonal porch on west portal. The spire on the crossing was built in 1868. Restored after 1945.

451 PALAIS DE JUSTICE   1493–1508
(law courts)
rue St.-Lo
R. le Roux

Richly decorated facade. Restored after 1945.

ST.-BENOÎT-SUR-LOIRE C4
35 km (22 mi) E of Orléans

452 BASILICA OF ST.-BENOÎT   11th–12th c

One of the most important Romanesque buildings in France. Belfry originally detached. Magnificent carved capitals. Chancel, crypt (restored ca. 1850), and transept built from 1065–1108. Try to see the carved north doorway (damaged during the Reformation).

ST.-BERTRAND-DE-COMMINGES F3
8 km (5 mi) S of Montréjeau

453 CATHÉDRALE DE NOTRE DAME   1304–50

Built over an earlier church, of which the Romanesque narthex (1120–40) and cloister survive.
•Many Roman remains in the village. Some statues are displayed in the Galerie du Trophée.

SAINTES E2

454 ST.-EUTROPE   1081–96
(church)
rue St.-Eutrope

Romanesque. Fine crypt. Tower added in 1496. •The contemporary church of the Abbaye aux Dames (ca. 1050), off rue G. Martel, has a fine Romanesque doorway. Also of interest is the Roman amphitheater (1st c A.D.) on rue Lacune.

SAINTES-MARIES-DE-LA-MER F5
38 km (24 mi) SW of Arles

455 FORTIFIED PILGRIMAGE CHURCH   12th c onward
on the seashore

ST.-GEORGES-SUR-LOIRE C2
25 km (16 mi) W of Angers

456 CHÂTEAU DE SERRANT   15th–18th c
2 km (1 mi) NE of St.-Georges-sur-Loire

Rich interiors. The chapel was built from the designs of J. Hardouin-Mansart. The mausoleum is by A. Coysevox.

ST.–GILLES F5
16 km (10 mi) W of Arles

457 ABBEY 12th C onward

The west front (1180–1240) is a superlative example of Romanesque carving. Fine spiral stair in the belfry.

ST.–JEAN–LES–PINASSE E3
42 km (26 mi) NW of Figeac

458 CHÂTEAU 1523 onward
      DE MONTAL

Renaissance. Built by Jeanne de Balsac for her son. Building stopped after his death, and only two of the four wings were completed. Excellent sculpture. Building was dismantled, and the pieces were sold to dealers around the world. M. Fenaille succeeded in repurchasing these pieces, and the building was restored in 1908.

ST.–NECTAIRE E4
26 km (16 mi) W of Issoire

459 CHURCH 12th C

Romanesque. •A more developed example is St.-Austremoine (1130–50, restored in 1862) in Issoire.

ST.–PAUL–DE–VENCE F6
8 km (5 mi) N of Cagnes-sur-Mer

460 FONDATION 1959–64
      MAEGHT
      J. L. Sert

Works by Miró, Calder, Braque, Giacometti, and others. •4 km (2.5 mi) further, in the walled town of Vence, is the lyrical Chapelle du Rosiare (1950, in avenue Matisse) with all decoration (stained glass, tile, and sculpture) by Matisse.

ST.–POL–DE–LÉON B1

461 ANCIENNE 13th–16th C
      CATHÉDRALE
(former cathedral)
place du Parvis

•The Chapelle du Kreisker (chapel, 14th–15th C) on the rue Verderel has a fine belfry modeled after St.-Pierre, Caen (entry 59).

ST.–QUENTIN B4

Museum: Musée Antoine Lecuyer, rue Antoine Lecuyer. Paintings, especially pastels by Q. de la Tour.

462 BASILIQUE 12th–15th C
(collegiate church)
rue St.-André

ST.–RÉMY–DE–PROVENCE F5

463 GLANUM ca. 100 B.C.–

(Roman town) ca. A.D. 200
1 km (0.6 mi) S of St.-Rémy

Interesting Roman remains include the well-preserved Mausoleum (ca. A.D. 40) and Triumphal Arch (ca. 20 B.C.). Exhibits from this site are on display in the Maison Sade in St.-Rémy.

ST.–SAVIN–SUR–GARTEMPE D3
41 km (25 mi) E of Poitiers

464 ST.–SAVIN 11th–12th C
(abbey church)

Excellent Romanesque paintings (ca. 1100). The crypt is decorated with equally fine paintings.

ST.–THÉGONNEC C1
13 km (8 mi) W of Morlaix

465 PARISH CLOSE 16th–17th C

Monumental grouping of a triumphal arch (1587) ossuary, Calvary (1610), and church pulpit (sculpted in 1683). This grouping is peculiar to Brittany and gave rise to much local rivalry between the villages. •A similar parish close is at Guimiliau (8 km/5 mi S).

ST.–TROPEZ F6

Museum: Musée de l'Annonciade, place Georges-Grammont. Collection of Georges Grammont. Paintings (1890–1940) by Bonnard, Matisse, Vuillard, and others.

466 ÉGLISE 18th C
(church)
rue de l'Église

Italian baroque.

SAN MARTIN–DU–CANIGOU G4
5 km (3 mi) W of Prades

467 MONASTERY 1009–26
      OF SAN onward
      MARTIN-DU-CANIGOU

Breathtaking site. Reconstructed hall church with barrel-vaulted nave and aisles. •The abbey of St.-Michel-de-Cuxa (955–74 onward) is 3 km (2 mi) south of Prades.

SAUMUR D3

468 NOTRE-DAME- 12th C
      DE-NANTILLY

(church)
rue de Nantilly

Romanesque. Flamboyant
south aisle (15th c) added by
Louis XI. 15th- and 16th-c
Aubusson tapestries.

469 CHÂTEAU   14th c
avenue du Docteur Peton

Museum of Decorative Arts
and Museum of the Horse
inside. •2 km (1.25 mi) SW of
Saumur is Bagneux, which has
an enormous dolmen
(prehistoric tomb) 20 m (66 ft)
long.

SÉES C3

470 CATHÉDRALE   13th–14th c
place Général de Gaulle

Fine interior. 13th-c stained
glass. West facade buttressed
in the 16th c.

SENLIS B4

471 CATHÉDRALE   1155–1556
DE NOTRE DAME
place Parvis-Notre-Dame

Transepts rebuilt in 1530–56
in the flamboyant style.

SENS C4

472 CATHÉDRALE   1140 onward
ST.-ÉTIENNE
rue de la République

Flamboyant Gothic transepts
(1490–1500) by M. Chambiges.
12th- to 17th-c stained glass
windows.

SOISSONS B4

473 CATHÉDRALE   1175–1225
ST.-GERVAIS-ET-
ST.-PROTAIS
rue de la Buerie/place Centrale

Badly damaged in WWI. Much
restored. Outstanding rose
window in the north transept.
•The west facade (15th c) of the
Abbaye de St.-Jean-des-Vignes
and a Gothic cloister, on
boulevard Jeanne d'Arc, are all
that remain of the ancient
abbey.

STRASBOURG C6

Museusms: Musée des Beaux-
Arts, Château des Rohan
(1731–42 by R. de Cotte), place
du Château. 14th- to 19th-c
paintings by de Keyser,
Memling, Corot, Rubens,
Goya, Vandyke, El Greco, etc.
  Museum of Modern Art,
Ancienne Douanne. 19th- and
20th-c painting and sculpture.

474 CATHÉDRALE   1176–1365
DE NOTRE DAME
place de la Cathédrale

Only the Romanesque apse and
crypt survived a fire in 1176.
Rebuilding began in 1230; nave
built 1250–90. The west facade
(1276–1365) was designed by

U. d'Ensinger; single tower
above was built from 1399–
1439. Damaged during the
French Revolution. Dome over
crossing built from 1878–89.
Superb sculpture on south
transept doorway and north
transept (facade of St.-
Laurent's chapel, 1495–1505).
12th- to 15th-c stained glass.

475 ST.-THOMAS   1270–1330
(church)
place St.-Thomas

Romanesque facade. Gothic
nave.

476 MAISON   1347 onward
DE L'OEUVRE
NOTRE-DAME
2, place du Château

The right-hand wing was built
in 1589. Museum of sculpture
from the cathedral. Also
K. Witz's painting of *St.
Catherine and St. Mary
Magdalene.*

SULLY-SUR-LOIRE C4

477 CHÂTEAU DE SULLY   1360

Moated fortress. Unique
unrestored chestnut timber
roof (1363) in the keep.

TANLAY C5
10 km (6 mi) E of Tonnerre

478 CHÂTEAU DE   1550
TANLAY

Renaissance. Additions (1643–
48) by P. Le Muet.

THIEPVAL B4
6 km (4 mi) N of Albert

479 MEMORIAL   1928–30
TO THE MISSING
OF THE SOMME
Sir E. Lutyens

TOULOUSE F3

Museum: Musée des Augustins,
2, rue d'Alsace-Lorraine.
Restored 14th-c Augustinian
cloister and church.
Romanesque and medieval
sculpture. Paintings by
Perugino, Rubens, Ingres,
Vandyke, Toulouse-Lautrec,
and others.

480 ST.-SERNIN   1060–1271
(church)
place St.-Sernin

Largest Romanesque church in
France. Brick. Octagonal
crossing tower. Porte des
Comptes (south transept
doorways). The Porte

Miegeville (1120) in the south
aisle has radiant carvings
depicting the Ascension.
Renaissance choir stalls (1670).

481 ÉGLISE DES   1260–92
     JACOBINS
     (church)
     off rue Pargaminières

Fortified brick church.
Octagonal bell tower modeled
after St.-Sernin.

482 CATHÉDRALE   11th–17th c
     ST.-ÉTIENNE
     place St. Étienne

Choir begun in 1272.
Flamboyant portal built in 1449.

483 TOULOUSE-LE-   1967–77
     MIRAIL
     (new suburb)
     off route de St.-Simon
     G. Candilis, A. Josic, and
     S. Woods

Hexagonal version of Le
Corbusier's *la Ville Radieuse.*

LA TOUR-
D'AIGUES F5
6 km (4 mi) NE of Pertuis

484 CHÂTEAU DE   ca. 1560
     LA TOUR-D'AIGUES

Ruined. The Triumphal Arch
(1571) and entrance pavilion
remain.

LA TOURETTE
See entry 96

TOURNUS D5

485 ST.-PHILIBERT   950–1120
     (church)   onward
     rue A. Thibaudet

Burgundian Romanesque. The
planning is advanced; most of
the problems of the medieval
cathedral have been solved in
this church, which precedes the
great Gothic cathedrals by a
century. Notable crypt.

TOURS C3

Museum: Musée des Beaux-
Arts, 18, place François-Sicard.
Former episcopal palace.
Furnishings from the Château
de Richelieu (and others).
Paintings by Rubens,
Rembrandt (*Fight into Egypt*),
Mantegna (*Christ in the Garden
of Olives* and *The
Resurrection*), Boucher, Degas,
and others. Sculpture by
Coysevox, Hoydon, etc.

486 CATHÉDRALE   1170–1507
     ST.-GATIEN
     place de la Cathédrale

Early Gothic through
Renaissance styles can be seen
in this cathedral. Choir, apse,
and east chapels completed
in 1260; west front and
towers (a most successful
vertical combination of
differing styles), in 1507.
Excellent 13th- to 15th-c stained
glass. Renaissance organ
gallery. Cloister adjacent.

TROYES C4

487 STE.-   12th c onward
     MADELEINE
     rue Général de Gaulle

Remodeled (1495–1508) by
J. Gailde, who executed the
flamboyant rood screen.
Renaissance choir.

488 CATHÉDRALE   1208–1429
     (St.-Pierre-et-St.-Paul)
     place St.-Pierre

Flamboyant west front by
M. Chambiges. Good 13th- and
14th-c stained glass. Choir
largely rebuilt.

489 ST.-URBAIN   1262 onward
     (church)
     rue G. Clemenceau

Refined, almost mannered
structure (especially the window
tracery). 13th- and 14th-c
stained glass. Never finished
beyond the choir and nave.
Facade built from 1875–1905.

490 ST.-JEAN-   14th–16th c
     AU-MARCHÉ
     (church)
     rue Molé

Exterior damaged. Altar by
F. Girardon.

491 ST.-NIZIER   16th c
     (church)
     rue de la Cité

Late Gothic. Renaissance
facade.

492 ST.-NICHOLAS   16th c
     (church)
     boulevard Victor-Hugo

LA TURBIE F6
W of Monte Carlo

493 TROPHÉE DES   6 B.C.
     ALPES
     (Roman trophy)

Reconstructed but still
impressive.

CHÂTEAU D'USSE
D3
14 km (8 mi) N of Chinon

494 CHÂTEAU   15th–17th c
     D'USSE

Medieval, with later
Renaissance additions. Grand
staircase (17th c). Renaissance
chapel (1520–38) on the grounds
in excellent condition.

VAISON-LA-
ROMAINE F5
27 km (17 mi) NE of Orange

495 ROMAN RUINS   1st C A.D.

A very interesting site with a
well-preserved theater (1st c
A.D.). The museum is in the
Puymin section; the Villasse
excavation is across avenue
Général de Gaulle. •St.-
Quentin, a curious church, is on
avenue St.-Quentin/Général
de Gaulle.

VALENCAY D3

496 CHÂTEAU DE   1540
     VALENCAY
P. de L'Orme

Replaced 12th-c fortress. West wing added in 17th c.

VALENCIENNES B4

497 MUSÉE DES   1782
     BEAUX-ARTS
place Verte

Paintings by Rubens (*The Story of St. Etienne*), Vandyke (*The Martyrdom of St. Jacques*), Watteau; sculptures and drawings by Carpeaux.

VAUX-LE-VICOMTE C4
4 km (2.5 mi) NE of Melun

498 CHÂTEAU DE   1656–61
     VAUX-LE-VICOMTE
L. Le Vau

A magnificent château in superb condition. Decorations by C. Le Brun. Outstanding garden design by A. Le Nôtre. Built for Fouquet, Louis XIV's finance minister. Shortly after the king had seen the château, he imprisoned Fouquet and invited Le Vau, Le Brun, and Le Nôtre to create a similar masterpiece for him at Versailles. Gardens restored in 1875.

VENDÔME C3

499 LA TRINITÉ   1150–ca. 1500
(abbey church)
rue de l'Abbaye

Romanesque belfry (1150). 13th-c polychrome statues at the transept crossing. Flamboyant west facade (ca. 1500) by J. de Beauce, architect of the later tower of the west front of Chartres cathedral. 12th-c Virgin-and-Child stained glass window in the chancel. Most of the abbey buildings have been demolished.

VERTEUIL-SUR-CHARENTE D3
5 km (3 mi) SE of Ruffec

500 CHÂTEAU   11th c onward
     DE VERTEUIL

Mostly 16th c. 11th-c chapel.

VÉZELAY C4
17 km (10 mi) W of Avallon

501 STE.-MADELAINE 1096–1137
(abbey church)

Built under the Cluny order. Remarkable sculpture in the narthex. Groined vaulted nave supported on transverse arches. Choir rebuilt in the Gothic style.

VIENNE E5

502 TEMPLE OF   25 B.C.
     AUGUSTUS AND LIVIA
place du Palais

Similar to the Maison Carrée, Nîmes, but less well preserved (used as a church and then as a Temple of Reason). •Close to the place de l'Hôtel-de-Ville are the remains of a Roman theater.

503 ST.-PIERRE   6th–10th c
(former church)
place St.-Pierre

Now the Musée Lapidaire Romain. Roman remains.

504 ST.-MAURICE   12th–16th c
(church)
place St.-Maurice

Flamboyant Gothic west front. Mausoleum of Cardinal de Montmorin (1713).

VILLANDRY D3
15 km (10 mi) W of Tours

505 CHÂTEAU DE   1532
     VILLANDRY

Medieval keep, incorporated in the present buildings, built by J. le Breton. Formal French Renaissance gardens reconstructed by Dr. Carvallo in the 19th c.

VILLARS E3

506 CHÂTEAU DE   16th c
     PUYGUILHEM
Champagnac-de-Belaire
(30 km/19 mi N of
Périgueux)

Richly decorated. Early Renaissance buildings. One wing added in the 18th c. Bleak surroundings.

VILLEGONGIS D3

507 CHÂTEAU   1530
     VILLEGONGIS
Levroux (20 km/12 mi N of
Châteauroux)

Renaissance. Much decoration derived from the château at Chambord.

VILLERS-COTTERÊTS B4

508 CHÂTEAU DE   1520
     VILLERS-COTTERÊTS
place A. Briand
J. and G. le Breton

Improved by Henry II. Renaissance facade. Park and gardens by A. Le Nôtre.

VITRÉ C2

509 CHÂTEAU   14th–15th c

Triangular plan. Well restored in the 19th c. •The old section of the town was surrounded by 15th-c ramparts (the north and east sides survive).

510 NOTRE-DAME   15th–16th c
(church)
rue Notre-Dame

•An interesting street, the rue Deaudrairie, is nearby.

West Germany

Schloss Linderhof; *see entry 331*

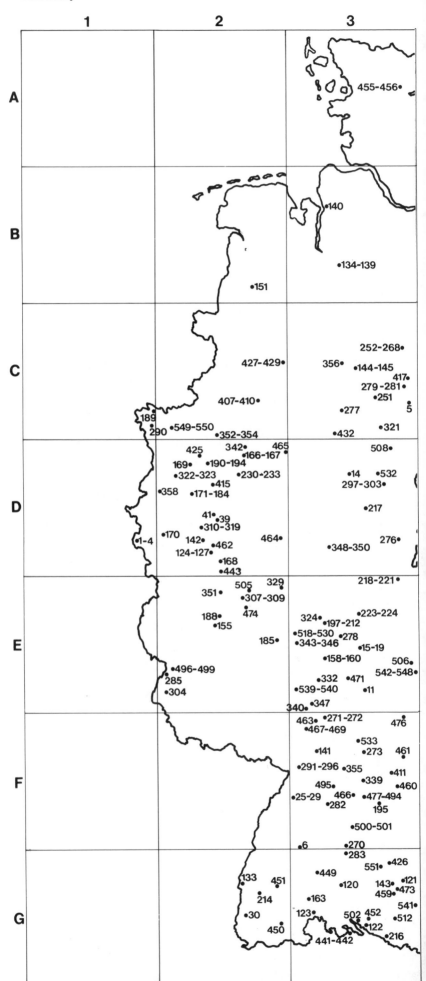

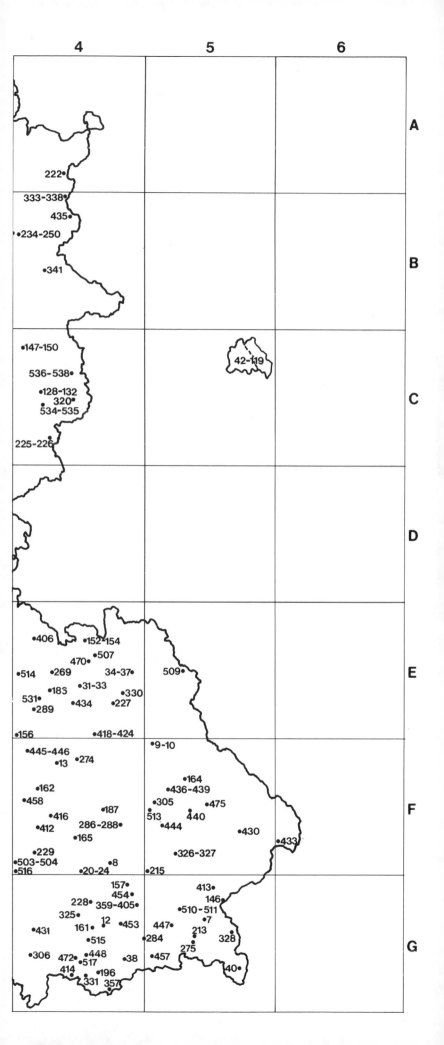

AACHEN D1

Museums: Suermondt-Ludwig Museum (1886, by E. Linse), Wilhelmstrasse 18. German 13th- to 18th-c sculpture. German and Flemish paintings from the 14th c onward.
Neue Galerie, Sammlung Ludwig, Kurhausstrasse 2. Good modern-art collection.

1 DOM   800 onward
(cathedral)
Domhof

The remarkable octagonal domed Palatine Chapel was built under Charlemagne's supervision (800–805). Gothic chancel added 1355–1414. The chapel was externally reroofed in the 17th c. Additional chapels were built in the 14th and 15th c. Pulpit (ambo) of Henry II and Karlsschrein (ca. 1215, Charlemagne's shrine). The treasury in the Domschatzkammer is extraordinarily rich.

2 ELISENBRUNNEN   1822
(fountain)
Friedrich-Wilhelm-Platz
J. P. Cremer and K. F. Schinkel

3 ST. JAKOBSKIRCHE 1877–86
(church)
Jakobstrasse
H. Wiethase

4 ST. FRONLEICHNAM   1931
(church)
Düppel-Strasse
R. Schwarz and H. Schwippert

ALFELD AN DER LEINE C3

5 FAGUSWERKE   1911–13
(Fagus factory)
Hannoversche-Strasse 58
W. Gropius and A. Meyer

ALPIRSBACH F3
18 km (11 mi) S of Freudenstadt

6 KLOSTERKIRCHE 11th–12th c
(abbey church)

Romanesque. Gothic apse and cloisters.

ALTENMARKT G5

7 KLOSTERKIRCHE   17th c
(abbey church)
Interior by C. and E. Asam

ALTOMÜNSTER F4

8 KLOSTERKIRCHE   1763–66
(Brigittine abbey church)
J. M. Fischer

AMBERG F5

9 ST. MARTIN   1421 onward
(church)
Marktplatz

10 DEUTSCHE   18th c
    SCHULKIRCHE
(church)
Deutsche Schulgasse

Elegant rococo interior.

AMORBACH E3
8 km (5 mi) S of Miltenberg

11 ABTEIKIRCHE   1742–47
(abbey church)
Schlossplatz
J. B. Neumann

Reworked Romanesque church. Frescoes by M. Günther.

ANDECHS G4
6 km (4 mi) S of Herrsching am Ammersee

12 KLOSTERKIRCHE   1751–55
(abbey church)

Gothic church totally remodeled (internally) in the rococo style by J. B. Zimmermann.

ANSBACH F4

13 RESIDENZ   14th c onward
(castle)

Baroque remodeling by G. de Gabrieli (1713–32) after a fire. Paintings by Titian, Rubens, and others.

AROLSEN D3

14 SCHLOSS   1714–28
(castle)

Modeled after Versailles.

ASCHAFFENBURG E3

15 STIFTSKIRCHE 12th c onward
(abbey church)
off Dalbergstrasse

Gothic. Romanesque west door and cloisters. Paintings by Grünewald (*Christ's Lamentation*, 1525) and Cranach (*Resurrection*).

16 SCHLOSS   1605–14 onward
    JOHANNISBURG
(rebuilt castle)
Riedingerstrasse
G. Riedinger

17 SCHÖNBUSCH   1775–80
(castle)
3 km (2 mi) W of Aschaffenburg
E. d'Herigoyen and F. L. von Sckell

Splendid gardens.

18 POMPEIANUM   1844–49
on the Main River, in the Schloss gardens
F. von Gärtner

A replica of the House of Castor and Pollux at Pompeii.

19 SCHULZENTRUM   1964–67
(school)
Leiderer-Stadtweg
G. Schlegel

AUGSBURG F4

Museums: Stadtische Kunstsammlungen, Maximilianstrasse 46. Housed in the Schätzlerpalais (rococo banquet hall; baroque paintings in the Deutsche Barock-Galerie) and connected Staatsgalerie

Augsburg (important 15th- and 16th-c Augsburg and Swabian works—Holbein, Burgkmair, Dürer, and others).

20 DOM 995 onward
(cathedral)
Fronhof

Romanesque basilica flanked by Gothic (1335–1431) side aisles.

21 ST. ANNA 1321 onward
(church)
St. Annastrasse

Flamboyant Gothic exterior, elaborate rococo interior. The Fuggerkapelle (Fugger funeral chapel, 1518) by H. Burgkmair is one of the earliest Renaissance works in Germany.

22 ST. ULRIC 1465–1500
UND ST. AFRA
(church)
Maximilianstrasse/Milchberg
V. Kindlin and B. Engelberg

Altered in the 17th c.

23 ZEUGHAUS 1602–7
(arsenal)
Zeughausgasse
E. Holl

Protobaroque. •Holl also remodeled the Rotes Tor (red gate), a fortification on Eserwallstrasse, in 1622.

24 RATHAUS 1615–20
(town hall)
Rathausplatz
E. Holl

BAD

See under proper (second) name

BADEN–BADEN F3

25 KURHAUS 1821–24
(casino)
Goetheplatz
F. Weinbrenner

Extended in 1855 and 1910. •The theater (1860–62) adjacent is by M. Derchy.

26 TRINKHALLE 1839–42
(pump room)
Kaiserallee, near the Kurhaus
H. Hübsch

27 EVANGELISCHE 1854–64
STADTKIRCHE
(church)
Augustaplatz
F. Eisenlohr

28 STOURDZA 1863–66
KAPELLE
(chapel)
Stourdzastrasse
L. von Klenze

29 WOHNHAUS 1961–62
EIERMANN
(own house)
Krippenhof 16–18
E. Eiermann

BADENWEILER G2

30 KURHAUS 1967–70
(spa)
K. Humpert

Built into the hillside below the castle ruins. A remarkable synthesis of site and structure.

BAMBERG E4

31 DOM 12th–13th c
(cathedral)
Domplatz

Romanesque with Gothic extensions. Double apse. The interior (restored ca. 1830) holds three masterpieces: the Bamberger Reiter (Bamberg Rider, ca. 1230); tomb of Heinrich II (1499–1513, by T. Riemenschneider); and St. Mary's Altar (1523, by V. Stoss). Chapter house (1730–32) by J. B. Neumann. •Statues from the Adam Portal are in the Diocesan Museum next door.

32 ST. MARTIN 17th c
(church)
Grüner Markt

Facade (1681–91) by G. Dientzenhofer. The former abbey buildings next door are by L. Dientzenhofer.

33 NEUE RESIDENZ 17th c
(new palace)
Obere Karolinenstrasse/
Domplatz

The baroque buildings (1697–1706) on the Domplatz are by L. Dientzenhofer. Splendid interiors. Now a museum. •The Alte Hofhaltung (old residence—a separate building with an outstanding Gothic courtyard) is on the south side of the Domplatz.

BAYREUTH E4

34 MARKGRÄFLICHES 1745–48
OPERNHAUS
(opera house)
Opernstrasse
A. Galli da Bibiena

Rococo. Wood construction throughout.

35 NEUES SCHLOSS 1753–54
(new castle)
Ludwigstrasse

Remodeling of existing buildings. Rococo interiors. Stuccowork by Pedrozzi.

36 FESTSPIELHAUS 1872–76
(festival theater)
Nibelungenstrasse
O. Brückwald

37 HAUS WAHNFRIED 1874
Richard-Wagner-Strasse 283
Wölfle

Richard Wagner's house. Wagner's grave is in the garden.

BENEDIKTBEUERN G4

38 KLOSTER 733 onward
(Benedictine monastery)

The Klosterkirche (abbey church, 1680–86) is decorated

with frescoes by H. G. Asam.
The Chapel of St. Anastasia
(1751–58) by J. M. Fischer, a
separate building, is an
admirable rococo work.

BENSBERG D2

39 RATHAUS   1962–68
(town hall)
Schlossberg
G. Böhm

Powerful forms that
complement the medieval
surroundings. •The Kinderdorf
(children's village, 1965–69)
close by is also by Böhm.

BERCHTESGADEN G5

40 SCHLOSS   13th c onward
(castle)
Schlossplatz

Former priory. Good
Romanesque cloisters, Gothic
dormitory (works by V. Stoss,
T. Riemenschneider, and
others). •The church on the
Schlossplatz was built from the
14th- to 16th c.

BERGISCH GLADBACH D2

41 COMMUNITY CENTER   1980
Marienplatz
G. Böhm

BERLIN C5

West Berlin

Tourist Information:
Verkehrsamt, Europa-Center,
Budapester Strasse (tel.
782–3031).

Architect's Institute: Bund
Deutsche Architekten, Mom-
msenstrasse (tel. 882–
2428).

Museums: Bauhaus-Archiv-
Museum für Gestaltung,
Schloss-strasse 1. Bauhaus arts
and crafts.
    Brücke-Museum (1965–67, by
W. Düttman), Bussardsteig 9.
Works by the Die Brücke group.
    Schloss Charlottenburg.
Guelph treasure in the
Decorative Arts Museum. 18th-
c French paintings (Frederick
the Great's collection):
Chardin, Watteau, and others.
See entry 42.
    Jagdschloss Grunewald
(1542, by C. Theyss),
Pücklerstrasse (continue
walking straight into the park).
17th-c Flemish and Dutch
paintings.
    Neue Nationalgalerie,
Potsdamer Strasse, 50. 19th-
and 20th-c paintings and
sculpture. See entry 96.
    Museum Dahlem, Arnimal-
lee. Enormous. Outstanding
13th- to 18th-c European
painting collection. See entry
67.

42 SCHLOSS   1695–1790
    CHARLOTTENBURG

(castle)
Spandauer Damm/Schloss-
    strasse *C4*
J. A. Nering, then E. von Göthe
(1702–13), then G. W. von
Knobelsdorff (1740–46), then
C. G. Langhans (1788–90)

In the Court of Honor is
A. Schlüter's statue of the
Great Elector (1703), a baroque
masterpiece. Fine rococo
interiors in the Knobelsdorff
wing (Golden Gallery). 18th-c
French paintings (second floor).
The Belvedere (1790, by
Langhans), Mausoleum and
Summer House (1810 and 1824,
both by K. F. Schinkel) are on
the grounds. The symmetrical
Antique and Egyptian Museums
(1855) opposite the Court of
Honor are by A. Stüler.

43 KÖNIGS-   1777–80
    KOLANNADEN
(street colonnades)
Kleistpark *D6*
K. von Gontard

44 SCHLOSS   1785
    BELLEVUE
(castle)
Spreeweg/Bellevueallee *D5*
P. Boumann

45 SCHLOSS   1794–97
(castle)
Pfaueninsel (island in the
    Wannsee) *F1*
J. Brendel

"Gothic ruin." •The Kavalier-
Haus (1824, by K. F. Schinkel)
is nearby. On the riverbank
opposite is Peter and Paul's
Church (1834–36) by A.
Schadow.

46 KREUZBERG   1821
    DENKMAL
(monument)
Kreuzbergstrasse *E6*
K. F. Schinkel

Enlarged in 1878.

47 HUMBOLDT   1822–24
    SCHLOSS
(castle)
Karolinenstrasse *A4*
K. F. Schinkel

48 SCHLOSS KLEIN   1826
    GLIENICKE
(castle)
Volkspark Klein Glienicke *G1*
K. F. Schinkel

49 ALTE NAZARETH-   1832
    KIRCHE
(church)
Leopoldplatz/Müller
    Chaussee *B6*
K. F. Schinkel

50 JOHANNESKIRCHE   1835
(church)
Alt-Moabit/Stromstrasse *C5*
K. F. Schinkel

Narthex added by A. Stüler in
1854.

51 MATTHÄI-KIRCHE   1845
(church)
Matthäikirchstrasse *D6*
A. Stüler

Berlin

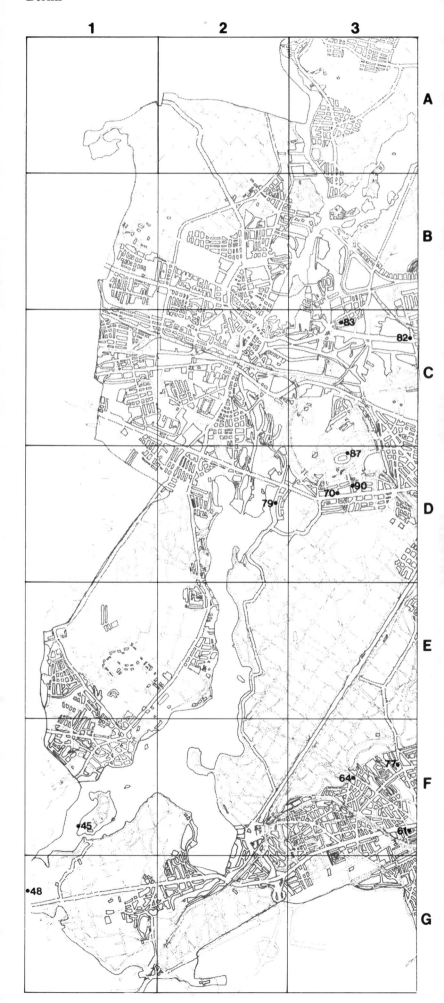

Berlin

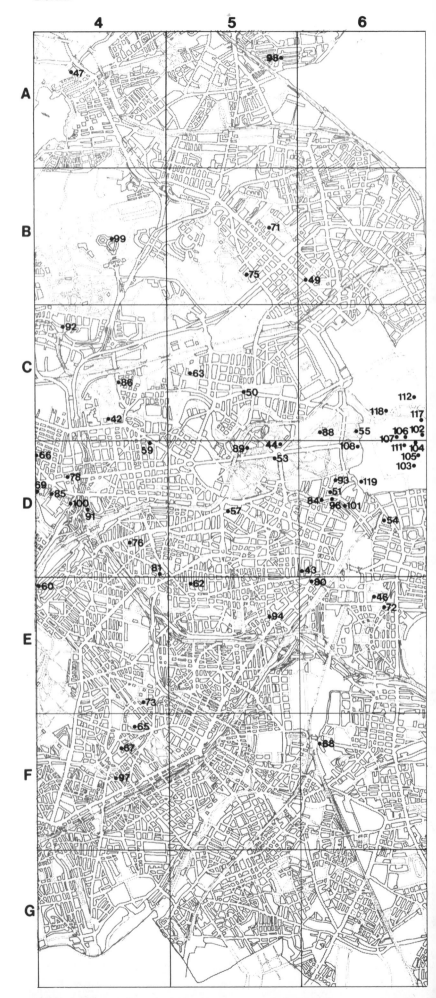

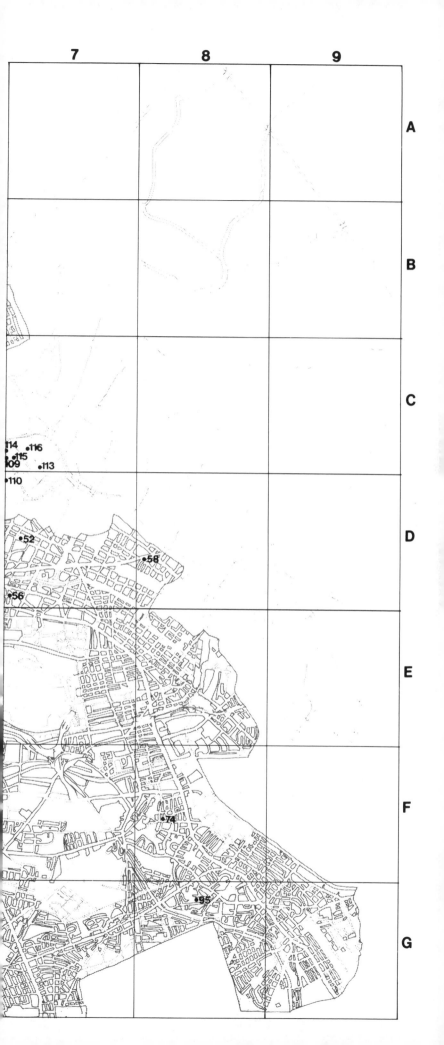

52 JAKOBI-KIRCHE 1845
(church)
Oranienstrasse/Lobeckstrasse
D7
A. Stüler

53 SIEGESSÄULE 1869–73
(victory column)
Grosser Stern *D5*
H. Strack

54 KUNSTGEWERBE- 1877–81
MUSEUM
(former museum)
Stresemannstrasse *D6*
M. Gropius

55 REICHSTAG 1884–94
(former parliament)
Platz der Republik *C6*
P. Wallot

Rebuilt with new interiors
(1962) by P. Baumgarten.

56 HEILIGKREUZKIRCHE
(church) 1885–88
Blücherstrasse, Kreuzberg *D7*
J. Otzen

57 KAISER WILHELM 1891–95
GEDÄCHTNISKIRCHE
(church)
Breidscheidplatz *D5*
F. H. Schwechten

Destroyed in 1944. The ruins
were incorporated in the new
church (1957–63) by
E. Eiermann.

58 U-BAHNHOF 1899
SCHLESISCHES TOR
(underground station)
Schlesische Strasse *D8*
H. Grisebach

59 RATHAUS 1899–1905
CHARLOTTENBURG
(town hall)
Otto-Suhr-Allee 100 *D4*
H. Reinhardt and G.
Süssenguth

60 VILLA 1905
Winklerstrasse 11 *E4*
H. Muthesius

•A. Messel built a villa nearby
(Wernerstrasse 10) in 1900.

61 VILLA MUTHESIUS 1906
(own house)
Potsdamer Chaussee 50 *F3*
H. Muthesius

•No. 48, Villa Freudenberg
(1907), is also by Muthesius.

62 HAUS STEINPLATZ 1906–7
(house)
Uhlandstrasse 197,
Charlottenburg *E5*
A. Endell

63 TURBINEHALLE AEG 1909
Huttenstrasse/
Berlichingenstrasse *C5*
P. Behrens

A key industrial building of
great visual power. •Behrens
also designed the motor factory
and high-tension plant
(1910–12) on Hussitenstrasse,
Voltastrasse, and Brunnen-
strasse.

64 VILLA PERLS 1911
(later Fuchs)
Hermannstrasse 14–18,
Zehlendorf *F3*
L. Mies van der Rohe

Extended in 1928.

65 VILLA WIEGAND 1911–12
Peter-Lenné-Strasse 28–30 *F4*
P. Behrens

Now the German Archeological
Institute.

66 PENSION WESTEND 1912
Kastanienallee 32 *D4*
A. Endell

67 STAATLICHE 1912–16
MUSEEN
(State Museum)
Arnimallee 23 *F4*
B. Paul

Since extended.

68 LINDENHOF 1918–19
(housing)
Arnulf Strasse/Röbling
Strasse *F6*
M. Wagner

69 TWO-FAMILY VILLA 1922
5a Karolingerplatz *D4*
E. Mendelsohn

70 VILLA STERNFELD 1923
Heerstrasse *D3*
E. Mendelsohn

71 SIEDLUNG 1925, 1928
SCHILLERPARK
(housing)
Bristolstrasse, Dublinerstrasse,
Windsorerstrasse, and
Oxforderstrasse *B5*
B. Taut

72 DEUTSCHEN 1925
BUCHDRUCKER
(office building)
Dudenstrasse 10 *E6*
M. Taut and F. Hoffmann

73 HOUSING 1925–27
Schorlemer Allee 7–23 *E4*
W. and H. Luckhardt

74 GROSS-SIEDLUNG 1925–31
BRITZ
(housing)
Fritz-Reuter-Allee, Parchimer
Allee, Onkel-Bräsig-Strasse,
and Stavenhagener Strasse *F8*
B. Taut and M. Wagner

75 APARTMENT 1926–27
BUILDING
Afrikanischestrasse 14–41 *B5*
L. Mies van der Rohe

76 WOGA 1926–28
BUILDING COMPLEX
Cicerostrasse/Lehniner Platz/
A.-Achilles-Strasse *D4*
E. Mendelsohn

77 GROSS-SIEDLUNG 1926–31
ONKEL-TOMS-HÜTTE *F3*
(housing)
Argentinische Allee,
Riemeisterstrasse,
Hochsitzweg
B. Taut

Eisvogelweg 1–84,
Riemeisterstrasse 57–112,
Am Fischtal 27–53
H. Häring

Am Fischtal 58–60
H. Tessenow

Am Fischtal 4
P. Schmitthenner

78 APARTMENT   1928–29
BUILDING
Kaiserdamm/Königin-
Elisabeth-Strasse *D4*
H. Scharoun

79 HOUSES   1928–35
Am Rupenhorn *D2*
No. 5 (Haus Lindeman, 1929)
B. Paul

No. 6 (own house, 1929)
E. Mendelsohn

No. 9 (1935)
L. Hilberseimer

No. 24 (1928)
H. and W. Luckhardt, with
A. Anker.
•Heerstrasse 55 (roof terrace
pergola removed) and 161,
nearby, are also by Anker
and the Luckhardts.

80 KATHREINER-   1929–30
HOCHHAUS
(office building)
Potsdamer Strasse/Kleistpark
E6
B. Paul

81 APARTMENT   1929–30
BUILDING
Hohenzollerndamm/
Fehrbelliner Platz *D4*
H. Scharoun

82 GROSS-SIEDLUNG 1929–31
SIEMENSSTADT *C3*
(housing)
Jungfernheideweg 1–47,
Mäckeritzstrasse
H. Scharoun

Jungfernheideweg,
Goebelstrasse
W. Gropius

Goebelstrasse 1–113
O. Bartning

Goebelstrasse 2–114
H. Häring

83 HASELHORST   1930–32
APARTMENTS
Haselhorsterdamm/
Nonnendammallee *C3*
W. Gropius

84 SHELLHAUS   1931
(office building)
Hitzigallee/Reichpietschufer
D6
E. Fahrenkamp

Extended (1965) by P.
Baumgarten.

85 HAUS DER   1931
RUNDFUNKS
(broadcasting studios)
Dag-Hammerskjöld-Platz *D4*
H. Poelzig

86 GUSTAV-ADOLPH   1934
KIRCHE
(church)
Brahestrasse/Herschelstrasse
C4
O. Bartning

87 OLYMPIA-STADION 1934–36
(Olympic stadium)
Olympischer Platz *D3*
W. March

88 KONGRESSHALLE   1955–57
(congress hall)
John-Foster-Dulles-Allee *C6*
H. Stubbins

89 HANSAVIERTEL   1957
INTERBAU
(housing exhibition)
Klopstock Strasse,
Bartningallee, and
Händelallee *D5*

Model units by W. Luckhardt,
W. Gropius, A. Aalto,
A. Jacobsen, O. Niemeyer,
E. Eiermann, and others.

90 UNITÉ   1957–58
D'HABITATION
(apartment building)
Heilsberger Allee *D3*
Le Corbusier

91 KIRCHE AM   1957–59
LIETZENSEE
(church)
Herbartstrasse 5 *D4*
P. Baumgarten

92 CHARLOTTENBURG 1957–60
NORD
(housing)
Heilmannring/Goebelplatz *C4*
H. Scharoun

93 PHILHARMONIE   1960–63
(symphony hall)
Kemperplatz *D6*
H. Scharoun

A splendidly convincing
example of Scharoun's
expressionist work. •The
Staatsbibliothek (library,
1964–78) across the road is
Scharoun's last work.

94 ST. NORBERT-   1961–62
   KIRCHE AND PAUL-
   GERHARDT-KIRCHE
   (two churches)
   Dominicusstrasse and
   Hauptstrasse 48 *E5*
   H. Fehling and D. Gogel

95 GROSS-SIEDLUNG   1962–69
   BRITZ-BUCKOW-
   RUDOW
   Löwensteinring *G8*
   TAC (W. Gropius)

   A large housing estate
   with community facilities.

96 NEUE   1963–68
   NATIONALGALERIE
   Potsdamer Strasse 50 *D6*
   L. Mies van der Rohe

19th- and 20th-c paintings and
sculpture.

97 FREIE   1963–74
   UNIVERSITÄT
   (Free University)
   Habelschwerdter-Allee *F4*
   G. Candilis, A. Josic, S.
   Woods, and M. Schiedhelm

98 MÄRKISCHES   1964–71
   VIERTEL
   (housing estate)
   Wilhelmsruher Damm/
   Tornowerweg *A5*
   H. Stranz, R. Plarre, K. Fleig,
   and others

   Housing in the tradition of the
   Hansaviertel (entry 89) and
   earlier estates.

99 CONTROL TOWER   1970–74
   Tegel Airport *B4*
   M. von Gerkan and V. Marg

100 INTERNATIONAL   1979
    CONGRESS CENTER
    Messedamm *D4*
    R. Schuler and U. Witte

101 WISSENSCHAFTS-   1979–85
    ZENTRUM
    (science center)
    Reichpietschufer *D6*
    J. Stirling and M. Wilford

    Under construction.

East Berlin

102 ZEUGHAUS   1694–1706
    (arsenal)
    Unter den Linden, opposite
    Oberwallstrasse *C6*
    J. A. Nering

    Completed by M. Grünberg,
    A. Schlüter, and J. de Bodt. The
    sculptured keystones were
    carved by Schlüter. Now the
    Museum of German History.
    •The Neue Wache (new

guardhouse, 1816–18) by
K. F. Schinkel is adjacent; the
interior (1930) is by
H. Tessenow.

103 FRANZÖSISCHER   1701–5
    DOM
    (French church)
    DEUTSCHER   1701–8
    DOM
    (German church)
    Platz der Akademie (former
    Gendarmenmarkt) *D6*

    Detached towers added by K.
    von Gontard from 1780–85.
    •Between the churches is the
    Schauspielhaus (theater, 1821)
    by K. F. Schinkel. The theater's
    interior has not yet been
    repaired.

104 DEUTSCHE   1741–43
    STAATSOPER
    (opera house)
    Unter den Linden /Bebelplatz
    D6
    G. W. von Knobelsdorff

105 HEDWIGS-KIRCHE   1747–73
    (church)
    Französische Strasse/
    Hedwigkirchgasse *D6*
    J. Legay

    Directly derived from the
    Pantheon. Remodeled by
    C. Holzmeister (1928), then by
    H. Schwippert (1952).

106 HUMBOLDT   1748–53
    UNIVERSITY
    Unter den Linden/
    Universitätsstrasse *C6*
    J. Boumann

    Built to the designs of G. W.
    von Knobelsdorff. Originally
    the palace of Prince Heinrich.

107 DEUTSCHE   1774–80
    STAATSBIBLIOTHEK
    (old library)
    Unter den Linden/
    Charlottenstrasse *C6*
    G. Unger and J. Boumann

108 BRANDENBURGER   1788–91
    TOR
    (Brandenburg Gate)
    Unter den Linden *D6*
    C. G. Langhans

    Extended by colonnades
    (1868, by H. Strack). Important
    neoclassic structure derived
    from the Propylum, Athens.
    Victory Quadriga (1781–94) by
    G. Schadow.

109 ALTES MUSEUM   1823–30
    (old museum)
    Museumstrasse *C7*
    K. F. Schinkel

    Schinkel's masterpiece
    (confirmed by Mies). 20th-c
    painting and sculpture.
    Restored (1958–65) by T.
    Voissem (architect) and F.
    Seiler (engineer).

110 FRIEDRICH   1824–30
    WERDERSCHE KIRCHE
    (church)
    Werderschermarkt *D7*
    K. F. Schinkel

111 KAISER   1834–36
    WILHELM I PALACE
Unter den Linden/
    Bebelplatz *D6*
C. G. Langhans

112 SYNAGOGUE   1859–66
(ruined)
Oranienburger Strasse *C6*
E. Knoblauch and A. Stüler

113 RATHAUS   1861–69
(town hall)
Rathausstrasse/Spandauer
    Strasse *C7*
H. F. Waesemann

114 NATIONAL-   1867–76
    GALERIE
Marx-Engels-Platz *C7*
A. Stüler

19th- and 20th-c paintings.

115 DOM   1892–1905
(cathedral)
Marx-Engels-Platz *C7*
J. Raschdorff

116 STADTGERICHT   1897–1900
(law courts)
Littenstrasse *C7*
O. Schmalz

117 PERGAMON   1906–10
    MUSEUM
Museumstrasse *C6*
A. Messel

An unrivaled collection
of oriental, Greek, and Roman
antiquities.

118 GROSSE   1919
    SCHAUSPIELHAUS
Am Zirkus *C6*
H. Poelzig

Spectacular interior.

119 REICHSCHANCELLERY
(ruins)   1938–39
Vossstrasse 4–6 *D6*
A. Speer

Rubble used by the Soviets to
construct the Soviet Memorial
in Treptow Park.

BEURON G3

120 ST. MAURUS-   1868–70
    KAPELLE
(chapel)
Sigmaringer Landstrasse
Beuroner Kunstschule

Neo-Byzantine, by the
Beuroner Art School.

BIBERACH G3
40 km (25 mi) S of Ulm

121 SCHMITZ HOUSES   1949–50
Mettenbergerweg 15–17
H. Häring

BIRNAU G3
5 km (3 mi) SE of Überlingen

122 WALLFAHRTSKIRCHE
(church)   1746–50
P. Thumb

Vorarlberg school rococo.
Sculpture and stuccowork
(1750–58) by J. A.
Feuchtmayr.

BLUMBERG-RANDEN G3

123 TASCHENTUCHWEBEREI
(handkerchief   1949–51
factory)
E. Eiermann

BONN D2

124 MÜNSTER   11th–13th c
(church)
Münsterplatz

11th-c crypt. Romanesque
towers, Gothic nave. 12th-c
cloisters.

125 POPPELSDORFER   1715–46
    SCHLOSS
(castle)
Poppelsdorfer Allee
R. de Cotte

•De Cotte also worked on the
university buildings (part of the
Kurfürstliche Residenz) at the
far end of the Poppelsdorfer
Allee.

126 AKADEMISCHES   1822
    MUSEUM
in the Hofgarten
K. F. Schinkel

Former Institute of Anatomy

127 GODESBERG HOTEL   1961
off Burgstrasse, Bad-
    Godesberg
G. Böhm

Built on the remains of a
medieval fortress.

BRAUNSCHWEIG C4
(Brunswick)

Museum: Herzog-Anton-
Ulrich Museum (1883–87, by
O. Sommer), Museumstrasse 1.
Paintings by Rubens, Vermeer,
Rembrandt (*Family Group*),
Veronese, and others.

128 DOM   1173 onward
(cathedral)
Burgplatz

Romanesque with Gothic
double aisles added (on the
south, 1322–46; north, 1469–
74). Imerwald Crucifix (ca.
1150) in north aisle. •The
castle on the Burgplatz was
almost totally rebuilt in 1884.

129 ST. MARTIN   12th–14th c
(church)
Altstadtmarkt/Sonnenstrasse

Romanesque west facade.
14th-c sculpture on gables.

130 ALTSTADTRATHAUS   1253
(old town hall)   onward
Altstadtmarkt

Rebuilt from 1393–96 and
1447–68. Restored from
1841–52 and later. Two open,
galleried wings with 15th-c
sculpture. Handsome gables.

131 VIEWEGSCHES 1801–5
HAUS
Burgplatz
D. Gilly

Early German Doric. •The
"Gothic" Rathaus (town
hall, 1896–99) opposite is by
Winter.

132 HAUS SALVE HOSPES 1805
(Villa Holland)
Lessingplatz/Augusttorwall
P. J. Krahe

BREISACH AM RHEIN G2

133 MÜNSTER 11th–14th c
(church)

Romanesque basilica. Gothic
chancel added from 1300–1330.
The high altar (1526) is an
emotional Gothic sculpture.
Last Judgment frescoes by
M. Schongauer.

BREMEN B3

Museums: Kunsthalle Bremen,
Am Wall 207. A varied
collection of paintings from
Cranach onward. Strongest in
the 19th and 20th c,
(P. Modersohn-Becker).
Paula Modersohn-Becker
Haus, Böttcherstrasse 8.
Paintings by P. Modersohn-
Becker and other Worpswede
artists (Worpswede is 25 km/
15 mi N of Bremen). •The
authentic 16th-c Roselius
Haus is next door at no. 6.

134 DOM ST. PETRI 1044–1101
(cathedral) onward
Marktplatz

Substantially altered in the
13th c. Flamboyant north aisle
added in the 16th c. Restored
in 1888.

135 RATHAUS 1405–10
(town hall)
Marktplatz

Gothic. Renaissance facade
added 1609–12.

136 HAUPTBAHNHOF 1886–88
(railway station)
Bahnhofsplatz
H. Stier

137 FOCKE-MUSEUM 1958–64
Schwachhauser Heerstrasse 240
H. Bartmann

138 WOHNHOCHHAUS 1959–62
NEUE VAHR
(high-rise apartments)
Berliner Freiheit
A. Aalto

139 STADTHALLE 1961–64
(town hall)
Auf der Bürger Weide
R. Rainer

Powerful, exposed roof
structure.

BREMERHAVEN B3

140 DEUTSCHES 1969–75
SCHIFFAHRTSMUSEUM
(National Maritime Museum)
Deichpromenade (on the
waterfront)
H. Scharoun

A brilliant and apt piece of
"marine" architecture.

BRUCHSAL F3

141 SCHLOSS 1720 onward
(castle)

The staircase (1731–32) is by
J. B. Neumann. The castle has
been restored after being
devastated in 1945. •Neumann
also extended the church of
St. Peter (1738) in the town.

BRÜHL D2
13 km (8 mi) S of Köln

142 SCHLOSS 1725 onward
(castle)

Begun by J. C. Schlaun, altered
by F. Cuvilliés. The staircase
(1743–48) is by J. B. Neumann.
On the grounds is Falkenlust
(1728), a delightful small house
by F. Cuvilliés. •The altar
(1745) in the Franziskanerkirche
is by Neumann.

BUCHAU AM FEDERSEE G3
12 km (7 mi) SE of Riedlingen

143 KATHOLISCHE 1774–76
KIRCHE
(church)
M. d'Ixnard

BÜCKEBURG C3

144 SCHLOSS 1601–8
BÜCKEBURG
(castle)
Golden Hall by Ebert and
Wolff.

145 STADTKIRCHE 1611–15

Gothic hall church. Baroque
facade.

BURGHAUSEN G5

146 SCHLOSS 12th c onward
(castle)

Gothic fortifications and
chapel. Defenses strengthened
in the 16th c. Picturesque lower
town.

CELLE C4

147 SCHLOSS 1300 onward
(castle)
Schlossplatz

Enlarged in 1521, again in
1670. Square plan, corner
towers, dominated by helmed
roofs. Renaissance east facade.
Peculiar chapel (1569) by M. de
Vos (also responsible for the
altarpiece). Baroque theater.
•The town has many medieval
half-timbered houses.

148 SIEDLUNG 1925–26
ITALIENISCHER
GARTEN
Stadtgebiet Blumlage
O. Haesler

Early row housing. •The Neue
Sachlichkeit aesthetic was
developed by Haesler in later
schemes in this neighborhood:
Seidlung Georgsgarten
(1926–27) and Siedlung
Blumläger Feld (1930–31).

149 ALTSTÄDTER 1927–28
SCHULE
(school)
Sägemühlenstrasse 7
O. Haesler

150 MUSTERHAUS 1930
Lüneburger Heerstrasse 2
O. Haesler

CLEMENSWERTH B2

2 km (1 mi) E of Sögel

151 CLEMENSWERTH 1736–50
(hunting lodge)
J. C. Schlaun

COBURG E4

152 ST. MAURICE 14th–16th c
(church)
off Steingasse

153 VESTE 16th c
(fortress)

Huge. Double ramparts. Art
museum inside the Kemenate
wing has some Cranach
paintings, many engravings,
and much furniture and glass.

154 SCHLOSS 1543 onward
EHRENBERG
(castle)
Schlossplatz

Renaissance. Main facade
remodeled (1816) in the English
Gothic style. The interesting
interiors are a showcase for
various architectural styles
and eras.

COCHEM E2

155 SCHLOSS 1869–77
(castle)
Festungstrasse

Destroyed in 1689. Rebuilt by
J. Raschdorff.

COLOGNE

See Köln

CORVEY

See Korvey

CREGLINGEN E4

17 km (10.5 mi) NW of
Rothenburg

156 HERRGOTTSKIRCHE 15th c
(church)
1.5 km (1 mi) S, on the road to
Blaufelden

Superb altarpiece (1505) by
T. Riemenschneider.

DACHAU G4

16 km (10 mi) NW of Munich

157 GEDENKSTÄTTE 1933–45
(concentration camp memorial
and museum)

The horrors of an extermination
camp can be realized in this
memorial. The Evangelische
Versöhnungskirche (church,
1965–67) is by H. Striffler.

DARMSTADT E3

Museum: Hessisches
Landesmuseum (1893, by A.
Messel), Friedenplatz 1.
15th- to 17th-c German,
Dutch, and Flemish paintings.
Some Jugendstil. •In the
picture gallery of Schloss
Darmstadt on Marktplatz is
Holbein the Younger's *Meyer
Madonna* (1526).

158 LUDWIGSKIRCHE 1822–27
(church)
Wilhelminenplatz
G. Moller

Circular plan. The dome has
been altered. •Moller also
executed the Hoftheater (1825,
rebuilt ca. 1871) in the
Hoftheaterplatz opposite the
Schloss.

159 MATHILDEN- 1898–1907
HÖHE
An artist's colony sponsored by
Grand Duke Ernst Ludwig. The
first exhibition was held in
1901. Most buildings are
reasonably well preserved.
Nikolaiweg: Russian
chapel (1898).

Alexandraweg: no. 17, Haus
Behrens: P. Behrens
(1900–1901); his first
building. All the remaining
buildings on Alexandraweg
are by J. M. Olbrich: no. 23,
Haus Glückert I (1899–1900);
no. 25, Haus Glückert II
(1900–1901); no. 26, Ernst-
Ludwig-Haus (1900–1901).
Statues by L. Habich. The
center of the colony with
eight artists' studios: no.
27, Haus Habich (1901);
no. 28, Haus Olbrich (1901);
no. 31, Haus Keller (1900).

Olbrichweg: Hochzeitsturm
und Ausstellungsgebäude
(Wedding Tower and exhi-
bition buildings, 1906–7)
by J. M. Olbrich. Built
for the 1908 exhibition and
to celebrate Ernst Ludwig's
marriage. Garden sculpture
(to the west) by B. Hoetger.
No. 15 Olbrichweg, Upper
Hessian House (1907), is also
by Olbrich.

160 HAUPTBAHNHOF 1908
(railway station) onward
Platz der Deutsche Einheit
F. Pützer

DIESSEN AM AMMERSEE G4

161 STIFTSKIRCHE   1732–39
(abbey church)

Rebuilt by J. M. Fischer.
Baroque. Decoration of superb
quality. Altar by F. Cuvilliés.

DINKELSBÜHL F4

162 ST. GEORG   1444–95
(church)

Romanesque tower. Triple-
aisled late Gothic hall church
interior.

DONAUE– SCHINGEN G3

Museum: Fürstlich-
Fürstenbergisches
Sammlungen, Karlsplatz.
German paintings by
Grünewald, Holbein the
Elder (*Passionsaltar*), Master
of Messkirch (Wildenstein
altarpiece), and others.

163 PFARRKIRCHE   18th c
(church)

Statue of the Virgin of
Donaueschingen (1522).

DONAUSTAUF F5

11 km (7 mi) E of Regensburg

164 WALHALLA   1830–42
(a German "Hall of Fame")
L. von Klenze

An archeologically correct
Greek temple set above a
grandiose series of stairs and
terraces.

DONAUWÖRTH F4

165 HEILIGKREUZKIRCHE 1720
(church)

Baroque. Wessobrunn
stuccowork.

DORTMUND D2

Museum: Ostwall Museum,
Ostwall 7. 20th-c and German
expressionist paintings.

166 NIKOLAIKIRCHE   1929–30
(church)
Lindemannstrasse 72
P. and P. Grund

Early use of exposed concrete.

167 ZENTRALFRIEDHOF   1966
(cemetery)
Pferdebachstrasse,
Witten/Ruhr
H. Kahlenborn

DRACHENBURG D2

house near Königswinter

168 DRACHENBURG   1879–85
(country house)
Tüshaus and Abbema

A neo-Gothic mansion.

DUISBURG D2

169 WILHELM-   1958–64
LEHMBRUCK–MUSEUM
Düsseldorferstrasse 51
M. Lehmbruck

Works by W. Lehmbruck and
German expressionist painters.
Good collection of modern
sculpture.

DÜREN D2

170 ST. ANNA   1951–56
(church)
St. Annaplatz/Oberstrasse
R. Schwarz

Built from war rubble.

DÜSSELDORF D2

Museums: Kunstmuseum,
Ehrenhof 5. Mainly German
works. Düsseldorf School and
20th-c expressionists.
Kunstsammlung Nordrhein-
Westfalen, Jacobistrasse 2.
Housed in the Schloss Jägerhof
(rebuilt by N. de Pigage in
1752–63). 20th-c paintings:
Picasso, Léger, Kandinsky,
Klee, and others.

171 LAMBERTIKIRCHE   14th c
(church)
Altestadt Ratinger Strasse/
Müller-Schlosser-Gasse

Gothic hall church. Interesting
belfry.

172 JOHANNISKIRCHE 1875–81
(church)
Martin-Luther-Platz
Kyllmann and Heyden

173 AKADEMIE   1879–81
DER KUNSTE
(art academy)
Fritz Roeberstrasse
H. Riffart

174 KAUFHAUS AG   1907–9
(formerly Tietz)
Königsallee 1
J. M. Olbrich

Early department store.

175 MANNESMANN   1911–12
HAUS
(office building)
Mannesmann Ufer
P. Behrens

176 RHEINHALLE   1925–26
(planeterium and exhibition
hall)
Hofgartenufer 7
W. Kreis

177 VERWALTUNGS–   1949–51
GEBÄUDE GLASHAUS
(headquarters)
Couvenstrasse 4
B. Pfau

178 THYSSENHAUS   1957–60
(office building)
Jan-Wellem-Platz
H. Hentrich

179 EVANGELISCHE   1962–63
JACOBUSKIRCHE
(church)

Am Schabernack (Düsseldorf-
Eller)
E. Schulze-Fielitz

180 GEMEINDEZENTRUM 1967
UND ALTENHEIM
(community center and
residence for the aged)
Riccarda-Huch-Strasse, Garath
G. Böhm

181 SCHAUSPIELHAUS 1968–70
(theater)
Bleichstrasse/Jan-Willem-Platz
B. Pfau

182 WABBEL HOUSE 1973
Schulweg 22
W. Döring

Outskirts of Düsseldorf

183 BENRATH CHÂTEAU 1768
10 km (6 mi) SE of Düsseldorf

Rococo interiors. Fine park.

184 ST. BENEDIKT 1844–47
KIRCHE
(church)
Düsseldorf-Heerdt (4 km W of
Düsseldorf)
H. J. Freyse

EBERBACH E2
7 km (4 mi) W of Eltville

185 EHEMALIGES 1135 onward
KLOSTER
(former abbey)

Romanesque abbey church
(1135–86). Gothic aisle added
on south side. Chapter house
(1345) and 14th-c dormitory.

EBRACH E4

186 EHEMALIGES 12th c onward
KLOSTER
(former abbey)

Totally remodeled by J. B.
Neumann. Gothic church
(Cistercian plan after Cîteaux)
with baroque interior. Now a
prison.

EICHSTÄTT F4

187 DOM 1042–1396
(cathedral)
Domplatz

Baroque west facade, Gothic
interior. Notable 15th-c
Pappenheim altarpiece. 15th-c
cloisters and mortuarium
(funeral chapel). •The adjacent
Residenzplatz is surrounded by
rococo houses.

ELTZ E2
10 km (6 mi) SW of Hatzenport

188 SCHLOSS 12th c onward
(castle)

Extended in the 16th c.
Restored after a fire in 1920.
Spectacular site.

EMMERICH C1

189 HEILIG- 1865–66
GEIST–KIRCHE
(church)

Wassenbergstrasse
D. G. Baumewerd

ESSEN D2

Museum: Folkwang Museum
(1956–60, by W. Kreutzberger),
Bismarckstrasse 64. A good
collection. French and German
impressionists (van Gogh,
Gauguin, etc.) and 20th-c
paintings.

190 MÜNSTER 10th c onward
(church)
Gildehafstrasse

Gothic hall church. West
chancel derived from Aachen.
Golden Madonna (ca. 980) in
the north chapel.

191 ABTEIKIRCHE 13th c
(abbey church)
Essen-Werden (8 km/5 mi S of
Essen)

Transitional late Romanesque/
Gothic. Unusual pierced gallery
in the crypt.

192 VILLA HÜGEL 1868–73
Bredeney
Schwarz

193 ESSENER 1957–60
STEINKOHLENBERG–
WERKE HEAD OFFICE
Huyssenallee/
Hohenzollernstrasse
E. Eiermann

194 KARSTADT HEAD 1969
OFFICE
Theodor-Althoff-Strasse 2
W. Brune

ESSLINGEN F3

195 LIEBFRAUENKIRCHE
(church) 1321–1526
Obere Beutau (on the hilltop)

An outstanding Gothic church.
Excellent sculpture on the three
entrance portals. Restored in
1862.

ETTAL G4
16 km (10 mi) N of Garmisch-
Partenkirchen

196 KLOSTER 14th c onward
(abbey)

The polygonally planned Gothic
church was transformed into a
baroque ensemble by E. Zuccalli
(facade and chancel, 1710–26)
and J. Schmutzer (cupola,
1744–48). Cupola painting by
J. J. Zeiller.

FRANKFURT AM MAIN E3

Museum: Städelsches Kunstinstitut, Dürerstrasse 2. An excellent collection with many important works, including those by van Eyck (*Lucca Madonna,* 1436), Rembrandt (*Blinding of Samson*), Rubens (*Dido and Aneas*), Hans Baldung Grien (*Nativity* and *Baptism of Christ*). Also Degas, Monet, Braque, Beckman, and other 20th-c painters.

197 DOM   13th–14th c
    (cathedral)
    Domplatz

    Gothic triple-aisled hall church. Fine tower, begun, 1415–1514; completed, 1867–83. Bombed in 1943. Since restored. Vandyke's *Deposition from the Cross* in the north transept.

198 STÄDELSCHES   1873–78
    MUSEUM
    Schaumainkai
    O. Sommer

199 FRANKFURTER   1875–76
    HOF HOTEL
    Friedensstrasse/Kaiserstrasse
    Mylius and Bluntschli

200 DREIKÖNIGSKIRCHE
    (church)   1875–81
    Sachsenhäuser Ufer
    F. J. Denzinger

201 BÖRSE   1879
    (exchange)
    Börsenplatz
    H. Burnitz and O. Sommer

202 FESTHALLE   1907–8
    Messegelände
    F. von Thiersch

203 SYNAGOGUE   1908–10
    Freiherr von Stein Strasse
    F. Roeckle

204 MAIN-GASWERKE   1911–12
    Schielestrasse 20 (Osthafen)
    P. Behrens

    Important early example of geometrical simplicity in industrial architecture.

205 WOHNSIEDLUNG   1927–29
    ZICKZACKHAUSEN
    (housing)
    Bruchfeldstrasse, Frankfurt-Niederrad
    E. May

    May was appointed City Architect in 1925 and introduced a large housing program (15,000 low-cost units were built). •This scheme was followed by other housing estates: Praunheim, Damaschke-Anger; Bornheimer Hang, Ketterallee; Westhausen at Ludwig-Landmann-Strasse/Heise Strasse/Egestrasse; Römerstadt; all built from 1927–31. May developed a prefabricated construction system (May System) and minimum housing standards (adopted by CIAM) to cope with the volume of construction.

206 IG FARBEN AG   1928–30
    OFFICES
    Bremer Strasse
    H. Poelzig

207 BUDGE   1928–30
    FOUNDATION OLD
    PEOPLE'S HOME
    Hansaallee/Edingerweg
    M. Stam and W. Moser

    Now a U.S. Army clinic.

208 PALMENGARTENS   1929
    GESELLSCHAFTSHAUS
    Palmengarten
    E. May and M. Elsässer

209 GEWERK-   1930–31
    SCHAFTSHAUS
    Wilhelm-Leuschner-Strasse 69
    M. Taut and F. Hoffmann

210 NECKERMAN   1958–60
    VERSAND AG
    (warehouse)
    Hanauer Landstrasse
    E. Eiermann

211 OLIVETTI   1968–72
    HEADQUARTERS
    Niederrad
    E. Eiermann

Outskirts of Frankfurt

212 FARBWERKE   1920–24
    HÖCHST AG
    (former head office of the dye works)
    Werkgelände, Frankfurt-Höchst (10 km/6 mi W of Frankfurt)
    P. Behrens

    Dramatic brick entrance hall.

FRAUENINSEL G5
island in the Chiemsee (near Prien)

213 BENEDICTINE   11th c
    CONVENT   onward

    The 13th-c church was rebuilt in the 15th c. An 11th-c portal has survived.

FREIBURG G2

Museum: Augustinermuseum, Augustinerplatz. Medieval art. Right wing of M. Grünewald's Aschaffenburg altarpiece (*St. Mary of the Snows*). 14th-c Adelhauser Kreuz (crucifix).

214 MÜNSTER   1200–1513
    (cathedral)
    Münsterplatz

    Romanesque transept crossing and lower sections of the twin crossing towers. The remainder is a superb Gothic structure. West front (1275–1340) with an exceptional tower and excellent sculpture in the porch. Fan-vaulted choir (1354–1513) begun by Hans Parler. South porch remodeled in the Renaissance fashion in the 17th c. The high altarpiece (*Coronation of the Virgin,* 1512–16) is by Hans Baldung Grien. On the reverse side is the grim *Crucifixion.*

FREISING F5

215 DOM   1161–1205
(cathedral)

Remodeled ever since. Only the crypt has remained unchanged. Principal appearance inside is baroque (by the Asam brothers). Flamboyant Gothic choir stalls. The cloisters (stuccowork by J. B. Zimmermann) give access to St. Benedict's Chapel, a Gothic structure reworked in a baroque manner.

FRIEDRICHSHAFEN G3

216 SCHLOSSKIRCHE 1695–1701
(church)
Schloss-strasse
C. Thumb

FRITZLAR D3

13th-c town ramparts in good condition. Picturesque (half-timbered) Marktplatz.

217 DOM   1171–1230
(collegiate church)
Domplatz

Some sections of an earlier church have been incorporated in the present structure. Good column capitals in the very large crypt. Gothic baldachin and cloisters.

FULDA E3

218 MICHAELSKIRCHE 791–822
(church)   onward
Pauluspromenade

Carolingian crypt. Romanesque nave.

219 KIRCHE   9th c onward
    AUF DEM PETERSBURG
(church)
4 km (2.5 mi) E of Fulda, on a
    mountaintop

Rebuilt in the 15th c. Carolingian crypt with frescoes. Good 12th-c low reliefs.

220 SCHLOSS   1607 onward
(former abbot's palace)
Schloss-strasse

Remodeled by J. Dientzenhofer and Gallasini in the 18th c. Orangery (1721–30) by M. von Welsch.

221 DOM   1704–12
(cathedral)
Pauluspromenade/
   Kastanienallee
J. Dientzenhofer

Baroque. Restored in 1896.

GARKAU A4
15 km (9.5 mi) N of Lübeck

222 GUT GARKAU   1924–25
(farm buildings)
by the Pönitzer See
H. Häring

An expressionist work, now in poor condition.

GELNHAUSEN E3

223 KAISERPFALZ   12th c
(ruined palace)
on an island in the Kinzig River

Romanesque carvings.

224 MARIENKIRCHE   13th c
(church)
Untermarkt

Good interiors. Restored in 1879.

GOSLAR C4

225 KAISERPFALZ   1050 onward
(imperial palace)
Kaiserbleek

Totally rebuilt in 1873. The 12th-c Chapel of St. Ulrich has survived. It has an interesting section: a Greek cross plan (lower floor) distorted into an octagon (upper gallery).

226 RATHAUS   15th c
(town hall)
Marktplatz

•Many other medieval houses, including an interesting street of carved timber houses, Münzstrasse, just off the Marktplatz.

GÖSSWEINSTEIN E4
40 km (25 mi) SW of Bayreuth

227 WALLFAHRTSKIRCHE
(church)   1730–37
J. B. Neumann

GRAFRATH G4
5 km (3 mi) N of Inning

228 KIRCHE   1686–94
(church)
M. Thumb

GÜNZBURG F4

229 FRAUENKIRCHE   1736–41
(church)
D. Zimmermann

HAGEN D2

230 KARL-ERNST   1900–1902
    OSTHAUS MUSEUM
Hochstrasse 73
H. van de Velde (interiors)

231 EDUARD MÜLLER   1906–7
    KREMATORIUM
Delstern (SE of Hagen)
P. Behrens, with E. R. Weiss (painter)

232 HOHENHOF VILLA   1906–8
(now a clinic)
Stirnband 10
H. van de Velde

233 CUNO HOUSE   1908–11
Hassleyer Strasse 35
P. Behrens

• Also by Behrens is the
Goedecke house (1910), on
Amselgasse.

HAMBURG B4

Museums: Kunsthalle,
Glockengiesserwall 1. Mainly
German and Dutch paintings:
Master Bertram (Grabow
Altarpiece, 1379), Cranach,
and other primitives.
Comprehensive collection of
works by the Die Brücke and
Der Blaue Reiter schools.
   Museum für Kunst und
Gewerbe, Steintorplatz.
Applied arts of all periods.

234 HAUPTKIRCHE   1751–62
      ST. MICHAELIS
(church)
Michaelisstrasse
J. Prey and E. Sonnin

Tower built in 1786.

235 BÖRSE   1836–59
(exchange)
Adolphsplatz
C. L. Wimmel and F. G. J.
Forsmann

236 PETRIKIRCHE   1843–49
(church)
Mönckebergstrasse/
   Bergstrasse
A. de Chateauneuf

237 PATRIOTISCHE   1844–47
      GESELLSCHAFT
Börsenbrücke
W. Bölau

238 ST. NIKOLAI   1844–60
(former church)
Hopfenmarkt
Sir George Gilbert Scott

Only the tower survived the
WWII bombings. Now a
memorial.

239 ALTE POST   1846
Poststrasse
A. de Chateauneuf

240 KUNSTHALLE   1867–69
Glockengiesserwall
von der Hude and
Schirmmacher

241 RATHAUS   1880–96
(town hall)
Rathausplatz
M. Haller

242 HAUPTBAHNHOF   1901–6
(railway station)
Glockengiesserwall/
   Steintordamm
H. Reinhardt and G.
Süssengut

Iron and glass shed after
Contamin and Dutert's Galerie
des Machines, Paris (now
destroyed).

243 BISMARCK   1902–6
      DENKMAL
(monument)
Helgoländer Allee
E. Schaudt

Sculpture by H. Lederer.

244 MUSIKHALLE   1904
Karl-Muck-Platz
M. Haller

245 KLÖPPERHAUS   1912–13
Mönckebergstrasse/
   Bugenhagenstrasse
F. Höger

246 CHILEHAUS   1923
(shipping offices)
Am Messberg
F. Höger

An obvious and extremely
effective symbol.

247 PFLANZEN-   1961–63
      SCHAUHAUS
Botanischer Garten
B. Hermkes and G. Becker

248 UNILEVERHAUS   1961–64
(office building)
Dammtorwall 15
H. Hentrich and H. Petschnigg

249 FINNLANDHAUS   1964–66
(office building)
Esplanade/Neuer Jungfernstieg
H. Hentrich and H. Petschnigg

Suspended steel structure
hung off a central core.

250 HAMBURGER   1967–68
      ELEKTRIZITÄTSWERKE
Übersee-Ring, City-Nord
A. Jacobsen

HÄMELSCHEN-
BURG C3
11 km (7 mi) S of Hameln

251 SCHLOSS   1588–1612
(castle)

Weser Renaissance. Horseshoe
plan.

HANNOVER C3
(Hanover)

Museums: Kestner Museum, Friedrichswall. A very good collection of Roman and Egyptian antiquities. Niedersächsisches Landesmuseum, Am Maschpark 5. Regional museum. The Landesgalerie (picture gallery) section has a good collection of Italian and German primitives. Also 17th-C Dutch and 20th-C German works.

252 MARKTKIRCHE   14th C
(church)
Am Markte

14th-C stained glass in the choir. Notable 15th-C Schnitzaltar (Passion Altarpiece).

253 ALTES RATHAUS   1435–80
(old town hall)   onward
Markt/Karmarschstrasse

Extended 1875–91 by C. W. Hase.

254 HERRENHÄUSER 1666–1710
    GARTEN
(gardens)
Herrenhäuser Allee

Four separate and splendid gardens: Grosser Garten (formal French), Berggarten (botanical), Georgengarten, and Welfengarten.

255 WANGENHEIM   1832
    PALAIS
Friedrichswall 1
G. L. F. Laves

Now a ministry.

256 OPERNHAUS   1845–52
(theater)
Opernplatz
G. L. F. Laves

Interior restored after 1945.

257 BÖRSE   1846–49
(exchange)
Opernhausplatz
E. Ebeling

258 KÜNSTLERHAUS   1852–55
Sophienstrasse 2
C. W. Hase

259 TECHNISCHE   1857 onward
    HOCHSCHULE
(school)
Welfengarten
H. Tramm

260 CHRISTUSKIRCHE 1859–64
(church)
Klagesmarkt
C. W. Hase

261 APOSTELKIRCHE 1875–84
(church)
Celler Strasse
C. W. Hase

262 HAUPTBAHNHOF 1876–79
(railway station)
Ernst-August-Platz
H. Stier

263 GARTENKIRCHE   1886–90
(church)
Marienstrasse
E. Hillebrand

264 NEUES   1898–1913
    RATHAUS
(new town hall)
Trammplatz
H. Eggert and G. Halmhuber

265 LANDESMUSEUM   1902
Am Maschpark
H. Stier

266 STADTHALLE   1911–14
Corvinusplatz
P. Bonatz

267 ANZEIGER   1927–28
    HOCHHAUS
(office building)
Goseriede 9
F. Höger

268 ALTERSHEIM   1931
    HEINEMANN-STIFTUNG
(old-age home)
Brabeckstrasse 86, Hannover-Kirchrode
H. van de Velde

HASSFURT E4

269 WALLFAHRTS-   1751–54
    KIRCHE MARIÄ
    HEIMSUCHUNG
(church)
J. B. Neumann

•8 km (5 mi) SE of Hassfurt, on the river Main (opposite Zeil am Main), is the church of Maria-Limbach (1747–52), also by Neumann.

HECHINGEN F3

270 ST. JAKOB   1780–83
    KATHOLISCHE KIRCHE
(church)
M d'Ixnard

HEIDELBERG F3

Museum: Kurpfälziches Museum, Hauptstrasse 97. General history of the region. In the art section is T. Riemenschneider's *Windsheimer Zwölfbotenaltar* (twelve apostles altarpiece).

271 SCHLOSS   14th–17th C
(castle)

A romantic ensemble of buildings of various ages, with some ruined sections. The Ottenheimrichsbau (1556–59) has a good late-Renaissance facade.

272 RITTERHAUS   1592
(knight's house)
Hauptstrasse

An excellent Renaissance building. •The Heilig-Geist-Kirche (1400–36) opposite is a flamboyant Gothic hall church.

HEILBRONN F3

273 KILIANSKIRCHE 13th–15th c
(church)
Kiliansplatz

Gothic. Noted Renaissance
tower (1513–29). •The
Rathaus (town hall, 1535–96)
in the Marktplatz is Gothic,
with some Renaissance detail.

HEILSBRONN F4

274 KLOSTERKIRCHE 1150–1435
(former abbey church)

Now Protestant. Nothelferaltar
(Veit Stoss school, ca. 1520).

HERRENINSEL G5
island in the Chiemsee (near
Prien)

275 SCHLOSS   1878–85
(castle)

Closely modeled after
Versailles (some interiors are
exact copies). Built for King
Ludwig II. Some interiors by
F. P. Stulberger.

HERSFELD (Bad) D3

276 ABTEIKIRCHE   10th–12th c
(abbey church, ruined)
Marktplatz

Destroyed in 1761. The roof
(1968) above the ruins is by
F. Otto (with Romberg, Röder,
and Krier).

HERMANNS–
DENKMAL C3
monument 6 km (4 mi) SW of
Detmold in the Teutoburger
Wald (forest)

277 HERMANNSDENKMAL
(monument)   1838–46
E. von Bandel

A colossal monument.

HEUSENSTAMM E3
8 km (5 mi) S of Offenbach

278 ST. CÄCILIA   1739–40
(church)
Schloss-strasse 8
J. B. Neumann

HILDESHEIM C3

Museum: Roemer-Pelizaeus
Museum, Am Stein. Egyptian
antiquities.

279 DOM   11th c
(cathedral)
Domhof

An exact replica was rebuilt
after 1945. Romanesque
cloisters.

280 ST. MICHAELIS–   11th c
KIRCHE
(church)
Michaelis-Platz

Completely rebuilt after 1945.

281 ST. GODEHARD–   12th c
KIRCHE
(church)
Godehardplatz

HIRSAU F3

282 KLOSTER   11th c onward
(abbey)

Destroyed in 1692. Romanesque
Eulenturm (tower). St. Mary's
chapel and cloisters are more
or less intact. St. Aurelian
(church, 1038–71) has been
restored.

HOHENZOLLERN
G3

283 SCHLOSS   1493 onward
(castle)

Rebuilt from 1850–67. Superb
site, and an interesting triple-
circled entry ramp. The 12th-c
Chapel of St. Michael has
survived (with some ancient
stained glass, originally in
Stetten monastery).

HOLZKIRCHEN G5

284 PROPSTEIKIRCHE   1726
(church)
J. B. Neumann

IGEL E2

285 IGEL COLUMN   3rd c A.D.
Carved Roman funeral
monument 23 m (75 ft) high in
very good condition.

INGOLSTADT F4

286 FRANZISKANERKIRCHE
(Franciscan church)   1380
Harderstrasse 4

Inside the monastery.

287 LIEBFRAUENMÜNSTER
(church)   1425–1527
Kreuzstrasse

Gothic with some later
Renaissance details. Hochaltar
(altarpiece, 1572) by H. Mielich.

288 MARIA-DE-   1732–36
VICTORIA-KIRCHE
(church)
Neubaustrasse

Rococo "renovation" by E. and
C. Asam.

IPHOFEN E4

289 PFARRKIRCHE   1351
(church)

Late Gothic.

KALKAR C1

290 NICHOLAIKIRCHE 15th c
(church)

Gothic hall church. Altarpiece
(1520) by Douvermann. Other
fine Gothic works of art.

KARLSRUHE F3

Museum: Staatliche Kunsthalle
(1836–46, by H. Hübsch),
Hans-Thoma-Strasse 2. 15th- to
20th-c European paintings:
Grünewald, Rembrandt,
Rubens, Claude, and others.

291 SCHLOSS 1715
(castle)
Schlossplatz

The center of a radial street
plan. Gardens to the north.
•On axis is the Marktplatz
(1804–24) and Rondellplatz
(1805–13), both by F.
Weinbrenner. The Mar-
gräfliches Palace on
Rondellplatz is also by
Weinbrenner.

292 EVANGELISCHE 1806
STADTKIRCHE
(church)
Markt
F. Weinbrenner

•Weinbrenner also designed the
town hall, opposite.

293 MÜNZE 1826–27
(mint)
Stephanienstrasse 28
F. Weinbrenner

294 LUTHERKIRCHE 1905–6
(church)
Durlacher Allee
H. Curjel and K. Moser

295 HAUPTBAHNHOF 1913–15
(railway station)
A. Stürzenacker

296 SIEDLUNG 1929
DAMMERSTOCK
(housing)
Ettlinger Allee
W. Gropius, O. Haesler,
W. Riphahn, and others

KASSEL D3

Museum: Neue Galerie,
Schöne Aussicht 1. 18th- to
20th-c German paintings.

297 WILHELMSHÖHE 1701–96
Wilhelmshöher Allee
Schloss (castle) 1787–94
S. L. du Ry
Completed by H. C. Jussow.
Rebuilt after 1945. Houses
the Staatliche Kunst-
sammlungen, which contains
excellent Dutch and Flemish
paintings, including works
by Rembrandt, Hals, Ter-
bruggen, Vandyke, Rubens,
and others. Also Italian,
German, and Spanish works.
Greek and Roman an-
tiquities.

Grounds 1701–18
The park was laid out by
G. Guernieri. Numerous
follies and fountains. The
Octagon (1714) overlooks an
enormous water cascade.
Above is the Hercules, a
gigantic statue (after the
Farnese Hercules) atop an
obelisk. Schloss Löwenburg
(1793–96) in the park, an
imitation of a Gothic castle,
is by Jussow.

298 KARLS-AUE 1701–28
(park)
Kleine Fulda

In the French style (1709
onward). The Orangerie (1701–
11) is next to the Marmorbad
(a former bathroom, 1720–28)
with marvelous interiors
(sculpture by P. Monnot).

299 MUSEUM 1769–79
FRIDERICIANUM
Friedrichsplatz
S. L. du Ry

300 RATHAUS 1902–9
(town hall)
Obere Königstrasse
K. Roth

301 HESSISCHES 1907–13
LANDESMUSEUM
Brüder-Grimm-Platz
T. Fischer

302 HEINRICH- 1928
SCHÜTZ-SCHULE
(school)
Wilhelmshöher Allee
H. Tessenow

303 MARIE-VON- 1930–32
ASCHROTT-
ALTERSHEIM
(old-age home)
Friedrich-Ebert-Strasse 178
O. Haesler and K. Völker

KASTEL E2
34 km (21 mi) S of Trier

304 KLAUSE 1835
(chapel)
K. F. Schinkel

Neo-Romanesque.

KELHEIM F5

305 BEFREIUNGS- 1843–63
HALLE
(Liberation Monument)
2 km (1 mi) W of Kelheim
L. von Klenze

A huge neoclassic rotunda.
•Weltenburg Abbey is nearby.

KEMPTEN G4

306 KLOSTERKIRCHE 1652
(abbey church)
Residenzplatz
M. Beer

KOBLENZ E2

307 SCHLOSS 1777 onward
(castle)
M. d'Ixnard

308 KAISER   1897
    WILHELM DENKMAL
    (monument)
    Am Deutschen Eck
    B. Schmitz

309 REGIERUNGS-   1902
    GEBÄUDE
    (government offices)
    Am Rhein
    F. H. Schwechten

KÖLN D2
(Cologne)

Museums: Römisch-
Germanisches Museum,
Domhof. Roman remains
including the 2nd-c Dionysos
Mosaic.
    Wallraf-Richartz-Museum,
An der Rechtschule. Paintings
by 14th- to 16th-c Köln
masters—Lochner, the Master
of St. Severin, etc., as well as
Rubens, Hals, Nolde, Munch,
Kandinsky, Rauschenberg, and
others.

310 ST. MARIA   1040–65 onward
    IM KAPITOL
    (church)
    Lichhof off Pipinstrasse

    Trefoil plan (transept).
    Renaissance rood screen.

311 DOM   1248–1447 onward
    (cathedral)
    Domhof
    G. von Riehl

    Modeled after Amiens. Nave
    and spires finally completed
    according to original design
    from 1842–80. Altarbild
    (Adoration of the Magi
    altarpiece, 1444), by S.
    Lochner, off the ambulatory.
    Notable Dreikönigenschrein
    (shrine), by Nicolas of Verdun,
    behind the main altar.

312 ST. APOSTELN   1035–1220
    (church)
    Apostelnstrasse/Mittelstrasse

313 ST. GEREON   1075–1227
    (church)
    Gereonstrasse

    Elongated plan. Romanesque
    choir. Apse added in 1160;
    decagonal domed nave,
    1218–27. 13th-c frescoes.
    Damaged in 1945; much rebuilt.

314 TRINITÄTISKIRCHE 1857–61
    (church)
    Filzengraben
    A. Stüler

315 HAUPTBAHNHOF   1889–94
    (railway station)
    Bahnhofsvorplatz
    G. Frentzen

316 ST. MICHAELS-   1902–6
    KIRCHE
    (church)
    Brüsseler Platz
    E. Endeler

317 DISCHHAUS   1929
    Brückenstrasse/Herzogstrasse
    B. Paul

318 OWN HOUSE   1958–59
    AND OFFICE
    Belvederestrasse 60, Köln-
    Müngersdorf
    O. M. Ungers

    Well scaled and detailed. Some
    brutalist influence visible.

319 ST. GERTRUD   1962–65
    (church)
    Krefelder Strasse 45
    G. Böhm

KÖNIGSLUTTER
AM ELN C4

320 ABTEIKIRCHE   11th c
    (former abbey church)

    Triple-aisled Romanesque
    basilica with good carvings.
    Contemporary cloisters.

KORVEY C3
2 km (1 mi) NE of Höxter

321 KLOSTERKIRCHE   873
    (abbey church)   onward
    West facade (873–85, middle
    section heightened in 1146).
    Carolingian entrance hall.
    Remainder reworked in
    baroque style.

KREFELD D2

322 ST. STEPHAN   1854–59
    (church)
    Stephanstrasse
    F. von Schmidt

323 LANGE HOUSE   1928
    Wilhelmshofallee 91
    L. Mies van der Rohe

    Badly damaged in 1945. Now a
    museum. •The Esters's house
    (1928) next door is also by Mies.

KRONBERG E3
8 km (5 mi) N of Frankfurt am
Main

324 SCHLOSS   1889–93
    FRIEDRICHSHOF
    E. Ihne

LANDSBERG G4

325 RATHAUS   1699–1702
    (town hall)

    Facade (1719) by D.
    Zimmermann. Zimmermann
    was the mayor of the town, a
    rare combination of civic and
    architectural ability. •The

Bayertor (1425) at the end of the Alte Bergstrasse is an outstanding example of a Gothic town gate.

LANDSHUT F5

326 ST. MARTINS-   1390–1495
    KIRCHE
    (church)
    Altstadt
    H. Stethaimer

Built in brick. The tower (also brick) is 133 m (436 ft) high. Madonna (1518) by H. Leinberger in the south aisle.

327 RESIDENZ   1536 onward
    (palace)
    Altstadt

Two linked sections. The Italian wing is one of the earliest Renaissance palaces in Germany. Facade added in 1780.

LAUFEN G5

328 KIRCHE   1330–38
    (church)

Gothic hall church.

LIMBURG AN DER LAHN E2

329 DOM   1213–42
    (cathedral)
    off the Nonnenmauer

Romanesque exterior, Gothic interior (modeled after Laon). Interior badly restored.

LINDENHARDT E4

15 km (9 mi) S of Bayreuth

330 PFARRKIRCHE   15th C
    (church)
    Altarpiece by M. Grünewald.

LINDERHOF G4

castle 14 km (9 mi) W of Oberammergau

331 SCHLOSS   1870–78
    LINDERHOF
    (castle)
    G. von Dollmann

Superb lush rococo interiors by F. von Seitz. The justly famous park makes full use of a magnificent site. Some follies, including a Grotto of Venus (a Wagnerian fantasy by F. Schabet) and Moorish pavilion.

LORSCH E3

332 KÖNIGSHALLE   ca. 800
    (monastery gatehouse)

Carolingian. Much restored. The monastery is ruined.

LÜBECK B4

Museum: St. Annen-Museum, St. Annen Strasse 15. Religious carvings. 15th-c works by B. Notke. Passion altarpiece (1491) by Memling.

333 DOM   1173 onward
    (cathedral)
    Mühlondamm

Romanesque. Gothic choir added 1251–91. Cross by B. Notke.

334 JAKOBIKIRCHE   13th C
    (church)
    Breitestrasse/Engelsgrube

Gothic hall church.

335 MARIENKIRCHE   1250–1330
    (church)
    Breitestrasse/Marienkirchhof

Gothic. Superb brickwork. Lady Chapel added in 1440.

336 HEILIGEN-   1286
    GEIST-HOSPITAL
    (former almshouse)
    Koberg

14th-c hall church inside.

337 HOLSTENTOR   1477
    (fortified gateway)
    Holstenstorplatz

338 BEHNHAUS   1779–83
    Königstrasse 11
    J. Lilie

Now a museum. Paintings by Overbeck and Munch.

LUDWIGSBURG F3

339 SCHLOSS   1764–67
    MONREPOS
    (castle)
    Monreposstrasse, off
        Frankfurterstrasse (route 27)
    P. L. P. de la Guêpière

Horseshoe-shaped plan. Interiors altered in 1804. •The enormous (and boring) castle in the town is by Nette and Frisoni.

LUDWIGSHAFEN AM RHEIN E3

340 FRIEDRICH-   1962–65
    EBERT-HALLE
    Ebert-Park
    R. Rainer

An elegant solution.

LÜNEBURG B4

341 RATHAUS   13th–18th C
(town hall)
Am Markt

Fürstensaal (Prince's Hall,
15th C), Gothic, with a good
ceiling. Grosse Ratsstube
(council chamber, 1566–84);
a fine Renaissance hall.

LÜNEN D2

342 GESCHWISTER-   1956–61
SCHOLL-GYMNASIUM
(school)
Holtgrevenstrasse 6
H. Scharoun

MAINZ E3

Museum: Mittelrheinisches
Landesmuseum Mainz, Grosse
Bleiche/Bauhofstrasse.
Regional history. The
Jupitersäule (Jupiter column,
A.D. 66) is unique.

343 DOM   975 onward
(cathedral)
Am Markt

Romanesque with later
additions.

344 THEATER   1828–32
Gutenbergplatz
G. Moller

345 CHRISTUS-   1896–1902
KIRCHE
(church)
Kaiserstrasse 56
F. Fredrikson

346 GUTENBERG-   1961–63
WELTMUSEUM DER
DRUCKKUNST
Liebfrauenplatz
R. Schell

Museum of typography.
Gutenberg forty-two line Bible.

MANNHEIM E3

Museum: Städtische Kunsthalle
(1907, by H. Billing),
Moltkestrasse/Berlinerstrasse.
19th- and 20th-C paintings by
Pissarro, Sisley, Cézanne
(*Execution of Maximilian,
Pipe Smoker*), Kokoschka, etc.
Modern sculpture.

347 SCHLOSS   1720–60
(castle)
Bismarckstrasse/
Kurpfalzstrasse

Baroque. Much rebuilt. Rococo
library.

MARBURG AN DER
LAHN D3

348 ELISABETHKIRCHE 1235–83
(church)
Elisabethstrasse

The first Gothic hall church in
Germany. Triple apse. Gold
shrine of St. Elisabeth (1250)
in the sacristy (left of central
apse). Good open Gothic rood
screen.

349 ALTE   1873–79
UNIVERSITÄT
(old university)
Universitätsstrasse
K. Schäfer

Gothic style.

350 KAISER WILHELM   1880
TURM
Spiegelslust
K. Schäfer

MARIA LAACH E2
by the Laacher See, 25 km
(15 mi) W of Koblenz

351 ABTEIKIRCHE   1130–56
(abbey church)

Atrium entrance added from
1220–30. Six towers. Basalt
blind arcading on exterior
(compare St. Michael,
Hildesheim). Austere interior.
13th-C hexagonal baldachin.

MARL C2

352 RATHAUS   1960–67
(town hall)
Bergstrasse
J. van den Broek and J. Bakema

353 WOHNHÜGEL   1964–67
(housing)
Brüderstrasse
P. Faller and H. Schröder

354 HAUPTSCHULE   1966–68
(high school)
Westfalenstrasse 68, Marl-
Drewer-Süd
H. Scharoun

MAULBRONN F3

355 ABTEI   1148–14th C
(former abbey)

Now a school. Uniquely well
preserved. The church
(1148–78) has a Romanesque
rood screen. The porch (13th C)
and fan vaulting (15th C) are
noticeably later additions.
Off the cloister are the
remaining buildings (chapter
house, kitchen, refectory, etc.).
All the outbuildings have
survived.

MINDEN C3

356 DOM   1062–1379
(cathedral)
Domhof

Tower (1062–72), nave, and
choir (1267–1379). Powerful
west facade. 11th-C crucifix
at the crossing. •The railway
station (1847) nearby is an
appealing neo-Gothic structure.

MITTENWALD G4

357 PFARRKIRCHE 1738–49
(church)
J. Schmutzer

Baroque. Good stuccowork.

MÖNCHEN-GLADBACH D2

358 MÜNSTER 10th–13th C
(church)

The Gothic choir is possibly by
G. von Riehl (architect of
Köln cathedral).

MÜNCHEN G4 (Munich)

Tourist Information:
Verkehrsamt, Bahnhofplatz 2
(tel 239–1256).

Architect's Institute: Bund
Deutsche Architekten,
Martiusstrasse 8 (tel 348–180).

Museums: Alte Pinakothek,
Barer Strasse 27. 14th- to 18th-C
paintings: Dürer, Cranach,
Memling, Rubens, El Greco,
Rembrandt, Titian, and others.
Neue Pinakothek and
Staatsgalerie Moderner Kunst
(1933–37, by P. L. Troost),
Prinzregentenstrasse 1.
19th and 20th C French and
German paintings.
Städtische Galerie, Lenbach
Villa (1887, by G. von Seidl),
Luisenstrasse 33. Paintings by
Lenbach, Kandinsky, Klee, and
other München painters.

359 FRAUENKIRCHE 1468–88
(church)
Frauenplatz *D5*

Rebuilt after 1945. Flamboyant
Gothic.

360 MICHAELSKIRCHE 1583–97
(church)
Neuhauser Strasse *D5*

Modeled after the Gesù, Roma.
Enormous barrel vault.

361 RESIDENZ 16th C onward
(palace)
Residenzstrasse/
Hofgartenstrasse *D5*

Renaissance Residenzstrasse
facade, Kaiserhof, Brunnenhof,
and Kapellenhof by H. Schön
and P. Candid (1602–19).
Reiche Zimmer (state rooms,
1729–37) and superb Altes
Residenztheater (theater,
1751–53) by F. Cuvilliés; both
damaged in 1944 and since
restored. The Königsbau
(1826–35) on Max-Joseph-
Platz by L. von Klenze is
modeled after the Pitti Palace,
Firenze. Festsaalbau (1832–42)
and Allerheiligen Hofkirche
(chapel, 1827–37, rebuilt after
1945) also by von Klenze.

362 THEATINER-KIRCHE 1661–88
(church of St. Cajetan)
Theatinerstrasse *D5*
E. Zuccalli

Facade (1767) by F. Cuvilliés.

363 SCHLOSS NYMPHENBURG 1663–1777
(castle)
Menzinger Strasse *C2*
A. Barelli and G. Viscardi

The scheme is modeled after
Versailles. Rococo banquet hall
by J. B. Zimmermann. Park by
Carbonet and Girard. On the
grounds are various pavilions:
the Badenburg (bathing
pavilion) is interesting.

Outstanding, however, is the
exquisite Amalienburg hunting
lodge (1734–39) by F. Cuvilliés,
a rococo masterpiece.

364 HEILIGEN GEIST KIRCHE 1724–30
(church)
Tal/Heiliggeiststrasse *D5*
J. G. Ettenhofer

Interior by C. and E. Asam.
Extended by three (western)
bays in 1885.

365 ST. ANNA AM LEHEL 1727–39
(church)
St. Anna Strasse 9 *D5*
J. M. Fischer

366 ASAMKIRCHE 1733–46
(Asam brothers, or St. John
Nepomuk, church)
Sendlinger Strasse *D5*
C. Asam (frescoes) and E.
Asam (stuccowork)

The private chapel of the Asam
brothers, who lived next door.

367 ST. MICHAEL 1737–43
(church)
St. Michaelstrasse, Berg am
Lain *E6*
J. M. Fischer

Interior by J. B. Zimmermann.

München

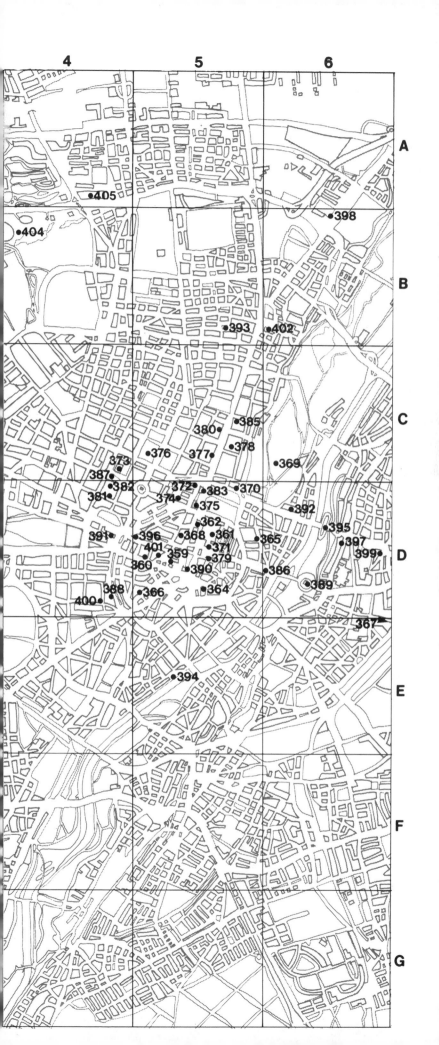

368 ERZBISCHÖFLICHES 1737
PALAIS
(archbishop's palace)
Kardinal-Faulhaber-Strasse *D5*
F. Cuvilliés

Formerly the Königsfeld Palace.

369 ENGLISHER 1789–1840
GARTEN
(park)
Prinzregentenstrasse *C6*

Chinese pavilion (1789, rebuilt
in 1952). English-style
landscape. Monopteros Temple
(1837) by L. von Klenze.

370 PRINZ–KARL–PALAIS 1803
(palace)
Königinstrasse 1/
Prinzregentenstrasse *D5*
K. von Fischer

371 BAYERISCHE 1811–18
STAATSOPER
Max-Joseph-Platz *D5*
K. von Fischer

Former national theater.
Reconstructed, 1823–25 by
L. von Klenze, and again,
1943–63.

372 LEUCHTENBERG 1816
PALAIS
Odeonsplatz 4 *D5*
L. von Klenze

•Ludwigstrasse 1–3 (1817–24) is
also by von Klenze.

373 GLYPTOTHEK 1816–30
(sculpture gallery)
Königsplatz 3 *C4*
L. von Klenze

374 PALAIS 1820
ARCO–ZINNEBERG
(palace)
Wittelsbacherplatz 1 *D5*
L. von Klenze

•Palais Ludwig Ferdinand
(1825), opposite, is also by von
Klenze.

375 ODEON 1826
Odeonsplatz 3 *D5*
L. von Klenze

Former concert hall.

376 ALTE 1826–36
PINAKOTHEK
(picture gallery)
Barer Strasse 27 *C5*
L. von Klenze

377 FORMER 1827–30
WAR OFFICE
Ludwigstrasse 14 *C5*
L. von Klenze

378 LUDWIGSKIRCHE 1829–40
(church)
Ludwigstrasse *C5*
F. von Gärtner

•The Staatsbibliothek (library,
1832–40), next door, is also by
von Gärtner.

379 HAUPTPOST 1834–38
Max-Joseph-Platz *D5*
L. von Klenze

Former Palais Törring.

380 LUDWIG- 1835–40
MAXIMILIANS
UNIVERSITÄT
(university)
Ludwigstrasse/Geschwister
Schollplatz *C5*
F. von Gärtner

381 BASILIKA 1835–50
ST. BONIFAZ
(church)
Karlstrasse 34 *D4*
G. F. Ziebland

Damaged in 1944.

382 NEUE 1838–45
STAATSGALLERIE
Königsplatz *D4*
G. F. Ziebland

Now the Antikensammlung.

383 FELDHERRNHALLE 1841–44
Odeonsplatz *D5*
F. von Gärtner

A replica of the Loggia dei
Lanzi in Firenze.

384 RUHMESHALLE 1843–53
Theresienwiese *E3*
L. von Klenze

A ponderous monumental
setting for the statue *Bavaria*.

385 SIEGESTOR 1843–52
(victory gateway)
Ludwigstrasse/Schackstrasse
C5
F. von Gärtner

386 STREET DESIGN 1848 onward
Maximilianstrasse *D6*
F. A. Bürklein

387 PROPYLÄEN 1848–60
(gateway)
Königsplatz *C4*
L. von Klenze

388 POSTSCHECKAMT 1850
(post office savings bank)
Sonnenstrasse *D4*
F. A. Bürklein

389 MAXIMILIANEUM 1865–67
Maximiliansbrücke *D6*
F. A. Bürklein

Now the regional council.

390 NEUES 1867–74 onward
RATHAUS
(new town hall)
Marienplatz *D5*
G. Hauberisser

391 JUSTIZPALAST 1891–97
Karlsplatz *D4*
F. von Thiersch

392 BAYERISCHES 1893–99
NATIONALMUSEUM
Prinzregentenstrasse *D6*
G. von Seidl

393 ST. URSULA 1894–97
(church)
Kaiserplatz, Schwabing *B5*
A. Thiersch

394 MAXIMILIANS- 1895–1901
KIRCHE
(church)

Wittelsbacherstrasse/
  Deutingerstrasse *E5*
H. von Schmidt

395 FRIEDENSENGEL   1896
  (monument)
  Prinzregentenstrasse, by the
    river *D6*
  M. Heilmaier

396 KÜNSTLERHAUS   1896–1900
  (artists' center)
  Lenbachplatz 8 *D5*
  G. von Seidl

397 STUCK VILLA   1897–98
  Prinzregentenstrasse 60 *D6*
  F. Stuck

  Stuck was a painter. Now a
  museum with contemporary
  (ca. 1900) paintings.

398 ERLÖSERKIRCHE 1899–1901
  (church)
  Ungererstrasse *B6*
  T. Fischer

399 THEATER   1900–1901
  Prinzregentenplatz *D6*
  M. Littmann

400 ALTE-ANATOMIE   1905–7
  Schillerstrasse/
    Pettenkoferstrasse *D4*
  M. Littmann

401 POLIZEIGEBÄUDE 1909–15
  Neuhauser Strasse/
    Augustinerstrasse *D5*
  T. Fischer

402 HYPOTHEKEN-   1964–66
    BANK
  Ungererstrasse 2 *B6*
  K. Ackerman

403 STIMMEN DER   1964–66
    ZEIT OFFICES
  Zucallistrasse 16 *C2*
  P. Scheider-Esleben

404 OLYMPISCHE   1968–72
    GESAMTANLAGE
  (Olympic park and sports
  facilities)
  Georg-Brauchle-Ring *B4*
  Behnish and Partners, with
  F. Otto

Superb cablenet roof covering
1.4 ha (3.5 acres) of parkland.
Velodrome by Beier, Dahms,
and Grube. Graphics by
H. Hollein.

405 BMW OFFICE   1970–72
    BUILDING
  Dostlerstrasse 9 *A4*
  K. Schwanzer

MÜNNERSTADT E4

406 KIRCHE   13th c
  (church)

  Altarpiece (1492) by T.
  Riemenschneider. Paintings
  (north aisle) by V. Stoss.

MÜNSTER C2

Museum: Landesmuseum für
Kunstgeschichte, Pferdgasse.
Regional medieval sculptures
and altarpieces.

407 DOM   1225–61 onward
  (cathedral)
  Domplatz

  14th-c cloisters.

408 RATHAUS   1335
  (town hall)
  Prinzipalmarkt

  Gothic. Facade rebuilt.

409 ÜBERWASSER-   1340–46
    KIRCHE   onward
  (church)
  Frauenstrasse

  Gothic.

410 RESIDENZSCHLOSS   1767
  (castle)
  Schlossplatz
  J. C. Schlaun

  Baroque. Fine garden. Now a
  university.

MURRHARDT F3

411 STADTKIRCHE   15th c
  (church)

  Noted for the (external)
  Romanesque Chapel of St.
  Walderich next to the church's
  north tower.

NERESHEIM F4

412 KLOSTERKIRCHE   1745–92
  (abbey church)
  J. B. Neumann

  Remodeled. Glorious baroque
  spaces. Earlier bell tower (1626).

NEUÖTTING G5

413 ST. NICHOLAS   1410–1510
  (church)

  Gothic. Begun by H.
  Stethaimer.

NEUSCHWANSTEIN G4

4 km (2.5 mi) E of Füssen

414 SCHLOSS   1869–86
    NEUSCHWANSTEIN
  (castle)
  E. Riedel, then G. von Dollman,
  then J. Hoffmann

  King Ludwig II's Wagnerian
  castle. Extraordinary site and
  interiors. •Schloss

Hohenschwangau (1832–37),
1 km (0.5 mi) east, is a neo-
Gothic reconstruction by J. D.
Ohlmüller on the ruins of an
earlier fortress. The interiors
are appropriately opulent.

NEVIGES D2
8 km (5 mi) SE of Velbert

415 WALLFAHRTSKIRCHE
(pilgrimage church)　　1966–68
G. Böhm

NÖRDLINGEN F4

416 ST. GEORG-　　1428–1505
　　KIRCHE
(church)
Marktplatz

Flamboyant Gothic hall church.
Altarpiece (1470) by F. Herlin
(some sections in the museum on
Baldinger Strasse). •The old
section of the town is still
surrounded by medieval
ramparts.

NORD-STEMMEN C3

417 SCHLOSS　　1857–67
　　MARIENBURG
C. W. Hase and E. Oppfer

NÜRNBERG E4 (Nuremberg)

Museum: Germanisches
Nationalmuseum, Kornmarkt 1.
Includes a very large (and
good) collection of German
paintings from the 14th to
20th c.

418 ST. LORENZ-　　1260–1477
　　KIRCHE
(church)
Lorenzer Platz

Nave widened 1403–45. Choir
rebuilt (1439–77) by K.
Heinzelmann. West facade with
fine rose window. Engelsgruss
(Annunciation, 1518) by V.
Stoss in the chancel. Baldachin
(1493–96) by A. Kraft.

419 ST. SEBALDUS-　　13th–14th c
　　KIRCHE
(church)
Rathausplatz

Romanesque west facade,
transitional nave, and Gothic
choir (1361–77). Much
sculpture by V. Stoss and
A. Kraft. The tomb of St.
Sebald (1519) is by P. Vischer.

420 FRAUENKIRCHE　　1354–61
(church)
Hauptmarkt

Rebuilt since 1945. Gothic hall
church.

421 ELISABETHKIRCHE　　1785
(Deutschhauskirche)
Jakobsplatz
I. M. Neumann

422 HAUPTBAHNHOF　　1901–11
(railway station)
Bahnhofsplatz
Zenger

423 THEATER　　1902–5
Frauentorgraben
H. Seeling

424 STADIUM　　1934
Zeppelinstrasse
A. Speer

OBERHAUSEN D2

425 LAGERHAUS DER　　1921–25
　　GUTEHOFFNUNGHÜTTE
(mining foundry depot)
Essenerstrasse 66
P. Behrens

OBERMARCHTAL G3

426 ABTEIKIRCHE　　1686–92
(abbey church)
C. Thumb and F. Beer

Early baroque work of the
Vorarlberg school.

OSNABRÜCK C2

427 DOM　　12th–13th c
(cathedral)
Domhof

Romanesque towers and
cloisters.

428 JOHANNISKIRCHE　　13th c
(church)
Johannisstrasse

Gothic hall church. Choir
built from 1256–92.

429 MARIENKIRCHE　　1306–1420
(church)
Marktplatz

OSTERHOVEN F5 (Osterhofen)

430 KLOSTERKIRCHE　　1726–40
(abbey church)
J. M. Fischer

Decorated by C. and E. Asam.

OTTOBEUREN G4

431 KLOSTER　　1711 onward
(abbey)

Magnificent baroque
remodeling (1711–31):
Kaisersaal (hall), library,
theater, chapel, etc. The
Klosterkirche (abbey church,
1748–66) is J. M. Fischer's
masterpiece. Frescoes by J. J.
and F. A. Zeiller. Stuccowork
by J. M. Feichtmayr. Sculpture
by J. Christian. Organ by K. J.
Riepp.

PADERBORN C3

432 DOM　　1143 onward
(cathedral)
Domplatz

Mainly Gothic. Romanesque
tower and crypt. The separate
Chapel of St. Bartholomew
(1017), a Romanesque structure
with some Byzantine detail, is
just north of the cathedral.

PASSAU F6

433 DOM 14th C onward
(cathedral)
Domplatz

Rebuilt (1665–95) in the baroque style by C. Lorago. The Gothic choir is intact. Frescoes in the ambulatory chapels by J. M. Rottmayr.

POMMERSFELDEN E4

6 km (3.5 mi) N of Höchstadt an der Aisch

434 SCHLOSS 1711–18
POMMERSFELDEN
J. Dientzenhofer

Spectacular baroque castle. Magnificent staircase (some contribution here by J. L. von Hildebrandt).

RATZEBURG B4

island town

435 DOM 1154 onward
(cathedral)

Romanesque. Brick. Notable altar (1430).

REGENSBURG F5

Museum: Museum der Stadt, Dachauplatz. Paintings by Altdorfer and others of the Danube school.

436 PORTA A.D. 179
PRAETORIA
(Roman gateway)
Unter den Schwibbogen, just E of the Alter Dom

437 ST. EMMERAMUS 12th C
(church)
St.-Emmeramus-Platz (S side)

Romanesque porch and sculpture. Remainder in poor rococo. Neo-Gothic funeral chapel (1841) in the cloisters. •The castle next door (formerly the St. Emmeramus abbey) has some good interiors (library, riding school).

438 ST. JAKOBSKIRCHE 12th C
(church)
Jakobsstrasse

Basilica. Good sculpture on the north portal.

439 DOM 1275–1534
(cathedral)
Domplatz

Splendid Gothic architecture. Unusual triangular porch on west front flanked by flamboyant towers (spires completed by F. J. Denzinger from 1858–69). Truncated transepts. Triple apse with 14th-C stained glass. Romanesque All Saints Chapel in the cloisters.

440 SCHLOSS 18th C
SÜNCHING
castle 33 km (20 mi) SE of Regensburg

Festsaal (banquet hall, 1761) by F. Cuvilliés.

REICHENAU G3

island in the Bodensee (Lake Constance)

441 MARIENMÜNSTER 754–819
(church) onward
Mittelzell (town)

Most of the existing building dates from the 11th- to 12th C. Gothic choir added from 1448–1551. •The church of St. Peter and St. Paul at Niederzell, 1.5 km (1 mi) north, is a 10th-C basilica.

442 ST. GEORGE 9th C
(church)
Oberzell (town)

Carolingian basilica, Gothic choir. Wall murals (ca. 1000) in the nave.

REMAGEN D2

23 km (14 mi) SE of Bonn

443 APPOLINARIS- 1839–43
KIRCHE
(church)
E. F. Zwirner

ROHR F5

444 KIRCHE 1718–25
(church)
C. and E. Asam

The Assumption of the Virgin altarpiece is an excellent example of the Asam brothers' emotional sculpture.

ROTHENBURG OB DER TAUBER F4

Well-preserved 16th-C town.

445 ST. JAKOB 1373–1471
KIRCHE
(church)
Kirchplatz

Double choir (east and west). Altarpiece of the Holy Blood (1504) by T. Riemenschneider in the south aisle. •The Franziskanerkirche on the Herrengasse is an early Gothic structure on a street of medieval houses.

446 RATHAUS 14th C onward
(town hall)
Marktplatz

Renaissance facade added ca. 1680.

ROTT AM INN G5

447 STIFTSKIRCHE 1759–63
(abbey church)
J. M. Fischer

Only the remodeled church remains. Stuccowork by J. M. Feichtmayr. Frescoes by M. Günther (completed in 1767).

ROTTENBUCH G4

448 MARIA   15th and 18th c
    GEBURTS KIRCHE
    (church)

Gothic transept. Remainder
remodeled (1737–42) in rococo
style by the Schmutzers
(stuccowork) and M. Günther
(frescoes).

ROTTWEIL G3

449 KAPELLENKIRCHE   ca. 1374
    (church)
    Hauptstrasse

Flamboyant Gothic tower and
loggia. Baroque interior.
•Excellent collection of Gothic
statuary in the Lorenzkapelle
on St. Lorenzgasse.

ST. BLASIEN G2

450 KLOSTERKIRCHE   1780
    (church of St. Blaise)
    M. d'Ixnard

Enormous domed rotunda with
a separate suspended inner
dome. Largely rebuilt after a
fire in 1874.

ST. PETER G2
16 km (10 mi) E of Freiburg

451 KLOSTERBIBLIOTHEK 1738
    (abbey library)
    P. Thumb

SALEM G3

452 KLOSTER   13th–18th c
    (abbey)

Now a school. The Gothic abbey
church (1299–1414) follows a
Cistercian plan. Baroque
interior. The castle (former
abbey buildings), also rebuilt
in the baroque style, has good
interiors.

SCHÄFTLARN G4
8 km (5 mi) N of
Wolfrathshausen

453 STIFTSKIRCHE   1733 onward
    (abbey church)
    F. Cuvilliés

SCHLEISSHEIM G4
15 km (9 mi) N of München

454 NEUES SCHLOSS   1701–27
    (castle)
    E. Zuccalli

Completed by J. Effner.
Excellent baroque and rococo
interiors. Great stairway by
Effner. 16th- and 17th-c Dutch
and Flemish paintings.

SCHLESWIG A3

455 DOM   12th c onward
    (cathedral)
    Süder-Domstrasse

Brick. Gothic hall church.
Bordesholm Altar (1514–21) by
H. Brüggeman in the choir.
Tomb of Frederick I (1552–55)
by C. de Vriendt.

456 SCHLOSS GOTTORP   1150
    (castle)   onward
    Gottorper Damm

Rebuilt since. Renaissance
chapel (1600) survives; now a
museum. 4th-c Nydam boat on
display.

SCHLIERSEE G5

457 PFARRKIRCHE   1712
    (church)

Baroque renovation.
Stuccowork and ceiling painting
by J. B. Zimmermann.

SCHÖNENBERG F4
2 km (1 mi) N of Ellwangen

458 WALLFAHRTS-   1682–95
    KIRCHE
    (pilgrimage church)
On the hilltop, above the castle
M. Thumb

SCHUSSENRIED G3

459 KLOSTER-   1754–61
    BIBLIOTHEK
    (abbey library)
    D. Zimmermann

Delightful rococo fantasy.
Stucco and sculpture by J. J.
Schwartzmann. The Gothic
church was transformed
internally into a baroque space
in the early 1700s. The
remaining buildings are now a
hospital.

SCHWÄBISCH-GMÜND F3

460 HEILIGKREUZMÜNSTER
    (cathedral)   1351–1521
    Münsterplatz

Begun by Heinrich Parler.
Vaulting built from 1491–1521.
Much sculpture.

SCHWÄBISCH-HALL F3

461 PFARRKIRCHE   1427–1525
    (St. Michael's church)
    Marktplatz

Gothic hall church (remodeled
Romanesque structure). •An
interesting ten-story
Romanesque dwelling tower
(now the Keckenburg Museum)
is in the Keuckenhof.

SCHWARTZ-RHEINDORF D2
3 km (2 mi) E of Bonn

462 KIRCHE   1151
    (church)
    Rheindorfer Strasse/
       Stiftsstrasse

Two-story Romanesque church.
Frescoes (1156) illustrating the
Book of Ezekiel.

SCHWETZINGEN F3
15 km (9 mi) SE of Mannheim

463 SCHLOSSGARTEN 1748–84
(castle park)

Begun in the French manner.
Theater (1752) by A. Galli da
Bibiena. Sections of the park
were remodeled in the "English
landscape" fashion from
1762–80. Many follies and
ruins, all by N. de Pigage.

SIEGEN D2

464 NIKOLAIKIRCHE 13th c
(church)
Am Markt

An unusual domed nave.

SOEST D2

465 PATROKLIDOM 11th–12th c
(cathedral)
Petrikirchhof

Refined Romanesque tower.
Interior totally restored. •The
Nikolaikapelle (chapel) nearby
displays K. von Soest's St.
Nicholas altarpiece (1400) in
the choir.

SCHLOSS SOLITUDE F3
castle 10 km (6 mi) W of
Stuttgart

466 SCHLOSS 1763–67
SOLITUDE
(castle)
P. L. P. de la Guêpière

Neoclassic. Interesting oval
plan. Some (French) rococo
interiors. •Schloss Ludwigsburg
(1704–33, by Nette and
Frisoni) lies across the valley.

SPEYER F3

467 DOM 1031 onward
(cathedral)
Domplatz/Maximilianstrasse

Enormous. Burned by the
French in 1689. Much of the
nave was rebuilt in the 19th c.
Unrivaled crypt (1031–61).
Groined nave (originally timber
roof). Four towers. Gothic
sacristy (1409). West work
(1858) by H. Hübsch.

468 GEDÄCHTNIS- 1893–1904
KIRCHE
(church)
Bartholomäusplatz
Flügge and Nordmann

469 HISTORISCHES 1907–8
MUSEUM DER PFALZ
Domplatz
G. von Seidl

STAFFELSTEIN E4

470 PFARRKIRCHE 768–814
(church)

Built under Charlemagne's
orders.

STEINBACH E3
5 km (3 mi) N of Michelstadt

471 EINHARDSBASILIKA 821
(church)

Built by Einhard. Sanctuary
preceded by lateral chapels
forming a primitive transept.

STEINGADEN G4

472 KLOSTERKIRCHE 1147
(abbey church) onward

Romanesque exterior; baroque
interior with rococo details.

STEINHAUSEN G3
15 km (9 mi) SW of Biberach

473 WALLFAHRTS- 1727–33
KIRCHE
(pilgrimage church)
D. Zimmermann

Baroque. Oval plan followed by
a smaller oval chancel. Frescoes
by J. B. Zimmermann (brother).

SCHLOSS STOLZENFELS E2
castle 6 km (4 mi) S of Koblenz,
near Kapellen

474 SCHLOSS 1836–42
STOLZENFELS
(castle)
K. F. Schinkel

An overrestored castle. Rich
interiors.

STRAUBING F5

475 URSULINEN- 1736–41
KIRCHE
(church)
Burggasse 9
C. and E. Asam

Rococo. •In complete contrast
is the brick Gothic hall church
of St. Jakob by the Stadtplatz.

STUPPACH F3
6 km (4 mi) S of Bad
Mergentheim

476 PFARRKIRCHE 15th c
(church)

Inside is Grünewald's *The
Virgin and the Infant Christ*
(central panel only, 1519),
originally in Aschaffenburg.
The one surviving wing (*St.
Mary of the Snows*) is in
Freiburg.

STUTTGART F3

Museum: Staatsgalerie (1842,
by G. Barth), Konrad-
Adenauer-Strasse 32. A good
representative collection of
European paintings.

477 ALTES SCHLOSS 1553–78
(old castle)
Schillerplatz
A. Tretsch

•The 15th-c Stiftskirche
(church) in the square was
largely rebuilt after 1945.
Interesting porch (1490–1530).

478 KURSAAL 1821
(casino)
König-Karl-Strasse, Bad
Cannstadt
N. F. von Thouret

479 WILHELMA 1842–53
(casino)
Neckartal Strasse
K. L. W. Zanth

480 VILLA BERG 1846–53
Sick Strasse
C. Leins

481 KÖNIGSBAU 1857–60
Schlossplatz
C. Leins

Stores, restaurants, and concert
hall.

482 JOHANNESKIRCHE 1866–76
(church)
Feuerseeplatz
C. Leins

Neo-Gothic.

483 MARIENKIRCHE 1876
(church)
Tübingerstrasse
J. Egle

484 GALATHEABRUNNEN 1890
(fountain)
Eugensplatz
O. Rieth

485 GUSTAV 1905–13
SIEGLE HAUS
Hardsplatz
T. Fischer

486 KUNSTVEREINS– 1909–12
GEBÄUDE
Schlossplatz
T. Fischer

487 HAUPTBAHNHOF 1911–28
(railway station)
Schillerstrasse
P. Bonatz and F. Scholer

Monumental. Neo-
Romanesque/Richardsonian
structure.

488 WEISSENHOF– 1926–27
SIEDLUNG
(housing)
Am Weissenhof/Rathenau-
Strasse/Friedrich-Ebert-
Strasse

Housing built for a Deutsche
Werkbund exhibition organized
by L. Mies van der Rohe.
Buildings by Mies, J. J. P. Oud,
V. Bourgeois, A. G. Schneck,
Le Corbusier and P. Jeanneret,
J. Frank, M. Stam, P. Behrens,
and H. Scharoun survive.

489 ROMEO UND JULIA 1954–59
(apartment blocks)
Schozacherstrasse,
S-Zuffenhausen
H. Scharoun

490 HOCHHAUS 1961–63
SALUTE
(high-rise apartments)
Sautterweg 5
H. Scharoun

491 INSTITUT FÜR 1965
LEICHTE
FLÄCHENTRAGWERKE
(institute of lightweight
structures)
Robert-Leicht-Strasse 211
F. Otto

Lightweight tensile structure.

492 F. L. LEITZ 1966–67
FACTORY
Siemensstrasse 64, S-Feuerbach
G. Heinrichs and H. C. Müller

493 IBM–GERMANY 1969–71
HEADQUARTERS
Pascal-Strasse 100, Valhingen
E. Eiermann

494 STAATSGALERIE 1977–84
EXTENSION
Konrad-Adenauer-Strasse
J. Stirling and M. Wilford

TIEFENBRONN F3
15 km (9 mi) SE of Pforzheim

495 PFARRKIRCHE 15th C
(church)

Altarpiece (1431) by L. Moser
in the south aisle. This is
the only work, known with
certainty, to be executed
by Moser. Other good
altarpieces.

TRIER E2

496 KAISERTHERMEN
(imperial baths) ca. 300 A.D.
Kaiserstrasse/Ostallee

Extensive remains. •The earlier
Barbarathermen on
Kaiserstrasse/Friedrich-
Wilhelm-Strasse are far less
impressive. Good Roman
section in the Rheinisches
Landesmuseum next to the
Kaiserthermen. Roman
amphitheater along Olewiger
Strasse. The Römer Brücke
(4th-C Roman bridge) was
rebuilt in the 17th C.

497 PORTA NIGRA 4th C
(Roman gateway)
Simeonstrasse

Fortified entrance in
outstanding condition.
Converted into a church in the
11th C. Restored in 1804 on
Napoleon's orders.

498 DOM 4th C onward
(cathedral)
Domfreihof

The central portion is an
authentic Roman structure.
West end added in 11th C, east
end in 12th C. •Next door is the
Liebfrauenkirche (1235–70), an
early Gothic church with a
Greek cross plan (after
Braisne). The interior is
exquisite.

499 ST. PAULIN 1734–54
(church)
Paulinstrasse
J. B. Neumann

TÜBINGEN F3

500 STIFTSKIRCHE 1470–1529
(St. George's church)
Holzmarkt

Flamboyant Gothic rood screen
and pulpit.

501 MENSA DER 1963–67
UNIVERSITÄT
(cafeteria)
Wilhelmstrasse 13
P. Baumgarten

•The library (1912) on
Wilhelmstrasse is by P. Bonatz.

ÜBERLINGEN G3

502 MÜNSTER 1353–1586
(cathedral)
Münsterplatz

ULM F4

503 MÜNSTER 1377–1492
(cathedral)
Münsterplatz
Parler and Ensinger families

Dominated by the single west
tower, 161 m (528 ft) high,
designed by U. Ensinger. The
upper section, designed
(ca. 1480) by M. Böblinger, was
finally built from 1880–90. The
twin-aisled nave was subdivided
into four aisles (and fan vaulted)
in 1507. Choir stalls (1469–74)
by J. Surlin the Elder.

504 EVANGELISCHE 1908–11
GARNISIONSKIRCHE
(church)
Frauenstrasse
T. Fischer

VALLENDAR E2
7 km (4 mi) N of Koblenz

505 KATHOLISCHE 1837
KIRCHE
(church)
J. C. Lassaulx

VEITSHÖCHHEIM E3
7 km (4 mi) N of Würzburg

506 SCHLOSS 1680 onward
(castle)

Rebuilt (1745–75) by J. B.
Neumann. Baroque gardens
with sculpture by d'Auvera,
Dietz, and Wagner.

VIERZEHN-HEILIGEN E4
30 km (18 mi) NE of Bamberg

507 WALLFAHRTS- 1743–72
KIRCHE
(pilgrimage church)
J. B. Neumann

Neumann's masterpiece. Altar
(1764) by J. J. M. Küchel.
•Directly across the valley is
Banz Abbey (1698–1772), begun
by L. Dientzenhofer. The
remarkable church (1710–18) is
by J. Dientzenhofer (brother).

WAHLSBURG-LIPPOLDSBERG D3
40 km (25 mi) SW of Höxter

508 KLOSTERKIRCHE 12th C
(former abbey church)

Very early vaulted Romanesque
church.

WALDSASSEN E5

509 STIFTSKIRCHE 1685–1704
(former abbey church)
G. Dientzenhofer

•6 km (4 mi) W at Kappel
(reached through Müchenreuth)
is G. Dientzenhofer's
pilgrimage Chapel of the
Trinity (1685–87).

WALHALLA
See Donaustauf

WASSERBURG AM INN G5

510 PFARRKIRCHE 1410–82
(church)
H. von Burghausen

511 PATRIZIERHAUS 18th C
Marienplatz

Baroque facade by J. B.
Zimmermann.

WEINGARTEN G3

512 STIFTSKIRCHE 1715–42
(abbey church)
K. Moosbrugger

Frescoes by C. Asam.

WELTENBURG F5

513 STIFTSKIRCHE 1718–21
(abbey church)
C. and E. Asam

Full-blown baroque. The
theatrical high altar of St.
George and the Dragon is by
E. Asam.

WERNECK E4

514 SCHLOSS 1734–45
(castle)
J. B. Neumann

WESSOBRUNN G4
17 km (10 mi) NW of Weilheim

515 KLOSTER 17th C
(former abbey)

Now a convalescent home. The
Fürstengang (Prince's Gallery)
is a splendid example of the
stuccowork done by the
Wessobrunn school in the 17th
and 18th C.

WIBLINGEN F4

516 STIFTSKIRCHE   1772–81
(abbey church)
J. M. Fischer

Baroque. Completed by J.
Specht. Outstanding rococo
library by C. Wiedemann.

WIES G4

517 WIESKIRCHE   1746–54
(church)
D. and J. B. Zimmermann

The zenith of the rococo style
in Germany.

WIESBADEN E3

518 SCHLOSS   1837
(now the Land Hessen)
Marktstrasse
G. Moller

519 ST. BONIFAZIUS   1844–49
(church)
Luisenplatz
P. Hoffmann

520 MARKTKIRCHE   1853–62
(church)
Am Markt
C. Boos

521 GRIECHISCHE   1855
    KAPELLE
(chapel)
Neroberg
P. Hoffmann

522 BERGKIRCHE   1877–79
(church)
Lehrstrasse
J. Otzen

523 RATHAUS   1884–87
(town hall)
Am Markt
G. Hauberisser

524 RINGKIRCHE   1891 onward
(church)
Bismarckring/Kaiser
    Friedrichring
J. Otzen

525 STAATSTHEATER   1892–94
(theater)
Wilhelmstrasse
F. Fellner and H. Helmer

526 HAUPTBAHNHOF   1904–6
(railway station)
Gustav-Stresemann-Ring
Klingelholz

527 SEKTKELLEREI   1907
    HENKELL
(champagne cellars)
Biebricher Strasse
P. Bonatz

528 KURHAUS   1907
(spa)
F. von Thiersch

529 MUSEUM   1912–15
Friedrich-Ebers-Allee
T. Fischer

530 OPELBAD   1934
(open-air swimming bath)
Am Neroberg
F. Schuster

WIESENTHEID E4

531 PFARRKIRCHE   1727–28
(church)
J. B. Neumann
Italianate murals by F.
Marchini.

WILHELMSTHAL (SCHLOSS) D3

castle 12 km (7 mi) N of Kassel

532 SCHLOSS   1747
    WILHELMSTHAL
(castle)
F. Cuvilliés

Rococo. Built by C. L. du Ry.

WIMPFEN IM TAL F3 (Bad)

533 STIFTSKIRCHE   12th–13th C
(St. Peter's church)

Romanesque west facade,
remainder Gothic. 13th- to
16th-C Gothic cloisters.

WOLFENBÜTTEL C4

534 HAUPTKIRCHE   1608–23
(St. Mary's church)
Kornmarkt

Gothic. Renaissance details.

535 TRINITÄTISKIRCHE 1705–18
(church)
Holzmarkt
H. Korb

Double-galleried octagonal
interior.

WOLFSBURG C4

536 KULTURZENTRUM   1958–62
(cultural center)
Rathausplatz
A. Aalto

•The town theater (1965–73) is
by H. Scharoun.

537 HEILIG-   1958–62
    GEIST-KIRCHE
(church)
Röntgenstrasse 81
A. Aalto

538 STEPHANUS-   1966–68
    KIRCHE
(church)
Marignanestrasse,
    W-Detmerode
A. Aalto

WORMS E3

539 DOM   1000–1224
(cathedral)
Andreasstrasse

Romanesque. Extremely well
preserved. Gothic sculpture in
the north aisle. Altar (1741) by
J. B. Neumann.

540 LUTHERS DENKMAL   1868
(monument)
Lutherplatz
E. Rietschel

WURZACH G3

541 PFARRKIRCHE   1777
(church)
French neoclassic.

WÜRZBURG E3

542 DOM   1034
(cathedral)
Domstrasse

Mostly rebuilt after 1945.
Romanesque with some interior
baroque detail.

543 FESTUNG   13th–17th C
   MARIENBURG
(fortress)
off the Höchberger Strasse

In the courtyard is a 13th-C keep
and a graceful circular chapel
with baroque stuccowork.

544 NEUMÜNSTER-   1710–19
   STIFTSKIRCHE
(church facade)
Schönbornstrasse
J. Dientzenhofer

545 RESIDENZ   1719–44
(palace)
Residenzplatz
J. B. Neumann

Neumann consulted R. de
Cotte, G. Boffrand, von
Welsh, and J. L. von
Hildebrandt about his design
for the palace; the inspiration
is his. Magnificent stairway
(designed 1735), Kaisersaal,
and chapel (1732–41), all
decorated by G. B. Tiepolo
and his sons (1752–54). Stuccowork by A. Bossi. •Neumann
also laid out the Theater-
strasse nearby.

546 KÄPPELE   1748–92
(pilgrimage chapel)
Nikolausstrasse
J. B. Neumann

Frescoes by M. Günther.
Stuccowork by J. M.
Feichtmayr.

547 OWN HOUSE   18th C
Kapuzinnergasse 7
J. B. Neumann

548 FRAUENGEFÄNGNIS
(women's prison)   1809–10
Burkharderstrasse
P. Speeth

Tough neoclassic building.
The influence of E. L. Boullée
and C. N. Ledoux's schemes is
clear.

XANTEN C2

549 DOM   12th–16th C
   ST. VIKTOR
(cathedral)

Excellent Gothic church. The
Romanesque west front,
incorporated from an earlier
church, still survives. Damaged
in 1945. 16th-C cloisters.

550 STIFTSKIRCHE   1738–53
(abbey church)
J. M. Fischer

Stuccowork by J. M.
Feichtmayr.

ZWEIFALTEN G3

551 STIFTSKIRCHE   1740–65
(abbey church)
J. M. Fischer

Frescoes by F. Spiegler;
stuccowork by J. M.
Feichtmayr.

Great Britain

Radcliffe Camera; *see entry 569*

Great Britain

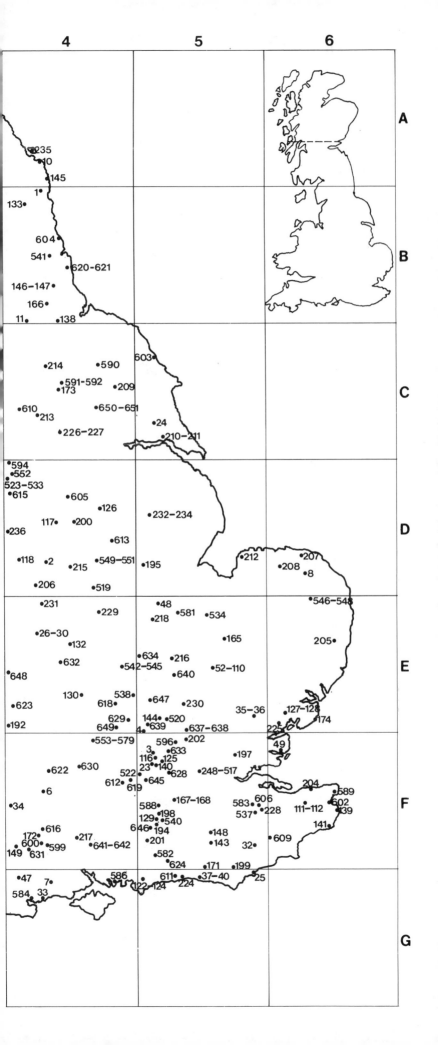

Historic Houses and Gardens:
An *Open to View* ticket
(available outside of Britain)
gives access to many historic
properties and monuments
throughout the country. Many
of these properties are
maintained by the National
Trust for Places of Historic
Interest or Natural Beauty, 42
Queen Anne's Gate, London.
Access to all National Trust
properties can be obtained by
becoming a member of this
organization (membership
applications available at any
National Trust property).
Access possible through this
group overlaps somewhat with
that provided by the *Open to
View* ticket. If you would like a
good guide to these structures,
buy the cheap and comprehensive *Historic Houses, Castles
and Gardens in Great Britain
and Ireland* (ABC Historic
Publications, updated
annually). A companion
volume, *Museums and
Galleries,* is also available.

Waterways and Canals: British
Waterways Board, Melbury
Terrace, London.

New Towns: Town and Country
Planning Association, 17
Carlton House Terrace,
London. Call before you visit a
new town.

Victoriana: Victorian Society,
1 Priory Gardens, London.

Architectural Periods: Anglo-
Saxon, ca. 700–1066; Norman,
1066–1154; Transitional,
1154–89; Early English,
1189–1307; Decorated,
1307–77; Perpendicular,
1377–1485; Tudor, 1495–1558;
Elizabethan, 1558–1603;
Jacobean, 1603–25; Stuart,
1625–1702; Georgian,
1702–1830; Victorian,
1830–90; Edwardian,
1890–1914; 20th-century,
1914–.

ALNWICK B4

1 ALNWICK   12th c onward
   CASTLE

Restored by A. Salvin in 1854.
Italian Renaissance interiors.

ALTON D4
(Staffordshire)
43 km (27 mi) S of Ashbourne

2 ALTON CASTLE   1847–51
A. W. N. Pugin

• Also by Pugin are the
Hospital of St. John (1840), the
village hall, and the school.

AMERSHAM F5

3 HIGH AND OVER   1929–31
(house)
E of Station Road
A. D. Connell

• Adjacent are four houses
designed by B. Ward (Connell's
partner) in 1934.

ASHRIDGE PARK E5
country house 5 km (3 mi) E of
Tring

4 ASHRIDGE PARK   1803–13
(country house)
J. Wyatt

Extravagent neo-Gothic
structure.

AUST F3

5 SEVERN BRIDGE   1966
Sir G. Roberts (Freeman, Fox
and Partners) with Mott, Hay
and Anderson

AVEBURY F4

6 AVEBURY   ca. 2000 B.C.
   CIRCLE

The village of Avebury is built
between three concentric
megalithic circles. An avenue
1.5 km (1 mi) long links
Avebury with Overton Hill,
where further ceremonial
megalithic circles can be seen.
• 13 km (8 mi) to the west of
Avebury is Lacock, a uniquely
well-preserved village with
many medieval houses, some
dating from the 14th c.

AVON TYRELL G4
country house, S of Ringwood

7 AVON TYRELL   1891–92
(house)
Thorney Hill
W. R. Lethaby

AYLSHAM D6
24 km (15 mi) N of Norwich

8 BLICKLING HALL   1626
R. Lyming

Jacobean mansion. Altered
from 1765–70.

BABBACOMBE G3
3 km (2 mi) from Torbay
(Torquay)

9 ALL SAINTS   1865–74
   CHURCH
W. Butterfield

All furnishings designed by
Butterfield. Stunning
polychrome interior, perhaps
his finest.

BAMBURGH A4
25 km (16 mi) N of Alnwick

10 BAMBURGH   12th c onward
   CASTLE

Romantic seaside location.
Norman keep. Fortifications
much restored.

BARNARD CASTLE
B4
25 km (16 mi) W of Darlington

11 BARNARD CASTLE   1869–74
(The Bowes Museum)
J. A. F. A. Pellechet

French second empire château.
Important painting collection:

late medieval to 19th-c works include El Greco, Goya (*Interior of a Prison*), Tiepolo, Fragonard, etc. Also furniture, tapestries, and decorative arts.

BATH F3

12 ROMAN BATHS   3rd C A.D.
York Street

Some portions of the baths are still in use today.

13 QUEEN SQUARE   1729–36
(housing/urban design)
J. Wood the Elder

This innovative design was one of the first to treat a number of separate houses as one building.

14 PRIOR PARK   1735–48
(country house)
Ralph Allen's Drive
J. Wood the Elder

Completed by R. Jones, who built the delightful Palladian Bridge (1755) on the grounds. Superb vista.

15 THE CIRCUS   1754 onward
(housing/urban design)
J. Wood the Elder

Wood died three months after laying the first stone. (This scheme was proposed by him twenty-nine years earlier). Executed by the younger Wood. Although the plan is a true circle, this is often referred to as "the Colosseum turned inside out" because of its Roman-style decoration.

16 ROYAL CRESCENT   1767–75
(housing/urban design)
J. Wood the Younger

The masterpiece of Bath. A semiellipse of houses forms a majestic ensemble that looks onto an open lawn. No. 1, now a museum, has been restored with 18th-c interiors.

17 THE ASSEMBLY   1768–71
    ROOMS
Bennett Street
J. Wood the Younger

The social center of polite society in 18th-c Bath. Restored in 1931 and 1963.

18 PULTENEY   1769–74
    BRIDGE
Bridge Street
R. Adam

Lined on both sides with shops. The original external south facade is reasonably well preserved.

19 THE GUILDHALL   1776
High Street
T. Baldwin

Greatly enlarged by J. M. Brydon in 1891. The Banqueting Hall is by Baldwin.

20 LANSDOWN   1789–93
    CRESCENT
(housing/urban design)
J. Palmer

Houses laid out along an undulating series of convex-concave curves based on Wood's Royal Crescent (entry 16).

21 THE PUMP ROOM   1786–95
Stall Street
T. Baldwin

Completed by J. Palmer (1793–95).

22 DODINGTON 1798–1813
HOUSE
16 km (10 mi) N of Bath, near
  Chipping Sodbury
J. Wyatt

Eclectic amalgam of diverse
styles. Fine stairway hall.
Landscaping by L. Brown.

BEACONSFIELD F5

23 HOLLY MOUNT 1906–7
(house)
Amersham Road, Knotty Green
C. F. A. Voysey

BEVERLEY C5

24 BEVERLEY 1225–1440
MINSTER
(cathedral)
SE of town center

Early English choir (ca. 1230).
The Percy Tomb (begun 1329) is
an outstanding decorated
shrine. •Another very fine
church is St. Mary's, along the
main street, with sculpture of an
equally high standard.

BEXHILL G5

25 DE LA WARR 1933–36
PAVILION
on the seafront
E. Mendelsohn and S.
Chermayeff

BIRMINGHAM E4

Museums: Barber Institute of
Fine Arts, University of
Birmingham. Bellini,
Tintoretto, Rubens, etc. A
comprehensive collection of
17th- to 19th-c masters.
  Birmingham City Museum
and Art Gallery, Congreve
Street. Uneven collection of
European works. Outstanding
Pre-Raphaelite collection.

26 CATHEDRAL 1711–15
Colmore Row
T. Archer

Some glass (1884–87) is by
E. Burne-Jones and W. Morris.

27 ST. CHAD'S 1839–41
CATHEDRAL
Bath Street
A. W. N. Pugin

28 BOURNVILLE 1894–1905
6 km (4 mi) S of Birmingham
A. Harvey

Model village for Cadbury's.
Early workers' housing built by
an enlightened company. This
preceded E. Howard's "Garden
Cities of Tomorrow."

29 EAGLE INSURANCE 1900
Colmore Row
W. R. Lethaby

Now Orion Insurance.

30 THE GOLDEN EAGLE 1935
Hill Street
J. P. Osborn

BLACKPOOL C3

31 CASINO 1937–38
South Shore
J. Emberton

Later enlarged.

BODIAM CASTLE F5
5 km (3 mi) S of Hawkhurst

32 BODIAM CASTLE 1386–89

Well-preserved medieval castle
surrounded by an enormous
moat.

BOURNEMOUTH G4

33 ST. ALBAN'S 1907–9
CHURCH
Charminster Road
G. H. Fellowes Prynne

BRADFORD-ON-AVON F4

34 ST. LAWRENCE 700
(church)

Roof restored in the 10th c;
otherwise unchanged.

BRAINTREE E5

35 CHURCH OF 1898
ST. FRANCIS
Convent Lane, Bocking
(1.5 km/1 mi NE of
Braintree)
J. F. Bentley

36 CRITTALL HOUSE 1928
Silver End, Braintree
T. S. Tait

BRIGHTON G5

37 ROYAL PAVILION 1815–20
(remodeling)
Grand Parade
J. Nash

Nash's oriental fantasy for the
Prince Regent. The state
apartments are furnished in the
Regency style.

38 ST. PETER'S 1823–28
CHURCH
The Steyne
Sir C. Barry

Gothic revival. Barry won the
commission for this building
in an open design competition.

39 ST. BARTHOLOMEW'S 1874
CHURCH
Ann Street
E. Scott

The very fine Byzantine
furnishings and altar (1897–
1908) are by H. Wilson.

40 EMBASSY COURT 1934
(apartments)
Sea front, Kemptown
W. Coats

BRISTOL F3

41 ST. MARY 13th c onward
REDCLIFF
(church)
Redcliff Street

Rebuilt continuously.
Hexagonal 13th-c porch.

42 BRISTOL   1306–1888
    CATHEDRAL
Deanery Road

The Norman chapter house
(1155–70) is original, as is the
Early English Elder Lady
Chapel (1215). The nave and
west tower (destroyed in the
16th c) were rebuilt by G. E.
Street from 1868–88. Unusual
hall church. The aisles are as
high as the nave but display the
most subtle spatial manipu-
lation in the treatment of the
exposed arches. This is
exploited even further in the
vaulting of the vestibule to the
Berkeley Chapel (1340).

43 CLIFTON   1836–64
    SUSPENSION BRIDGE
Bridge Road
I. K. Brunel

"Egyptian" pylons support a
clear span of 212 m (700 ft).
Completed after Brunel's death
by W. H. Barlow.

44 CENTRAL LIBRARY   1906
Deanery Road, College Green
C. Holden

Compare with C. R.
Mackintosh's Glasgow School
of Art.

45 EDWARD VII   1906–11
    BUILDING
Bristol Royal Infirmary,
    Marlborough Hill
H. P. Adams and C. Holden

Powerful massing that has
suffered from later alterations.

BROCKHAMPTON E3
near Ross-on-Wye

46 ALL SAINTS'   1900–1902
    CHURCH
W. R. Lethaby

Tiny, with extraordinary
power. Thatched roof over
massive, yet refined, stonework. The forms are symbolic
of meanings attributed to them
by Lethaby in his book,
*Architecture, Mysticism and
Myth.* Supervised by R. Wells.
• Wells also built the church of
St. Edward the Confessor
(1903, furnishings by E.
Gimson, lectern by E.
Barnsley) at Kempley, a few
miles away, which is visibly
influenced by Lethaby's design
for All Saints'.

BRYANSTON HOUSE G4
near Blandford Forum

47 BRYANSTON   1889–94
    HOUSE
R. N. Shaw

BURGHLEY HOUSE E5
SE of Stamford

48 BURGHLEY   1556–87
    HOUSE

Large Elizabethan house.
Picturesque roofline.

BURNHAM-ON-CROUCH F6

49 ROYAL CORINTHIAN   1931
    YACHT CLUB
The Quay
J. Emberton

A convincing modern-
movement building.

CAERNARVON D2

50 CAERNARVON   1270–1306
    CASTLE
(ruined)

Begun by Edward I. •Other
castles built by Edward in Wales
are Harlech, Beaumaris, Bere,
Criccieth, and Conway.

CAERPHILLY F3

51 CAERPHILLY   1271 onward
    CASTLE
(ruined)

Begun by G. de Clare.
Enormous and elaborate water
defenses.

CAMBRIDGE E5

Access to many of the
buildings and colleges is limited.
Check with the tourist office
first. Colleges are listed
chronologically by founding
date. Because of continuous
changes and renovations, the
buildings are (unless completely
discrete) listed under the
relevant college.

Tourist Information: British
Tourist Authority, Wheeler
Street (tel. 358977).

Museums: Fitzwilliam Museum,
Trumpington Street. Excellent
collection of 16th- to 20th-c
British painters (Reynolds,
Gainsborough, Augustus John,
etc.). French, Dutch, German,
and Italian (Titian) schools are
well represented.
    Rubens's *Adoration of the
Magi* is in King's College
Chapel.

52 CHURCH OF THE   1130
    HOLY SEPULCHRE
Bridge Street/Round Church
    Street *C3*

Drastically restored in the
Norman fashion by A. Salvin.

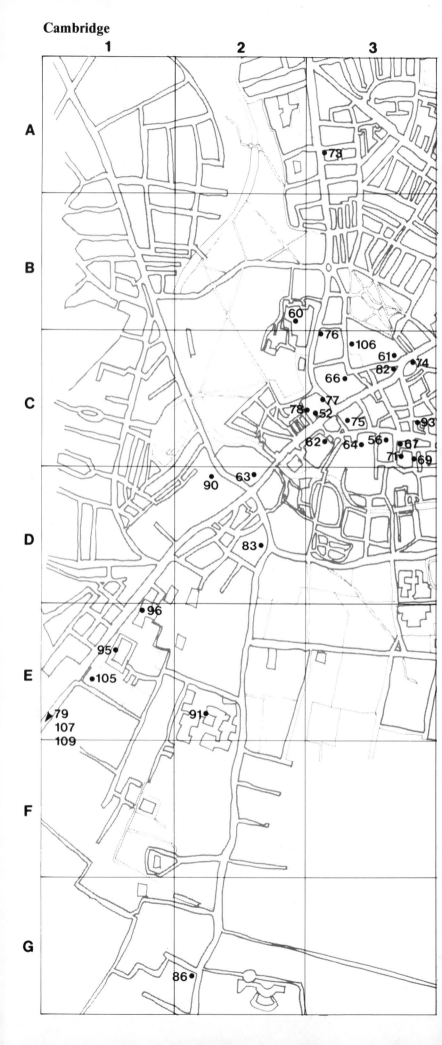

Cambridge

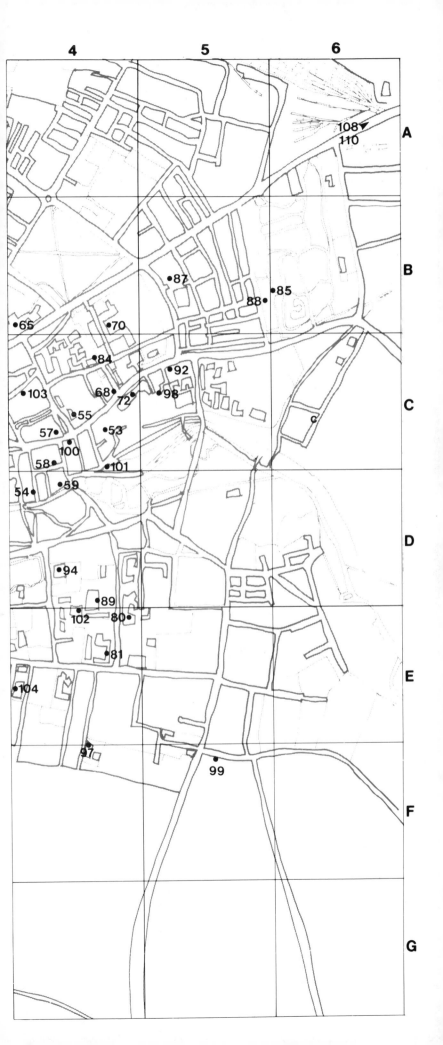

53 PETERHOUSE   founded 1284
COLLEGE
Trumpington Street, next to the
Fitzwilliam Museum *C4*

The oldest college in
Cambridge.
First court: South side—
original hall incorporated in
the "new" hall. The 17th-c
Laudian Chapel is in the
court's center.
Second (Gisborne) court:
South side—hall and
combination room (1871) by
George Gilbert Scott, Jr.
The stained glass is by W.
Morris from designs by F. M.
Brown and E. Burne-Jones.

54 CLARE   founded 1338
COLLEGE
Trinity Lane *D4*

Originally founded as
University Hall in 1326. The
present buildings (1638–1715)
were built by J. Wesley, then
R. Grumbold. Behind is Clare
Bridge (1640). The Chapel
(1763–69) is by J. Burrough.

55 PEMBROKE   founded 1347
COLLEGE
Trumpington Street/Pembroke
Street *C4*

Chapel   1663–64
Sir Christopher Wren
Wren's first complete
building (commissioned by
his uncle, the Bishop of Ely).
Extended by George Gilbert
Scott, Jr., in 1880.

Hall, library, and   1873–75
master's lodge
A. Waterhouse
Rooms added above the hall
by M. Webb (1926).

New building   1883
(on the east)
George Gilbert Scott, Jr.

56 GONVILLE   founded 1348
AND CAIUS COLLEGE
Trinity Street *C3*

Original entry through Gate of
Humility. Tree Court
(1868–70) by A. Waterhouse.
Pass through Gate of Virtue
(1567) to Caius Court, added

by Dr. Caius in 1557. The Gate
of Honour exits onto Senate
House Passage. Gonville Court
(14th c), refaced in 1753, is to
the north.

57 CORPUS   founded 1352
CHRISTI COLLEGE
Trumpington Street/Pembroke
Street *C4*

Front Court (1823–27) by
W. Wilkins. The Old Court
(enter through NE corner of
Front Court) is the most
complete example of a medieval
college court in Cambridge.

58 KING'S   founded 1441
COLLEGE
King's Parade *C4*
Great Court

Chapel   1446–1515
(north side)
The glory of the university.
Fan vaulting by J. Wastell.
The wooden choir screen
(1531– 36) and organ (1688)
divide the chapel into two.
Rubens's *Adoration of the
Magi* is behind the altar.

Fellows' Building   1723–29
(west side)
J. Gibbs

South Range,   1824–28
gatehouse, and screen
W. Wilkins

59 QUEEN'S   founded 1448
COLLEGE
Silver Street/Queen's Lane *D4*
First court: Hall (18th-c
woodwork), library, and
chapel.

Cloister court: North
side—President's Lodge
(1460–95). The timbered
galley above was added in
1537. Off this court is the
Mathematical Bridge (1749)
over the Cam designed by
W. Etheridge. Rebuilt in
1867.

Erasmus Building (1959) by
B. Spence and Partners.

60 JESUS   founded 1496
COLLEGE
Jesus Lane *B2*
Chapel   1849–53
(renovation)
A. W. N. Pugin
Screen, stalls, and altar by
Pugin. Ceiling (1867) by
W. Morris. Stained glass
windows by F. M. Brown and
E. Burne-Jones.

New North Court   1963–65
D. Roberts and Partners

61 CHRIST'S   founded 1505
   COLLEGE
   St. Andrews Street *C3*

Fellows' Building   1640–42
(in the second court)
Hall rebuilt in 1876 by George
Gilbert Scott, Jr.

62 ST. JOHN'S   founded 1511
   COLLEGE
   St. John's Street *C3*

First court: Built 1510–20. On
the north side is the Chapel
(1864–69) by Sir George
Gilbert Scott.

Second court: Built
1598–1602 by R. Symons.

New court: Built by T.
Rickman and H. Hutchinson
in the Gothic style (1825–31).
Hutchinson's Bridge of Sighs
over the river Cam joins the
New Court to the older
buildings.

Cripp's Building (1963–68),
between New court and
Magdalene College, is by
Powell and Moya.

63 MAGDALENE   founded 1542
   COLLEGE
   Magdalene Street *D2*

17th-c Pepysian library.

64 TRINITY   founded 1546
   COLLEGE
   Trinity Lane *C3*

Great Court: Great Gate
(1518–35). The fountain
(1602) in the center was
rebuilt in 1715. The Chapel
(1564) is on the north. On
the west is King Edward's
Gate (1428– 32), moved by
Nevile in 1599, and the Hall
(1604–8), a copy of the

Middle Temple Hall,
London, also by Nevile.
Nevile's Court (1612). The
west side was closed by the
Library (1676–95, by Sir
Christopher Wren). The
bookcases inside were carved
by G. Gibbons. Note that the
library floor is level with the
bottom of the (mannerist)
arches of the ground-floor
arcade.

New Court (1823–25)
by W. Wilkins.

Senior combination rooms
(1963–65) by T. Dannat.

65 EMMANUEL   founded 1584
   COLLEGE
   Emmanuel Street/St.
   Andrew's Street *B4*
   Chapel and cloister   1666–74
   Sir Christopher Wren

66 SIDNEY   founded 1596
   SUSSEX COLLEGE
   Sidney Street *C3*
   R. Symons

Extended by Sir J. Wyatville,
1831–32. Chapel enlarged and
altered by T. H. Lyon (1912).

67 SENATE HOUSE   1722–30
   King's Parade *C3*
   J. Gibbs

68 FITZWILLIAM   1727
   HOUSE
   32 Trumpington Street *C4*

69 OLD SCHOOLS   1754–58
   (East Range)
   King's Parade *C3*
   J. Burrough

Built by S. Wright.

70 DOWNING   founded 1800
   COLLEGE
   Regent Street *B4*
   W. Wilkins

Greek revival. Begun 1807–21.
Ultimately completed by Sir
H. Baker. Combination Room
(1972) by Howell, Killick,
Partridge, Amis.

71 UNIVERSITY   1836–42
   LIBRARY
   Senate House Passage *C3*
   C. R. Cockerell

Now the Squire Law Library.
Only the north range of
Cockerell's scheme was built.

72 FITZWILLIAM   1837–47
   MUSEUM
   Trumpington Street *C4*
   G. Basevi

Completed by E. M Barry and
C. R. Cockerell. Extension
(1959–65) by D. Roberts and
Partners.

73 CHRIST CHURCH   1839
   Newmarket Road *A3*
   A. Poynter

74 ST. ANDREW   1843
   THE GREAT
   (church)
   St. Andrew's Street *C3*
   A. Poynter

75 WHEWELL'S   1859–68
    COURT
Trinity College (between Trinity
    Street and Sidney Street) *C3*
A. Salvin

76 ALL SAINTS   1864
(church)
Jesus Lane *C3*
G. F. Bodley

The interior decoration is by
Morris and Company.

77 PITT CLUB   1865
Jesus Lane *C3*
Sir M. D. Wyatt

78 UNION SOCIETY   1866
Round Church Street *C3*
A. Waterhouse

79 GIRTON COLLEGE   1873–87
Huntingdon Road *E1*
A. and P. (son) Waterhouse

Woodlands Court (1931) is by
M. Waterhouse (grandson).

80 NEWNHAM COLLEGE   1875
Sidgwick Avenue *E4*
B. Champneys

Library extension (1961) by
C. Grillet.

81 SELWYN COLLEGE   1882
Sidgwick Avenue *E4*
Sir A. Blomfield

82 LLOYDS BANK   1891
Sidney Street *C3*
A. and P. Waterhouse

Extended (south section) in
1935.

83 WESTMINSTER   1899
    COLLEGE
Queen's Road *D2*
H. T. Hare

84 ZOOLOGY BUILDING 1901–4
Downing Street *C4*
E. S. Prior

85 DIRECTOR'S   1924
    HOUSE
Botanic Gardens
Bateman Street *B6*
M. H. Baillie Scott

•Also by Baillie Scott are nos.
29, 30, 48, 54, and 56 Storeys
Way (behind Wychfield; see
entry 105).

86 WHITE HOUSE   1931
1 Conduit Head Road *G2*
G. Checkley

•Also by Checkley on Conduit
Head Road is Thurso (1932,
now Willow House). Further
along is Shwams (1939), a house
by J. B. White.

87 SCOTT POLAR   1933–34
    RESEARCH INSTITUTE
Lensfield Road *B5*
Sir H. Baker

88 ST. MARY'S   1953–64
    CONVENT SCHOOL
Bateman Street *B5*
D. Roberts and Partners

89 ARTS FACULTY   1956–64
Sidgwick Avenue *D4*
Casson, Conder and
Partners

90 CASTLE HILL   1957–58
    HOSTEL
Clare College, Chesterton
    Lane *D2*
D. Roberts and Partners

91 CHURCHILL   1958–73
    COLLEGE
Storey's Way *E2*
Richard Sheppard, Robson and
Partners

92 SCHOOL OF   1958–59
    ARCHITECTURE
(extension)
Scroope Terrace *C5*
C. St. John Wilson and A.
Hardy

93 MARKET HOSTEL   1960–62
King's College, Market Hill,
    St. Edwards Passage *C3*
Architect's Co-Partnership

94 HARVEY COURT   1960–62
Gonville and Caius College
West Road *D4*
Sir L. Martin, C. St. John
Wilson, and P. Hodgkinson

95 FITZWILLIAM   1961 onward
    HOUSE
Huntingdon Road *E1*
Denys Lasdun and Partners

96 NEW HALL   1962–64
Huntingdon Road *E1*
Chamberlin, Powell and Bon

97 LECKHAMPTON   1963–64
    HOUSE
Corpus Christi College
Grange Road *F4*
P. Dowson of Arup Associates

98 WILLIAM STONE   1963–64
    BUILDING
Pembroke College (behind St.
    Peter's Terrace) *C5*
Sir L. Martin and C. St. John
Wilson

99 TWO HOUSES   1963–64
2, 2a Grantchester Road *F5*
C. St. John Wilson

100 KEYNES HALL   1963–67
King's College and St.
    Catherine's College
King's Parade *C4*
F. Atkinson of James Cubitt
and Partners

101 UNIVERSITY   1964–68
    CENTRE
Granta Place *C4*
Howell, Killick, Partridge
and Amis

102 HISTORY FACULTY 1964–69
between West Road and
Sidgwick Avenue *E4*
J. Stirling and M. Wilford

Weathering very badly.

103 MATHEMATICAL 1966–69
LABORATORY
Corn Exchange Street *C4*
P. Dowson of Arup Associates

104 CLARE HALL 1966–69
Herschel Road *E4*
R. Erskine (in association with
Twist and Whitley)

105 WYCHFIELD 1967–69
Trinity Hall
Huntingdon Road *E1*
P. Dowson of Arup Associates

106 CHRIST'S 1967–70
COLLEGE HOSTEL
King Street *C3*
Denys Lasdun and Partners

Outskirts of Cambridge

107 MANOR HOUSE 1848–51
Wilburton (29 km/18 mi N of
Cambridge) *E1*
A. W. N. Pugin

108 MIDDLEFIELD 1908
(country house)
Stapleford (8 km/5 mi SE of
Cambridge) *A6*
Sir E. Lutyens

109 VILLAGE COLLEGE 1938
Impington Hall Estate (just N
of Cambridge) *E1*
W. Gropius and M. Fry

110 PATSCENTRE 1976
Melbourn (16 km/10 mi S of
Cambridge) *A6*
R. Piano and R. Rogers

CANTERBURY F6

111 CANTERBURY 1070
CATHEDRAL onward

Rebuilt for the next four
hundred years after a fire in
1174. The Norman crypt (1093–
1107) has survived. The choir
(1175–85) begun by William of
Sens is the first authentic
Gothic building in England.
Choir screen built in 1304.
Nave rebuilt (1375–1421) in
Perpendicular style. Crossing
tower built from 1495–1503.
Thomas à Becket (martyred in
the NW transept in 1170) was
canonized in 1173. The Trinity
Chapel (1178–80), a shrine to his
memory, has many 13th-c
stained glass windows. The very
fine circular Corona Chapel
beyond is also known as
Becket's Crown.
•Take the Brick Walk (N of
Cathedral), pass first through
the Infirmary Court, then the
Dark Entry, into the Green
Court, a unique arcaded
Norman courtyard.

112 ST. AUGUSTINE'S 1846–73
COLLEGE
Monastery Road
W. Butterfield

CARDIFF F3

Museums: National Museum of
Wales, Cathays Park. Welsh
and British 18th- to 20th-c
works. Excellent French
impressionist collection.

113 CARDIFF 1090 onward
CASTLE
Castle Street

Built on a Roman fortified
site (some parts of which still
survive). Completely restored
in the Gothic style by W.
Burges (1868–81) for the
Marquis of Bute. Magnificent
interiors. •Castle Coch
(1875–81) at Tongwynlaif
(10 km/6 mi N of Cardiff),
again by Burges for the Marquis
of Bute, is an equally lavish
Gothic fantasy with interiors
more opulent than those in
Cardiff Castle.

114 CITY HALL   1897–1906
       AND LAW COURTS
    Cathays Park
    H. Lanchester and E. Rickards

Vigorous baroque building.

CARLISLE B3

115 CARLISLE   1123–1419
       CATHEDRAL
    Abbey Street

    Norman south transept.
    Decorated choir (1292–1362)
    with fine east window (ca.
    1380).

CHALFONT ST. GILES F5
6 km (4 mi) NE of Beaconsfield

116 SHRUB'S WOOD   1934–35
    (house)
    5 km (3 mi) ENE of Chalfont
       St. Giles
    E. Mendelsohn and
    S. Chermayeff

CHATSWORTH HOUSE D4
6 km (4 mi) E of Bakewell

117 CHATSWORTH   1687–1707
       HOUSE
    W. Talman

    Talman rebuilt the south and
    east facades. Baroque interiors
    and chapel. Wall and ceiling
    paintings by A. Verrio and L.
    Laguerre.

CHEADLE D4
15 km (9 mi) SE of Stoke-on-
Trent

118 ST. GILES   1841–46
    (church)
    A. W. N. Pugin

CHESTER D3

119 CHESTER   ca. 1100–1490
       CATHEDRAL
    Northgate Street

    Totally restored (1868–78)
    by Sir George Gilbert Scott.
    Magnificent 14th-c choir stalls
    and fine Lady Chapel.

120 ROWS   13th c onward
    Eastgate Street/Bridge Street

    Half-timbered houses linked by
    a continuous second-floor
    gallery overlooking the street.

121 TOWN WALLS   14th c

    The towers were rebuilt in the
    19th c. The walls, which are
    complete, are original.

CHICHESTER G5

122 ROMAN PALACE   A.D. 75
       OF FISHBOURNE
    between Chichester and Bosham

    A large palace with some
    excellent mosaics.

123 CHICHESTER   1080 onward
       CATHEDRAL
    St. Richard's Lane

    Burned in 1114 and 1186. Lady
    Chapel, 1288–1302; 14th-c
    cloisters; 15th-c bell tower;
    spire rebuilt, 1861–66.

124 FESTIVAL   1961–62
       THEATRE
    Broyle Road, Oaklands Park
    Powell and Moya

CHORLEYWOOD F5
24 km (15 mi) NW of London

125 THE ORCHARD   1899
    (house)
    Shire Lane
    C. F. A. Voysey

    Own house. •Also by Voysey
    are Hollybank (1904) next door
    and an extension to Hill Cottage
    on Shire Lane.

CLUMBER PARK D4
8 km (5 mi) SE of Worksop

126 CLUMBER CHAPEL   1886–89
    G. F. Bodley

COLCHESTER E6

127 TOWN HALL   1898–1902
    High Street
    Sir J. Belcher

128 UNIVERSITY   1965 onward
       OF ESSEX
    8 km (5 mi) NE of Colchester
    Architects' Co-Partnership

COMPTON F5
5 km (3 mi) SW of Guildford

129 G. F. WATTS   1896
       MEMORIAL CHAPEL
    Cemetery on the Guildford
       Road
    M. Watts, assisted by local
    workshops organized by her.

COMPTON WYNYATES E4
16 km (10 mi) W of Banbury

130 COMPTON   1480–ca. 1520
       WYNYATES

    Tudor mansion.

CONWAY D2

131 CONWAY CASTLE   1283–88

    Built for Edward I. An
    impressive ruin.

COVENTRY E4

132 NEW CATHEDRAL   1956–62
    Priory Street
    Sir B. Spence

The design incorporates the remains of the old cathedral (destroyed in 1940). Many works in glass and tapestry by modern artists.

CRAGSIDE B4
house 0.8 km (0.5 mi) E of Rothbury

133 CRAGSIDE   1870–85
(house)
R. N. Shaw

Spectacular site and architecture.

CULZEAN CASTLE A2
19 km (12 mi) SW of Ayr

134 CULZEAN CASTLE 1777–92
R. Adam

Dramatic site on the coast. Massive exteriors in deliberate contrast to the delicate interiors.

CUMBERNAULD A2
new town

135 PARISH CHURCH   1962
Kildrum
A. Reiach and S. Renton

136 CUMBERNAULD   1967
TOWN CENTRE
Hugh Wilson, Dudley Leaker and Associates, with G. Copcutt

137 OUR LADY'S   1968
HIGH SCHOOL
Dowanfield Road
Gillespie, Kidd and Coia

DARLINGTON B4

138 CUMMINS ENGINE   1965
COMPANY PLANT
Yarm Road
Kevin Roche, John Dinkeloo and Associates

DEAL F6

139 DEAL CASTLE   16th c
on the seashore

Artillery fort.

DENHAM F5

140 RANK LABORATORIES 1936
on the A412
W. Gropius and M. Fry

DOVER F6

141 DOVER   1180–86 onward
CASTLE

Keep by Henry II. Outer defenses strengthened ca. 1240. Inside are the Pharos (lighthouse—lower part Roman) and St. Mary, a Saxon church.

DREWSTEIGNTON G2
3 km (2 mi) NE of Chagford.

142 CASTLE DROGO   1910–30
Sir E. Lutyens

An interpretation of a medieval castle overlooking the river Teign. Only half the projected scheme was built. Tiny chapel with massive stonework of great power. Superb formal rose garden and croquet lawn.

DUDDLESWELL F5
10 km (6 mi) S of East Grinstead

143 THE CROW'S NEST   1904
(house)
Ashdown Forest
M. H. Baillie Scott

DUNSTABLE E5

144 GLIDING CLUB   1935–36
Tring Road
C. Nicholson

DUNSTANBURGH CASTLE A4
on the coast, 3 km (2 mi) E of Embleton

145 DUNSTANBURGH   1313
CASTLE   onward

Now ruined. Magnificently sited.

DURHAM B4

146 DURHAM   1093–1490
     CATHEDRAL

The finest Norman building in
the country. The choir, transept, west towers, and nave
are Norman (built 1093–1133).
The nave is outstanding in its
skillful use of compound
piers attached to the wall,
alternating with vigorously
patterned round piers. The
nave and transept vaulting are
possibly the earliest pointed
ribbed vaulting to be built in
Europe. Unusual Lady Chapel
(Galilee) added by H. de
Puiset, 1170–75. The Chapel of
Nine Altars (1242–80), added
by Bishop Poore, replaced the
east apse. The central tower
was built from 1465–90; the
cloisters, 1400–1490. The
cathedral was unfortunately
"restored" (1778–99) by J.
Wyatt ("The Destroyer"), who
demolished the 12th-c chapter
house. A replica was built in
1895. Further restoration by
Sir George Gilbert Scott, ca.
1870. •Durham Castle, now
part of the university, is close
by.

147 DUNELM HOUSE   1964
     Durham University
     Architects' Co-Partnership

EAST GRINSTEAD F5

148 STANDEN   1892
     (house)
     near Saint Hill
     P. Webb

EAST KNOYLE F4
8 km (5 mi) N of Shaftesbury

149 CLOUDS   1879–91
     (house)
     P. Webb

Altered.

EDINBURGH A3

Museums: National Gallery of
Scotland (1850, by W. H.
Playfair), The Mound. An
outstanding collection of
European paintings from the
15th to 19th c.
   Scottish National Gallery of
Modern Art, Royal Botanic
Gardens. 20th-c paintings.

150 CASTLE   11th c onward
     Esplanade

Magnificently sited. The tiny
St. Margaret's Chapel (1090)
inside is the oldest building in
Edinburgh. Scottish National
War Memorial (1918–27) by
Sir R. Lorimer.

151 ST. GILES'   1385–1495
     CATHEDRAL
     High Street

Badly restored from 1830–33.
The interior, which had been
divided into four sections, was
restored from 1873–83. The
Thistle Chapel (1909–11) in the
Gothic style is by Sir
R. Lorimer.

152 HOLYROOD   1670–79
     PALACE
     Canongate
     Sir W. Bruce

State apartments within. The
ruined 13th-c Chapel Royal
is adjacent.

153 REGISTER HOUSE   1774–92
     Princes Street (opposite North
       Bridge)
     R. Adam

154 UNIVERSITY   1789 onward
     Chambers Street
     R. Adam

Monumental facade.
Completed (1815–30) by W. H.
Playfair after Adam's death in
1792. Dome added by Sir
R. Anderson in 1887.

155 CHARLOTTE SQUARE   1791
     R. Adam

Many fine streets with
Georgian houses are in this
area, including George Street,
Princes Street, Queen Street,
Royal Circus, and a grand
sequence (by G. Graham) from
Randolph Circle through
Ainsley Place to Moray Place.

156 NATIONAL   1822–25
     MONUMENT
     Calton Hill
     C. R. Campbell and W. H.
     Playfair

Unfinished copy of the
Parthenon.

157 ROYAL HIGH   1825–29
     SCHOOL
Regent Road
T. Hamilton

Greek revival.

158 DEAN BRIDGE   1832
(stone)
off Queensferry Road
T. Telford

159 SIR WALTER   1840–46
     SCOTT MONUMENT
Princes Street Garden
G. Meikle Kemp

160 ST. MARY'S   1874–79
     EPISCOPAL
     CATHEDRAL
Palmerston Place
Sir George Gilbert Scott

161 NUFFIELD   1968
     TRANSPLANTATION
     SURGERY UNIT
Western General Hospital
P. Womersley

Outskirts of Edinburgh

162 ROSSLYN CHAPEL   1446
Roslin (13 km/8 mi S of
   Edinburgh)

Remarkable carvings.

163 HOPETOUN   1721–54
     HOUSE
South Queensferry (3 km/2 mi
   W of the Forth Road Bridge)
W. Adam

164 FORTH RAILWAY   1882
     BRIDGE
Queensferry (10 km/6 mi W of
   Edinburgh town center)
Fowler and Baker

A magnificent structure. •The
Forth Road Bridge (suspension)
next to it was built from
1960–64 by Mott, Hay and
Anderson with Freeman, Fox
and Partners.

ELY E5

165 ELY CATHEDRAL   1083
                          onward

Norman nave, extended six
bays (eastward) in 1240. The
central tower collapsed in 1322.

The splendid octagonal lantern
(1322–40) that replaced it, ''the
only Gothic dome in existence,'' was built in wood by
W. Hurly. The three Decorated
choir bays adjacent to the
tower were rebuilt after its
collapse. The Lady Chapel
(1321–49) contains exceptional
carving, originally poly-
chromed. (Every statue's head
was cut off during the Reformation.) The West front,
once symmetrical, is now
missing the northwest transept;
the porch (1198–1215) in front
is Early English.

ESCOMB B4

3 km (2 mi) W of Bishop
Auckland

166 ST. JOHN'S CHAPEL   ca. 700

Saxon. Built from Roman
materials.

ESHER F5

167 CLAREMONT   1734
(country house)
1 km (0.5 mi) SE of Esher
W. Kent

Transformed into a Palladian
mansion by L. Brown in 1772.
Interiors by H. Holland and
Sir J. Soane. The garden, the
earliest (surviving) to be
designed in the English
landscape manner, was begun
by Sir J. Vanbrugh in 1720,
extended and improved by
Kent.

168 THE HOMEWOOD   1938
(house)
P. Gwynne

Built for himself.

EWENNY PRIORY F3

3 km (2 mi) S of Bridgend

169 EWENNY   1141 onward
     PRIORY

Fortified Norman church.

EXETER G3

170 EXETER   1107–1394
     CATHEDRAL
Cathedral Yard

Outstanding Geometric
Decorated cathedral. Norman
transeptal towers (1107–37).

FALMER F5

171 FALMER HOUSE   1960
     AND PHYSICS BUILDING
University of Sussex
Spence, Bonnington, and
Collins

FONTHILL ABBEY
F4
16 km (10 mi) NW of Wilton

172 FONTHILL 1796–1812
 ABBEY
J. Wyatt

Enormous neo-Gothic mansion,
now totally ruined.

FOUNTAINS ABBEY
C4
6 km (4 mi) SW of Ripon

173 FOUNTAINS 1132–1500
 ABBEY

Cistercian monastery now in
ruins. The buildings, although
roofless, are well preserved and
hauntingly beautiful.

FRINTON–ON–SEA
E6

174 THE HOMESTEAD 1905
(house)
Second Avenue/Holland Road
C. F. A. Voysey

GALASHIELS A3

175 BERNAT KLEIN 1972
 DESIGN STUDIO
P. Womersley

GLASGOW A2

Art Society: Charles Rennie
Mackintosh Society, 866
Garscube Road (tel. 546-6600).

Museums: Glasgow Art Gallery
and Museum, Kelvingrove
Park. One of the best art
galleries in Britain. Outstanding
French impressionist paintings.
   Hunterian Art Gallery,
University of Glasgow.
Rembrandt, Whistler,
Mackintosh (two reconstructed
interiors), etc.
   Pollock House, Pollock
Park. Built by W. Adam. The
Stirling Maxwell Collection
includes El Greco, Goya, and
other Spanish masters. The
Burrell Collection is to be
installed here soon (at present in
the Glasgow Art Gallery).

176 CATHEDRAL 1200–ca. 1500
Castle Street/Cathedral Street

Exceptionally well preserved.
The crypt (1233–56) is a Gothic
masterpiece. •The Necropolis
behind the cathedral is worth a
visit.

177 CALEDONIA 1856–57
 ROAD FREE CHURCH
Caledonia Road
A. Thomson

Greek revival. Burned in
1965. Unrestored.

178 CHURCH 1859
St. Vincent Street
A. Thomson

Greek revival. •Also by
Thomson is the church (1867)
in Queen's Park.

179 GLASGOW 1893
 HERALD BUILDING
60 Mitchell Street
C. R. Mackintosh

180 GLASGOW 1896–99
 SCHOOL OF ART
167 Renfrew Street
Garnethill
C. R. Mackintosh

The Library wing was added
from 1907–9.

181 CRANSTON 1897
 TEA-ROOMS
Buchanan Street
C.R. Mackintosh

Now Mackintosh Gift Shop.

182 QUEEN'S 1897–99
 CROSS CHURCH
866 Garscube Road, Woodside
C. R. Mackintosh

Now the Charles Rennie
Mackintosh Society.

183 WILLOW TEA-ROOMS 1903
217 Sauchiehall Street
C. R. Mackintosh

The facade is altered, and the
interior has been rebuilt in the
Glasgow University Museum.

184 SCOTLAND 1904–6
 STREET SCHOOL
225 Scotland Street
C. R. Mackintosh

185 CHURCH OF OUR 1964
 LADY OF GOOD
 COUNCIL
Dennistoun
Gillespie, Kidd and Coia

Good use of a very small site.
Face brick walls. The off shutter
concrete columns support an
asymmetric roof clad in
redwood.

186 LIBRARY 1969
Glasgow University
W. Whitfield

Outskirts of Glasgow

   The following entries
(187–91) are listed here because

of their proximity to Glasgow. They are indicated on the general map of Great Britain.

187 WINDYHILL   1899–1901
       (house)
       Rowantree Hill Road,
         Kilmacolm (25 km/15 mi W
         of Glasgow) A2
       C. R. Mackintosh

188 WHITE HOUSE   1899–1900
       5 Upper Colquhoun Street,
         Helensburgh (32 km/20 mi
         NW of Glasgow) A2
       M. H. Baillie Scott

189 HILL HOUSE   1902–4
       8 Upper Colquhoun Street,
         Helensburgh A2
       C. R. Mackintosh

Original interiors and furnishings. Open to visit.

190 ST. BRIDE'S CHURCH   1960
       East Kilbride A2
       Gillespie, Kidd and Coia

191 ST. PETER'S   1966
       COLLEGE
       Cardross A2
       Gillespie, Kidd and Coia

This seminary is well integrated with Kilmahew House (1870 by J. Burnet, Sr.) next door. The obvious (and successful) influence of Le Corbusier is apparent.

GLOUCESTER E4

192 GLOUCESTER   1089–1498
       CATHEDRAL
       St. Mary's Street

Norman interior (1089–1164). Exterior rebuilt from 1329–37 in the Perpendicular style. West facade, south porch, and crossing tower (1420–57); Lady Chapel (1457–98). Richly decorated choir. Huge east window (glass ca. 1350). Very early fan-vaulted cloister (1351–1412).

Outskirts of Gloucester

193 ST. MARY'S   ca. 9th c
       CHURCH
       Deerhurst (14 km/9 mi W of
         Gloucester) E3

Well-preserved Saxon church incorporated into the later Norman extension.

GODALMING F5

194 CHAPEL   1922–27
       Charterhouse School
       Sir Giles Gilbert Scott

GRANTHAM D5

195 HARLAXTON   1834–55
       MANOR

Exterior (1834–37) by A. Salvin. Satisfyingly garish Victorian baroque interiors (1838–55) by W. Burn.

GREAT MALVERN E3

196 MEMORIAL LIBRARY   1924
       Malvern College
       Sir A. Webb

GREAT WARLEY F5
near Brentwood

197 ST. MARY   1904
       THE VIRGIN
       (church)
       C. H. Townsend

The art nouveau decoration in silver, bronze, and mother-of-pearl is by Sir W. R. Stephens.

GUILDFORD F5

198 COURT III   1968–71
       HOUSING
       University of Surrey,
         Stag Hill
       R. Maguire and K. Murray

HALLAND F5

199 BENTLEY WOOD   1934
       (house)
       1 km (0.5 mi) SW of Halland
       S. Chermayeff

Very badly altered.

HARDWICK HALL D4
house 3 km (2 mi) S of Chesterfield

200 HARDWICK HALL   1591–97
       R. Smythson

Elizabethan manor ("more glass than wall") with most original furnishings intact.

HASLEMERE F5

201 OLIVETTI   1969–73
       TRAINING CENTER
       J. Stirling

Sophisticated extension, using glass-reinforced polyester wall and roof components.

HATFIELD F5
34 km (21 mi) N of London

202 HATFIELD HOUSE 1607–11

Jacobean. Partly designed by
R. Lyming. Good interiors.
Portrait of Elizabeth I by
I. Oliver.

HEREFORD E3

203 HEREFORD ca. 1070–1530
     CATHEDRAL
Castle Street

Norman nave, south transept
and choir. North transept
rebuilt (1250–88). 15th-c
cloisters. Badly restored by
J. Wyatt. Reworked by Sir
George Gilbert Scott (1856–63).
New facade in 14th-c style
(1902–8) by J. O. Scott (son).
Mappa Mundi (ca. 1290), an
early map of the world, is in the
choir.

HERNE BAY F6

204 ST. BARTHOLOMEW 1908
(church)
King Edward Avenue
W. D. Caröe

HEVENINGHAM HALL E6
house 6 km (4 mi) SW of
Halesworth

205 HEVENINGHAM 1778–87
     HALL
Sir R. Taylor
Interiors by J. Wyatt

HOAR CROSS D4
3 km (2 mi) E of Abbot's
Bromley

206 HOLY ANGELS' 1872–76
(church)
G. Bodley and T. Garner

HOLT D6
(Norfolk)
16 km (10 mi) W of Cromer

207 HOME PLACE 1903–5
Cromer Road
E. S. Prior

Supervised by R. Wells and D.
Blow. Now a convalescent
home.

HOUGHTON HALL D6
house 16 km (10 mi) E of
Fakenham

208 HOUGHTON HALL 1722–26
(house)
C. Campbell

Interiors by W. Kent.

CASTLE HOWARD C4
24 km (15 mi) NE of York

209 CASTLE 1699–1726
     HOWARD
Sir J. Vanbrugh and
N. Hawksmoor

Fine entry hall. Uneven interiors
(some left unrestored after a
fire). The mausoleum (1729) is
by Hawksmoor.

HULL C5
(Kingston upon Hull)

210 SCHOOL OF ART 1902–4
Anlaby Road
H. Lanchester and E. Rickards

211 UNIVERSITY 1958 onward
     OF HULL
Northgate, Cottingham

Master plan by Sir L. Martin,
also Middleton Hall and Faculty
of Arts. Brynmor Library
(1957–59) by Forsyth and
Partners. Gulbenkian Centre by
P. Moro (1966–68). Grant and
Reckitt Hall by Gillespie, Kidd
and Coia (1969).

HUNSTANTON D5

212 SECONDARY 1950–53
     MODERN SCHOOL
Downs Road
A. and P. Smithson

Inspired by L. Mies van de
Rohe but with a strongly English
sensibility, this was a key
postwar building that led
directly to the New Brutalism
movement.

ILKLEY C4

213 HEATHCOTE 1906
(house)
King's Road
Sir E. Lutyens

JERVAULX ABBEY C4
6 km (4 mi) NW of Masham

214 JERVAULX ABBEY 1156
(ruined) onward

Beautiful surroundings.

KEDLESTON HALL D4
house 8 km (5 mi) NW of Derby

215 KEDLESTON 1759–65
     HALL
(house)
M. Brettingham and J. Paine

Completed and vastly improved
by R. Adam. The two south
wings were never built. The
garden facade and monumental
hall are by Adam.

KIMBOLTON E5
22 km (14 mi) N of Bedford

216 KIMBOLTON   1708–20
     CASTLE
     Sir J. Vanbrugh

Complete remodeling.
Gatehouse by R. Adam.

KING'S SOMBORNE F4
near Stockbridge

217 MARSHCOURT   1901–4
     (country house)
     Sir E. Lutyens

Extended in 1924.

KIRBY HALL E5
house E of Corby

218 KIRBY HALL   1570–75
     (country house)

Dignified courtyard. Very
early use of giant Corinthian
order. Partly roofed.

KNUTSFORD D3

219 BEXTON CROFT   1895–96
     (house)
     Toft Road
     M. H. Baillie Scott

220 THE KING'S   1907–8
     COFFEE HOUSE
     King Street
     R. H. Watt

•Watt was also responsible
for the Ruskin Rooms (1904)
and the Gaskell Memorial
Tower (1907–8). Other houses
by Watt on Legh Road include
The Old Croft (1895, tower
1907) and Moorgarth (1898).

LANCASTER C3

221 TOWN HALL   1906–9
     Dalton Square
     E. Mountford

222 ASHTON   1907–9
     MEMORIAL
     Williamson Park
     Sir J. Belcher

Outstanding baroque building
that dominates its hilltop site.

223 UNIVERSITY   1963 onward
     OF LANCASTER
     Bailrigg, S of Lancaster
     Bridgewater, Shepheard and
     Epstein

LANCING G5
1.5 km (1 mi) inland from
Worthing

224 LANCING   1848–58
     COLLEGE
     R. C. Carpenter

•The French Gothic chapel
(begun in 1868) is by R. H.
Carpenter (son).

LAYER MARNEY E6
5 km (3 mi) SE of Tiptree

225 LAYER MARNEY   1500–1520
     TOWER
     (house)

Eight-story Tudor gatehouse.

LEEDS C4

226 TOWN HALL   1853–58
     Victoria Square
     C. Brodrick

227 CORN EXCHANGE   1861–63
     Kirkgate
     C. Brodrick

Oval plan. Spectacular iron
dome.

LEEDS CASTLE F5
9 km (6 mi) SE of Maidstone

228 LEEDS   13th c onward
     CASTLE

Built in the middle of a lake.

LEICESTER E4

229 ENGINEERING   1960–63
     LABORATORIES
     Leicester University, off
     University Road, Victoria
     Park
     J. Stirling and J. Gowan

University laid out by Sir
L. Martin.

LETCHWORTH E5

230 LETCHWORTH   1903
     GARDEN CITY   onward
     B. Parker and R. Unwin

Letchworth was the first garden
city in Britain. Based on
E. Howard's city-planning
concepts, outlined in his book,
Garden Cities of Tomorrow.
Became the prototype of
thousands of garden-city
schemes around the world.

LICHFIELD E4

231 LICHFIELD   1200–1360
     CATHEDRAL

Triple spires. The red
sandstone interior was
drastically restored, first by
J. Wyatt, then by Sir
George Gilbert Scott.

LINCOLN D5

232 NEWPORT ARCH   ca. A.D. 50
     Bailgate

Original Roman city-gate. The
Bailgate (street) was the center
of the Roman town.

233 STONEBROW 15th c
(gatehouse)
High Street

Guildhall above. •Many
attractive old buildings are
in this quarter, some dating
the 12th c.

234 LINCOLN 1070 onward
CATHEDRAL
Minster Yard

A magnificent building. Rebuilt
after fire (1141) and earthquake
(1185). The choir and east
transepts (1187–1200) are
among the earliest examples of
true Gothic architecture in
England. The west transepts
(notable Rose Windows north
and south), decagonal chapter
house and nave were built from
1209–53. The superb Angel
Choir (notable East Window)
extended the choir east,
1258–79. The north range of
the cloisters (fine view) and
library above (1280–99) were
rebuilt by Sir Christopher
Wren.

LINDISFARNE A4
on Holy Island (8 km/5 mi E of
Beal)

235 LINDISFARNE 1903 onward
CASTLE
Sir E. Lutyens

The castle, built in 1550, was
renovated by Lutyens for
E. Hudson, the owner of
Country Life magazine. •The
remains of Lindisfarne Priory
nearby date from 1090.

LITTLE MORETON HALL D4
house 6 km (4 mi) SW of
Congleton

236 LITTLE MORETON 16th c
HALL
(country house)

Outstanding half-timbered
house.

LIVERPOOL D3

Museum: Walker Art Gallery,
William Brown Street. Excellent
British collection. Also
Rembrandt, Corot, Degas,
Rubens, Martini, etc.

237 ALBERT DOCK 18th c
near Canning Place
J. Hartley

The docks are magnificent.

238 TOWN HALL 1754
Water Street
J. Wood the Younger (of Bath)

Extended in 1789.

239 ST. GEORGE'S 1839–54
HALL
Lime Street
H. L. Elmes

Interiors by C. R. Cockerell.

240 ORIEL CHAMBERS 1864–66
16 Cook Street
P. Ellis

The elevations clearly express
the cast-iron frame of the
building. A historic example
of functionalism, named in
innumerable histories of
architecture as a precursor of
the Chicago School.

241 ANGLICAN 1904–78
CATHEDRAL
St. James's Mount
Sir Giles Gilbert Scott

Scott won the design
competition to build this at the
age of twenty-two. Much
changed by Scott during
construction.

242 STUDENTS' UNION 1910–13
Bedford Street
Sir C. Reilly

Enlarged in 1935 and 1961.

243 CUNARD 1914–16
BUILDING
Pier Head
Mewès and Davis

244 METROPOLITAN 1929–60
**CATHEDRAL OF CHRIST
THE KING**
Mount Pleasant
Sir E. Lutyens

Lutyens won the commission
for this building in an open
design competition with a
superb design. Only the crypt
(1933–41) was built, however. A
second competition, held after
WWII, was won by Frederick
Gibberd. New design completed
in 1960.

Outskirts of Liverpool
The following entries
(245–47) are listed here because
of their proximity to
Liverpool. They are indicated
on the general map of Great
Britain.

245 PORT 1888 onward
SUNLIGHT
10 km (6 mi) S of Liverpool
(via the Mersey Tunnel) D3
W. H. Lever

Model village for the employees
of the Lever soap factory. The
architectural centerpiece of
the village, the Lady Lever
Gallery, has works by Turner,
Gainsborough, Reynolds,
Milais, Burne-Jones, etc.

246 ST. HELENS 1922–26
(church)
Church Street, St. Helens
(19 km/12 mi E of Liverpool)
D3
W. D. Caröe

247 ST. MONICA 1936
(church)
Fernhill Road, Bootle (5 km/
3 mi SE of Liverpool) D3
F. X. Velarde

LONDON F5

Tourist Information: British Tourist Authority, 64 St. James's Street (tel. 499-9325).

Architect's Institute: Royal Institute of British Architects, 66 Portland Place (tel. 580-5533). The institute has one of the finest architectural libraries in the world. (The Drawing Collection is at 21 Portman Square.)

Bookstores: Foyles, Charing Cross Road.
Zwemmer, 78 Charing Cross Road.

Maps: Geographers Map Company, 26 Gray's Inn Road.
Geographia, 63 Fleet Street.
Cook, Hammond and Kell, 22 Caxton Street (Ordnance Survey maps).

Museums: British Museum, Great Russell Street. Museum of history, archeology, and art. See entry 366.
Courtauld Institute Galleries, Woburn Square. Important impressionist works.
Dulwich College Picture Gallery. See entry 357.
Iveagh Bequest. See entry 344.
Hayward Gallery, South Bank. Arts Council of Great Britain.
William Morris Gallery in Water House, Lloyd Park, Forest Road, Walthamstow. Works by Morris and his school.
The National Gallery, Trafalgar Square. An outstanding collection of European art.
National Portrait Gallery, St. Martin's Place. Portraits of the English nation.
Queen's Gallery. See entry 303.
Tate Gallery, Millbank. British art from 1550 until today. Some 20th-c European works.
Victoria and Albert Museum, Thurloe Place. Decorative arts from all ages and countries. The finest collection in its field in the world. See entry 402.
The Wallace Collection, Hertford House, Manchester Square. Outstanding 18th-c French furniture and art. Also Hals (*Laughing Cavalier*), Rembrandt, Rubens, etc.

248 WESTMINSTER   11th c
    ABBEY   onward
Broad Sanctuary *E5*

Totally rebuilt from 1245 by H. de Reynes (for Henry III).

Nave completed (1375) by H. Yevele. The Henry VII chapel (1503-19) displays the most spectacular Late Perpendicular vaulting ever built. The tombs of Henry VII and Elizabeth of York (1512-18, by P. Torrigiano) in this chapel mark the beginning of the Renaissance in Britain. West towers (1722-45) by Sir Christopher Wren and N. Hawksmoor. Major restoration (1849-78) by Sir George Gilbert Scott, completed by J. L. Pearson in 1897.

249 TOWER   1066 onward
    OF LONDON
Tower Hill *C9*

White Tower (central keep) and Chapel of St. John (1077-97); Queens House (1540); Waterloo Barracks (1845) by A. Salvin.

250 WESTMINSTER   1097-99
    HALL
Palace of Westminster
Old Palace Yard *E6*

Rebuilt (1394-1401) by H. Yevele and H. Herland (the master carpenter for the hammerbeam roof).

251 ST. BARTHOLOMEW   1123
    THE GREAT
(church)
West Smithfield *B7*

Rebuilt by G. Dance the Younger (1789) and then again by T. Hardwick (1823). Restored by Sir A. Webb (1893-97).

252 THE TEMPLE   12th c onward
(offices) *C7*

Inner Temple Gateway, 16-17 Fleet Street (1610, rebuilt 1908); Temple Church (1160-1240), altar screen (1682) by Sir Christopher Wren; King's Bench Walk (1678) by Wren; Middle Temple Hall (1660-74); New Court (1676) by Wren; Middle Temple Gateway (1684) by R. North.

253 ST. HELEN   12th-17th c
    BISHOPGATE
(church)
Great St. Helen's *C9*

254 JEWEL TOWER   1364-66
Old Palace Yard *E5*
H. Yevele

London

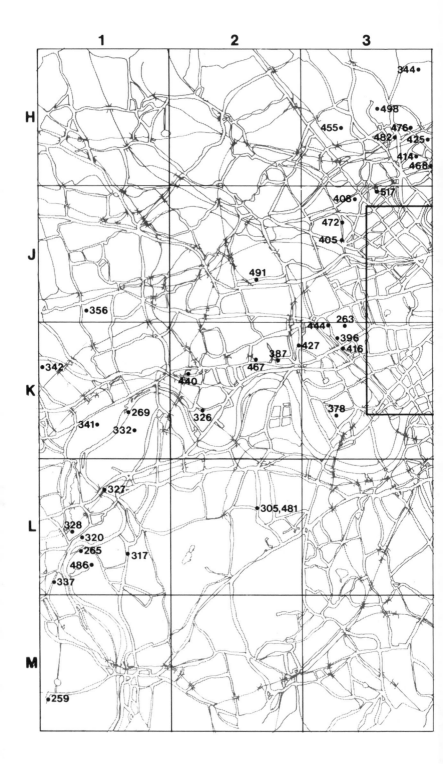

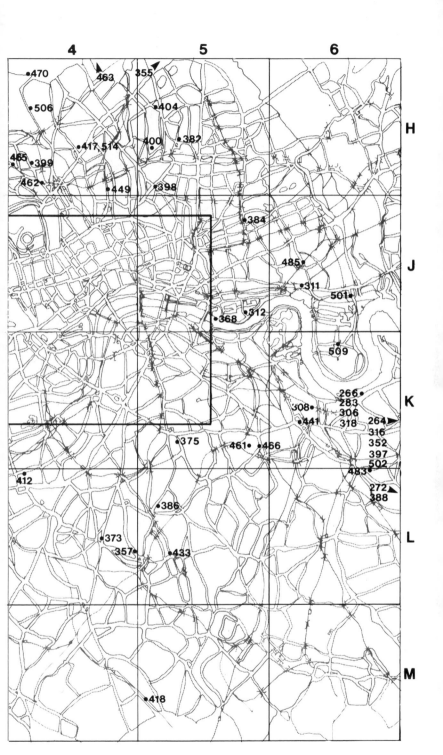

London detail

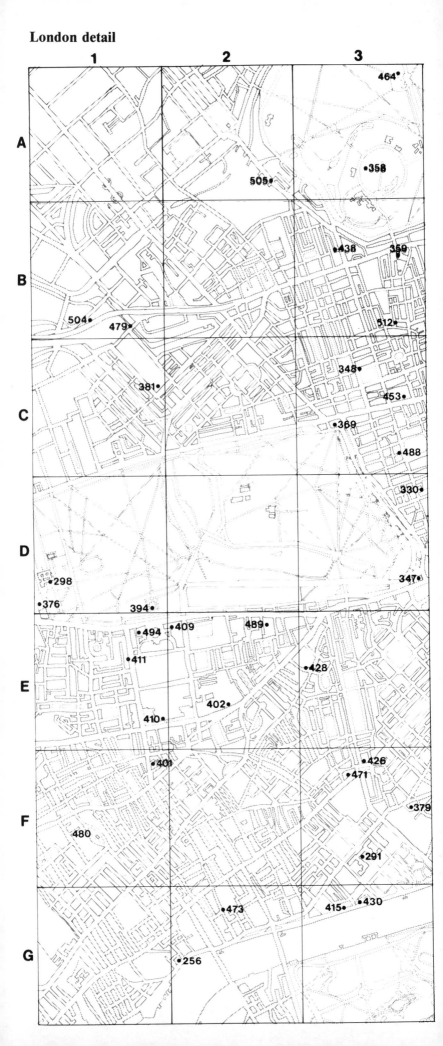

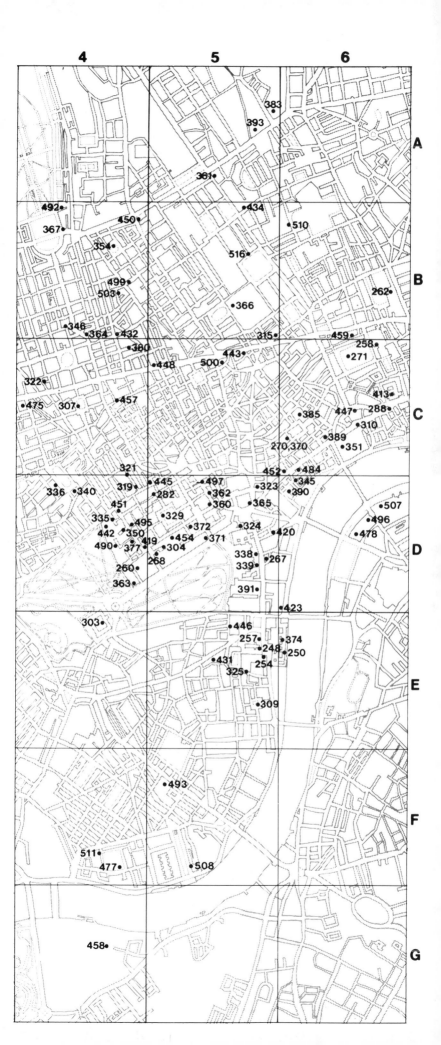

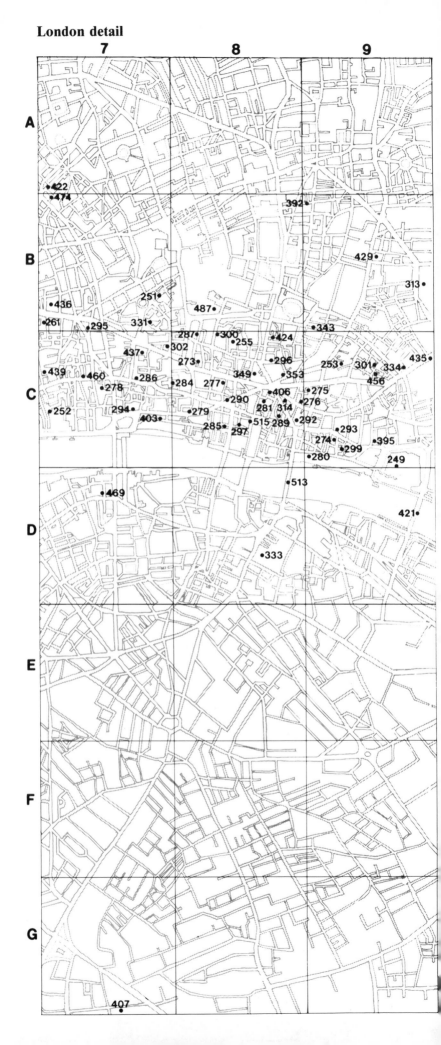

London detail

255 GUILDHALL   1411–40
Gresham Street *C8*

Restored (1789) by G. Dance
the Younger. 13th-c crypt,
originally restored by Sir
Christopher Wren. Rebuilt
1940–54.

256 CROSBY HALL   1466–75
Cheyne Walk *G2*

The great hall of Sir John
Crosby's residence. Moved
from Bishopsgate to present site
in 1908.

257 ST. MARGARET'S   1488–1523
(church)
Parliament Square *E5*

Major renovation and
alteration to the Perpendicular
style by Sir George Gilbert
Scott in 1877.

258 LINCOLN'S INN   1490
(offices)   onward
Chancery Lane *C6*

Old Hall (1490–92); Gatehouse
(1518); Chapel (1619–23); New
Square (1685–97); New Hall and
Library (1843–45) by P.
Hardwick.

259 HAMPTON   1514 onward
   COURT PALACE
Richmond *M1*

South and east ranges, state
apartments, and Fountain
Court by Sir Christopher Wren
(1689–94). The Banqueting
House (to the south, on the
river side) is also by Wren.
Painting collection includes
Mantegna's *Cartoons of the
Triumph of Caesar* in the Lower
Orangery. The Tijou Screen, a
remarkable ironwork screen by
J. Tijou, is at the south end of
the Privy Garden.

260 ST. JAMES'S   1530 onward
   PALACE
St. James's *D4*

Stable Court (1717) by
N. Hawksmoor. The Chapel
Royal, Gatehouse, and
Ambassadors' Court are open
to the public (restricted
times).

261 STAPLE INN   1586–96
(offices)
Holborn *B7*

The front range (back rebuilt
in 1937) survived the Great Fire
in 1666. The hall was added in
1581, then the east (1731–34)
and west (1757–59) ranges.

262 GRAY'S INN   16th c onward
(offices)
Gray's Inn Road *B6*

Many buildings rebuilt since
1945. The hall (1556–60) adjoins
South Square, an elegant
courtyard.

263 HOLLAND HOUSE   1605–7
Holland Park *K3*

Now a youth hostel. Much
altered.

264 CHARLTON   1607–12
   HOUSE
Charlton Park Road *K6*

The finest Jacobean mansion
in London.

265 HAM HOUSE   1610
Ham Street, Petersham
Richmond *L1*

Enlarged and redecorated from
1675–78. Restored since to
original condition, including
the interiors and the
furnishings.

266 QUEEN'S   1616–1737
   HOUSE AND ROYAL
   NAVAL COLLEGE
Greenwich *K6*

This magnificent group of
buildings was laid out by Sir
Christopher Wren. Its
inspiration was Queen Mary's
requirement that the Queen's
House and its view of the river
be preserved.

Queen's House   1616–62

I. Jones (1616–19), completed
in 1635. The first classical
building in England. The
entrance hall is a perfect
cube. The East and West
Bridge rooms were added by
J. Webb in 1662. The
Colonnades and East and
West Wings were added in

1807. Collection of marine paintings. Now part of the National Maritime Museum.

Royal Naval   1664–1737
College
Former Royal Naval Hospital. Kings Charles Block (1664–69) by J. Webb. King William, Queen Mary, and Queen Anne Buildings designed by Wren (1696–99), built by N. Hawksmoor (1698–1735) and T. Ripley (1735–37).
 Wren designed the Chapel (redecorated, 1780–88, by J. Stuart and W. Newton after a fire in 1779) and the Painted Hall (baroque ceiling and wall paintings by Sir J. Thornhill, executed 1708–27).

267 BANQUETING   1619–22
    HALL
    Whitehall *D5*
    I. Jones

Double cube room. The splendid ceiling was painted by Rubens in 1629. North entry added by J. Wyatt in 1809. Exterior refaced by Sir J. Soane in 1829.

268 QUEEN'S CHAPEL   1623–25
    St. James's Palace
    Marlborough Road *D5*
    I. Jones

England's first classical church.

269 DUTCH HOUSE   1631
    (Kew Palace)
    Kew Gardens *K1*
    S. Fortry

270 ST. PAUL   1631–33
    (church)
    Covent Garden *C6*
    I. Jones

Covent Garden, also by Jones (1631), was the first consciously designed urban square to be built in London.

271 LINCOLN'S   1650 onward
    INN FIELDS *C6*

Laid out in 1650
    Nos. 12–14: Sir J. Soane (1792–1824). Now the Sir John Soane Museum. No. 12 (1792–94) was Soane's own house; no. 13 (1813), his museum; and no. 14 (1824), an annex. Unchanged since his death by an Act of Parliament requested by Soane. The building, painting, sculpture, and antiquities collection (*The Rake's Progress* by Hogarth) give a fascinating insight into Soane's delightfully esoteric predelictions.
    Nos. 17–18: A. Waterhouse (1871–72)

No. 19: P. Webb (1868)

Nos. 59–60 (Lindsey House): I. Jones (1650). Originally exposed brickwork, now plastered.

South Side: Royal College of Surgeons (1836–38) by Sir C. Barry. Extended in 1888.

272 ELTHAM LODGE   1664
    Court Road *L6*
    H. May

273 ST. VEDAST   1670–73
    (church)
    Foster Lane *C8*
    Sir Christopher Wren

Interiors rebuilt to Wren's design.

274 ST. MARY-AT-HILL 1670–76
    (church)
    St. Mary-at-Hill, off Eastcheap *C9*
    Sir Christopher Wren

Well-concealed courtyard entrance. Magnificent carved woodwork.

275 ST. MICHAEL   1670–77
    (church)
    Cornhill *C9*
    Sir Christopher Wren

Tower completed (1718–24) by N. Hawksmoor. Remodeled (1857–60) by Sir George Gilbert Scott. •St. Peter upon Cornhill (1677–87), at Cornhill/Gracechurch Street, is also by Wren.

276 ST. EDMUND   1670–79
    THE KING AND MARTYR
    (church)
    Lombard Street *C8*
    Sir Christopher Wren

277 ST. MARY-LE-BOW 1670–83
    (church)
    Cheapside *C8*
    Sir Christopher Wren

Original tower (the sound of Bow bells) and steeple. Church rebuilt after 1941.

278 ST. BRIDE   1670–84
    (church)
    Fleet Street *C7*
    Sir Christopher Wren

Original steeple. Church rebuilt after 1941.

279 ST. NICHOLAS   1671–81
    COLE ABBEY
    (church)
    Queen Victoria Street *C8*
    Sir Christopher Wren

280 ST. MAGNUS   1671–87
    MARTYR
    (church)
    Lower Thames Street *C9*
    Sir Christopher Wren

Much changed internally by renovations in 1886 and 1924.

281 ST. STEPHEN   1672–77
    (church)
    Walbrook *C8*
    Sir Christopher Wren

Prototype dome for St. Paul's Cathedral. Marvelously complex articulation of the church's interior by the eight arches supporting the dome.

282 ST. JAMES   1674–84
(church)
Piccadilly/Church Place *D5*
Sir Christopher Wren

Restored 1947–54. Organ case,
altarpiece, and font carved by
G. Gibbons.

283 ROYAL   1675–76
OBSERVATORY
Blackheath Avenue, Greenwich
Park
Greenwich *K6*
Sir Christopher Wren

284 ST. PAUL'S   1675–1708
CATHEDRAL
St. Paul's Churchyard *C8*
Sir Christopher Wren

The triple-layered dome is an
ingenious solution to the
differing internal and external
requirements. The altar and
choir (carved by G. Gibbons)
were designed by Wren. The
sanctuary screens are by
J. Tijou. Wren is buried in the
cathedral walls.

285 ST. JAMES   1676–83
GARLICKHYTHE
(church)
Garlick Hill/Upper Thames
Street *C8*
Sir Christopher Wren

17th-c woodwork. Spire built
in 1713.

286 ST. MARTIN   1676–84
LUDGATE
(church)
Ludgate Hill *C7*
Sir Christopher Wren

Splendid steeple and spire.

287 ST. ANNE AND   1676–87
ST. AGNES
(church)
Gresham Street/Noble Street
C8

Rebuilt by Sir Christopher
Wren. Steeple built in 1714.
•St. Lawrence Jewry (1670–87),
also by Wren, is at Gresham
Street opposite King Street.

288 ST. CLEMENT   1680–82
DANES
(church)
Strand/Aldwych *C6*
Sir Christopher Wren

The upper spire (1719) is by
J. Gibbs. Pulpit by G. Gibbons.
Burned in 1941, rebuilt 1955–58.

289 ST. MARY   1681–86
ABCHURCH
(church)
Abchurch Lane off Cannon
Street *C8*
Sir Christopher Wren

Central dome on pendentives
that spring from the
perimeter walls. Damaged in
1940.

290 ST. MARY   1681–87
ALDERMARY
(church)
Queen Victoria Street/Watling
Street *C8*
Sir Christopher Wren

Gothic. Pulpit and swordrest
by G. Gibbons.

291 ROYAL HOSPITAL   1682–92
Hospital Road
Chelsea *F3*
Sir Christopher Wren

Stables (1814–17) by Sir
J. Soane.

292 ST. CLEMENT   1683–87
EASTCHEAP
(church)
Clement's Lane *C8*
Sir Christopher Wren

The fine interior is original.

293 ST. MARGARET   1684–89
PATTENS
(church)
Rood Lane, off Eastcheap *C9*
Sir Christopher Wren

Needle-sharp spire. Superb
woodwork.

294 ST. ANDREW–   1685–95
BY-THE-WARDROBE
(church)
Queen Victoria Street/
St. Andrew's Hill *C7*

Rebuilt by Sir Christopher
Wren. Gutted in 1940.

295 ST. ANDREW   1686–87
HOLBORN
(church)
Holborn Circus *B7*
Sir Christopher Wren

296 ST. MARGARET   1686–90
(church)
Lothbury (facing the Bank of
England) *C8*
Sir Christopher Wren

The screen was designed by
Wren.

297 ST. MICHAEL   1686–94
PATERNOSTER ROYAL
(church)
College Hill, off Cannon Street
C8
Sir Christopher Wren

298 KENSINGTON   1689–95
PALACE
Palace Avenue *D1*
Sir Christopher Wren

Interiors reworked by W. Kent
(1723–27). The Orangery by
Wren was remodeled by Sir
J. Vanbrugh in 1705.

299 ST. DUNSTAN–   1697
IN-THE-EAST
(church tower only)
Dunstan's Hill, off Great
Tower Street *C9*
Sir Christopher Wren

300 ST. ALBAN   1697–98
(church tower only)
Wood Street *C8*
Sir Christopher Wren

301 SPANISH AND   1701
PORTUGUESE
SYNAGOGUE
Heneage Lane, off Bevis Marks
C9
J. Avis

302 CHRIST CHURCH 1704
(tower only)
Newgate Street/King Edward
Street *C7*
Sir Christopher Wren

303 BUCKINGHAM 1705–1913
PALACE *E4*

The mansion (1705) was
remodeled by J. Nash (1825–
30), completed by E. Blore in
1837. Blore added the east
wing (1847–50), which was
enlarged by J. Pennethorn
(1853–55). Sir A. Webb
raised (and faced in Portland
stone) the east wing facade in
1913.
•The Queen's Gallery, on
Buckingham Palace Road,
displays temporary exhibitions
drawn from the Royal
Collection. The Royal Mews,
further down, are by J. Nash.

304 MARLBOROUGH 1709–11
HOUSE
St. James's *D5*
Sir Christopher Wren

Interiors remodeled (1771–74)
by Sir W. Chambers. Attic
added 1861–63.

305 ROEHAMPTON 1710–12
HOUSE
Roehampton Lane *L2*
T. Archer

Now part of Queen Mary's
Hospital.

306 ST. ALPHEGE 1712–14
(church)
Nelson Road/Greenwich
Church Street
Greenwich *K6*
N. Hawksmoor

Upper tower (1730) by J. James.

307 ST. GEORGE'S, 1712–25
HANOVER SQUARE
Hanover Square *C4*
J. James

Freestanding portico, giant
Corinthian columns.

308 ST. PAUL 1712–30
(church)
Deptford High Street *K6*
T. Archer

309 ST. JOHN 1713–28
(church)
Smith Square *E5*
T. Archer

Gutted by fire in 1941.
Restored since.

310 ST. MARY– 1714–17
LE-STRAND
(church)
Strand *C6*
J. Gibbs

Baroque. (Gibbs studied under
C. Fontana in Roma).

311 ST. ANNE, 1714–26
LIMEHOUSE
(church)
St. Anne Street *J6*
N. Hawksmoor

This church is dominated by an
extraordinarily aggressive
baroque tower. Restored by
P. Hardwick (1854) after a fire.

312 ST. GEORGE– 1714–29
IN-THE-EAST
(church)
Cable Street *J5*
N. Hawksmoor

Distinctive steeple. Burned in
1942, since restored with a
modern interior.

313 CHRIST CHURCH, 1714–29
SPITALFIELDS
Commercial Street/Fournier
Street *B9*
N. Hawksmoor

The spire was slightly altered
when rebuilt in the 19th c.
Currently being restored.

314 ST. MARY 1716–24
WOOLNOTH
(church)
Lombard Street/King William
Street *C8*
N. Hawksmoor

Massive steeple (after Pliny's
description of a mausoleum).
The interior was altered by
W. Butterfield in 1875.

315 ST. GEORGE'S 1716–31
BLOOMSBURY
(church)
Bloomsbury Way, near New
Oxford Street *B5*
N. Hawksmoor

316 MILITARY 1716–1819
BUILDINGS
Woolwich *K6*
Royal Arsenal, Warren Lane:
Sir J. Vanbrugh (1716–19)

Royal Artillery Barracks,
Artillery Place: (1775–82)

Royal Military Academy,
Academy Road: J. Wyatt
(1800–1806)

The Rotunda, Woolwich
Common: J. Nash (1814–19)

317 SUDBROOKE 1717–20
PARK
(house)
Petersham Road, Richmond *L1*
J. Gibbs

318 VANBRUGH 1717–26
CASTLE
Maze Hill
Greenwich *K6*
Sir J. Vanbrugh

His own house. Pastiche of a
medieval fortress.

319 BURLINGTON 1718–19
　　　HOUSE
　　　Piccadilly *D4*
　　　C. R. Campbell

Remodeled for Lord
Burlington, a fanatical believer
in Palladianism as the only
correct style. Internal
alterations (1815–18) by
S. Ware. Piccadilly facade
(1874) by R. R. Banks and
C. Barry, Jr. •The delightful
Burlington Arcade (1815–18)
alongside is by S. Ware.

320 OCTAGON, 1720
　　　ORLEANS HOUSE
　　　Richmond Road
　　　Twickenham *L1*
　　　J. Gibbs

Plasterwork by G. Artari and
G. Bagutti. Now a gallery. The
house was demolished in 1926.

321 QUEENSBURY 1721–23
　　　HOUSE
　　　Burlington Gardens *C4*
　　　G. Leoni

This became the model for
innumerable Palladian town
houses. Refaced in 1792. Now
the Royal Bank of Scotland.

322 ST. PETER'S 1721–24
　　　CHAPEL
　　　Vere Street *C4*
　　　J. Gibbs

323 ST. MARTIN- 1722–26
　　　IN-THE-FIELDS
　　　(church)
　　　St. Martin's Place *D5*
　　　J. Gibbs

Gibbs's magnum opus is known
for its steeple rising above a
Corinthian portico.

324 THE ADMIRALTY 1722–26
　　　Whitehall *D5*
　　　T. Ripley

The screen in front is by R.
Adam (1759–61).

325 WESTMINSTER 1722–30
　　　SCHOOL DORMITORY
　　　Great College Street *E5*
　　　R. Boyle, Earl of Burlington

Altered during restoration in
1941. Very little of the original
building has survived.

326 CHISWICK HOUSE 1723–29
　　　Burlington Lane *K2*
　　　R. Boyle, Earl of Burlington

Palladio (Villa Rotunda) in
England. Interiors (1726–29)
by W. Kent, Burlington's
protégé.

327 MAIDS OF HONOUR 1724
　　　ROW HOUSING
　　　The Green
　　　Richmond *L1*

Perfect proportions. The
Green itself is charming.

328 MARBLE HILL 1724–29
　　　HOUSE
　　　Richmond Road
　　　Twickenham *L1*
　　　R. Morris, with the Earl of
　　　Pembroke.

329 ST. JAMES 1726 onward
　　　SQUARE *D5*
　　　No. 4: Built in 1676,
　　　remodeled in 1726.

No. 5: M. Brettingham
(1748–50). Refaced in
1854.

No. 10: H. Flitcroft
(1734–36).

No. 15 (Lichfield House):
J. Stuart (1764–66).

No. 20: R. Adam (1771–74).
Refaced in 1936.

No. 32: S. P. and C. R.
Cockerell (1819–21). Porch
added in 1931.

330 GROSVENOR 1730
　　　CHAPEL
　　　South Audley Street *D3*
　　　B. Timbrell

331 ST. BARTHOLO- 1730–59
　　　MEW'S HOSPITAL
　　　West Smithfield *B7*

J. Gibbs and others. Staircase
murals by Hogarth in the north
wing. See entry 251.

332 KEW 1730 onward
　　　GARDENS *K1*

The landscaping begun by
W. Kent in 1730 was completed
by L. Brown in 1774. The
garden buildings by Sir
W. Chambers include the
Orangery (1757–61), Temple
of Bellona (1760), and
Pagoda (1761). The Palm
House (1844–48) by
D. Burton and R. Turner
(engineer) is outstanding.
The Temperate House (1864) is
also by Burton.

333 GUY'S HOSPITAL 1738–78
　　　St. Thomas Street *D8*

Begun by J. Steere (1738–40)
and completed by R. Jupp
(1774–78).

334 ST. BOTOLPH 1741–44
　　　ALDGATE
　　　(church)
　　　Aldgate *C9*
　　　G. Dance the Elder

Interiors completely reworked
by J. F. Bentley in 1889.

335 WIMBOURNE 1741–50
　　　HOUSE
　　　22 Arlington Street *D4*
　　　W. Kent

336 HOUSE   1742–44
44 Berkeley Square *D4*
W. Kent

A spectacular stairway. •No. 45
is by H. Flitcroft.

337 STRAWBERRY   1747–76
      HILL
Waldegrave Road
Twickenham *L1*
H. Walpole, with J. Chute and
R. Bentle

A Gothic villa with fascinatingly
willful interiors, all completely
different. This was a major
influence on the Gothic revival
style in Britain. Refurbished
and enlarged from 1855–73.
Now St. Mary's College.

338 HORSE GUARDS   1750–58
Whitehall *D5*
W. Kent

Built after Kent's death by
J. Vardy.

339 DOVER HOUSE   1754–58
(Scottish Office)
Whitehall *D5*
J. Paine

Screen and porch (1787) by
H. Holland.

340 LANSDOWNE   1762–68
      HOUSE
Fitzmaurice Place, off
      Berkeley Square *D4*
R. Adam (interiors)

Sculpture gallery (1788–91, by
G. Dance the Younger)
remodeled by Sir R. Smirke
from 1816–19. Now
Landsdowne Club.

341 SYON HOUSE   1762–69
(remodeling)
London Road
Isleworth *K1*
R. Adam

Notable interiors. The screen
(1773) by the road is also by
Adam.

342 OSTERLEY   1763–80
      PARK HOUSE
Thornbury Road, off the Great
      West Road *K1*
R. Adam

The unique interiors (many
personally designed by Adam

down to the last doorknob) are
intact.

343 ALL HALLOWS   1765–67
(church)
London Wall *B9*
G. Dance the Younger

344 KENWOOD HOUSE   1767–69
(Iveagh Bequest)
Hampstead Lane *H3*
R. Adam

Completely remodeled by
Adam. Superb interiors and
library room. Paintings by
Rembrandt (*Self-Portrait
in Old Age*), Hals, Vermeer,
Turner, Gainsborough (*Mary,
Lady Howe*), Reynolds, etc.

345 THE ADELPHI   1768–72
Adam Street *D6*
R. and J. Adam

Little remains of this very fine
riverside scheme; however,
no. 8 John Adam Street, off
Adam Street (built for the Royal
Society of Arts), by the
Adam brothers, has survived.

346 CHANDOS HOUSE   1771
Chandos Street *B4*
R. Adam

347 APSLEY HOUSE   1772–78
(Wellington Museum)
1 Piccadilly *D3*
R. Adam

Totally altered and enlarged by
B. Wyatt in 1829. Only the
Portico Room and Piccadilly
Drawing Room by Adam have
survived. Paintings by
Correggio (*The Agony in the
Garden*), Velásquez (*Water
Seller of Seville*), Wilkie, etc.

348 HOME HOUSE   1773–76
20 Portman Square *C3*
R. Adam

349 FREDERICKS   1775–76
      PLACE
Old Jewry *C8*
R. and J. Adam

350 BROOK'S CLUB   1776–78
61 St. James's Street *D4*
H. Holland

•Boodle's Club (no. 28),
opposite, is by J. Crunden
(1765). White's Club (no. 37,
possibly by J. Wyatt) was
built in 1778, renewed in 1852.

351 SOMERSET HOUSE   1776–96
Strand *C6*
Sir W. Chambers

Completed by J. Wyatt in
1801. Extended by Sir R.
Smirke (east wing, 1830–35) and
J. Pennethorne (west wing,
1851–56).

352 SEVERNDROOG   1784
      CASTLE
Shooter's Hill *K6*
R. Jupp

An appealing folly.

353 BANK OF ENGLAND 1788–1808
Threadneedle Street *C8*
Sir J. Soane

Only the south and west screens remain. The present structure (1924–39) that unfortunately replaced Soane's masterpiece is by Sir H. Baker.

354 FITZROY SQUARE *B4* 1790–94
R. Adam

South and east sides (in Portland stone) by Adam. Other sides completed in 1844.

355 GROVELANDS 1797
(house)
The Bourne
Southgate *H5*
J. Nash

356 PITZHANGER MANOR 1800–1803
Walpole Park *J1*
Sir J. Soane

Most interiors have survived. Now the Ealing Public Library.

357 DULWICH COLLEGE PICTURE GALLERY 1811–14
College Road *L4*
Sir J. Soane

The gallery includes the mausoleum of the two founders. Very skillful handling of the interior spaces. The collection includes Gainsborough, Rembrandt, Rubens, Vandyke, and others.

358 REGENT'S PARK *A3* 1811–30
J. Nash

Nash's design linked Carlton House on Waterloo Place (demolished 1829) to Regent's Park through a planned series of superb vistas along Regent Street and Portland Place (1776, by R. and J. Adam). Regent Street survives in plan only, All Souls church excepted. The terraces of houses behind continuous giant colonnades that line Regent's Park have mostly survived. They were designed by D. Burton and others and submitted to Nash for approval. Nash personally designed Park Crescent and Park Village West.

359 ST. MARY 1813–17
(church)
Marylebone Road, opposite York Gate *B3*
T. Hardwick

The Corinthian portico was added by J. Nash to complete a vista down York Gate from Regent's Park.

360 ROYAL OPERA ARCADE 1816–18
off Pall Mall East *D5*
J. Nash and G. S. Repton

361 ST. PANCRAS 1819–22
(church)
Upper Woburn Place/ Euston Road *A5*
H. W. and W. (father) Inwood

Meticulously accurate Greek revival.

362 THEATRE ROYAL 1820–21
Haymarket, opposite Charles II Street *D5*
J. Nash

363 LANCASTER HOUSE 1820–27
Stable Yard Road *D4*
Sir R. Smirke

Completed by J. Wyatt. Fine stairway by Sir C. Barry.
•Clarence House, opposite, is by J. Nash (1825).

364 ALL SOULS 1822–25
(church)
Langham Place *B4*
J. Nash

The round church, in a pivotal position on Nash's Regent Street design, "turns the corner" into Portland Place, which continues to Regent's Park (also by Nash).

365 ROYAL COLLEGE OF PHYSICIANS 1822–27
Trafalgar Square/Pall Mall Street *D5*
Sir R. Smirke

Now Canada House.

366 BRITISH MUSEUM 1823–46
Great Russell Street *B5*
Sir R. Smirke

Reading Room (1852–57) by S. Smirke (brother). Edward VII Gallery (1904–14) by Sir J. Burnet.

367 HOLY TRINITY 1826–27
(former church)
Marylebone Road *B4*
Sir J. Soane

Now offices of the SPCK.

368 ST. KATHERINE DOCK 1827–29
East Smithfield *J5*
T. Telford and P. Hardwick

The architect's favorite. Compare with Liverpool Docks. Recent conversions have begun to revitalize this area. A good example is the Ivory Warehouse (1852, by G. Aitchison, Sr.), converted to residential apartments in 1966 by Renton Howard Wood Levin.

369 MARBLE ARCH *C3* 1828
J. Nash

Designed as a gateway to

Buckingham Palace. Moved to its present position in 1851.

370 COVENT   1828–30
    GARDEN MARKET
Covent Garden *C6*
C. Fowler

Floral Hall (1858–60) by E. M. Barry. Renovated since 1974. Now shops and offices.

371 CARLTON   1829–33
    HOUSE TERRACE
The Mall *D5*
J. Nash

Carlton House, the centerpiece of Nash's Regent Street plan, rather ironically was demolished and replaced by this terrace overlooking St. James's Park.

372 TRAVELLERS   1830–32
    CLUB
106 Pall Mall *D5*
Sir C. Barry

• The Reform Club next door (No. 104), also by Barry, is modeled after the Farnese Palace, Roma.

373 CHRIST   1840–41
    CHURCH, STREATHAM
Christchurch Road *L4*
J. Wild

A "Romanesque" masterpiece.

374 PALACE OF   1840–65
    WESTMINSTER
St. Margaret Street *E6*
Sir C. Barry and A. W. N. Pugin

Plan by Barry; Gothic details and decorations by Pugin.

375 ST. GILES   1842–44
    (church)
Peckham Road
Camberwell *K5*
Sir George Gilbert Scott

376 KENSINGTON   1843 onward
    PALACE GARDENS *D1*
J. Pennethorne (layout)
Nos. 6, 7: T. H. Wyatt and D. Brandon; no. 8: D. Burton; no. 13: C. J. Richardson (1852); no. 14: T. Cubitt.

Palace Green No. 1: P. Webb (1863); no. 2: F. H. Thackeray (1861).

377 CONSERVATIVE   1844
    CLUB
74 St. James's Street *D4*
G. Basevi and S. Smirke

378 ST. THOMAS   1847–49
    OF CANTERBURY
(church)
Rylston Road *K3*
A. W. N. Pugin

379 ST. BARNABAS   1847–50
    (church)
Pimlico Road *F3*
T. Cundy II and W. Butterfield

380 ALL SAINTS   1849–59
    (church)
Margaret Street *C4*
W. Butterfield

High-Victorian emphasis on patterned flat surfaces. Brilliantly colored brickwork.

381 PADDINGTON   1850–52
    RAILWAY STATION
Praed Street *C1*
I. K. Brunel and Sir M. D. Wyatt

The Great Western Hotel (1851–53, P. Hardwick) forms the main facade of the station.

382 ST. MATTHIAS   1851–53
    (church)
Wordsworth Road
Stoke Newington *H5*
W. Butterfield

383 KING'S CROSS   1852
    RAILWAY STATION
Euston Road *A5*
L. Cubitt

384 BETHNEL GREEN   1857
    MUSEUM OF
    CHILDHOOD
Cambridge Heath Road *J5*
J. Wild and W. Cubitt

Toys, dolls, and a good collection of Rodin's sculpture. The prefabricated iron and glass galleries were the first buildings of the present Victoria and Albert Museum. They were rebuilt here in 1872 and faced with a brick exterior.

385 ROYAL OPERA   1858
    HOUSE
Bow Street *C6*
E. M. Barry

386 ST. PAUL   1858
    (church)
Herne Hill *L5*
G. E. Street

387 ST. JOHN   1859
    (church)
Glenthorne Road *K2*
W. Butterfield

Tower built in 1882.

388 THE RED HOUSE   1859
Red House Lane
Bexleyheath *L6*
P. Webb

Built for William Morris. Glass by E. Burne-Jones.

389 ST. MICHAEL'S   1859–60
    VICARAGE
Burleigh Street *C6*
W. Butterfield

390 CANOVA HOUSE 1860
22 Buckingham Street *D6*
R. P. Pullan

Gothic. Offices for William
Burges.

391 HOME OFFICE, 1861–73
FOREIGN OFFICE
Whitehall *D5*
Sir George Gilbert Scott

Scott was a confirmed
Gothicist. This Italianate-style
building was demanded and
obtained by Lord Palmerston.

392 ST. MICHAEL 1863–65
(church)
Mark Street *B9*
J. Brooks

Polychrome brickwork after
W. Butterfield.

393 ST. PANCRAS 1863–65
RAILWAY STATION
MIDLAND 1868–74
GRAND HOTEL
(now offices)
Euston Road *A5*
Sir George Gilbert Scott

The train shed is by W. H.
Barlow.

394 ALBERT 1863–72
MEMORIAL
Kensington Gore (opposite
Albert Hall) *D1*
Sir George Gilbert Scott

The Victorian Gothic
monument.

395 OFFICE BUILDING 1864
59–61 Mark Lane *C9*
G. Aitchison the Younger

396 LEIGHTON HOUSE 1865
12 Holland Park Road *K3*
G. Aitchison the Younger

The Arab Hall inside by W. de
Morgan incorporates antique
oriental tiles to form a
remarkable interior.

397 CROSS NESS 1865
PUMPING STATION
near Woolwich *K6*
J. Bazalgette

Wonderful ornate ironwork
behind an Italian Romanesque
facade.

398 PEABODY BUILDINGS 1865
(housing)
Greenman Street
Islington *H5*
H. Darbishire

399 ST. MARTIN 1865
(church)
Vicar's Road *H4*
E. Lamb

400 ST. SAVIOUR'S 1865–66
(church)
Aberdeen Park *H5*
W. White

401 ST. AUGUSTINE 1865–77
(church)
Queen's Gate *F1*
W. Butterfield

402 VICTORIA 1866–1909
AND ALBERT MUSEUM
Thurloe Place *E2*

Captain F. Fowke (North
Court). Completed by Sir
A. Webb (1891–1909). Huxley
Building (1867–71) by Major-
General H. Y. D. Scott.

403 BRITISH AND 1867–69
FOREIGN BIBLE SOCIETY
146 Queen Victoria Street *C7*
E. l'Anson, Jr.

404 ABBEY MILLS 1868
PUMPING STATION
Abbey Lane *H5*
J. Bazalgette and E. Cooper

Spectacular interiors.

405 ST. MARY 1868–72
MAGDALENE
(church)
Rowington Close
Paddington *J3*
G. E. Street

The Chapel of St. Sepulchre
(1895) is by Sir. J. N. Comper.

406 MAPPIN AND WEBB 1870
(Mansion House)
Queen Victoria Street/
Poultry *C8*
Sir J. Belcher

•The Albert Buildings (1871)
next door at no. 39–49 are by
F. J. Ward. Two Victorian
gems.

407 ST. JOHN THE 1871–74
DIVINE, KENNINGTON
(church)
Vassall Road *G7*
G. E. Street

408 ST. AUGUSTINE 1871–80
(church)
Kilburn Park Road *J3*
J. L. Pearson

Tower and spire built in 1898.

409 LOWTHER LODGE 1873–79
Albert Court *E2*
R. N. Shaw

Now the Royal Geographic
Society.

410 NATURAL 1873–81
HISTORY MUSEUM
Cromwell Road *E1*
A. Waterhouse

Grim and powerful. East wing
extension (1975) by
J. Pinckheard.

411 HOUSE 1874–76
196 Queen's Gate *E1*
R. N. Shaw

•No. 170 (1888–90) is also by
Shaw.

412 ASCENSION 1874–78
(church)
Lavender Hill *L4*
J. Brooks

413 ROYAL COURTS 1874–82
OF JUSTICE
(Law Courts)
Strand *C6*
G. E. Street

Exceedingly picturesque Gothic.
Designed in 1866, completed
by A. Street (son) after Street
died (from overwork on this
building).

414 HOUSE 1875
6 Ellerdale Road *H3*
R. N. Shaw

The architect's own house.

415 SWAN HOUSE 1875–76
17 Chelsea Embankment *G3*
R. N. Shaw

416 TOWER HOUSE 1875–80
9 Melbury Road *K3*
W. Burges

Gothic. The architect's own
house. •Nos. 8 (1876) and 11
(1877) are by R. N. Shaw;
15–17 (1891–93), by H.
Ricardo.

417 ST. MICHAEL 1880–81
(church)
Camden Road *H4*
G. Bodley and T. Garner

418 ST. MICHAEL 1880–85
(church)
Poplar Walk
Croydon *M5*
J. L. Pearson

419 ALLIANCE 1881–83
ASSURANCE OFFICES
1–2 St. James's Street *D4*
R. N. Shaw

•An extension at no. 88 St.
James's Street, also by Shaw,
was built from 1901–6.

420 NATIONAL 1885–87
LIBERAL CLUB
Whitehall Place *D5*
A. Waterhouse

421 TOWER 1886–94
BRIDGE *D9*
I. K. Brunel and Sir J. W. Barry

422 HOLY REDEEMER 1887–88
(church)
Exmouth Market *A7*
J. D. Sedding

Completed by H. Wilson.

423 NEW SCOTLAND 1889–90
YARD
Victoria Embankment *D6*
R. N. Shaw

South annex added in 1905.

424 INSTITUTE OF 1888–93
CHARTERED
ACCOUNTANTS

Great Swan Alley, off
Moorgate *C8*
Sir J. Belcher and A. B. Pite

Enormously influential.
External sculpture by H.
Thornycroft and H. Bates.
Exterior inspired from Belcher's
study of Genoese baroque
architecture. The interiors are
equally powerful and original.
Extended (Great Swan Alley) by
J. J. Joass in 1930. Extended
by Whitfield Partners in 1970.

425 ALL HALLOWS, 1889–1901
GOSPEL OAK
(church)
Savernake Road *H3*
J. Brooks

426 HOLY TRINITY 1890
(church)
Sloane Street *F3*
J. D. Sedding

The stained glass windows
were designed by E. Burne-
Jones, executed by W. Morris.

427 STUDIO HOUSE 1891
14 South Parade
Bedford Park *K2*
C. F. A. Voysey

•A similar studio house by
Voysey is at 17 St. Dunstan's
Road.

428 HOUSE 1894
12 Hans Road *E3*
A. H. Mackmurdo

•Nos. 14 and 16 Hans Road
(1894) are by C. F. A. Voysey.

429 BISHOPSGATE 1894
INSTITUTE
Bishopsgate *B9*
C. H. Townsend

The first (exterior) use of
Arts and Crafts ornament in
Britain.

430 HOUSES 1894–1905
38, 39 Cheyne Walk *G3*
C. R. Ashbee

431 WESTMINSTER 1895–1903
CATHEDRAL
Victoria Street *E5*
J. F. Bentley

Byzantine.

432 TOWN HOUSE 1896
82 Mortimer Street *B4*
A. B. Pite

Tiny. Sculpted facade figures
modeled after the style of
Michelangelo.

433 THE HORNIMAN 1896–1902
MUSEUM
100 London Road
Forest Hill *L5*
C. H. Townsend

A powerful and very satisfying
building.

434 MARY WARD 1897–98
HOUSE
(Passmore Edwards
Settlement)
Tavistock Place *B5*
D. Smith and C. Brewer

Smith and Brewer won the commission for this building in an open design competition (R. N. Shaw was the assessor).

435 WHITECHAPEL 1897–99
ART GALLERY
Whitechapel High Street *C9*
C. H. Townsend

436 PRUDENTIAL 1899–1906
ASSURANCE COMPANY
Holborn *B7*
A. Waterhouse

437 CENTRAL 1900–1906
CRIMINAL COURTS
Old Bailey/Newgate Street *C7*
E. Mountford

Edwardian baroque in the grand manner.

438 ST. CYPRIAN'S 1901–3
CHURCH
Ivor Place/Glentworth Street *B3*
Sir J. N. Comper

Delicate interiors in Comper's very personal interpretation of Perpendicular Gothic.

439 LAW SOCIETY 1902
LIBRARY
Chancery Lane *C7*
H. P. Adams and C. Holden

The influence of A. B. Pite can be seen in the slightly mannerist detailing.

440 SANDERSON'S 1902
WALLPAPER FACTORY
Barley Mow Passage, off Turnham Green
Chiswick *K2*
C. F. A. Voysey

Now Alliance Assurance.

441 DEPTFORD 1902–4
TOWN HALL
New Cross Road, Deptford *K6*
H. Lanchester and E. Rickards

442 RITZ HOTEL 1903–6
Piccadilly *D4*
Mewès and Davis

Davis was largely responsible for the magnificent interiors.

443 OFFICE BUILDING 1904
127–29 High Holborn *C5*
C. Holden

444 DEBENHAM HOUSE 1905–7
8 Addison Road
North Kensington *K3*
H. Ricardo

Brightly colored glazed tile exterior. Mannerist interiors executed by the Art Workers' Guild (glass by E. S. Prior). Now the Richmond Fellowship.

445 PICCADILLY 1905–8
HOTEL
Piccadilly *D5*
R. N. Shaw

Only the brilliantly original Piccadilly and Regent Street facades are by Shaw.

446 CENTRAL HALL 1905–11
(Methodist)
Storey's Gate
Westminster *E5*
H. Lanchester and E. Rickards

The originally planned entrance facade towers were never built.

447 MORNING POST 1906–7
BUILDING
(Inveresk House, now Lloyds Bank)
Aldwych *C6*
Mewès and Davis

Badly altered when additional top floors were added in 1924.

448 MAPPIN HOUSE 1906–8
158 Oxford Street *C5*
Sir J. Belcher and J. J. Joass

Steel frame with strained mannerist details by Joass.

449 CARNEGIE 1906–8
PUBLIC LIBRARY
Thornhill Square *H4*
A. B. Pite

450 EDINBURGH AND 1906–8
GLASGOW ASSURANCE
Euston Road/Euston Square *B4*
A. B. Pite

Classic Greek turned inside out. Now government offices.

451 ROYAL 1907–8
INSURANCE BUILDING
St. James's Street/
Piccadilly *D4*
Sir J. Belcher and J. J. Joass

Now Bradford and Bingley Building Society.

452 BRITISH 1907–8
MEDICAL ASSOCIATION
429 Strand *C6*
C. Holden

Now Rhodesia House.

453 SELFRIDGE'S 1907–28
DEPARTMENT STORE
Oxford Street *C3*
F. Swayles, D. Burnham (Chicago), F. Atkinson, and Sir. J. Burnet

454 ROYAL 1908–11
AUTOMOBILE CLUB
Pall Mall *D5*
Mewès and Davis

455 WATERLOO COURT 1909
(housing)
Heath Close, Hampstead Way
Hampstead Garden Suburb *H3*
M. H. Baillie Scott

•Baillie Scott also designed nos. 6, 8, and 10 Meadway and 22 Hampstead Way. The suburb was laid out by B. Parker and R. Unwin in 1906. The Free Church and Vicarage (1910) on North Square and St. Jude's Church (1909–13) on Central Square are by Sir E. Lutyens.

456 HOLLAND HOUSE 1914
32 Bury Street *C9*
H. P. Berlage

457 IDEAL HOUSE 1928
Great Marlborough Street/
Argyll Street *C4*
R. Hood with G. Jeeves

Now Palladium House.

458 BATTERSEA 1929–34
POWER STATION
off Cringle Street *G4*
Halliday and Agate with Sir Giles Gilbert Scott

459 CRAWFORD'S 1930
232 High Holborn *B6*
F. Etchells and Welch

460 DAILY EXPRESS 1931
BUILDING
Fleet Street *C7*
Ellis, Clarke and Atkinson, with Sir O. Williams

Big, bold, and black.

461 SASSOON HOUSE 1932
Belfort Road/St. Mary's Road
Camberwell *K5*
M. Fry

462 KENT HOUSE 1932
Ferdinand Street *H4*
A. D. Connell and B. Ward

463 ARNOS GROVE 1932
UNDERGROUND
STATION
(for London Transport)
Bowes Road
C. Holden (Adams, Holden, and Pearson)

464 GORILLA HOUSE 1933, 1934
AND PENGUIN POOL
London Zoo, Prince Albert Road *A3*
B. Lubetkin and Tecton

A virtuoso demonstration of the spatial potential of reinforced concrete. •Elephant and Rhinoceros House (1964) by Casson, Conder & Partners (Elephant House shown in illustration). Aviary (1964) by Lord Snowdon, A. Armstrong-Jones; Price; and F. Newby

465 ISOKON 1934
APARTMENTS
Lawn Road
Hampstead *H4*
W. Coats

466 PIONEER 1934–35
HEALTH CENTRE
St. Mary's Road
Camberwell *K5*
Sir O. Williams

Now adult-education institute.

467 ROYAL MASONIC 1935
HOSPITAL
Ravenscourt Park *K2*
Sir J. Burnet, Tait and Lorne

468 SUN HOUSE 1935
9 Frognal Way
Hampstead *H3*
M. Fry

•No. 66 (1938) is by Connell, Ward and Lucas.

469 SAINSBURY'S 1935
WAREHOUSE
Rennie Street
Southwark *D7*
Sir O. Williams

470 HIGHPOINT I 1935, 1938
AND II
(apartment buildings)
North Hill
Highgate *H4*
B. Lubetkin and Tecton

Highpoint I was the first modern point block in Britain. Three years later Lubetkin was already abandoning the regulation modern-movement style in Highpoint II with a caryatid porte cochere and other decorative elements.

471 PETER JONES 1936
(department store)
Sloane Square
Chelsea *F3*
W. Crabtree, Slater and Moberly, with C. H. Reilly

Extended in 1964.

472 KENSAL HOUSE 1936
Ladbroke Grove *J3*
M. Fry

473 HOUSE   1936
   66 Old Church Street *G2*
   W. Gropius and M. Fry

   •No. 64 (1936) is by
   S. Chermayeff and E.
   Mendelsohn

474 FINSBURY HEALTH   1938
      CENTRE
   Pine Street
   Finsbury *B7*
   B. Lubetkin and Tecton

   Some of Le Corbusier's
   influence is visible here. Poorly
   maintained.

475 HIS MASTER'S   1938–39
      VOICE
   363–367 Oxford Street *C4*
   J. Emberton

476 HOUSES   1940
   1–3 Willow Road
   Hampstead *H3*
   E. Goldfinger

477 CHURCHILL   1950–62
      GARDENS
   Grosvenor Road/Lupius Street
   Pimlico *F4*
   Powell and Moya

   12-ha (30-acre) site with
   1,700 housing units.

478 ROYAL   1951
      FESTIVAL HALL
   Belvedere Road *D6*
   R. Matthew and Sir L. Martin

479 HALLFIELD   1954–56
      ESTATE
   Bishops Bridge Road *B1*
   Tecton, L. Drake, and D.
   Lasdun

   The school off Porchester
   Terrace (1955) is by Drake and
   Lasdun.

480 BOUSFIELD   1955
      PRIMARY SCHOOL
   The Boltons *F1*
   Chamberlin, Powell and Bon

481 ALTON WEST   1955–59
      ESTATE
   (housing)
   Roehampton Lane
   Roehampton *L2*
   LCC Architect's Department

   Alton East estate, 1952–55.

482 HOUSES   1956
   80–90 South Hill Park
   Hampstead *H3*
   Howell, Killick, Partridge and
   Amis

483 SPAN HOUSING   1957
   Blackheath Park *L6*
   E. Lyons

484 PETER ROBINSON   1958
   65 Strand *C6*
   D. Lasdun and Partners

   Now New South Wales House.

485 CLUSTER BLOCK   1958
      HOUSING
   (Keeling House)
   Claredale Street, Bethnal
      Green *J6*
   D. Lasdun and Partners

486 LANGHAM CLOSE   1958
   (apartments)
   Ham Street, Ham Common *L1*
   J. Stirling and J. Gowan

487 BARBICAN ESTATE   1959–79
   London Wall *B8*
   Chamberlin, Powell and Bon

   Housing for 5,000 people, a
   school, and a major arts center.

488 UNITED STATES   1960
      EMBASSY
   Grosvenor Square *C3*
   Eero Saarinen and Associates,
   with Yorke Rosenberg Mardall

489 LINSTEAD HALL 1960–63
Imperial College, Princes
Gardens *E2*
Richard Sheppard, Robson and
Partners

490 APARTMENTS 1961
26 St. James's Place *D4*
Denys Lasdun and Partners

An excellent answer to the
problem posed by a luxury
apartment building.

491 WOLFSON INSTITUTE 1961
Hammersmith Hospital
Du Cane Road *J2*
Lyons Israel Ellis Partnership

492 ROYAL COLLEGE 1961–64
OF PHYSICIANS
11 St. Andrew's Place,
Regents Park *B4*
Denys Lasdun and Partners

493 LILINGTON 1961–71
GARDENS
Vauxhall Bridge Road *F5*
Darbourne and Darke

A large housing estate built in
three phases. Red brick.
Excellent landscaping.

494 ROYAL 1962–64
COLLEGE OF ART
Kensington Gore *E1*
H. T. Cadbury-Brown, Sir
H. Casson, and R. Y. Gooden

495 ECONOMIST 1962–64
BUILDING
25 St. James's Street *D4*
A. and P. Smithson

An important example of
sensitive urban planning. Three
towers (of differing heights
on a plaza) respond to the scale
and character of the historic
buildings around them.

496 SOUTH BANK 1963
ARTS CENTRE
South Bank/Waterloo Bridge
D6
G.L.C. Department of
Architecture and Civic Design

497 NEW ZEALAND 1963
HOUSE
Haymarket *D5*
Matthew, Johnson-Marshall
and Partners

498 SCHREIBER 1963–64
HOUSE
9 West Heath Road
Hampstead *H3*
J. Gowan

The rather witty swimming pool
was added in 1966.

499 POST OFFICE 1963–66
TOWER
Howland Street *B4*
Ministry of Public Buildings
and Works

500 CENTREPOINT 1965
OFFICE BUILDING
St. Giles Circus *C5*
R. Seifert and Partners

501 ROBIN HOOD 1966–72
GARDENS
(housing)
Robin Hood Lane, off East
India Dock Road *J6*
A. and P. Smithson

This actual example of the
Smithsons' diagrams of the
1950s—see *Team 10 Primer*—
is disappointing.

502 THAMESMEAD 1966 onward
(new community)
Woolwich, Erith *K6*
G.L.C. Department of
Architecture and Civic Design

Planned for 50,000 people.
The earlier areas are typical for
their time: point blocks, very
heavy precast concrete panels,
raised walkways, etc. This has
changed over time to more
traditional housing types and
materials. •The Modern Art

Glass Ltd. Warehouse (1973) on Hailey Road is by Foster Associates.

503 POLYTECHNIC 1967
COLLEGE OF
ENGINEERING AND
SCIENCE
New Cavendish/Cleveland Streets *B4*
Lyons Israel Ellis Partnership

504 PADDINGTON 1968
MAINTENANCE DEPOT
117 Harrow Road *B1*
Bicknell and Hamilton

Powerful massing in response to an elevated freeway immediately adjacent.

505 MERCURY HOUSING 1968
SOCIETY APARTMENTS
125 Park Road, Regents Park *A2*
Farrell/Grimshaw Partnership

Shiny corrugated-aluminum cladding.

506 ARCHITECT'S HOUSE 1969
81 Swain's Lane *H4*
John Winter and Associates

Huge windows in a Cor-ten steel frame. No compromise.

507 NATIONAL 1969–72
THEATRE
South Bank/Waterloo Bridge *D6*
Denys Lasdun and Partners

508 PIMLICO 1970
SECONDARY SCHOOL
St. Georges Square *F5*
G.L.C. Department of Architecture

Sunken below street level. The teaching spaces are strung along both sides of a central "main street."

509 OLSEN SHIPPING 1970
TERMINAL
Millwall Dock, Glengall Grove Isle of Dogs *K6*
Foster Associates

A crisp high-tech building. Appropriate use of reflective glass curtain wall.

510 FOUNDLING ESTATE 1970
(housing)
Brunswick Square *B6*
P. Hodgkinson and Sir L. Martin (with Bickerdike, Allen and Rich)

Massing reminiscent of Sant' Elia's futurist schemes.

511 SCHOOL 1971
Lupus Street *F4*
G.L.C. Department of Architecture

512 DESIGN RESEARCH 1972
UNIT
32 Aybrook Street *B3*
R. and S. Rogers.

Colorful renovation of a Victorian warehouse.

513 LONDON BRIDGE 1973
H. King *D8*

Concrete. This replaced J. Rennie's bridge (1831), which is now in Arizona.

514 CAMDEN ROAD 1974
HOUSING
Camden Road *H4*
Darbourne and Darke

An immensely livable scheme of terraced houses.

515 BUSH LANE HOUSE 1976
80 Cannon Street *C8*
Arup Associates

Exposed diagonal stainless-steel grid that visibly supports the floor slabs. Rather forced.

516 INSTITUTES OF 1976
EDUCATION AND LAW
Bedford Way *B5*
Denys Lasdun and Partners

Uneven. A monumental, exterior, terraced staircase.

517 ALEXANDRA 1977
ROAD DEVELOPMENT
Abbey Road (NW8) *J3*
Camden Department of Architecture (N. Brown and others)

Terraced housing alongside a railway line. •Children's home (1977) at east end by Evans and Shalev.

LONGLEAT HOUSE
F3
8 km (5 mi) SE of Frome

518 LONGLEAT 1556–80
HOUSE

Elizabethan country house. Altered (1801–11) by Sir J. Wyatville. Grounds by L. Brown.

LOUGHBOROUGH D4

519 UNIVERSITY   1967
    OF TECHNOLOGY
    Arup Associates

LUTON E5

520 LUTON HOO   17th c onward
    (country house)
    Park Street

17th-c house remodeled by R. Adam (1763), Sir R. Smirke (1827), and Mewès and Davis (1903). Landscaping by L. Brown.

MAIDEN CASTLE G3
3 km (2 mi) SW of Dorchester

521 MAIDEN   ca. 400 B.C.
    CASTLE

Gigantic hill fort. Four concentric glacis ramparts encircle the site. Sophisticated gate defense. •There is a Roman amphitheater in the center of Dorchester.

MAIDENHEAD F5

522 ALL SAINTS   1854–57
    CHURCH
    Boyne Hill
    G. E. Street

Built for an ideal Christian community. •The vicarage, school, and some housing are also by Street.

MANCHESTER D3

Museums: Manchester City Art Gallery, Mosley Street. See entry 523.
  Whitworth Art Gallery, Oxford Road. Good contemporary collection. Also works by Turner, Blake, and other English painters.

523 ROYAL INSTITUTE   1824
    OF FINE ARTS
    Mosley Street/Princess Street
    Sir C. Barry

Greek revival. Now the Manchester City Art Gallery. The strength of the painting collection is in British work from the 17th c to the present. Outstanding Pre-Raphaelite works: Watts, Millais (*Autumn Leaves*), Burne-Jones, etc. Some 15th-to 17th-c Italian, Dutch, and French paintings. •The Atheneum (1836) on Princess/Mosely Street is also by Barry.

524 TOWN HALL   1867–77
    Albert Square
    A. Waterhouse

Built in the Early English style. Superb stairway. Murals in the great hall by F. M. Brown.

•The main buildings (now somewhat altered) of the Manchester University, Oxford Street, are also by Waterhouse (1870–73).

525 RYLANDS   1890–99
    MEMORIAL LIBRARY
    Deansgate/Cumberland Street
    B. Champneys

Gothic with marvelous interiors.

526 METHODIST   1899–1902
    CHURCH AND SCHOOL
    Long Street, Middleton
    E. Wood and J. H. Sellers

Lovely massing. Compare with C. R. Mackintosh's Glasgow School of Art. •Nearby are two more schools by Wood and Sellers, on Durnford Street and Elm Street (both built 1908–10).

527 FIRST CHURCH   1903
    OF CHRIST, SCIENTIST
    Daisy Bank, Victoria Park
    E. Wood

528 LONGFORD CINEMA 1936
    Chester Road, Stretford
    H. Elder

529 ST. MICHAEL'S   1937
    CHURCH
    Orton Road, Northenden
    Cachmaille, Day and Lander

530 DAILY EXPRESS   1939
    BUILDING
    Great Ancoats Street
    Sir O. Williams

A replica of the Daily Express in London, also by Williams.

531 WILLIAM TEMPLE   1964–65
    MEMORIAL CHURCH
    Simonsway, Wythenshawe
    G. G. Pace

Outskirts of Manchester

532 HEATON HALL   1772
    Heaton Park (10 km/6 mi N of
      city center)
    J. Wyatt

Now a museum.

533 ROYD HOUSE   1914–16
    224 Hale Road, Hale (16 km/
      10 mi S of Manchester)
    E. Wood

The architect's own house. •Other houses by Wood include Halecroft, Hale Road, and 116 and 117–121 Park Road.

MARCH E5
25 km (16 mi) E of Peterborough

534 ST. WENDREDA   15th c
    (church)

Superb double hammerbeam roof decorated with carved angels.

MELROSE A3

535 ABBEY   1150 onward
    (ruins)

Present remains date from ca. 1450. The choir is exquisite.
•Three other abbeys (all ruined) in this area were founded at the same time. They are at Dryburgh (also very beautiful), Kelso, and Jedburgh (the church remains are well preserved).

MENAI STRAIT D2

536 MENAI   1818–26
    SUSPENSION BRIDGE
    T. Telford

•The Britannia Bridge (1846–50) close by is by R. Stephenson.

MEREWORTH CASTLE F5
5 km (3 mi) S of Addington

537 MEREWORTH   1722–25
    CASTLE
    C. Campbell

Directly inspired by Palladio's Villa Rotunda. Campbell published the influential *Vitruvius Britannicus,* a survey of English buildings, in 1715.

MILTON KEYNES E4

538 MILTON KEYNES   1969
    (new town)   onward
    Planners: Llewelwyn-Davies-Weeks-Forrestier-Walker
    Chief architect: D. Walker

MORECAMBE C3

539 MIDLAND   1932–33
    HOTEL
    Marine Road
    O. Hill

The first international-style hotel to be built in Britain.

MUNSTEAD F5
3 km (2 mi) SE of Godalming

540 ORCHARDS   1897–99
    (country house)
    Sir E. Lutyens

NEWCASTLE UPON TYNE B4

541 BYKER   1970–80
    2 km (1 mi) E of city center
    R. Erskine with V. Gracie and R. Tillotson

Rehousing of 10,000 people. For once, a real solution. The Byker Wall, a superb conception is a continuous cranked wall of housing 7.5 km (4.5 mi) long.

NORTHAMPTON E4

542 NEW WAYS   1925–26
    (house)
    508 Wellingborough Road
    P. Behrens

One room from the Basset-Lowke house by C. R. Mackintosh has been rebuilt in this house.

Outskirts of Northampton

543 CHURCH   ca. 670
    Brixworth (10 km/6 mi N of Northampton)

Basilican-type plan. Built from Roman materials.

544 ALL SAINTS   11th c
    (church tower)
    Earl's Barton 10 km (6 mi) ENE of Northampton

"Long and short" decoration.

545 CASTLE   1572 onward
    ASHBY
    10 km (6 mi) E of Northampton

Fourth side of courtyard enclosed in 1635, possibly by I. Jones.

NORWICH E6

546 NORWICH   1096 onward
    CATHEDRAL
    Tombland Market

Entrance through St. Ethelbert's Gate (1272). Most of the original Norman structure (1096–1145) is intact. The spire was rebuilt in 1364. Nave and choir revaulted in the Perpendicular style from 1446–99. The two-story cloister (1295–1430), off the south aisle, is the largest in England.

547 ST. GEORGE   1459–99
    COLEGATE
    (church)
    Colegate Street

548 UNIVERSITY   1962–68
    OF EAST ANGLIA
    2 km (1 mi) W of Norwich
    Denys Lasdun and Partners

A "megastructure" of terraced concrete units dominating the surrounding countryside.

•Inside this complex, in complete contrast, is the Sainsbury Centre for the Performing Arts (1974–78) by Foster Associates.

NOTTINGHAM D4

549 WOLLATON HALL 1580–88
3 km (2 mi) W of city center
R. Smythson

550 ROMAN 1842–44
CATHOLIC CATHEDRAL
Derby Road
A. W. N. Pugin

551 BOOTS 1932, 1938
FACTORY
Beeston
Sir O. Williams

A superbly confident building.
Reinforced-concrete structure
with mushroom-headed
columns enclosed by a totally
glazed curtain wall. •The head
office (1966–68) next door is by
Skidmore, Owings and Merrill.

OLDHAM D4

552 DRONSFIELD'S 1906–7
OFFICES
King Street
J. H. Sellers with E. Wood

The first flat concrete roof
used by Wood and Sellers.

OXFORD F4

Tourist Information: British
Tourist Authority, St. Aldates
Chambers, St. Aldates (tel.
48707).

Bookstore: Blackwell's Art
Bookshop, 48 Broad Street.

Museums: Ashmolean Museum,
Beaumont Street. A great
collection in the oldest museum
in Great Britain. Antiquities
(Arundel Marbles, Cretan
works collected by Sir A.
Evans), decorative arts and fine
arts (Raphael, Rembrandt,
Rubens, Vandyke, Uccello,
Claude, etc. Good Pre-
Raphaelite works).
    Christ Church Picture
Gallery. (See under Christ
Church, entry 562.)
    University Museum, South
Parks Road. Geological and
other scientific collections.

533 ST. EDMUND founded 1220
HALL
Queen's Lane/High Street

Only surviving medieval hall.

554 MERTON founded 1274
COLLEGE
Merton Street

Chapel: choir built in 1277;
transept added in 1414.

Mob Quad: (Enter from front
quad under the Treasury).
The Library on the south side,
built in 1378, is still in use.

555 BALLIOL founded 1282
COLLEGE
Broad Street

None of the original buildings
have survived. The chapel
(1858) by W. Butterfield
incorporates the plan of an

earlier 16th-c chapel. The
hall (1876) is by A. Waterhouse.

556 EXETER founded 1314
COLLEGE
Turl Street

16th-c front quad. The Chapel
(1857) by Sir George Gilbert
Scott is modeled after Ste.-
Chapelle, Paris.

557 QUEEN'S founded 1340
COLLEGE
High Street/Queen's Lane

Front Quad (1710–59) designed
by N. Hawksmoor.

558 NEW COLLEGE founded 1379
New College Lane

Chapel: Pure Perpendicular
with 14th-c stained glass.
The cloisters were completed
in 1400.

Garden Quad: Built in 1684
and very beautiful.

559 DIVINITY SCHOOL 1426–80
W of Radcliffe Square

Remarkable groined ceiling.
Restored by Sir Christopher
Wren.

560 ALL SOULS founded 1437
COLLEGE
Catherine Street

Front Quad: The original
buildings from 1437 have
survived. The chapel has most
of the original stained glass.

Great Quad: Built by N.
Hawksmoor in 1730.

561 MAGDALEN founded 1458
COLLEGE
High Street

Magdalen Tower built 1482–
1504. The front quad, St.
Swithin's Quad, and the
Cloisters are all beautiful
courtyards.

562 CHRIST founded 1525
CHURCH
(college)
Aldate's Street

Tom Tower: Built by Sir
Christopher Wren in 1682

over Cardinal Wolsey's gatehouse.

Tom Quad: The largest quad in Oxford. The fan-vaulted stairway (1630) in the SE corner ascends to the Hall (built by Cardinal Wolsey in 1529).

Cathedral: 12th c onward. West end demolished and shortened by Cardinal Wolsey to make room for the quad. West window in south aisle by W. Morris. The 13th-c Lady Chapel has stained glass (east window) by E. Burne-Jones.

Peckwater Quad: Palladian. Built by Dean H. Aldrich, 1705–14. Baroque library (1761) on south side by Dr. G. Clarke.

Canterbury Quad: J. Wyatt (1773–78).

The Christ Church Picture Gallery (1967 by Powell and Moya), in the Deanery Garden, has a fine collection of Italian and European paintings.

563 TRINITY COLLEGE   founded 1555
Broad Street

Kettell Hall: The Chapel (1690–94) is by Dean H. Aldrich. The gardens designed by Sir Christopher Wren are altered beyond redemption.

564 ST. JOHN'S COLLEGE   founded 1555
St. Giles' Street

Front Quad: Portions date from a previous college built in 1440.

Canterbury Quad: Built by Archbishop W. Laud, 1631–36. Modeled after the Ospedale Maggiore, Milano. The Gardens by L. Brown are delightful. Sir Thomas White Building (1980) by P. Dowson of Arup Associates.

565 WADHAM COLLEGE   founded 1610
Parks Road

Little changed. Noteworthy hall. The chapel's 17th-c stained glass windows are intact.

566 SHELDONIAN THEATRE   1664–69
Broad Street
Sir Christopher Wren

Modeled after the Theatre of Marcellus, Roma.

567 CLARENDON BUILDING   1711–24
Catherine Street
N. Hawksmoor

568 WORCESTER COLLEGE   founded 1714
Walton Street/Beaumont Street

Chapel (1864–70) by W. Burges.

569 RADCLIFFE CAMERA   1737–48
Radcliffe Square
J. Gibbs

One of Gibbs's finest buildings.

570 ASHMOLEAN MUSEUM AND TAYLORIAN INSTITUTE   1841–45
Beaumont Street/St. Giles' Street
C. R. Cockerell

The St. Giles' facade and statuary are worth a close study.

571 UNIVERSITY MUSEUM   1855–59
South Parks Road
T. Deane and B. Woodward

572 KEBLE COLLEGE   1867–83
Keble Road
W. Butterfield

Notable chapel.

573 LIBRARIES   1963
Manor Road/St. Cross Road
Sir L. Martin, C. St. John Wilson, and P. Hodgkinson

574 WOLFSON BUILDING   1964
St. Anne's College, Woodstock Road
Howell, Killick, Partridge, Amis

575 ST. CATHERINE'S COLLEGE   1964
Manor Road
A. Jacobsen

576 GARDEN BUILDING   1967–70
St. Hilda's College, Cowley Place
A. and P. Smithson

577 FLOREY BUILDING   1968–71
Queen's College, York Place, off St. Clements
J. Stirling

A tour de force.

Outskirts of Oxford

578 ST. MARY (church)   1175–80
Iffley (3 km/2 mi S of Oxford)

Norman west front.

579 BLENHEIM PALACE   1705–24
Woodstock (13 km/8 mi N of Oxford)
Sir J. Vanbrugh

Park (and lake) by L. Brown.

PEMBROKE F2

580 PEMBROKE CASTLE   1105 onward

Norman castle. The walls of the keep are 5 m (16 ft) thick.

PETERBOROUGH E5

581 PETERBOROUGH CATHEDRAL   1171 onward

Norman, with a unique painted ceiling (1220) in the nave. The Early English West front, a magnificent screen of three huge arches, was added from 1200–1222. The porch in the central arch was built in 1370. Fan-vaulted retrochoir built from 1483–1500. Central tower rebuilt in 14th c, then again by J. L. Pearson, 1884–86.

PETWORTH HOUSE F5
10 km (6 mi) E of Midhurst

582 PETWORTH HOUSE   1688–96

Park by L. Brown. Important collection of paintings by Turner, Vandyke, Titian, Reynolds, etc. Turner painted many views of this house, which can be seen in the Turner Room.

PLATT F5
2 km (1 mi) E of Borough Green

583 THE HOPFIELD   1933
(house)
SE of the village
C. Lucas

POOLE G4

584 ST. OSMUND'S CHURCH   1913–16
Bournemouth Road, Parkstone
E. S. Prior with A. Grove

PORTMEIRION D2

585 PORTMEIRION   1926–66
Tremadog Bay (just E of Porthmadog)
C. Williams-Ellis

A pastiche of assorted historical and vernacular buildings, many built at reduced scale.

PORTSMOUTH G4

586 IBM ADVANCE HEAD OFFICE   1970
Foster Associates

A refined solution.

PRESTON C3

587 AVENHAM ESTATE   1959–61
Russell Street and Oxford Street
J. Stirling and J. Gowan

PYRFORD F5
near Woking

588 VODIN   1902
(now Little Court)
Old Woking Road, Pyrford Common
C. F. A. Voysey

RAMSGATE F6

589 ST. AUGUSTINE   1845–50
(church)
A. W. N. Pugin

Pugin paid for this building himself. •His own house, the Grange (1844), is next door.

RIEVAULX ABBEY C4
4 km (2.5 mi) NW of Helmsley

590 RIEVAULX ABBEY   12th–13th c
(ruined)

Evocative ruins surrounded by a semicircular 18th-c grassed terrace (classical temple at each end) on the hillside. Views of the ruins from the terrace are framed by mature groves of trees alternating with open avenues.

RIPON C4

591 CATHEDRAL   1150–1538

Early English through Perpendicular. Restored (1862–72) by Sir George Gilbert Scott. Screen (1923) by Sir J. N. Comper.

592 NEWBY HALL   1765–85
6 km (4 mi) SE of Ripon
R. Adam

ROCHDALE C3

593 ST. MARY   1909–11
(church)
Toad Lane
Sir J. N. Comper

ROCHESTER D4

594 ROCHESTER   11th–15th c
     CATHEDRAL

Norman west front and
doorway, ca. 1160. Choir,
1201–27. Notable decorated
doorway (1340–60) to chapter
house. Large Early English
crypt.

RUNCORN D3

595 SOUTHGATE   1970–73
     HOUSING
S of town center
J. Stirling and M. Wilford

ST. ALBANS F5

596 CATHEDRAL   1077–1328
     Abbey Mill Lane

Much altered. Drastically
restored, 1879–84.

ST. ANDREWS A3

597 ANDREW   1964
     MELVILLE HALL
(student residence)
University of St. Andrews
J. Stirling

ST. DAVID'S E1

598 CATHEDRAL   1180 onward

The main body of the cathedral
dates from 1290–1350. West
front restored by J. Nash,
1789. Exterior restored by Sir
George Gilbert Scott and J. O.
Scott in 1862–78. Lady Chapel
finally reroofed in 1901. The
rich interior has a fine 15th-c
oak ceiling.

SALISBURY F4

599 CATHEDRAL   1220–80
     North Walk

Remarkably consistent Early
English (built in sixty years).
Double transepts. The

Decorated tower (1330–70) is
the tallest in England. Interior
destroyed by J. Wyatt's
"restoration" (1778–92). Sir
George Gilbert Scott attempted
to correct this in his restoration
(ca. 1859). Lady Chapel (1220–
26), cloisters (1364–80).

600 WILTON HOUSE   1636, 1650
     Wilton (4 km/2.5 mi W of
     Salisbury)

South front (1636) by I. de
Caux. Interiors by I. Jones
(double cube room with ten
Vandyke paintings) and
J. Webb. Appealing Palladian
Bridge (1736) in garden by
R. Morris.

SALTRAM HOUSE G2

5 km (3 mi) E of Plymouth

601 SALTRAM   16th c onward
     HOUSE

Two good rooms (1768–69) by
R. Adam.

SANDWICH F6

602 THE SALUTATION   1911
(country house)
Sir E. Lutyens

Queen Anne. Garden and house
laid out on an axial plan.

SCARBOROUGH C5

603 GRAND HOTEL   1865–67
St. Nicholas Cliff
C. Brodrick

SEATON DELAVAL B4

10 km (6 mi) N of Newcastle-
upon-Tyne

604 SEATON   1718–29
     DELAVAL HALL
3 km (2 mi) NE of Seaton
Delaval
Sir J. Vanbrugh

Rebuilt in 1862 and 1962.

SHEFFIELD D4

605 PARK HILL   1956
     HOUSING ESTATE
Duke Street/South Street
Sheffield City Architect (L.
Womersley with J. Lynn, I.
Smith, and F. Nicklin)

The continuous blocks of
apartments cranked around
traffic-free green spaces are
linked by a series of elevated

pedestrian decks. Based on
A. and P. Smithson's Golden
Lane scheme. The Hyde Park
extension was built from
1962–65.

SHIPBOURNE F5
5 km (3 mi) S of Borough Green

606 THE WOOD HOUSE   1937
S of the green
W. Gropius and M. Fry

SHREWSBURY E3

607 COALBROOKDALE 1777–79
BRIDGE
11 km (7 mi) S of Shrewsbury
T. Pritchard

The first bridge to be built
in cast iron.

608 ST. CHAD'S   1790–92
(church)
St. Chad's Terrace
G. Steuart

Massive contrasting volumes
slam into each other in this
brutally successful composition.

SISSINGHURST CASTLE F6
3 km (2 mi) NE of Cranbrook

609 SISSINGHURST   ca. 1550
CASTLE

Little remains of the castle.
The gardens, however, are very
beautiful and were laid out by
V. Sackville-West and H.
Nicholson in the 1920s.

SKIPTON C4

610 GLEDSTONE HALL   1923–27
(house)
Sir E. Lutyens

Lutyens's planning at its best.
The garden planting is by
G. Jekyll, Lutyens's life-long
collaborator.

SOMPTING G5
5 km (3 mi) NE of Worthing

611 ST. MARY   10th c
(church)

Unique gabled Saxon helm
tower.

SONNING F4

612 DEANERY GARDEN   1901
(house)
Thames Street
Sir E. Lutyens

SOUTHWELL D4
35 km (22 mi) NE of
Nottingham

613 SOUTHWELL   1108 onward
MINSTER
(cathedral)

The nave, transept, and three
towers are Norman (1108–40).
Choir rebuilt from 1234–44.

The East window contains
16th-c glass from the Temple
Church, Paris. The Chapter
House (1280–99) has exquisite
carvings and a superb doorway.

STIRLING A2

614 STIRLING   1966 onward
UNIVERSITY
Airthrey (3 km/2 mi N of
Stirling)
Matthew, Johnson-Marshall,
and Partners

Built around a small lake.
Pedestrian footbridge over the
lake links the student residences
(staggered for lake views) to the
teaching buildings. •Airthrey
Castle, by R. Adam, is nearby.

STOCKPORT D4

615 HOLLY COTTAGE   1905
Woodford Road/Holly Road,
Bramhill
E. Wood

STONEHENGE F4
11 km (7 mi) N of Salisbury

616 STONEHENGE   ca. 1800–
1400 B.C.

Two concentric circles of
standing stones surround a
horseshoe formation. Theories
as to its use range from a
religious temple to an
astronomical observatory. A
barrier stops the visitor from
walking among the stones.

STOURTON F3
5 km (3 mi) NW of Mere

617 STOURHEAD   1722
(country house)
C. Campbell

Palladian. The exquisite garden
by H. Hoare is the apotheosis
of the English landscape garden.

STOWE E4

house, now a school, 5 km (3 mi)
N of Buckingham

618 STOWE   1730–36
    (house)

Magnificent south facade by
R. Adam (completed and
altered by T. Pitt in 1774).
Superb elliptical state hall. The
garden by W. Kent, J. Gibbs,
and L. Brown is poorly kept.
The "Elysian Fields" by Kent
include a Temple of Ancient
Virtue (after the Temple of
Vesta) in the spirit of ideal
rusticity then current.

SULHAMSTEAD F4

619 FOLLY FARM   1906, 1912
    (country house)
    Sir E. Lutyens

Extended twice by Lutyens.

SUNDERLAND B4

620 ST. ANDREW'S   1906–7
    CHURCH
    Roker (just NE of Sunderland)
    E. S. Prior and R. Wells

621 CIVIC CENTRE   1968–72
    Burdon Road
    Sir Basil Spence, Bonnington
    and Collins

SWINDON F4

622 RELIANCE   1967
    CONTROL FACTORY
    Drakes Way
    Greenbridge Industrial Estate
    N. and W. Foster, R. Rogers

TEWKESBURY E4

623 TEWKESBURY   1092–1430
    ABBEY

Norman. Stained glass windows
(ca. 1400). Important tombs
(Beauchamp Chantry and Hugh
le Despenser).

THAKEHAM F5

near Pulborough

624 LITTLE   1902
    THAKEHAM
    (house)
    Sir E. Lutyens

TINTERN ABBEY F3

8 km (5 mi) N of Chepstow

625 TINTERN ABBEY   1131
    (ruined)   onward

A romantic and highly
evocative ruin. The church
(1270–1325), missing its roof
and north wall, is otherwise
well preserved.

TOTNES G3

626 DARTINGTON   1933–36
    HALL
    G. Howe and W. Lescaze

The gymnasium, headmaster's
house (Curry House), and a
private house in the warren are
by Lescaze.

TRURO G2

627 TRURO   1880–1910
    CATHEDRAL
    St. Mary Street
    J. L. Pearson

Incorporates the remains of a
16th-c church (south aisle of
choir).

UXBRIDGE F5

628 HILLINGDON   1976–78
    CIVIC CENTRE
    High Street
    Matthew, Johnson-Marshall
    and Partners

Suburban image consciously
evoked by broken roofline and
massing. Red tile roofs and
face brick.

WADDESDON MANOR E4

10 km (6 mi) NW of Aylesbury

629 WADDESDON   1875–89
    MANOR

A 19th-c "Loire Château."
Noted painting collection:
Rubens, Gainsborough,
Reynolds, Cuyp, de Hooch, etc.

WANTAGE F4

630 WHITE LODGE   1898–99
    on the grounds of St. Mary's
    Convent, Denchworth Road
    M. H. Baillie Scott

The simple exterior belies a very
rich interior decoration.

WARDOUR CASTLE F4

24 km (15 mi) W of Salisbury

631 WARDOUR CASTLE 1770–76
J. Paine

Notable interiors. Now a
school.

WARWICK E4

632 WARWICK CASTLE 14th c

One of the finest medieval
castles in Britain. Imposing
site overlooking the Avon.

WATFORD F5

633 CHURCH OF 1883–90
THE HOLY ROOD
Market Street
J. F. Bentley

WELLINGBOROUGH E5

634 ST. MARY 1906, 1908–30
(church)
Knox Road
Sir J. N. Comper

English Perpendicular and
Italian Renaissance, along with
Comper's own personal
decorations, unite to
convincingly demonstrate his
principle of Unity by Inclusion.

WELLS F3

635 WELLS 1174–1425
CATHEDRAL

Early English north porch
(1213) and west front (350
medieval statues, originally
polychromed). Three (eastern)
choir bays, retrochoir and
Lady Chapel rebuilt (1300–30)
in the Decorated style. Unique
double strainer arch (1338) to
support crossing tower. Superb
octagonal Chapter House (ca.
1320) reached by a remarkable
staircase.

636 HOLKHAM 1734 onward
HALL
3 km (2 mi) W of Wells
W. Kent with Lord Burlington

Outstanding interiors based on a
monumental reconstruction of
the components of various
ancient buildings.

WELWYN E5

637 WELWYN 1920 onward
GARDEN CITY
R. Unwin and L. de Soissons

638 PENTLEY PARK 1948
PRIMARY SCHOOL
C. H. Aslin (County Architect)

One of a series of prefabricated
schools built by the County
Architect's Department.
•Others at Cheshunt, East
Barnet, Essendon, Hemel
Hempstead, Hertford, Hitchin,
Oxley, St. Albans, Stevenage,
and Ware.

WHIPSNADE E5

639 ZOO 1934–35
B. Lubetkin and Tecton

Most of the animal shelters are
by Lubetkin and Tecton, who
also designed two small houses
on the zoo grounds.

WILLINGTON E5

8 km (5 mi) E of Bedford

640 TIRLEY GARTH 1906–7
(house)
1 km (.75 mi) E of Willington
C. E. Mallows

WINCHESTER F4

641 WINCHESTER 1079–1486
CATHEDRAL

Choir completed in 1093.
West front and nave alteration
(to the Perpendicular style)
executed 1350–1486. Restored
1905–12. Windows by W.
Morris (design by E. Burne-
Jones) in the Epiphany Chapel.

642 WAR MEMORIAL 1924
CLOISTER
Winchester College
Kingsgate Street
Sir H. Baker

WINDERMERE C3

643 BROADLEYS 1898–1900
(house)
Cartmel Fell
C. F. A. Voysey

•Moor Crag, close by, was built
by Voysey at the same time.

644 BLACKWELL 1898–99
SCHOOL
Bowness (3 km/2 mi S of
Windermere)
M. H. Baillie Scott

WINDSOR F5

645 WINDSOR 1160 onward
CASTLE

Restored to its present
appearance by Sir J. Wyatville
from 1824–37. The state
apartments have works by
Holbein, Vandyke (*Triple*

Portrait of Charles I),
Rembrandt, Rubens, etc.,
including *Queen Mary's Doll
House* (1921) by Lutyens.
St. George's Chapel (1477–
1540) is an outstanding example
of the Late Perpendicular
style; 16th-c stained glass
windows.

WITLEY F5
2.5 km (1.5 mi) S of Milford

646 TIGBOURNE   1899
      COURT
      (house)
      Sir E. Lutyens

WOBURN ABBEY E5
house 13 km (8 mi) NW of
Dunstable

647 WOBURN ABBEY   1746
      (house)   onward
      H. Flitcroft

      Interiors by H. Holland.

WORCESTER E4

648 WORCESTER   1062–1374
      CATHEDRAL
      College Street

      The exterior has suffered from
      Sir George Gilbert Scott's
      restoration (1857–73). Norman
      crypt (1084–92). Fine Early
      English choir. Off the Cloisters
      is the circular Chapter House
      (1150–ca. 1460).

WOTTON HOUSE E4
NW of Aylesbury

649 WOTTON HOUSE   1704

      Wrought ironwork by J. Tijou.
      Interiors (1820) by Sir J. Soane.

YORK C4

The old town is bounded by
14th-c walls that follow the
original Roman defenses. York
has an enormous amount of old
stained glass work; some of the
churches with stained glass
include St. Michael's,
Spurriergate; St. Martin-le-
Grand, Coney Street; All Saints,
North Street, and St. Denys,
Walmgate.

650 YORK MINSTER   1070
      (cathedral)   onward
      Petergate

      Magnificent stained glass.
      Decorated nave (1291–1354)
      with 14th- and 15th-c stained
      glass windows; the roof (rebuilt
      in 1840) is of timber, painted to
      resemble stone. The Five Sisters
      (lancet windows glazed from
      1305–25) are in the north
      transept. Perpendicular choir
      (east window, glazed 1405–8,
      is the largest medieval window
      in the world). Lady Chapel
      (1361–73). Splendid Chapter
      House (1280–1330, glass 1300–
      1320).

651 ROWNTREE   1904 onward
      GARDEN SUBURB
      New Earswick, 6 km (3.5 mi) N
        of York
      R. Unwin

Italy

Siena Duomo; *see entry 479*

Italy

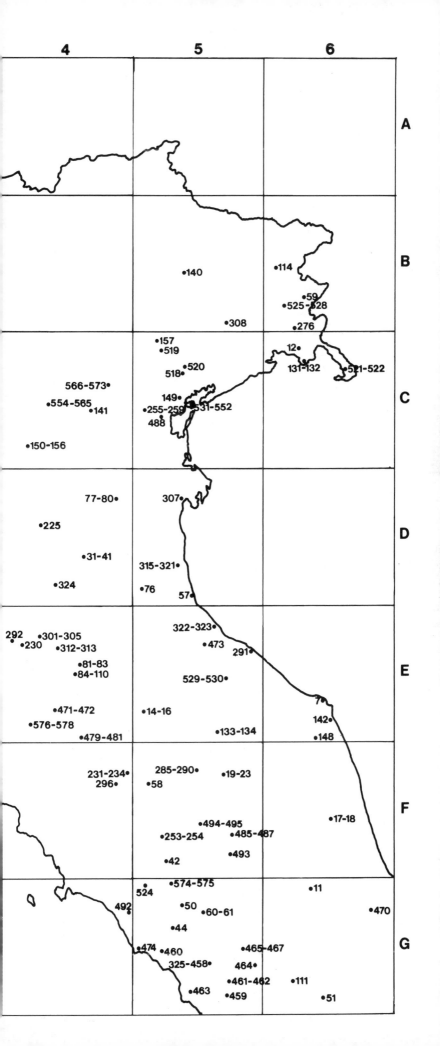

Italy

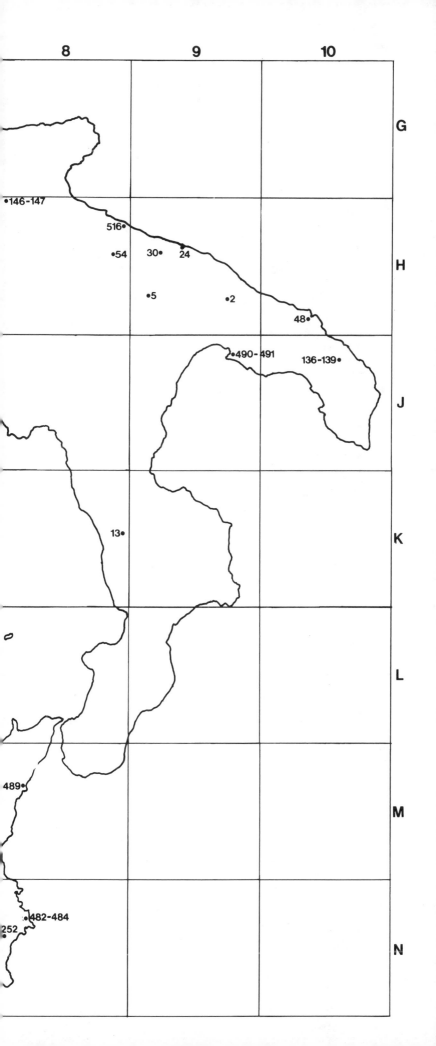

AGRIGENTO N6

1 VALLATA   6th–1st C B.C.
     DEI TEMPLI
(Valley of the Temples)
Along route 118 and the Strada
     Panoramica

   Tempio di Ercole   6th C B.C.
   (Temple of Hercules/Temple
   A)
   Eight re-erected columns.

   Tempio di   5th C B.C.
     Giunone Lacinia
   (Temple of Juno/Temple D)

   Tempio di Giove   ca. 480 B.C.
   (Temple of Jupiter)
   Destroyed by an earthquake.
   Architrave originally
   supported by telemones
   (giant male figures acting as
   columns). One figure, reconstructed by C.R. Cockerell,
   is in the Archaeological
   Museum behind San Nicola.

   Tempio della   450–440 B.C.
     Concordia
   (Temple of Concord/Temple
   F)

   Enormous and well pre-
   served.

   Tempio dei   5th C B.C.
     Dioscuri
   (Temple of Castor and
     Pollux/Temple I)

   Oratorio di   1st C B.C.
     Falaride
   (Oratory of Phalaris)
   Behind San Nicola; a 13th C
   church.

ALBEROBELLO H9

2 ZONA MONUMENTALE

Has 1000 *trulli:* traditional,
round, whitewashed houses
with drystone conical roofs.

ALESSANDRIA C2

3 ANTITUBERCU–   1935–38
     LOSIS DISPENSARY
Via Burgonzio
I. Gardella

•The adjacent hygiene
laboratory (1937–39) is also by
Gardella.

4 RESIDENTIAL   1951
     BUILDINGS
Corso Teresio Borsalino 11, 15,
17
I. Gardella

ALTAMURA H9

5 DUOMO   ca.1230
(cathedral)

A beautiful Romanesque building. Renaissance belfries.

AMALFI J7

6 SANT' ANDREA   12th–13th C
(cathedral)

West front (1204, rebuilt ca.
1860). Campanile (1276, lower
section Romanesque). The
cloister (1268) has a markedly
Arabic appearance.

ANCONA E6

7 DUOMO SAN   11th–13th C
     CIRIACO
(cathedral)
Via Giovanni XXIII

Romanesque with Byzantine
influence. Gothic porch. Greek
cross plan, central dome. •The
Roman Arch of Trajan (A.D.
115) is to the east, near the
waterfront.

AOSTA C1

8 ARCO DI AUGUSTO 23 B.C.
(Arch of Augustus)
Piazza di Augusto

•A Roman bridge from this period is across the river.

9 PORTA PRETORIA   1st C B.C.
(gateway)
Via Porta Pretoria

•The remains of a Roman
theater (restored) and amphitheater lie to the north.

10 COLLEGIATA   11th–16th C
     DI SANT'ORSO
(church)
Via Sant'Orso

12th-C Romanesque cloisters.
Renaissance priory (1506).

AQUILA G6

11 SAN BERNARDINO   1454–72
(church)
Via San Bernardino

Facade (1527) by C. dell
'Amatrice.

AQUILEIA C6

12 BASILICA   1021–61

Built by Poppone over an
earlier church. 4th-C mosaic
floors. Romanesque frescoes in
the 9th-C crypt. 1st- to 4th-C
mosaics in the Cripta degli
Scavi.

ARCAVACATA K8

10 km (6 mi) N of Cosenza

13 UNIVERSITA   1974 onward
     DELLA CALABRIE
(university)
V. Gregotti and Associates

Under construction. Multiuse
building by M. Pica Ciamarra.

AREZZO E5

14 SANTA MARIA   12th C
     DELLA PIEVE
(church)
Via dei Pileati

Interesting facade: Five blind
arches surmounted by three

superimposed loggias. Campanile built in 1330. •The Piazza Grande behind is an attractive urban space.

15 SAN FRANCESCO   1322
(church)   onward
Via Madonna del Prato
G. da Pistoa

Gothic. Frescoes (1452–66) by P. della Francesca in the chancel.

16 CASA VASARI   ca. 1540
Via 20 Settembre 55

Bought by G. Vasari and decorated with his own frescoes. Now a museum.

ARICCIA
See entry 459

ASCOLI PICENO F6

Attractive town and old quarter (Via delle Torri) surrounded by medieval ramparts.

17 DUOMO   12th c onward
(cathedral)
Piazza Arringo

Much restored. 12th-c baptistry.

18 SAN FRANCESCO 1262–1371
(church)
Piazza del Popolo

Dome added in 1549. •The 13th-c Palazzo del Popolo is opposite (facade altered in 1549 by C. dell 'Amatrice).

ASSISI F5

19 SANTA   1st c onward
MARIA SOPRA MINERVA
(church)
Piazza del Comune

Former Temple of Minerva. The Corinthian pronaos is intact. Enlarged (at rear) in 1540. •The remains of a Roman amphitheater can be seen off the Piazza Matteotti.

20 DUOMO SAN   1140–1228
RUFINO
(cathedral)
Piazza San Rufino

Powerful facade. Interior rebuilt in 1571 by G. Alessi.

21 SAN FRANCESCO   1228–53
(church and monastery)
Piazza San Francesco
Frate Elia

Two churches, one above the other. Lower church has frescoes by S. Martini and

Cimabue. 15th-c Chiostro dei Morti (Cloisters of the Dead). Upper church contains *Crucifixion* by Cimabue (north transept) and *The Life of St. Francis* frescoes by Giotto.

22 SANTA CHIARA   1260–65
(church)
Piazza Santa Chiara
F. da Campello

23 ROCCA MAGIORE   1367
(fortress)
Via della Rocca Perlici

BARI H9

24 SAN NICOLA   1087–1197
(church)
Via Venezia

Norman. Internal traverse arches added later. Much rebuilt.

BENEVENTO H7

25 ARCO DI   A.D. 114
TRAIANO
(Arch of Trajan)
Via di Circonvallazione

One of the best preserved Roman arches in existence. •Roman theater (1st c A.D.) off Via Torre (near the cathedral).

26 SANTA SOFIA   8th c onward
(church)
Corso Garibaldi

Circular/polyagonal plan. Rebuilt ca. 1688. 12th-c cloister.

BERGAMO C3

The well-preserved medieval Città Alta (upper town) is reached by the funicular. The center of the new town was laid out in 1922 by M. Piacentini.

Museum: Accademia Carrara, Via San Tomaso. 14th- to 19th-c paintings: Lotto, Bellini, etc.

27 SANTA   1137 onward
MARIA MAGGIORE
(church)
Piazza del Duomo

Romanesque basilica. Porch (1353) and freestanding octagonal baptistry by G. da Campione. •On the right is the Colleoni Chapel (1470–76) by G. Amadeo, with frescoes by G. B. Tiepolo.

28 OFFICE AND   1970–71
APARTMENT BUILDING
Rotonda dei Mille 2
G. Gambirasio

29 HOUSING   1976–80
Via Carducci/Via Loreto
G. Gambirasio

BITONTO H9

30 DUOMO   1175–1200
(cathedral)

Romanesque. Early rose window.

BOLOGNA D4

Museum: Pinoteco Nazionale, Via della Belle Arti 56. Many 14th- to 18th-c paintings. Works by Carracci, Raphael (*St. Cecilia*), and others.

31 SANTA STEFANO 8th–12th c
(church)
Via Santa Stefano/Via Farini

The church consists of a group of separate chapels facing a square surrounded by 16th-c palaces.

32 TORRI DEGLI 1109–19
ASINELLI AND DELLA
GARISENDA
Piazza di Porta Ravegnana

Two adjacent residential towers both slightly out of true.

33 SAN DOMENICO 1221–33
(church)
Piazza San Domenico

Tomb (1267, sixth chapel, right) by N. Pisano. Flamboyant arch above (1473) by N. da Bari. Three statuettes– *St. Procalus, St. Petronius,* and the *Kneeling Angel*–are attributed to Michelangelo.

34 SAN FRANCESCO 1236–63
(church)
Piazza de Marchi

Gothic. Badly damaged in 1943. Fine altarpiece (1392).

35 SAN GIACOMO 1267
MAGGIORE onward
(church)
Via Zamboni

Rebuilt in the 15th and 18th c. The Cappela Bentivoglio (chapel, ca. 1445), an exceptional Renaissance work, has an altarpiece by F. Francia and frescoes by L. Costa. Further frescoes in the Oratorio di Santa Cecilia.

36 SAN PETRONIO 1390–1659
(church)
Piazza Maggiore
A. di Vicenzo

Gothic. Unfinished (only the nave was built). Central entrance portal (1425–38) by J. della Quercia. •The Piazza Maggiore and Piazza del Nettuno (fountain, 1566, by G. di Bologna) interlock in a manner that resembles the Piazza and Piazzetta of San Marco, Venezia.

37 PALAZZO 1638
DAVIA-BARGELLINI
Strada Maggiore, 44
B. Provaglia

38 HOPKINS 1962
UNIVERSITY BUILDING
Via Belmelloro, 11
E. Zacchiroli

39 L'ESPRIT NOUVEAU 1977
PAVILION
Piazza della Constituzione

An exact replica of the pavilion by Le Corbusier at the Paris Exposition in 1925.

40 OFFICE 1975 onward
COMPLEX
Zona Fiera
(Fiera district)
K. Tange and others

Outskirts of Bologna

41 MADONNA DI 1723–57
SAN LUCA
(church)
5 km (3 mi) W of Bologna
C. F. Dotti

BOMARZO F5
21 km (13 mi) NE of Viterbo

42 PALAZZO ORSINI 1525–83
P. Ligorio

Fantastic carvings (giant faces and figures) in the Bosco Sacro (Sacred Wood) in the park.

BRA D1

43 SANTA CHIARA 1742–48
(church)
Via Barbacana
B. Vittone

BRACCIANO G5

44 CASTELLO 15th c
ORSINI-ODESCALCHI
Fortress. Pentagonal plan.

BRESCIA C3

Museums: Museo Civico Età Romana, Via dei Musei. Incorporates the ruins of the Capitoline Temple (A.D. 72). 1st-c *Winged Victory*.

Pinoteca, Via Martinengo da Barco. Brescian school paintings.

45 SAN SALVATORE 8th c
(church)
Via Veronica Gambara (access through the Museo dell' Età Cristiana)

46 DUOMO NUOVO ca. 1604
(new cathedral)
Piazza dell Duomo

•The circular 12th-c Rotondo (old cathedral) is entered through the new cathedral.

47 LOGGIA 1492–1574
Piazza della Loggia

After designs by A. Sansovino and A. Palladio.

BRINDISI H10

48 OFFICES AND   1958–61
     CANTEEN
     Montecatini-Edison
       Petrochemical Plant, Via
       Fiume Grande
     E. Sgrelli

CAMPO DEI FIORI B2
10 km (6 mi) NW of Varese

49 GRAND HOTEL TRE   1908
     CROCI
     G. Sommaruga

CAPRAROLA G5

50 PALAZZO   1530–73
     FARNESE
     G. da Vignola

     Begun by B. Peruzzi.
     Pentagonal plan enclosing an
     elegant circular courtyard.
     Monumental entrance up an
     elaborate series of staircases
     Notable (internal) spiral stair.
     Formal garden.

CASAMARI G6
abbey 14 km (9 mi) E of
Frosinone

51 ABBAZIA DI   1203–17
     CASAMARI
     (abbey)

     Cistercian.

CASERTA H7

52 PALAZZO REALE   1752–74
     (royal palace)
     L. Vanvitelli

Huge baroque palace and
gardens modeled after
Versailles.

53 INDUSTRIAL CENTER   1963
     (SIAG Plant)
     Marcianise (10 km/6 mi S of
       Caserta)
     A. Mangiarotti

CASTEL DEL MONTE H8
castle 50 km (31 mi) W of Bari

54 CASTEL DEL MONTE ca. 1240
     (castle)

     Built by Frederick II. Gothic
     structure, Roman detail,
     octagonal plan. Much restored.

CASTELSEPRIO C2
6 km (4 mi) S of Castiglione
Olona (near Varese)

55 SANTA MARIA   7th C
     (church)

     7th-c frescoes.

CEFALÙ M7

56 DUOMO   1133–48 onward
     (cathedral)

Superb Romanesque church
begun by King Roger II. Facade
(1240) by G. Panettera. 15th-c
portio by A. da Como. Splendid
12th-c Byzantine mosaics in the
apse.

CERVETERI
See entry 460

CESENATICO D5
29 km (18 mi) E of Forlì

57 AGIP HOLIDAY   1938
     CENTER
     G. Vaccaro

CHIUSI F5

Museum: Museo Civico
Etrusco. Etruscan sarcophagi
and other burial objects.

58 MONKEY TOMB   5th C B.C.

     Etruscan tomb with 5th-c B.C.
     murals. •The Grand Duke and
     Casaccini tombs are two other
     notable tombs in this
     necropolis.

CIVIDALE DEL FRIULI B6
18 km (11 mi) NE of Udine

59 TEMPIETTO   8th–9th C
     LONGOBARDO
     (Oratory of Sante Maria
       in Valle)
     Piazza San Biagio

     Traditionally ascribed to
     Petrulda. The rich interior is
     well preserved. Remarkable
     8th-c stucco relief frieze of six
     figures.

CIVITA CASTELLANA G5

60 DUOMO   11th–12th C
     (cathedral)
     Via Garibaldi

     Romanesque. Portal (1210)
     and pulpits by the Cosmati
     family.

61 ROCCA   1494–1500
     (fortress)

     Pentagonal plan. Keep (1512)
     added by A. da Sangallo the
     Elder.

COMO C2

62 SAN ABBONDIO   1095
(church)
Via San Abbondio

Romanesque. Twin aisles.

63 DUOMO   1396–1770
(cathedral)
Piazza del Duomo

Apse by C. Solari. Facade
(1487) by the Rodari family.
Dome (built 1770) designed by
F. Iuvara in 1734.

64 NOVOCOMUM   1927–28
APARTMENT BUILDING
Via Vacchi/Via Sinigallia
G. Terragni

•The war memorial (1933,
shown below) by Terragni after
Sant' Elia's design is nearby at
the end of Via Vittorio Veneto
(by the lake shore).

65 CASA DEL FASCIO   1932–36
(now Casa Del Popolo)
Piazza del Popolo 4
G. Terragni

Terragni's magnum opus.
•Another Casa del Fascio (1939)
by Terragni is at Lissone, 30 km
(19 mi) S of Como. At Seveso,
3 km (2mi) NW of Monza, is
Villa Bianco (1937, by Terragni), now a restaurant.

66 ASILO SANT'ELIA   1936–37
(nursery)
Saint'Elia district
G. Terragni

Sensitive building scaled down
to an appropriate size.

67 CASA GIULIANI   1939–40
FRIGERIO
(apartment building)
Via Rosselli 4
G. Terragni

Outskirts of Como

68 APARTMENT   1939
BUILDING
Via Regina 41, Cernóbbio
(5km/3mi NW of Como)
C. Cattaneo

Compare with G. Terragni's
Casa Giuliani Frigerio (entry
67).

69 APARTMENT   1939
BUILDING
Via Garibaldi 4, Fino Mornasco
(10 km/6 mi S of Como)
A. Magnaghi and M. Terzaghi

70 STABILIMENTO LEMA 1970
(factory)
Alzate Brianza (8 km/5mi SE of
Como)
A. Mangiarotti

71 B & B ITALIA   1971
OFFICE BUILDING
Novedrate (20 km/12.5 mi S of
Como)
R. Piano and R. Rogers

72 IBM TRAINING   1972
CENTER
Via Europa Unita, Novedrate
B. Morassutti and others

CREMONA C3

73 DUOMO   1107–14th c
(cathedral)
Piazza del Comune

Romanesque/Gothic. The lofty
Torrazzo (campanile, 1261–84)
is connected to the cathedral by
a Renaissance loggia (1525).
•The Piazza, a splendid space,
is enclosed by the octagonal
Baptistry (1167), Palazzo
Comunale (1245, remodeled
1575), and Gothic Loggia dei
Militi (1292).

DOGLIANI D1

74 BIBLIOTECA CIVICA   1963
     LUIGI EINAUDI
(library)
B. Zevi

ERCOLANO H7
(Herculaneum)

75 ROMAN TOWN
A complete Roman town buried
in A.D. 79 by an eruption of
Mount Vesuvius. Many well-
preserved houses, amphi-
theaters, temples, forums, etc.

FAENZA D5

76 DUOMO   1474
(cathedral)
Piazza della Libertà/Corso
   Garibaldi
G. da Maiano

Tuscan. Incomplete facade.
•The Museo della Ceramica,
Via Campidori, has a good
ceramics collection.

FERRARA D4

77 DUOMO   1135 onward
(cathedral)
Corso Martiri della Libertà/
   Piazza Trento Trieste

Tripartite facade; lower section
Romanesque, upper Gothic.
Campanile (1412–1594) by
L. B. Alberti.

78 PALAZZO   1391 onward
     SCHIFANOIA
Via Scandiana 23

Completed (1467–69) by B.
Rossetti. Frescoes by F. del
Cossa. Now a museum.

79 PALAZZO DEL   1492–1565
     DIAMANTI
Corso Rossetti/Corso Ercole
   d'Este
B. Rossetti

Facade clad in projecting
marble pyramids. Now the
Pinoteca Nazionale (picture
gallery).

80 PALAZZO DI   1447–1516
     LUDOVICO IL MORO
Via 20 Settembre/Via Porta
   d'Amore
B. Rossetti

FIESOLE E4

81 TEATRO ROMANO ca. 80 B.C.
(Roman theater and ruins)
N of the Piazza (past the E end
   of the Duomo)

82 SANT'   ca. 6th c
     ALESSANDRO
(church)
Via San Francesco

Converted from an earlier
Etruscan, then Roman, temple.
Continue up the road to the
church of San Francesco (good
view of Firenze).

83 SAN DOMENICO   1405–35
     DI FIESOLE
(church)
2.5 km (1.5 mi) S of Fiesole

Frescoes by Fra Angelico. •Just
south is the abbey church Badia
Fiesolana (1028, rebuilt 1466).
The unfinished facade incorporates the earlier Romanesque
facade. Interiors in the style of
F. Brunelleschi.

FIRENZE E4
(Florence)

Museums: Galleria dell'
Accademia di Belle Arti, Via
Ricasoli 60. *David* (original)
and the four unfinished *Slaves*
by Michelangelo. Florentine
paintings.
    Museo Archeologico, Via
Gino Capponi 2. Antiquities;
strong Etruscan section.
    Museo Bardini, Piazza dei
Mozzi 1. Antiquities, art, and
sculpture.
    Museo della Casa Buonar-
roti, Via Ghibellina 70. The
house of Michelangelo. Early
works, drawings, etc.
    Museum della Fondazione
Horne (Palazzo Corsi, by G.
da Sangallo), Via dei Benci 6.
Primitive and Renaissance
paintings and furnishings.
    Museo Nazionale (Bargello
or Palazzo del Podestà, ca.
1255), Palazzo Bargello, Via
del Proconsolo 4. Sculpture by
Donatello, Michelangelo,
Brunelleschi, Bernini, and
others.

    Palazzo Pitti (shown above,
1458 onward, after F.
Brunelleschi's plans), Piazza
Pitti. The Galleria Palatina
(remodeled in 1640–47 by P. da
Cortona) has a superb collection of paintings by Raphael,
Titian, Rubens, etc. Also in the
palace is the Museo degli
Argenti (decorative arts) and
Galleria d'Arte Moderna (19th-
and 20th-c works). Behind the
palace are the Boboli Gardens
(interesting grotto).
    Galleria degli Uffizi, Log-
giata degli Uffizi 6. The most
important collection of pain-

tings in Italy. Opposite the entry is the Loggia dei Lanzi (1376–82, by S. Talenti), an open-air museum containing Giambologna's *Rape of the Sabines* and *Hercules and Nessus,* as well as Cellini's *Perseus.*

84 DUOMO   1296–1462
(Santa Maria del Fiore
    cathedral)
Piazza del Duomo
A. di Cambio, then F. Talenti

Dome (1420–34, lantern 1436–62) by F. Brunelleschi. Facade rebuilt 1875–77. Interior: dome frescoes by G. Vasari and F. Zuccari, *Pietà* (north transept) by Michelangelo. •On the right of the cathedral is the campanile (1334–59) by Giotto, then A. Pisano, then F. Talenti, each changing his predecessor's design. Reliefs by Pisano and L. della Robbia on lower sec-

tion. The octagonal Baptistry (San Giovanni) across the piazza dates from the 5th C (rebuilt in the 11th). South door (1330–36) by A. Pisano. North (1403–24) and east ("Doors of Paradise," 1425–52) doors by L. Ghiberti. The baptistry interior has 13th-C mosaics (dome) and tomb of John XXIII by Donatello. The Museo dell 'Opera del Duomo, Piazza del Duomo 9 (behind the cathedral apse), has models and important sculpture from the cathedral, including Donatello's *Cantorie, Jeremiah,* and *Habakuk.*

85 SAN MINIATO   1018–62
    AL MONTE
(church)
on the hilltop overlooking Viale Galileo Galilei

Superb Florentine Romanesque facade. Cardinal of Portugal's chapel (1459–66, left aisle) by A. Manetti and other artists.

86 OGNISSANTI   1239 onward
(church)
Piazza Ognissanti

Restored in the 17th C. Botticelli's fresco *St. Augustine*

(1480, between the third and fourth altars, right). In the monastery refectory, entrance to the left of the church, is Ghirlandaio's *Last Supper.*

87 SANTA   1268 onward
    MARIA DEL CARMINE
(church)
Piazza del Carmine

Baroque interior (1771). Brancacci Chapel (end, right transept) with frescoes by Masaccio, Masolino, and Fra Lippi. Saint Andrea Corsini Chapel (1683) at the opposite end of the transept.

88 PALAZZO   1298–1314
    DELLA SIGNORIA
(Palazzo Vecchio)
Piazza della Signoria
A. di Cambio

Powerful tower. On the entry steps is Donatello's *Judith and Holofernes.* Other works by A. del Verrocchio, G. Vasari, etc., inside.

89 SANTA MARIA   1278–1360
    NOVELLA
(church)
Piazza di Santa Maria Novella

Completed by I. Talenti. The facade (1456–70) is by L. B. Alberti. Important frescoes by Masaccio, Orcagna, Ghirlandaio, etc. Notable crucifix by F. Brunelleschi in the Gondi Chapel (first, left chancel). Frescoes in the cloisters, especially in the Cappellone degli Spagnoli (ca. 1355, by A. Buonaiuto).

90 SANTA CROCE   1294–1442
(church)
Piazza Santa Croce

Begun by A. di Cambio. Modern facade (1863). Many works by Giotto, A. Orcagna, A. Veneziano, Donatello (Crucifix, end chapel, north transept), and others. In the cloisters is the Pazzi Chapel (1429–42) by F. Brunelleschi; also the church's museum with additional works of art.

91 ORSANMICHELE 1337–1404
(oratory)
Via de' Calzaiolo
F. and S. Talenti

Transitional Gothic-Renaissance. Exterior statues by L. Ghiberti, Donatello, A. del Verrocchio (*Doubting St. Thomas*). Inside is a remarkable Tabernacle (1359, right aisle) by A. Orcagna.

92 PONTE VECCHIO   1345
(old bridge)
T. Gaddi

Lined on both sides with shops.
•The corridor above (1564, by
G. Vasari) links the Uffizi with
the Pitti Palace.

93 OSPEDALE   1421–25
    DEGLI INNOCENTI
(foundling hospital)
Piazza Santissima Annunziata
    (E side)
F. Brunelleschi

The first Renaissance building.
Elegant loggia. •The matching
facade opposite (1518) is by A.
Sangallo the Elder. The church
of Santissima Annunziata
(1250, restored from 1441–55
by Michelozzo) is on the north
side. Portico added in 1601.

94 SAN LORENZO   1421–46
(church)
Piazza San Lorenzo
F. Brunelleschi

Interior (1447–60) by A.
Manetti. Latin cross plan.
Sagrestia Vecchio (old sacristy,
1421–28, off left transept) by
Brunelleschi, decoration by
Donatello. Access to the
Laurentian Library (1524–68,
by Michelangelo) is through
the cloisters at no. 9, left of the
church. The staircase in the
library vestibule is by B.
Ammanati after Michelangelo's
design. In the Medici Chapels
(access off the Piazza Madonna degli Aldobrandini, right of
the church) is the Sagrestia
Nuova (new sacristy, 1520–38)
by Michelangelo, who also
sculpted the tombs.

95 CONVENTO DI   1436–53
    SAN MARCO
(enlargement)
Piazza San Marco
Michelozzo

Cloisters, sacristy, and library.
Now a museum. Numerous
frescoes by Fra Angelico
throughout the building.

96 PALAZZO   1444–60
    MEDICI-RICCARDI
Via de' Gori/Via de' Ginori
Michelozzo

Main facade extended in 1680.
Notable chapel (frescoes by B.
Gozzoli). Frescoes by L.
Giordano in the gallery.

97 SANTO SPIRITO   1444–87
(church)
Piazza Santo Spirito
F. Brunelleschi

Completed by A. Manetti.
Sacristy (1489–92) by G. da
Sangallo and Il Cronaca. •The
Palazzo Guadagni (1490–1506)
opposite is also by Il Cronaca.

98 PALAZZO PAZZI   1445–72
    QUARATESI
Via del Proconsolo 10
F. Brunelleschi

Executed by G. da Maiano.

99 PALAZZO   1446–51
    RUCELLAI
Via Vigna Nuova
B. Rossellino

Built to L. B. Alberti's design.
•In the Via della Spada,
behind, is the Rucellai Chapel.
Inside is the Edicola del Santo
Sepulcro (1467), a templelike
shrine by Alberti.

100 PALAZZO   1489–1539
    STROZZI
Via de Tornabuoni/Via degli
    Strozzi
B. da Maiano

Completed by Il Cronaca.

101 PALAZZO   1520–27
    PANDOLFINI
Via San Gallo 74/Via Micheli
Raphael

Executed by G. F. Sangallo.

102 PONTE SANTA   1567–70
    TRINITA
(bridge)
over the Arno River
B. Ammanati

Destroyed in 1944. Rebuilt in
1958.

103 SAN GAETANO   1604–48
(church)
Via de Tornabuoni/Via del
    Campidoglio
M. Nigetti

104 SAN FIRENZE   1715–74
(church)
Piazza San Firenze
F. Ruggieri

Completed by Z. del Rosso

105 VILLA GIULIO   1908–12
    LAMPREDI
Via Giano della Bella
G. Michelazzi

Art nouveau. •Other villas by Michelazzi are Broggi-Caraceni (1911), Via Scipione Ammirato; and Ravazzini (1912) and Toccafondi (1913), both on Via XX Settembre.

106 STADIO   1930–32
    COMMUNALE BERTA
    (stadium)
    Viale Manfredo Fanti (N of
      Viale Pasqualé Padi)
    P. L. Nervi

Beautiful exposed staircase.

107 STAZIONE   1936
    FERROVIARA DI SANTA
    MARIA NOVELLA
    (railway station)
    Piazza della Stazione
    G. Michelucci and others

108 CHIESA SAN   1964
    GIOVANNI
    (church)
    Autostrada del Sole/Autostrada
    Firenze-Mare
    G. Michelucci

Too much of a good thing.

109 APARTMENT   1965
    BUILDING
    Via Piacentina 129
    L. Savioli and D. Santi

110 PONTE GIOVANNI   1967–70
    DA VERRAZZANO
    (bridge)
    over the Arno River
    L. Savioli, C. Damerini, and V.
    Scalesse

FIUGGI G6
27 km (17 mi) N of Frosinone

111 COMPLESSO   1965–70
    TERMALE FONTI DI
    BONIFACIO VIII
    (spa)
    L. Moretti

FLORENCE
See Firenze

FOSSANOVA H6
abbey 4 km (2.5 mi) S of
Priverno

112 ABBAZIA   1163–ca. 1200
    DI FOSSANOVA
    (abbey)

Cistercian. Restored but still fairly authentic.

FRANCAVILLA AL MARE G7
3 km (2 mi) S of Pescara

113 SAN FRANCO   1948–58
    (church)
    L. Quaroni

FRASCATI
See entry 461

GEMONA DEL FRIULI B6
26 km (16 mi) N of Udine

114 DUOMO   13th–14th c
    (cathedral)
    G. Griglio

Transitional Romanesque Gothic.

GENOVA D2 (Genoa)

115 CATTEDRALE   11th c
    DI SAN LORENZO   onward
    (cathedral)
    Piazza San Lorenzo

Chapel of St. John (1478) by E. and D. Gagini. Treasury museum (1952) by F. Albini.

116 SANTO STEFANO   12th c
    (church)
    Via 20 Settembre/Corso A.
      Podesta

Reconstructed after 1945.

117 SANTA   1552–1603
    MARIA DI CARIGNANO
    (church)
    Piazza Carignano
    G. Alessi

Greek cross plan after Bramante's scheme for St. Peter's.

118 PALAZZO ROSSO   1613–83
    Via Garibaldi 18
    P. A. Corradi

Rich frescoes. Fine painting collection. •Other palaces on Via Garibaldi are at nos. 4 (Cataldi, 1558, by G. Alessi); 9 a splendid mansion, (Doria Tursi, now Municipale [1501–93] by R. Lurago. Offices at rear [1961] by F. Albini); and 11 (Bianco, by G. Orsolino and D. Ponzello. Good paintings.)

119 PALLAZZO DELL'   1640
    UNIVERSITA
    Via Balbi 5
    B. Bianco

Fine stairway. •Also by Bianco on Via Balbi are nos. 4 (Senarega) and 1 (Durazzo Pallavicini).

120 PALAZZO REALE   1650
    Via Balbi 10
    P. F. Cantoni

Altered (1705) by C. Fontana. 17th-c paintings.

121 TEATRO   1827
   COMMUNALE
   (Carlo Felice theater)
   Piazza Fontane Marose
   C. Barabino

   Interior damaged in 1945.

122 CIMITERIO DI   1835
   STAGHENO
   (cemetery)
   Via Piaceza
   C. Barabino

123 CHIESA DELLA   1956
   SACRE FAMIGLIA
   (church)
   Via Chiappazzo
   A. de Carlo, A. Mor, and L.
   Quaroni

124 HIGHWAY   1960–67
   VIADUCT
   Polcevera River, between
   Autostrade dei Fiori and
   Autostrade di Savara
   R. Morandi

125 REDIGLIONE IRI   1962
   (Steel Pavilion)
   Fiera del Mare, Strada
   Sopraelevata
   A. Mangiarotti

126 SIP SKYSCRAPER   1969
   Via San Lorenzo/Via Fiume
   M. Bega, P. Gambacciani, and
   A. Viziano

127 STUDIO WORKSHOP   1968
   Via Melen 71, Cornigliano
   R. Piano

128 MUSEO   1976 onward
   SANT'AGOSTINO
   (museum)
   Piazza Sarzano
   F. Albini, F. Helg, and others

Outskirts of Genova

129 PUNTA SAN   1956
   MARINO HOTEL
   Arenzano Pineta, Arenzano
   (25 km/16 mi W of Genova)
   I. Gardella and M. Zanuso

130 CASA AROSIO   1959
   (house)
   Arenzano Pineta, Arenzano
   V. Magistretti

GRADO C6

131 DUOMO   6th c
   (cathedral)

   Basilica. Built of Roman
   fragments. 6th-c mosaic floor.
   Venetian altarpiece (1372).
   5th-c baptistry.

132 ZIPSER CENTER   1962
   by the sea
   M. d'Olivo

GUBBIO E5
   An attractive hill town. A
   well-preserved Roman theater
   has survived.

133 PALAZZO DEI   1332–46
   CONSOLI
   Piazza della Signoria
   M. Gattaponi

134 PALAZZO   1476 onward
   DUCALE
   Via Ducale

   Built by Frederico da Montefel-
   tro, Duke of Urbino. Fine
   courtyard (almost identical to
   L. da Laurana's courtyard in
   Urbino).

HERCULANEUM
See Ercolano

IVREA C1
42 km (26 mi) N of Torino

135 OLIVETTI   1934 onward
   FACTORY AND
   FACILITIES
   Via Jervis

   Office building (1934–37), Asili
   Nido (nursery, 1939–41), Servizi
   Sociali (social services building,
   1954–57), all by L. Figini and
   G. Pollini. The mensa (canteen,
   1953–59) is by I. Gardella;
   the ICO plant (1953–61), by
   E. Vittoria. Multiuse building
   (1967–75) by I. Cappai, P.
   Mainardis, and G. Chiodini.
   New factory (1971) by M.
   Zanuso and E. Vittorio.

LECCE J10

136 SANTI NICOLA   1180
   E CATALDO
   (chapel)
   in the Cemetery, off Via
   d'Aurio/Viale degli
   Studenti

   Built by Tancredi. Roman-
   esque/Norman. Baroque facade
   added in 1716.

137 BASILICA DI   1549–1691
   SANTA CROCE
   (church)
   Piazza Castromediano/Via
   Umberto I
   G. Riccardi, then C. Penna,
   then F. and G. Zimbalo.

   Powerful baroque facade. Rich
   interior. •The adjacent Palazzo
   del Governo (1695) is attributed to G. Zimbalo.

138 SANT'IRENE   1591–1639
(church)
Corso Vittorio Emanuele
F. Grimaldi

139 DUOMO   1659–70
(cathedral and campanile)
Piazza del Duomo
G. Zimbalo

Part of a magnificant baroque
square. •The surrounding
buildings include the Bishop's
Palace (1632) and Seminary
(1694–1709, by G. Cino).
Another church by Zimbalo in
Lecce is San Giovanni Battista
(or del Rosario, 1691–1728).

LONGARONE B5
10 km (6 mi) N of Belluno

140 CHIESA   1978
(church)
G. Michelucci

LONIGO C4
24 km (15 mi) SW of Vicenza

141 ROCCA PISANA   ca. 1576
(villa)
V. Scamozzi

Palladian influence. Superb
views carefully framed by
meticulous siting and align-
ment.

LORETO E6

142 SANCTUARIO   1468–18th C
    DELLA SANTA CASA
(church)
Piazza della Madonna

Begun by G. da Maiano. Dome
(ca.1500) by A. da Sangallo the
Younger; side chapels (1511)
by Bramante. Facade (1570–87)
by G. Boccalini, then G. B.
Ghioldi. The doors (1590–
1610), by many artists, are
exquisite. Note the figures of
Adam and Eve (central door by
A. Lombardo). The Santa
Casa under the dome is by
Bramante, decoration by
others. •The facade of the Palazzo Apostolico (ca. 1510) on
the piazza is by A. Sansovino.

LUCCA E3

143 ANFITEATRO   2nd C A.D.
    ROMANO
(Roman amphitheater)
Piazza dell'Anfiteatro Romano

144 DUOMO   11th C onward
(cathedral)
Piazza San Martino

Superb Romanesque facade
(upper section, 1204–10 by G.
Como). Gothic interior. Tomb
(left transept) of Ilaria del
Carretto by J. della Quercia.

145 SAN MICHELE   12th C
(church)
Piazza San Michele

Pisan Romanesque.

LUCERA H8
18 km (11 mi) W of Foggia

146 FORTEZZA   1269–83
    ANGIOINA
(castle)

Built by Charles I. The earlier
castle (1233) by King Frederick
II is inside the defenses.

147 DUOMO   1302–17
(cathedral)
P. d'Angicourt

French Angevin to the last
detail.

MACERATA E6

148 SFERISTERION   ca. 1835
(arena)
Piazza Nazario Savro
I. Aleandri

Neoclassic arena.

MALCONTENTA C5
just S of Mestre

149 VILLA FOSCARI   1560
(Malcontenta)
1.5 km (1 mi) out of town, on
the Brenta Canal
A. Palladio

Only the central block remains.

MANTOVA C4
(Mantua)

150 SAN LORENZO   ca. 1080
(church)
Piazza delle Erbe

Circular. Romanesque
brickwork.

151 PALAZZO   1290–1708
    DUCALE   onward
Piazza Sordello

Vast. Cortile della Cavallerizza
by G. Romano. Frescoes by A.
Mantegna in the Camera degli
Sposi. Paintings by Rubens
and others. •The Duomo opposite, rebuilt in 1545 by G.
Romano, has a baroque facade
(1756) by N. Baschiera. The
Chapel of the Incoronata inside (north aisle) is by L. B.
Alberti.

152 SAN SEBASTIANO   1459
(church)
Via Acerbi

Designed by L. B. Alberti;
built by L. Fancelli. First
Renaissance church to employ
a Greek cross plan. •Opposite,

at no. 45, is the Casa del Mantegna, which has a very fine courtyard.

153 SANT'ANDREA   1472–94
(church)   onward
Piazza Mantegna

Designed by L. B. Alberti; built by L. Fancelli. Dome (1732–82) by F. Iuvara. Frescoes by G. Romano.

154 PALAZZO DEL TÈ   1525–35
(Palace)
Viale Tè
G. Romano

Frescoes (Sala dei Giganti) by Romano and his school. Stuccowork by F. Primaticcio (see Fontainebleau, France).

155 OWN HOUSE   1544
Via C. Poma 18
G. Romano

An influential mannerist building. •The Palazzo di Giustizia (law courts) at Via Poma 7 was built to Romano's designs.

156 BURGO PAPER   1960–62
     FACTORY
Strada Montata 13
P. L. Nervi

MASÈR C5
30 km (19 mi) NW of Treviso

157 VILLA BARBARO   1555–59
A. Palladio
Frescoes by P. Veronese.

MILANO C2
(Milan)

Museums: Pinacoteca Ambrosiana (within the library), Piazza Pio XI. Paintings by Bramantino, Botticelli, da Vinci, Lombard, and Venetian schools. Also Raphael's cartoons for the Athenean School frescoes (in the Vatican).
    Pinacoteca di Brera, Via Brera 28. Excellent collection: Mantegna's *The Dead Christ,* Bellini, Titian, Raphael, etc.
    Galleria d'Arte Moderna, Via Palestro 16. 19th- and 20th-c paintings. The extension (no. 8) is by I. Gardella (1953).
    Museo Poldi Pezzoli, Via Morone 10. A fine collection. Italian paintings, mainly 15th and 16th c. Pollaiuolo, Mantegna, Bellini, and others.

158 SAN LORENZO   4th c
(church)   onward
Corso di Porta Ticinese *F3*

Octagonal plan. Reconstructed in the 16th c.

159 SANT' EUSTORGIO   9th c
(church)   onward
Piazza Sant' Eustorgio *E3*

Romanesque basilica. The Capella Portinari (chapel, 1462) behind the apse is by Michelozzo (stucco and frescoes by V. Foppa).

Milano

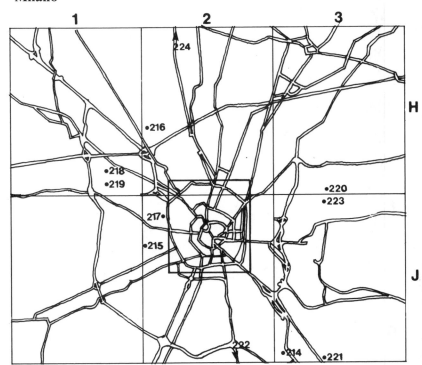

Milano detail

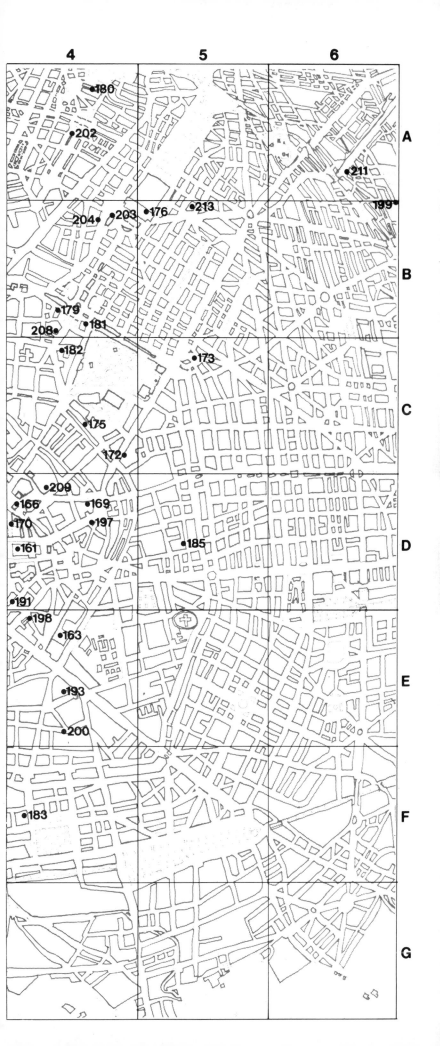

160 SANT' AMBROGIO 1098–1128
(church)
Piazza Sant' Abrogio *D2*

Founded 386, extended
789–859, rebuilt 1098–1128,
and restored after being
bombed in 1943. Rare atrium
(ca. 1150) entrance. Pro-
totypical Lombardian basilica.
Campaniles: left, 9th c; right,
ca. 1128. Interior: 5th-c chapel
(seventh, right) of San Vittore
in Ciel d'Oro with fine
mosaics. Portico della
Canonica (1492, rebuilt since
1945) by Bramante, who also
designed two of the cloisters.

161 DUOMO 1386–1813
(cathedral)
Piazza del Duomo *D4*

Immense. Initially directed by
French and German masters.
Bare interior. The exterior is
covered with rather archeological Gothic detailing (2,245
statues, etc.). Fascinating roof-
top promenade. Tomb of
G. G. de Medici (1565, south
transept) by L. Leoni.

162 CASTELLO 1450
SFORZESCO
(castle)
Piazza Castello *C3*

Contains the Museo d'Arte
Antica (Museum of Antique
Art). Antique, medieval, and
Renaissance sculpture.
Unfinished *Pietà* by
Michelangelo. Italian paint-
ings. Museum design (1956–64)
by BBPR Architectural Studio.

163 OSPEDALE 1457–1624
MAGGIORE
(hospital)
Via Francesco Sforza *E4*
A. Filarete

Renaissance building completed
in the Gothic style by C. Solari
and then F. M. Ricchini. Now a
university.

164 SANTA MARIA 1465–97
DELLE GRAZIE
(church)
Corso Magenta/Via Caradosso
D2

Apse, dome, cloisters, and old
sacristy by Bramante (1492–
97). On the left, in the
Cenacolo Vinciano, is the *Last
Supper* fresco by Leonardo da
Vinci, in very poor condition.
See Geel, Belgium.

165 SAN SATIRO 1476–1514
(church)
Via Torino/Via Speronari/Via
Falcone *D3*
Bramante

The original 9th-c church and
campanile remain. A false
perspective in stucco creates
illusionary apses. Octagonal
sacristy (1488).

166 PALAZZO MARINO 1560
(town hall)
Piazza San Fedele *D4*
G. Alessi

Facade (1888–90) on the Plaza
della Scala by L. Beltrami.

167 SAN ALESSANDRO 1602
IN ZEBEDIA
(church)
Piazza San Alessandro *D3*
L. Binago

168 LA SCALA 1776–78
(opera house)
Piazza della Scala *D3*
G. Piermarini

Interior (1830) by A.
Sanquirico.

169 SAN CARLO 1844–47
(church)
Corso Vittorio Emanuele II/
Piazza San Carlo *D4*
C. Amati

Modeled after the Pantheon.
•An interesting hotel (1905) by
A. Cattaneo and G. Santamaria
is at no. 15 Corso Vittorio
Emmanuele II.

170 GALLERIA 1865–77
VITTORIO EMMANUELE
Piazza del Duomo, through to
Piazza della Scala *D4*

A superb iron and glass gallery
linking the two piazzas.
Cruciform plan, central dome.

171 CIMITERO 1866 onward
MONUMENTALE
(cemetary)
Piazzale Cimitero Monumentale
B3

Interesting tombs and
monuments. (Monument to
the victims of the German
concentration camps by BBPR
Architectural Studio.)

172 CASA CASTIGLIONI   1903
     (apartment building)
     Corso Venezia 47 *C4*
     G. Sommaruga

     Art nouveau. Monumental
     staircase.

173 GALIMBERTI   1905
     APARTMENT BUILDING
     Via Malphigi *C5*
     G. B. Bossi

     Clad in decorative glazed tiles
     (Liberty figures).

174 CLINICA COLUMBUS   1909
     (clinic, former Villa Romeo)
     Via Buonarroti 48 *D1*
     G. Sommaruga

175 CASA TOSI   1910
     Via Senato 28 *C4*
     A. Campanini

176 STAZIONE CENTRALE 1931
     (railway station)
     Piazza Duca d'Aosta *B5*
     E. Montuori

Reminiscent of the film sets of
F. Lang's *Metropolis*.

177 PALAZZO DELLE   1932
     ARTI
     (Triennale Building)
     Viale E. Alemagna 6 *C2*
     G. Muzio

     •The steel frame tower (1933)
     nearby is by C. Chiodi, E.
     Ferrari, and G. Ponti.

178 CASA RUSTICI   1934
     (house)
     Corso Sempione 34 *B2*
     G. Terragni and P. Lingeri

     A pioneering modern building.

179 APARTMENT   1934–35
     BUILDING
     Via Marcora 11 *B4*
     G. Mucchi and G. Prearo

180 APARTMENT   1934–35
     BUILDING
     Via Perrone di San Martino 8
     A4
     L. Figini

181 CASA FELTRINELLI   1935
     (apartments)
     Via Manin 37 *B4*

     BBPR Architectural Studio

182 MONTECATINI   1936
     OFFICE BUILDING
     Via della Moscova/Via F.
     Turati *C4*
     G. Ponti, A. Fornaroli, and E.
     Soncini

     •A second building (1951–58)
     by Ponti is on Via F. Turati/Via
     Principe Amedeo.

183 BOCCONI   1938–40
     UNIVERSITY
     Via R. Sarfatti 25 *F4*
     G. Pagano

184 APARTMENT   1947–48
     AND OFFICE BUILDING
     Via Broletto 37 *D3*
     L. Figini and G. Pollini

185 CORRIDONI   1947–50
     RESIDENTIAL HOTEL
     Via Corridoni 22 *D5*
     L. Moretti

186 APARTMENT   1949
     BUILDING
     Via Paleocapa 5 *D2*
     I. Gardella

187 FARMITALIA   1951–53
     FACTORY
     Viale E. Bezzi 24 *E1*
     G. Giordani and I. M. Valeri

188 OFFICE AND   1951–53
     APARTMENT BUILDING
     Corso Italia 15 *E3*
     L. Moretti

189 HOUSING   1951
     Quartiere 8 Triennale (QT8) *C1*
     P. Lingeri and L. Zuccoli, M.
     Zanuso and R. Menghi

     •The church of Sante Maria
     Nascente (1957) on Via Sal-
     moiraghi is by V. Magistretti
     and M. Tedeschi.

190 CHIESA DELLA   1952–56
     MADONNA DEI POVERI
     (church)
     Piazza Madonna dei Poveri, off
     Via Forze Armate *D1*
     L. Figini and G. Pollini

191 ZANOLETTI   1953
     OFFICE BUILDING
     Via Albricci 8 *D4*
     M. Asnago and C. Vender

192 OLIVETTI OFFICE   1954
     BUILDING
     Via Clerici 4 *D3*
     G. Bernasconi, A. Fiocchi, and
     M. Nizzoli

193 APARTMENT   1954
     BUILDING
     Via Marchiondi 7 *E4*
     A. Castelli, I. Gardella, and
     R. Menghi

194 SAN ILDEFONSO   1955
     (church)
     Piazza le Chiesa *B1*
     C. de Carli

195 LORO & PARSINI   1956
     OFFICE BUILDING
     Via Savona 129 *F1*
     L. C. Dominioni and V. Dubini

Twenty-eight stories high. A
successful interpretation of the
spirit of a medieval tower (the
cathedral is close by). Attacked
for these very same qualities by
Team 10 members when built.

An elegant, slender, high-rise
building that clearly displays its
structure.

Outskirts of Milano

Asterian abbey. 17th c porch.
Polygonal crossing tower.

Off shutter concrete
throughout.

216 CHIESA MATRI 1956–57
    MISERICORDIAE
    (church)
    Via Trieste, Baranzate *H2*
    A. Mangiarotti and B.
    Morassutti

217 MULTIUSE 1969–76
    SPORTS BUILDING
    Via Tesio 26 *J2*
    Gilberto and Tommaso Valle

218 MONTE 1968–73
    AMIATA HOUSING
    Via Falck 37, Gallarate *H1*
    A. Rossi

219 MONTE 1968–74
    AMIATA HOUSING
    Via Cilea 34, Gallarate *H1*
    C. and M. Aymonino, A. De
    Rossi, S. Messare, and others

220 SEDE IBM 1968–75
    (headquarters)
    Via Rivoltana, Tregarezzo
        di Segrate *H3*
    M. Zanuso and P. Crescini

221 SNAM OFFICES 1970–73
    AND CANTEEN
    Viale De Gasperi, San Donato
        Milanese (8 km/5 mi SE of
        Milano) *J3*
    F. Albini, F. Helg, and others

222 CENTRO CIVICO 1971–80
    (civic center)
    Pieve Emanuele (15 km/9 mi
        S of Milano) *J2*
    G. Cannella and M. Achilli

223 MONDADORI 1973–75
    HEADQUARTERS
    Via Marconi 27, Tregarezzo di
        Segrate *J3*
    O. Niemeyer, L. Pozzo, and
    G. Campello

224 SCUOLA 1974–76
    ELEMENTARE
    (primary school)
    Quartiere San Giorgio, Meda
        (22 km/13 mi N of Milano)
        H2
    V. Magistretti and G. Aulenti

MODENA D4

Museum: Palazzo dei Musei,
Largo Porta San Augustino.
Good Italian paintings in the
Galleria Estense.

225 DUOMO 1099–13th C
    (cathedral)
    Piazza Grande

Begun by Lanfranco. Important
Romanesque building. 12th-C
sculpture on west (central)
portal and south side by
Wiligelmo and his school.

MONDOVI D1

226 CHIESA DELLA ca. 1650
    MISSIONE
    (church)
    Mondovi-Piazza (upper town)
    G. Boetto

Baroque. Rich interiors (1697)
by A. Pozzo. •Close by is the
Cattedrale di San Donato (1743)
by F. Gallo.

227 SAN FILIPPO ca. 1750
    (church)
    Mondovi-Breo (lower town)
    F. Gallo

228 SANCTUARIO 1596–19th C
    DI VICO FORTE
    on the outskirts of the town
    A. Vittozzi

Splendid baroque interior. Oval
dome (ca. 1750) by F. Gallo.
19th-C corner towers.

MONREALE M6

229 DUOMO 1174–89
    (cathedral)

Norman/Sicilian fusion.
Superb interior, 12th-C
mosaics. Rich exterior; bronze
doors (1186) by B. da Pisa.
Beautiful cloisters.

MONTECATINI-TERME E4

19 km (12 mi) W of Pistoia

230 CIMITERO 1968 onward
    (cemetery)
    Montecatini Alta
    L. Savioli, D. Santi, and E.
    Brizzi

MONTEPULCIANO F4

231 PORTA AL PRATO 16th C
    (gateway)
    Via Roma
    A. da Sangallo the Elder

•No. 37, the Palazzo
Avignonesi, is attributed to
G. da Vignola. The facade of
Sant' Agostino, further on,
is by Michelozzo

232 PALAZZO CERVINI 16th C
    Via Cavour 9
    A. da Sangallo the Elder

233 PALAZZO 1519–35
    CONTUCCI
    Piazza Grande (E side)
    A. da Sangallo the Elder

Completed by B. Peruzzi. •On
the north side of the piazza is the
Palazzo Tarugi, possibly by G.
da Vignola. The cathedral
(1592–1630) opposite is by I.
Scalza.

234 MADONNA DI 1518–29
    SAN BIAGIO
    (church)
    1 km (0.5 mi) S of the Porta al
        Prato
    A. da Sangallo the Elder

His masterpiece. Greek cross
plan, high dome. •The canon's
residence opposite is also by
Sangallo.

MONZA C2

235 DUOMO   13th–14th c
(cathedral)
Piazza del Duomo

Facade (1390–96) by M. di
Campione. Interior rebuilt ca.
1650.

236 VILLA REALE   1780
Viale Regina Margherita
G. Piermarini

Neoclassic. "English" park
(1806) by E. de Beauharnais.
Now a museum.

237 ELMAG   1964
    INDUSTRIAL BUILDING
beginning of the Superstrada
    Milano-Lecco
A. Mangiarotti

NAPOLI H7
(Naples)

Museums: Museo Archeologico
Nazionale, Piazza Museo
Nazionale. Collection of
antique sculpture and art
discovered at Pompeii and
Ercolano.
    Museo Nazionale di Capodi-
monte, Parco di Capodimonte.
Former royal palace. Good
collection of Italian paintings
by Bellini, Masaccio, Titian,
Caravaggio, etc. Also Cranach,
Brueghel, and others. Imitation
Trianon (Versailles) in the
park.

238 CASTEL NUOVO   1279–82
(castle)
Via Vittorio Emanuele III
P. de Chaulnes

Totally rebuilt (ca. 1440) by G.
Sagrera. Triumphal Arch
(1455–68) designed by F.
Laurana.

239 DUOMO DI   1294–1393
    SAN GENNARO   onward
(cathedral)
Via del Duomo/Via Tribunali

Modern facade (1905). Chapel
of San Gennaro (1608–37, third
right).

240 SANTA CHIARA   1310–28
(church)
Via B. Croce (S side, E of
    Piazza del Gesù Nuovo)

Rebuilt after 1943. Tomb
(1345) of Robert the Wise by
G. and P. Bertini behind the
altar. Cloister transformed in
1742 into a rather surreal
garden.

241 SAN PAOLO   1583
    MAGGIORE
(church)
Via dei Tribunali/Via
    Cinquesanti
F. Grimaldi

242 GESÙ NUOVO   1584
(church)
Piazza del Gesù Nuovo
G. Valeriani

243 PALAZZO   1600–1602
    REALE
(palace)
Piazza del Plebiscito
D. Fontana

Interior stair (1651) by F. A.
De Vita. Restored 1841, 1945.
•Opposite is San Francesco di
Paolo (church, 1816–24, by P.
Bianchi), a replica of the
Pantheon, in the center of a
semielliptical colonnade.

244 SANTA MARIA   1602–13
    DELLA SANITÀ
(San Vincenzo church)
Via della Sanità
G. Donzelli (Fra Nuvolo)

Greek cross plan.

245 SAN GIORGIO   1640
    MAGGIORE
(church)
Via Pietro Colletta
C. Fansago

246 CERTOSA DI SAN   17th c
    MARTINO
(monastery)
Via Angelini (on the hilltop;
    funicular access)

Neapolitan baroque. Many
good paintings: Reni, Stanzione
(*Pietà*), Ribera, and others.

247 TEATRO SAN   1809–17
    CARLO
(opera house)
Piazza Trento e Triste
E. C. Leconte

Rebuilt by A. Niccolini (1816–
17).

248 VILLA   1817–19
    FLORIDIANA
Via A. Falcone
A. Niccolini

Neoclassic. Now a ceramic
museum.

249 GALLERIA   1887–90
    UMBERTO I
Via Roma/Via Sante Brigita
E. Rocco

A rather dusty copy of the
Galleria in Milano.

250 APARTMENT 1966
BUILDING
Via San Giacomo dei Capri 179
A. L. Rossi

251 BORSA MERCI 1972
(stock exchange)
Corso Meridionale
M. Capobianco, R. Dalisi, and
M. P. Ciamarra

NOTO N8
27 km (17 mi) SW of Siracusa

252 NOTO 1695 onward
(rebuilt town)

The 18th-c town was replanned
after an earthquake in 1693.
Many baroque villas along the
Corso. Fine cathedral
(1710–70, by V. Sinatra).

ORVIETO F5
Well-preserved medieval
town. Spectacular hilltop site.

253 DUOMO 1290–ca. 1600
(cathedral)
Piazza del Duomo

Begun by A. di Cambio. The
facade, a synthesis of Gothic
structure and rich Italian
ornament, was begun by L.
Maitani (1310–30), continued
by A. Pisano, then A. Orcagna
(1354). Completed in 1600.
Inside (south transept) is the
Capella di San Brizio, a chapel
with frescoes by Fra Angelico
(begun in 1447, completed by
L. Signorelli ca. 1504).

254 POZZO DI SAN 1528–37
PATRICIO
(well)
off the Piazza Cahen, near the
upper funicular station
A. da Sangallo the Younger

Two concentric spiral stairs.

OSTIA ANTICA
See entry 463

PADOVA C5
(Padua)

Museum: Museo Civico, Piazza
del Santo. 14th- to 18th-c Italian
paintings by Bellini, Tintoretto,
Tiepolo, etc.

255 BASILICA DEL 1232–1307
SANTO ANTONIO
(church)
Piazza del Santo

Gothic/Byzantine hybrid. The
plan is essentially that of San
Marco, Venezia, with a French
chevet added at the rear. High
altar (1450) by Donatello. •The

equestrian statue of Gatta-
melata (1453) outside is
Donatello's masterpiece.

256 CAPELLA DEGLI 1303
SCROVEGNI
(Madonna dell'Arena chapel)
Corso Garibaldi

Outstanding fresco cycle by
Giotto.

257 CAFFÉ PEDROCCHI 1816
Via 8 Febbraio
G. Japelli

258 MORASSUTTI 1957
INDUSTRIAL BUILDING
Via Venezia 71
A. Mangiarotti and B. and G.
Morassutti

259 BANCA 1966–72
D'ITALIA
(bank)
Via Roma
G. Samona

PAESTUM J7
Greek colony founded in the
6th c B.C. Many ruined
buildings, agora, amphitheater,
etc.

Museum: Sculpture and
artifacts from this site.
Metopes from the Temple of
Hera. (The temple itself is 9
km [5.5 mi] away at the mouth
of the Sele River.)

260 BASILICA 6th c B.C.

Archaic column capitals.

261 TEMPIO DI 6th c B.C.
CERERE
(Temple of Ceres)

•127 m (140 yd) to the south is
the underground Temple of
Hera.

262 TEMPIO DI 5th c B.C.
NETTUNO
(Temple of Neptune)

Remarkably well preserved.
The proportions of the temple
create an overwhelming
impression of strength and
power.

PALERMO M6

Museums: Museo Nazionale
Archeologico, Via Roma/Via
Bara. Antiquities, Greek
sculpture, etc. Metopes from
Temples C and E, Selinus.
  Galleria Nazionale, Palazzo
Abbatellis (1495, by M. Carne-
livari), Via Alora (E of Via
Butera). 15th- to 18th-c
Sicilian paintings. Fresco of
Death Triumphant. The
arrangement of the interiors is
by C. Scarpa (1954).

263 PALAZZO DEI   ca. 1130
    NORMANNI   onward
    (Palazzo Reale)
    Corso Vittorio Emanuele/
      Porta Nuova

Now the Sicilian Parliament.
The central section and Torre
Pisano (Pisan Tower) are
original. Inside is the Capella
Palatina (Palatine Chapel,
1132–40), built by Roger II:
Norman-Saracen fusion,
original mosaics, superb stalac-
tite ceiling. Royal apartments:
original mosaics (1140) in the
Sala di Re Ruggero.

264 SAN GIOVANNI   1132
    DEGLI EREMITI
    (church)
    Via dei Benedettini/Via A.
      Mongitore

Arabic domes. Picturesque
cloisters.

265 LA MARTORANA   1143–51
    (S.M. dell'Ammiraglio, church)
    Piazza Bellini

12th-c mosaics and campanile.
Greek cross plan, extended ca.
1680. •On the north side of the
piazza is San Cataldo (church,
1161, since restored). Santa
Caterina (16th c), east side, is
an attractive baroque church.

266 PALAZZO   1154–66
    DELLA ZISA
    Via dei Normanni

267 CATTEDRALE   1170–85
    (cathedral)   onward
    Piazza della Cattedrale/Corso
      Vittorio Emanuele

Much restored and rebuilt. The
east end is the oldest surviving
section. Dome (1801) by F.
Fuga.

268 SAN FRANCESCO   13th c
    D'ASSISI
    (church)
    Via Paternostro

Renaissance choir stalls (1524).
Interior damaged in 1943.

•Next door at no. 5 is the
Oratorio della Compagnia di
San Lorenzo; fine interior
(1687–96) by G. Serpotto.

269 SANTA MARIA   15th c
    DELLA CATENA
    (church)
    Via Vittorio Emanuele/Piazza
      Marina (NE side)

Gothic/Renaissance. Possibly
by M. Carnelivari.

270 CHIESA DE LA   1689
    PIETÀ
    (church)
    Via Torremuzza
    Fra G. Amato

271 VILLINO BASILE   1904
    Via Siracusa 15
    E. Basile

272 BANK   1908–13
    Piazza Cassa di Risparmio
    E. Basile

273 OFFICE BUILDING   1959
    Viale della Regione/Via
      Marchese di Villabianca
    G. Samona

274 INSTITUTI   1979 onward
    DI SCIENCE
    (Science Faculty, Palermo
      University)
    Parco d'Orleans
    V. Gregotti and Associates

Outskirts of Palermo

275 VILLA PALAGONIA   1715
    Bagheria (16 km/10 mi E of
      Palermo)
    M. T. Napoli and A. Daidone

Baroque. Grotesque sculpture
on the grounds. •Other 18th-c
villas (Butera, Valguarnera,
etc.) in the town.

PALESTRINA
See entry 464

PALMANOVA B6

276 PALMANOVA   1593 onward
    (town plan)

Fortified star-shaped "ideal
city." •The Duomo (cathedral,
1615 onward) in the exact
center of the town was begun
by B. Longhena and completed
by V. Scamozzi.

PARMA D3

277 DUOMO   12th c
    (cathedral)
    Piazza del Duomo

Romanesque. 13th-c porch and
campanile. Dome frescoes
(1522–30) by Correggio.
Superb octagonal Romanesque/
Gothic baptistry (1196–1260)
enclosed by four superimposed
loggias. •Behind the Duomo is
the church of San Giovanni
Evangelista with frescoes
(dome) by Correggio. Other
frescoes by Correggio are in
the Camera di San Paolo (NE
of the Piazza Marconi).

278 MADONNA 1521–39
DELLA STECCATA
(church)
Via Garibaldi (E side)/Via
Dante
B. and G. Zaccagni

Greek cross plan. Frescoes by
Il Parmigianino.

279 PALAZZO 1583 onward
DELLA PILOTTA
Piazza Pilotta
G. Boscoli

Inside is the Galleria Nazionale
(paintings by Correggio, Fra
Angelico, Il Parmigianino,
and others) and the Teatro
Farnese (1618, by G. B.
Aleotti), which was severely
damaged in 1944. Restored
(1969–78) by G. Canali.

280 OFFICE BUILDING 1953
Via Cavour/Via San Biagio
F. Albini

281 CASA DI 1969–72
RISPARMIO
(bank)
Via Emilia
G. Canali and V. Banzola

PAVIA C2

282 SAN MICHELE 1100–1155
(church)
Via P. Diacono

Lombard, rebuilt in the Romanesque style. Good facade.

283 SAN PIETRO IN 1132
CIELO D'ORO
(church)
Via Liutprando, off Viale
Matteotti

Rich facade. Arca di Sant'
Agostino (tomb of St. Augustine, 1362) in the choir.

284 CERTOSA DI 1396–1497
PAVIA
(Carthusian monastery)
9 km (5.5 mi) N of Parma

Perfectly preserved. The
church (1453–97, by Giovanni
and Guiniforte Solari) is
Gothic with Renaissance detail.
The superbly executed Renaissance facade (1490–1560) is by
G. Amadeo, then B. Briosco,
then C. Lombardo. Inside are
the tombs of Lodovico il Moro
and Beatrice d'Este (left
transept, 1497–99, by G.
Solari) and Gian Galeazzo
Visconti (right transept,
1493–97, by G. C. Romano).
Little and great cloisters off the
refectory. •The Palazzo Ducale
(1625, now the museum) is by
M. Richino.

PERUGIA F5

285 IPOGEO DEI 2nd C B.C.
VOLUMNI
(Etruscan cemetery)
6 km (4 mi) S of Perugia

Very well preserved rock-cut
tombs.

286 ARCO 3rd C B.C.
ETRUSCO
(Etruscan Arch, also of
Augustus)
Via Rocchi, off Piazza
Fortebraccio

Upper part Roman. •Many of
the ancient city walls have
survived. Another Etruscan
gateway, the Porta Marzia, off
Via Marzia (only the arch
remains), gives entry to a
strange subterranean street, the
Via Bagliona Sotterannea. The
Palazzo Gallenga Stuart (1758,
by F. Bianchi) is in the Piazza
Fortebraccio.

287 SAN PIETRO 10th C onward
(church)
Borgo 20 Giugno

Reconstructed in the Renaissance style. Campanile dates
from 1468. Good view through
east door.

288 PALAZZO DEI 1293–1443
PRIORI
Piazza 4 Novembre
G. di Servado and G. di
Benvenuto

Inside is the Galleria Nazionale
dell' Umbria, with an
important collection of 13th- to
17th-C Umbrian paintings.
•The fountain in the piazza
(1278, design by Fra Bevignote,
execution by N. and G. Pisano)
has been much restored, most
recently in 1949. The Collegio
di Cambio (exchange, 1452–
57), just south of the Palazzo
dei Priori, on Corso Vannucci,
has a council chamber
decorated with frescoes by Il
Perugino (and pupils).

289 SAN DOMENICO 1305
(church)
Corso Cavone

Totally rebuilt (1605–32) by C.
Maderna. Archeological
museum in the monastery.

290 ORATORIA DI 1457–61
SAN BERNARDINO
(oratory)
Piazza San Francesco
A. di Duccio

Exquisite carvings. •The Porta
di San Pietro is also by di
Duccio.

PESARO E5

Museum: Musei Civili, Via
Toschi Mosca, off Via Rossini.
Paintings: Italian primitives,
Bellini, and others. Good
ceramic collection.

291 VILLA RUGGERI   1902–7
Via A. Vespucci
G. Brega

Art nouveau.

PESCIA E4
19 km (12 mi) E of Lucca

292 MERCATO DEI FIORI   1948
(flower market)
E. Brizzi, L. Ricci, L. Savioli,
and others

•The new flower market (1972–
81) on Via Mammianese is by
Savioli and others.

PIACENZA C3

293 DUOMO   1122–1233
(cathedral)
Via Legnano

Later altered. Transitional
Romanesque/Gothic structure.

294 PALAZZO DEL   1281
    COMMUNE
(Palazzo Pubblico)
Piazza dei Cavalli

Lombardian Gothic.

PIAZZA ARMERINA N7
21 km (13 mi) SSE of Enna

295 VILLA OF   4th C A.D.
    MAXIMIAN
3 km (2 mi) S of Piazza
    Armerina

Interesting plan. Some well-
preserved mosaic floors.

PIENZA F4

296 DUOMO AND   1460–63
    PALAZZO PICCOLOMINI
(cathedral and palace)
Piazza Pio II
B. Rossellino

Rossellino designed the piazza
and laid out the town, all for
Pope Pius II.

PISA E3

Museum: Museo Nazionale, in
the Monastero di San Matteo,
Lungarno Mediceo. Medieval
sculpture and paintings of the
Pisan schools: G. and N.
Pisano, S. Martini, Masaccio,
etc.

297 PIAZZA DEL DUOMO
    Duomo   1063–1118
    (cathedral)

Begun by Buscheto.
Enlarged (including a new
facade) by Rainaldo. Pulpit
(1311, rebuilt in 1926) by G.
Pisano. Splendid Roman-
esque transept doors (1180,
opposite the campanile) by
B. Pisano.

    Battistero   1152–1263
    (baptistry)
Diotisalvi, then N. and G.
Pisano, then C. di Nese.

Pulpit (1260) a masterpiece
by N. Pisano.

    Campanile   1173–1271
    (leaning tower)
    B. Pisano (possibly).

Continued (third floor up
and already leaning) by G. di
Simone. Belfry added in
1350.

    Campo Santo   1278–83
    (cemetery)   onward
G. Pisano. 14th- and 15th-c
frescoes, tombs, etc. Damaged in 1944.

298 SAN PAOLO A RIPA   1148
    D'ARNO
(church)
Piazza San Paolo a Ripa d'Arno

Restored since 1944. Magnificent facade.

299 SANTA   1251–1300
    CATERINA
(church)
Piazza Santa Caterina

Facade (1330). Saltarelli tomb
(left wall) and sculpted columns
flanking the altar by N. Pisano.

300 SANTA MARIA   1323
    DELLA SPINA
(church)
Lungarno Gambacorti
(by the bridge)

Decoration by pupils of N. and
G. Pisano. Inside, *Madonna
and Child* by N. Pisano.

PISTOIA E4

301 DUOMO   12th C
(cathedral)
Piazza del Duomo

Romanesque facade. Entry atrium added in 1311. •The baptistry (begun in 1337 by C. di Nese), Palazzo Pretorio (1367), and Palazzo Communale (1294–1385) surround the piazza.

302 SANT' ANDREA   1166
(church)
Via di Sant'Andrea

Pulpit (1301) and crucifix (third altar, left) by G. Pisano.

303 SAN GIOVANNI   12th–14th C
FUORCIVITAS
(church)
Via Cavour

Facade (ca. 1160). Restored since 1945.

304 SANTA MARIA   1469
DELLA GRAZIE
Via del Ceppo
Michelozzo

305 BORSA MERCI   1965
(stock exchange)
Piazetta San Leone
G. Michelucci

POMPEII H7

306 ROMAN RUINS

An entire Roman town buried by an eruption of Mount Vesuvius in A.D. 79. Many important buildings of all types; forum, amphitheater, baths, villas, etc. Historic remains in the Antiquarium (museum).

POMPOSA D5

307 ABBAZIA DI   9th C
POMPOSA
(abbey)

Frescoes (c. 1340) by V. da Bologna. Superb campanile (1069). •The contemporary Palazzo della Ragione (law court) is opposite.

PORDENONE B5

308 ZANUSSI-REX   1959–60
OFFICES
Gino Valle

PORTESE C3
40 km (25 mi) E of Brescia, on Lake Garda

309 CASA LA SCALA   1955–57
(house)
Baia de Vento
V. Vigano, L. Finzi, and E. Nova

POZZUOLI H7

310 TEMPIO DI   1st C B.C.
SERAPIDE
(Temple of Serapis)
Piazza di Serapide (by the seashore)

More accurately a market.

311 ANFITEATRO   1st C A.D.
ROMANO
(Roman amphitheater)
Via Rossini

Well preserved (basement especially).

PRATO E4

312 DUOMO   10th C onward
(cathedral)
Piazza del Duomo

Facade (1211) by G. da Coma. Exterior pulpit (1439) by Donatello and Michelozzo. Frescoes by Fra Lippi in the choir. •The Museo Civico in the Palazzo Pretorio, Piazza del Commune, has further works by Lippi and other Tuscan painters.

313 SANTA MARIA   1485–91
DELLE CARCERI
(church)
Piazza Santa Maria delle Carceri
G. da Sangallo

Modeled after F. Brunelleschi's Pazzi Chapel, Firenze.

RAVELLO J7

314 DUOMO   1086
(cathedral)
Piazza del Duomo

Remodeled in 1786. Bronze doors (1179, by B. da Trani). Pulpits right (1272, by N. da Foggia) and left (1131, Byzantine, mosaic of Johah and the whale). •The Palazzo Rufolo, a 13th-c Norman-Saracen villa on Piazza Vescouada, has an extraordinary site (and view). Villa Cimbone, built from antique fragments, possesses a belvedere with a breathtaking vista.

RAVENNA D5

315 BATTISTERO   400–450
DEGLI ORTODOSI
(Neoni or Orthodox Baptistry)
Via Rasponi

Dome decorated with excellent 5th-c mosaics.

316 MAUSOLEO DI   ca. 420
GALLA PLACIDIA
(mausoleum)
Via Galla Placidia

Greek cross plan. Fine mosaics.

317 BATTISTERO   5th C
DEGLI ARIANI
(baptistry)
Via Diaz

5th-C mosaics.

318 SANT'   493–520
    APOLLINARE NUOVO
    (church)
    Via di Roma, opposite Via E.
    Negri

Built by Theodoric. Superb
6th-c mosaics; 10th-c campanile; 16th-c portico.

319 MAUSOLEO DI   520–26
    TEODORICO
    (Tomb of Theodoric)
    Via delle Industrie/Via Dorsena

Chiefly remarkable for the
shallow-domed roof, a single
block of limestone 10m (36 ft)
in diameter.

320 SANT'   535–38
    APOLLINARE IN CLASSE
    (church)
    5 km (3 mi) S of Ravenna

Basilica. Superb 6th- and 7th-c
mosaics on the triumphal arch
and choir. The 9th-c campanile
is the earliest surviving in Italy.

321 SAN VITALE   526–47
    (church)
    Via San Vitale/Via Galla
      Placidia
    G. Argentarius

An extraordinarily sophisticated solution to the problem
of designing a centralized
space. Central octagon (dome
above carried on squinches)
surrounded by an ambulatory.
Glorious mosaics. •Museum of
Antiquities in the former
monastery next door.

RIMINI E5

322 ARCO D'AUGUSTO   27 B.C.
    (Arch of Augustus)
    Piazzale Giulio Cesare

•Another Roman relic, the
Porta di Tiberio (A.D. 14–21),
still spans the Marecchia River.

323 TEMPIO   13th c onward
    MALATESTIANO
    (church)
    Via 4 Novembre/Via Tempio
      Malatestiano

L. B. Alberti converted this
church (San Francesco) in 1446
into a monument to Scais-
mondo Malatesta. The
enormously influential facade
(still unfinished) was the first
to employ the motif of a
Roman triumphal arch on a
church. Interior by M. de
Pasti. The relief carving and
tombs are by A. di Duccio.

RIOLA DI VERGATO D4
40 km (25 mi) SE of Bologna

324 CHIESA   1966–78
    PARROCCHIALE
    (parish church)
    A. Aalto

ROMA G5 (Rome)
The Vatican City follows the
Roma entries.

Tourist Information: Ente
Nazionale Italiano per il
Turismo, Via Marghora 2 (tel.
49711).

Architect's Institute: Consiglio
Nazionale degli Architetti, Via
Arenula 71 (tel. 655–145).

Museums: Galleria Borghese,
Piazzale Museo Borghese, off
Via Pinciana. Housed in the
Villa Borghese (1613 by G.
Vansanzio). Three masterpieces
by Bernini: *David, Rape of
Proserpine,* and *Apollo and
Daphne.* Also Canova's
Pauline Borghese. Paintings by
Bellini, Raphael, Titian (*Sacred
and Profane Love*), Veronese,
Caravaggio, and others.
    Pinateca Capitolina, Palazzo
dei Conservatori, Piazza del
Campidoglio (S side).
Paintings by Titian, Rubens,
Caravaggio (*St. John the
Baptist*), da Cortona, and
others. Antique sculpture
(*Dying Gaul*) in the Museo dei
Conservatori (same building,
lower floors). Further antique
sculpture in the Museo
Capitolino, opposite. See entry
367.
    Galleria Doria Pamphili,
Piazza del Collegio Romano.
18th-c mansion. Rich interiors.

Paintings by Velásquez, Raphael, Caravaggio, and others. Antique sculpture.

Galleria Nazionale d'Arte Moderna, Palazzo delle Belle Arti (1882, by P. Piacentini), Viale delle Belle Arti 131. Italian 19th- and 20th-c paintings.

Galleria Nazionale d'Arte Antica, Palazzo Barberini. See entry 384.

Galleria Nazionale d'Arte Antica, Palazzo Corsini (1732, by F. Fuga), Via della Lungara 10. Paintings by Caravaggio, Guercino, and the Neopolitan and Genoese schools.

Galleria Pallavicini, Palazzo Rospigliosi, Via 24 Maggio. Paintings by Botticelli, Lotto, Reni, etc. Restricted admission; check before visiting.

Galleria Spada, Palazzo Spada (1540, by G. Mazzoni), Piazza di Capo di Ferro 3. 17th-c painting collection housed in a suite of rooms designed for this purpose by F. Borromini. Colonnade (false perspective) in the second courtyard by Borromini.

San Pietro in Vincoli (church), Piazza San Francesco di Paolo. At the end of the right aisle is Michelangelo's *Moses,* flanked by *Leah* and *Rachel* (from Pope Julius II's unfinished tomb).

325 FORO ROMANO
(Roman Forum)
Via dei Fori Imperiali *E7*

Temple of   ca. 500 B.C
Saturn

Eight granite columns remain.

Temple of   484 B.C
Castor and Pollux
(Temple of the Dioscuri)

Rebuilt by Augustus. Three Corinthian columns in white marble remain.

Basilica Emilia   179 B.C.

Basilica Guilia   54–44 B.C.
Built by Julius Caesar, completed by Augustus.

House of   ca. A.D. 66
the Vestal Virgins

Temple of   A.D. 81
Vespasian
Three Corinthian columns remain.

Arch of Titus   A.D. 81

Temple of   A.D. 141
Antonius and Faustina

Converted into the church of San Lorenzo in Miranda in 1602. Baroque facade.

Arch of   A.D. 203
Septimus Severis

Temple of   A.D. 205
the Vestal Virgins
Partial reconstruction (ca. 1930). The base is original.

Curia   A.D. 303
Rebuilt by Julius Caesar, then by Diocletian.
Converted into the church of Sant' Adriano in A.D. 638.

Basilica   A.D. 306–12
di Massenzio
(St. Maxentius or Constantine)

Completed by Constantine. Three huge arches from the north aisle remain standing.

Column of Phocas   A.D. 608

Roma

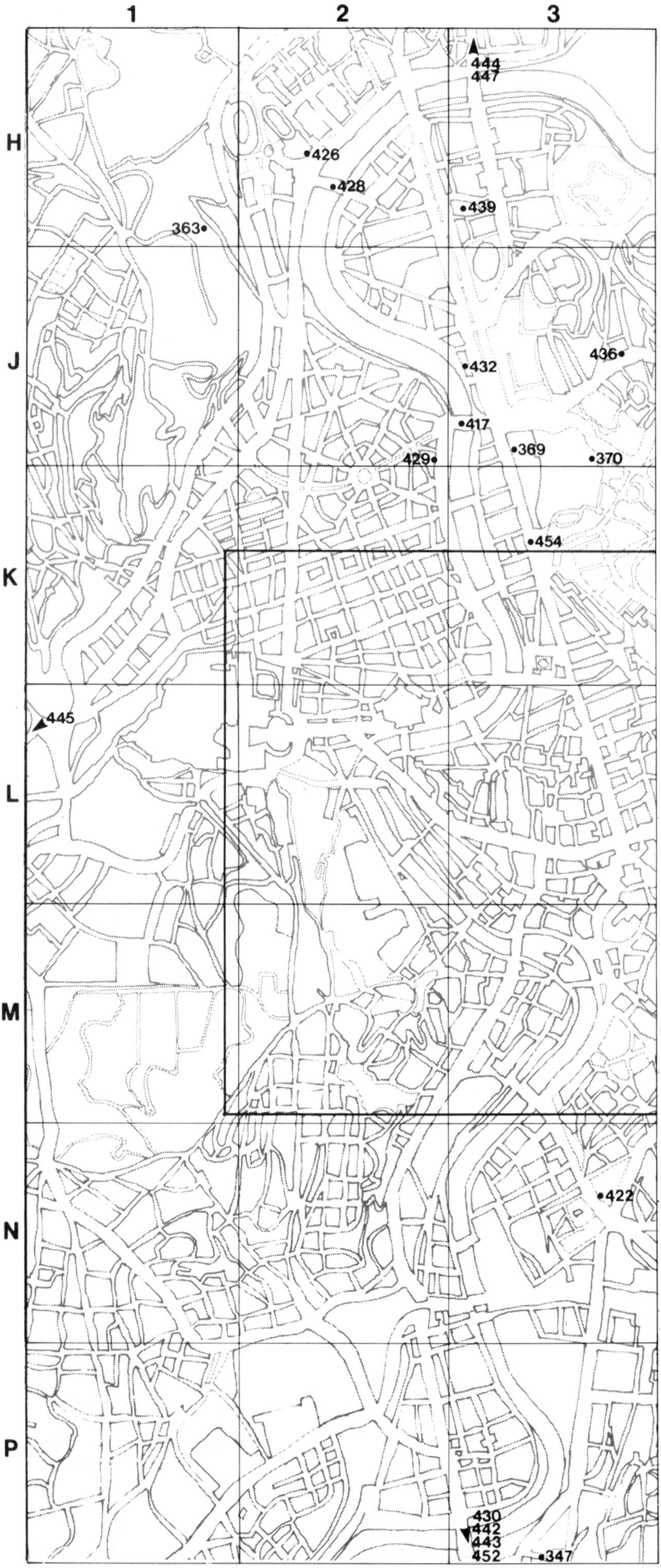

- •426
- •428
- 363•
- •439
- •432
- •436•
- •417
- •429•
- •369
- •370
- •454
- ▲445
- •422
- 444
- 447
- 430
- 442
- 443
- 452
- •347

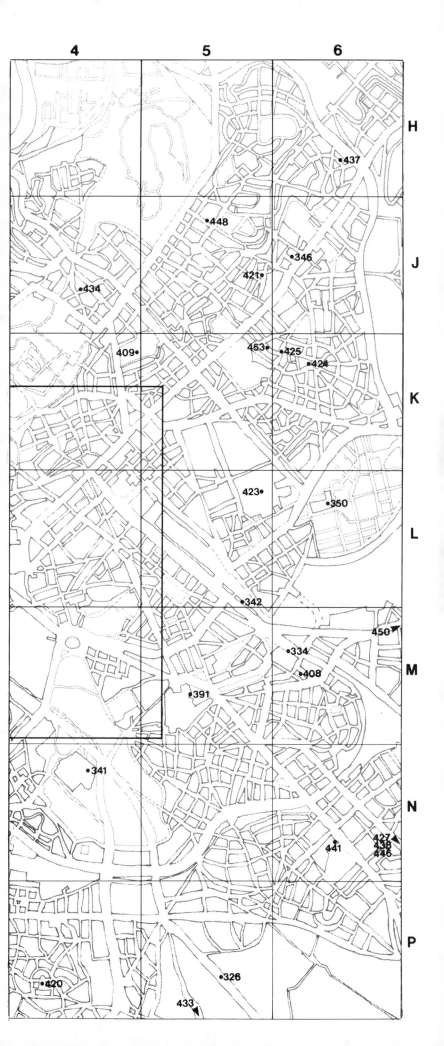

Roma detail

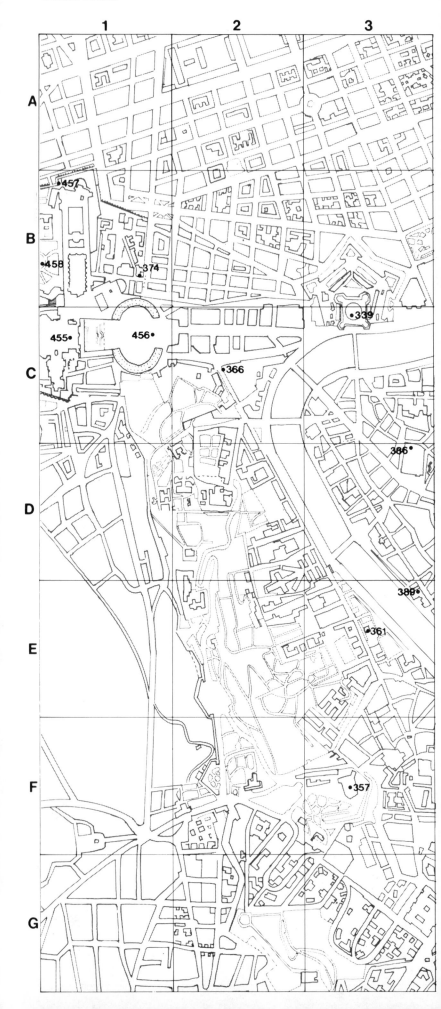

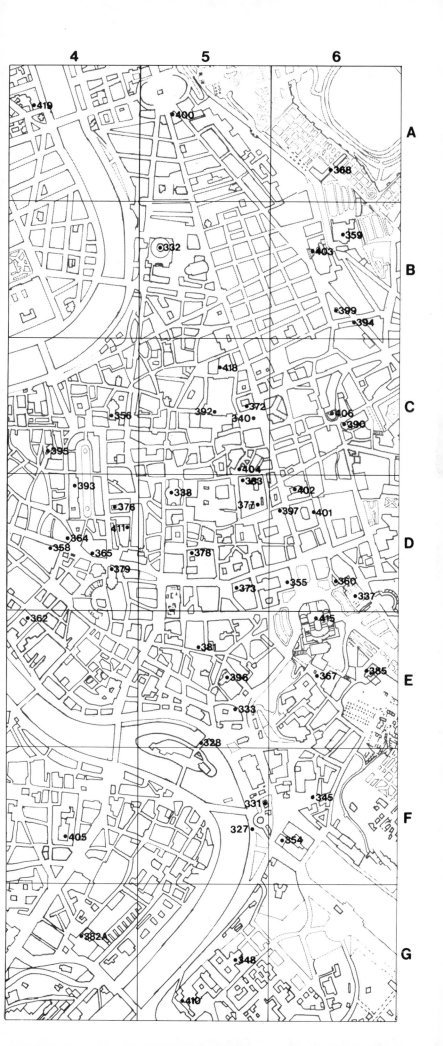

Roma detail

	7	8	9
			•440
A	451•		•371
B	•416	•382 •380	•343
C	•388 •384 •387 •396 •375 •412	•413	435•
D	•407 •414		349 •352
E	•449 •330 431•	335	
F	•325 336 344• •329		•353
G		351•	

326 VIA APPIA   312 B.C.
     ANTICA *P5*
     (Roman road)

Exit through the Porta San Sebastiano. •3 km (2 mi) further on is the Tomb of Caecilia Metella. The section beyond this is the best preserved, with further tombs beside the ancient roadway.

327 CLOACA   ca. 184 B.C.
     MAXIMA *F5*
     (Roman drainage system)

View from the Ponte Palatino (bridge) over the Tiber River (on the east bank). Built (ca. 6th C B.C.) to drain the area that later became the Roman Forum. Roofed over in ca. 184 B.C. with three concentric rings of voussoirs.

328 PONTE   61–21 B.C.
     FABRIZIO *E5*
     (bridge)

Spans half the Tiber River to the Isola Tiberna in midstream. Still in use today.

329 PALATINE HILL
     entry off the Piazza del
     Colosseo *F7*

The remains of the palaces of the Emperors were incorporated into the Villa Farnese and its grounds. The most interesting sections are the Casa di Livia (House of Livia, ca. 55 B.C., interesting frescoes), Domus Flavia (Palace of the Flavians, or of Domitian, A.D. 85), Domus Augustus (Palace of Augustus), and the large hippodrome.

330 FORO   42–2 B.C.
     D'AUGUSTO
     (Forum of Augustus)
     Via Alessandrina *E7*

Inside are the remains of the Temple of Mars Ultor (14–2 B.C.).

331 TEMPIO DELLA   ca. 40 B.C.
     FORTUNA VIRILIS
     (Temple of Manly Fortune)
     Lungot Aventino, opposite the
     Ponte Palatino *F5*

In the Forum Boarum in very good condition. •Adjacent is the circular Temple of Vesta or of Portunus (ca. 31 B.C., now Santa Maria del Sole, shown), one of the best-preserved Roman temples extant. Built of marble. Original roof replaced. The remains of the Ponte Rotto, the oldest bridge in Rome (179 B.C., rebuilt in 1575), can be viewed from the Ponte Palatino.

332 MAUSOLEO   ca. 25 B.C.
     D'AUGUSTO
     (Augustan Mausoleum)
     Via di Ripetta *B5*

Built by Augustus for himself and his family, converted into a fort by the Colonna family (12th C), then a formal garden, bullring, theater, and finally concert hall, which was removed in 1934.

333 TEATRO DI   23–13 B.C.
     MARCELLO
     (Theatre of Marcellus)
     Via del Mare *E5*

Begun by Julius Caesar, completed by Augustus, this is one of the earliest uses of the superimposed orders of architecture (Doric, with Ionic above). •The third level has been absorbed by the Palazzo Orsini (1523–27, by B. Peruzzi).

334 AQUA CLAUDIA   A.D. 38–52
     (Roman aqueduct)
     Via Casilina *M6*

Built by Caligula and Claudius to bring water from Subiaco to Rome. The best-preserved sections are out in the Campagna.

335 DOMUS AUREA   A.D. 65
   (Nero's Golden House)
   Parco Oppio *E8*

   The underground rooms with
   frescoes remain.

336 COLOSSEO   A.D. 72–82
   (Colosseum)
   Piazza del Colosseo *F8*

   Built under the emperors Vespasian, Titus, and Domitian.

337 FORO TRAIANO   111–14
   (Forum of Trajan)
   Via Alessandrina *D6*
   Apollodorus of Damascus

   Only part of the Basilica Ulpia
   and Trajan's Column (A.D.
   113) remain. The column's
   carved frieze describes Trajan's
   Dacian campaign. The statue
   of Trajan was replaced by one
   of St. Peter in 1567. The
   entrance to Trajan's Market is
   off the Via 4 Novembre.

338 PANTHEON   117–25
   Piazza del Rotonda *D5*

   The best-preserved antique
   monument in Rome. Founded
   by Agrippa (27 B.C.), rebuilt by
   Hadrian, as a temple to all the
   gods. The bronze doors, 12 m
   (40 ft) high, are original. The
   tomb of Raphael is under the
   altar. •Just behind the
   Pantheon, in the church of
   Santa Maria sopra Minerva,
   Piazza di Minerva, is
   Michelangelo's *Risen Christ*
   (left, foot of stairs to choir)
   and Bernini's *Tomb of Maria
   Raggi.*

339 CASTEL SANT'   135
   ANGELO
   (Mausoleum of Hadrian)
   Lungotev Castello/Ponte S.
   Angelo *C3*

   Converted into a fort during
   the Middle Ages, now a
   museum. Interesting spiral
   ramp (Roman) inside. Chapel
   of Leo X by Michelangelo.
   Papal apartments by A. da
   Sangallo the Younger.

340 COLUMN OF   174–93
   MARCUS AURELIUS
   Piazza Colonna *C5*

   To commemorate Aurelius's
   victory against the German
   tribes at the Danube. The original statue was replaced by one
   of St. Paul in 1589. Spiral
   reliefs similar to Trajan's
   Column show various scenes
   from the campaign.

341 TERME DI   206–17
   CARACALLA
   (Baths of Caracalla)
   Via delle Terme di Caracalla *N4*

   Built under the emperors
   Septimus Severus and
   Caracalla, the remains give a
   good impression of the gigantic
   scale of the Roman baths.

342 TEMPLE OF   253–68
   MINERVA MEDICA
   (ruined)
   Via G. Giolitti/Via P. Micca *L5*

   Generally regarded as a precursor of the centralized church
   (e.g., San Vitale, Ravenna).
   Very early use of rough
   pendentives to support a dome.

343 SANTA MARIA   284–302
   DEGLI ANGELI
   (church)
   Piazza della Republica *B9*

   The Baths of Diocletian were
   converted into this church by
   Michelangelo in 1563. This
   became the transept of L.
   Vanvitelli's enlarged scheme
   (1749). The central hall is
   covered with the original
   Roman concrete vaulting. The
   National Museum of Rome is
   in the remaining parts of the
   baths.

344 ARCO DI   312
   CONSTANTINO
   (Arch of Constantine)
   Via di San Gregorio/Piazza del
   Colosseo *F7*

Built to commemorate
Constantine's victory over his
rival, Maxentius.

345 ARCO DI GIANO   315
(Arch of Janus Quadrifrons)
Via de Velabro *F6*

346 SANTA CONSTANZA   330
(church)
Via Nomentana/Viale 21 Aprile
J6

Built by Constantine as a
mausoleum for his daughter
Constantia. Circular dome
supported by twelve pairs of
coupled granite columns. 4th-c
mosaics. Converted into a
church in 1256. •Adjacent is
the Church of Sant'Agnese
fuori le Mura (324, rebuilt ca.
630) with a 7th-c Byzantine
mosaic in the apse.

347 SAN PAOLO FUORI   386
LE MURA
(church)
Piazzale di San Paolo *P3*

Immense interior. Totally
rebuilt from 1823–54. Richly
decorated cloisters (1193–
1241).

348 SANTA SABINA   425–30
(church)
Piazza Pietro d'Illiria/Via
Santa Sabina *G5*

Restored in the 16th c. 5th-c
carved wooden entry door.

349 SANTA MARIA   432–40
MAGGIORE   onward
(church)
Piazza dell'Esquilino *D9*

Extended and restored in the
17th and 18th c. Main facade
(1743) by F. Fuga. Apse facade
(1673) by C. Rainaldi. 5th-c
mosaics in the nave. Three
notable chapels are the Sforza
(ca. 1560) by Michelangelo
(executed by others), Sistine
(1586) by D. Fontana, and
Borghese (Paolina, 1611)
Chapel by F. Ponzio.

350 SAN LORENZO   432, 578
FUORI LE MURA
(church)
Piazzale di San Lorenzo *L6*

Two churches, originally back
to back, were combined to
form one church in 1216.
Restored since 1945.

351 SANTO STEFANO   468–83
ROTONDO
(church)
Via Santo Stefano Rotondo/
Piazza Navicella *G8*

Large circular church.

352 SANTA PRASSEDE   822
(church)
Via Santa Prassede *D9*

Byzantine mosaics. Chapel of
St. Zeno (third, right).

353 SAN CLEMENTE   1099–1108
(church)
Via di San Giovanni/Via
Celimontana *F9*

An earlier 4th-c church had
been built over a Roman
temple dedicated to Mithras
(remains visible in the crypt).
An atrium and ambulatory
form a forecourt to the church.
12th-c mosaics on apse
vaulting inside. Frescoes by
Masolino (first chapel, left).

354 SANTA MARIA IN   12th c
     COSMEDIN
(church)
Via Santa Maria in Cosmedin/
   Via di Greca *F6*

4th-c church, enlarged by
Adrian I (772–95), restored
(and campanile built) in 12th c.
Basilica interior decorated by
the Cosmati family in the late
13th c.

355 PALAZZO DI   ca. 1455–64
     VENEZIA
Piazza Venezia *D6*

Attributed to L. B. Alberti.
Now a museum.

356 SANT'AGOSTINO   1479–83
(church)
Via Sant'Agostino *C4*
G. di Pietrasanta

Built from materials removed
from the Colosseum. Interior
(altered by L. Vanvitelli in
1750) has works by Caravaggio
(*Virgin of the Pilgrims,* first
chapel, left), Raphael (*Isaiah,*
third pillar, left), and
Sansovino (*Madonna,* right of
entrance).

357 SAN PIETRO IN   15th c
     MONTORIO
(church)
Via Garibaldi *F3*

Rebuilt with Renaissance
facade. In the courtyard is the
circular Tempietto (1502) by
Bramante, a tiny, perfect
Renaissance building. The
circular peristyle that would
have surrounded the Tempietto
was never built. •Up the Via
Garibaldi is F. Ponzio's Fonta
Paolo (1612, fountain).

358 PALAZZO DELLA   1486–98
     CANCELLERIA
Piazza della Cancelleria *D4*

Attributed to Bramante. First
important Renaissance building
in Rome. Incorporates the
basilica of San Lorenzo in
Damaso. *Salon of 100 Days*
(1525) by G. Vasari inside.

359 CHIESA DELLA   1502–87
     TRINITA DEI MONTI
(church)

Viale della Trinita dei Monti *B6*
D. Fontana

Facade (1587) by C. Maderna.

360 SANTA MARIA DI   1507
     LORETO
(church)
Piazza del Foro Traiano *D6*
A. da Sangallo the Elder

The lantern (1582) is by G. del
Duca.

361 VILLA FARNESINA   1509–11
Via della Lungara 230 *E3*
B. Peruzzi

Trompe l'oeil frescoes inside
by Raphael (*Galatea*), Peruzzi,
and Il Sodoma (*Marriage of
Alexander and Roxana*).

362 PALAZZO   1514–89
     FARNESE
Piazza Farnese *E4*

A. da Sangallo the Younger is
responsible for the lower two
floors. Michelangelo added the
third floor and cornice in 1546.
Completed by G. da Vignola
and G. della Porta (rear
loggia). Frescoes by the
Carracci family and Il Domenichino in the first floor loggia.
Now the French Embassy.

363 VILLA   1516 onward
     MADAMA
Via di Villa Madama *H1*
Raphael

Executed by G. Romano. Com-
pleted by A. Sangallo the
Younger. Stuccowork by G. da
Udine and paintings by G.
Romano in the loggia.

364 PICCOLA   1523
     FARNESINA
(palazzo)
Piazza San Pantaleo *D4*
A. da Sangallo the Younger

Now the Barracco Museum.
Ancient sculpture from Baby-
lon, Greece, Egypt, etc.

365 PALAZZO MASSIMO 1532–36
     ALLE COLONNE
Corso Vittorio Emanuele II/
   Corso del Rinascimento *D4*
B. Peruzzi

Ingenious plan. Curved
mannerist facade follows the
street boundary.

366 SANTO SPIRITO   1538–44
     IN SASSIA
(church)
Borgo Santo Spirito *C2*
A. da Sangallo the Younger

Facade (1585) by Mascherino.

367 PIAZZA DEL   1538–1655
     CAMPIDOGLIO *E6*

Michelangelo positioned the statue of Marcus Aurelius in 1538, planned the piazza in 1546, and built the approach stair and double stair opposite. The Palazzo di Conservatori was built to his design (1564–68). C. Rainaldi built the Palazzo del Senatore (1592) and the Capitoline Museum (1644–55), adhering closely to Michelangelo's original design.

368 VILLA MEDICI   1540–44
     (French Academy)
     Viale della Trinita dei Monti *A6*
     A. Lippi

369 SANT'ANDREA   1550–55
     DELLA VIA FLAMINIA
     (church)
     Via Flaminia *J3*
     G. da Vignola

•The villa of Pio IV (1552, by da Vignola or P. Ligorio) is adjacent.

370 VILLA GIULIA   1550–55
     Viale delle Belle Arti *J3*
     G. da Vignola

Built for Pope Julius III, this is a masterpiece. Now an Etruscan museum. (In the garden is a well-preserved Etruscan temple from Alatri.)

371 PORTA PIA   1561–65
     (gateway)
     Via 20 Settembre/Corso d'Italie
     A9
     Michelangelo

Restored (1853) by V. Vespignani, who executed the outer face from 1861–68.

372 PALAZZO CHIGI   1562
     Piazza Colonna (N side) *C5*
     G. della Porta

Completed by C. Maderna.

373 IL GESÙ   1568–84
     (church)
     Via del Plebiscito/Piazza del
     Gesù *D5*
     G. da Vignola

Completed by G. della Porta, who altered the facade. Baroque interior (1668). The trompe l'oeil ceiling fresco by G. B. Gaulli repays close study. Altar by A. Pozzo (1695–99).

374 SANTA ANNA   1572
     DEI PALAFRENIERI
     (church)
     Via Santa Anna *B1*
     G. da Vignola

375 PALAZZO   1574–1615
     DEL QUIRINALE
     Piazza del Quirinale *C6*
     F. Ponzio

Completed by D. Fontana, C. Maderna, G. L. Bernini (main portal) and F. Fuga. Capella dell'Annunciata frescoes (1610) by G. Reni. Residence of the president of the Italian Republic.

376 PALAZZO   1575–1660
     DELLA SAPIENZA
     Corso del Rinascimento *D4*

Begun by G. della Porta. Completed by F. Borromini, who added the superb baroque Chapel of Sant'Ivo (1642–50) in the courtyard.

377 COLLEGIO   1582–84
     ROMANO
     Piazza del Collegio Romano *D5*
     B. Ammanati

378 PALAZZO   ca. 1590
     MARESCOTTI
     Via dei Cestari 21 (entry off
     Via della Pigna) *D5*
     G. della Porta

379 SAN ANDREA   1591
     DELLA VALLE
     (church)
     Corso Vittorio Emanuele II/Via
     de Chiavari *D4*
     F. Grimaldi and G. della Porta

Completed by C. Maderna and C. Rainaldi (facade built 1661–65). Frescoes by Lanfranco (1627, dome) and Il Domenichino (1628, pendentives). •On the left is the Palazzo Vidoni-Caffarelli (1515). The rear facade (on Via del Sudario) is attributed to Raphael.

380 SANTA   1595–1603
     SUSANNA
     (church facade)
     Piazza San Bernardo *B8*
     C. Maderna

381 PALAZZO   1598–1618
     MATTEI
     Piazza Mattei 17 *E5*
     C. Maderna

382 SANTA MARIA   1605
     DELLA VITTORIA
     (church)
     Via 20 Settembre/Via Santa
     Susanna *B8*
     C. Maderna

The baroque interior is mostly original. Bernini's *Ecstasy of St. Teresa,* a unique masterpiece combining sculpture and architecture of genius, is in the fourth chapel (left). •A similar

sculptural program by Bernini
is the treatment of the statue
*Death of the Blessed Ludovica
Albertoni* in the Altieri Chapel
(fourth, left) in the church of
San Francesco a Ripa in Piazza
San Francesco d'Assisi
(marked 382A, map coordinate
G4).

383 SANT'IGNAZIO   1626–85
(church)
Piazza Sant'Ignazio/Via del
    Caravita *D5*

After plans by Il Domenichino.
Facade by A. Algardi. Trompe
l'oeil ceiling fresco (1691–94)
by A. Pozzo.

384 PALAZZO   1628–38
    BARBERINI
Via Quattro Fontane *C7*
C. Maderna

Executed by G. L. Bernini.
Houses the collection of the
Galleria Nazionale d'Arte
Antica. Frescoes by P. da Cor-
tona in the Great Hall. Paint-
ings by Fra Angelico, Lippi,
Raphael, Fragonard, and
others.

385 SANTI LUCA E   1634–47
    MARTINA
(two churches)
Via della Curia *E6*
P. da Cortona

Two superimposed churches.
Da Cortona is buried in the
crypt.

386 ORATORY OF   1637–40
    SAN FILIPPO NERI
Piazza d'Orologio (off the
    Corso Vittorio Emanuele II)
    D3
F. Borromini

•At the rear (on the Corso) is
the Chiesa Nuova (church,
1575–1605) with decorations by
P. da Cortona (vault, apse,
dome, and sacristy ceiling).
Three paintings by Rubens in
the apse.

387 SAN CARLO   1638–41
    ALLE QUATRO FONTANE
(church)
Via del Quirinale/Via della
    Quattro Fontane *C7*
F. Borromini

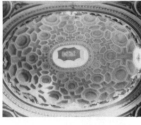

The spatial equivalent of a
fugue by Bach. Complex
baroque geometrical scheme
that had enormous influence.
Borromini added the west
(main) facade from 1660–67.
The cloisters date from 1635.

388 FONTANA DEL   1640
    TRITONE
(Triton fountain)
Piazza Barberini *B7*
G. L. Bernini

389 PALAZZO   ca. 1640
    FALCONIERI
Via Giulia/Via dell'Armato V
    E3
F. Borromini

390 SANTI   1646–50
    VICENZO E ANASTASIO
(two churches)
Via della Lavatore/Via dei
    Lucchesi *C6*
M. Longhi the Younger

391 SAN GIOVANNI   1646–1736
    IN LATERANO
(church)
Piazza di Porta San Giovanni
    M5
F. Borromini

Originally built in 330. Burned
down several times, the church
was totally restored by
Borromini in 1646. The facade
was added by A. Galilei in
1733–36. Transept by G. della
Porta. The 13th-c cloisters
have survived. •The adjacent
Palazzo Laterano (1568) is by
D. Fontana. On the SE corner
of the piazza is the Baptistry of
Constantine (432–40, more
accurately, of St. John), rebuilt
by Sixtus III, incorporating
various antique building
fragments.

392 PALAZZO   1650 onward
    MONTECITORIO
Piazza Montecitorio *C5*
G. L. Bernini

Completed by C. Fontana.

393 SANT'AGNESE   1652–66
    IN AGONE
(church)
Piazza Navone *D4*
C. Rainaldi and F. Borromini

Begun by Rainaldi, the church's appearance largely resulted from Borromini's efforts (1653–55). Completed by others. •The Fountain of the Rivers outside is by G. L. Bernini, as is the Triton Fountain on the south end of the piazza. The Palazzo Pamphili (1650, by Rainaldi) to the left of the church has frescoes in the long gallery by P. da Cortona.

394 SANT'ANDREA   1653–65
      DELLE FRATE
(church)
Via Capo le Case *B6*

Completed by F. Borromini. Facade (1826) by G. Valadier. In the choir are two angels carved by G. L. Bernini.

395 SANTA MARIA   1656–58
      DELLA PACE
(church)
Vicolo della Pace *C4*
P. da Cortona

Reconstructed, with new facade, by da Cortona, who also remodeled the flanking houses to relate to his new facade. Octagonal interior. Fresco by Raphael (1574, arch of first chapel, right). The cloisters with a two-story arcade by Bramante (1500–1504) are entered through the sacristy.

396 SANTA MARIA   1657–65
      IN CAMPITELLI
(church)
Piazza Campitelli *E5*
C. Rainaldi

397 SANTA MARIA   1658–62
      VIA LATA
(facade)
Via del Corso/Via Lata *D6*
P. da Cortona

398 SANT'ANDREA   1658–70
      AL QUIRINALE
(church)
Via del Quirinale *C7*
G. L. Bernini

Elliptical plan entered on short axis. Similar to the Pantheon in the organization of the

surrounding chapels. Emotional sculpture. Considered by Bernini to be his masterpiece.

399 PALAZZO   1660
      PROPAGANDA FIDE
(facade)
Via di Propaganda/Vie Due
      Macelli *B7*
F. Borromini

400 SANTA MARIA   1662–79
      DEI MIRACOLI AND
      DI MONTE SANTO
Piazza del Popolo *A5*
C. Rainaldi

Twin churches designed to give a symmetrical appearance when seen from the piazza. As the sites are of differing widths, the Monte Santo church is elliptical in plan; the Miracoli, circular. G. L. Bernini completed the Monte Santo church. •The piazza was completed (1816–22) by G. Valadier. On the north side is the church of Santa Maria del Popolo, built in 1412–17; apse (1505–9) by Bramante. In the Chigi Chapel (1513–20, second left), built according to plans by Raphael, are the statues *Daniel* and *Habbakuk,* by Bernini. The adjacent Porta del Popolo (gateway) is by G. da Vignola (outer face, 1561) and Bernini (inner face, 1625).

401 PALAZZO   1664
      ODESCALCHI
Piazza Santi Apostoli *D6*
G. L. Bernini

The facade was doubled in length in 1745 by N. Salvi and L. Vanvitelli.

402 SAN MARCELLO   1683
(facade)
Via del Corso/Via dell'Umiltà
      D6
C. Fontana

403 SCALINATA DI   1721–23
      TRINITÀ DEI MONTI
(Spanish Steps)
Piazza di Spagna *B6*
F. De Sanctis

•At the foot of the steps is a lovely boat-shaped fountain (1628) by P. Bernini. Above is

the church of the Trinità dei
Monti (1495) by A. Specchi
(the "Roman" obelisk in the
square is a modern copy).

404 PIAZZA SAN   1723–28
    IGNAZIO *C5*
    F. Raguzzini

405 SAN GALLICANO   1724–26
    (church and hospital)
    Via di San Gallicano/Viale
    Trastevere *F4*
    F. Raguzzini

406 FONTANA DI   1732–62
    TREVI
    (Trevi fountain)
    Via della Stamperia/Via della
    Muratte *C6*
    N. Salvi

Urban sculpture at its best.

407 PALAZZO   1733–38
    DELLA CONSULTA
    Via Quirinale/Via della
    Consulta *D7*
    F. Fuga

408 SANTA CROCE IN   1743
    GERUSALEMME
    (church)
    Piazza di Sante Croce in
    Gerusalemme *M6*

    Baroque interior (church
    completely redecorated in
    1743). 12th-C campanile.

409 VILLA ALBANI   1760
    (now Torlonia)
    Via Salaria/Via Adda *K4*
    C. Marchionni

410 SANTA MARIA DEL   1765
    PRIORATO
    (church)
    Piazza dei Cavalieri di Malti *G5*
    G. B. Piranesi

    •The piazza is also by Piranesi.

411 TEATRO VALLE   1821
    (theater)
    Via del Teatro Valle *D4*
    G. Valadier

412 EXHIBITION HALL   1880–83
    Via Nazionale *C7*
    P. Piacentini

413 PIAZZA DELL'   1885
    ESEDRA
    (now della Republica) *C8*
    G. Koch

    Fountain of the Naiads by
    Guerrieri. A very successful
    piece of urban design.

414 BANK OF ITALY   1885–94
    Via Nazionale 183 *D7*
    G. Koch

415 MONUMENTO   1885–1911
    VITTORIO EMANUELE II
    (monument)
    Piazza Venezia *E6*
    G. Sacconi and others

A colossal pile dominating the
city skyline.

416 PALAZZO   1886–90
    MARGHERITA
    Via Vittorio Veneto/Via
    Bissolati *B7*
    G. Koch

    Now the American embassy.

417 PONTE DEI   1911
    RISORGIMENTO
    (bridge)
    Piazzale delle Belle Arti *J3*
    F. Hennebique

418 BANK OF ITALY   1918
    OFFICE BUILDING
    Piazza del Parlamento *C5*
    M. Piacentini

419 DE'SALVI HOUSE   1929–31
    Piazza della Libertà 20 *A4*
    P. Aschieri

420 GARBATELLA   1929
    NEIGHBORHOOD
    Piazza S. Eurosia, Piazza
    Damiano Sauli, etc. *P4*
    P. Aschieri, M. De Renzi, and
    others

    Plan by P. Marconi.

421 ISTITUTO ROMANO   1930
    DEI CIECHI DI GUERRA
    (Institute for the Blind)
    Via Parenzo 5 *J5*
    P. Aschieri

422 POST OFFICE   1932
    Via Marmorata/Porta San
    Paolo *N3*
    M. De Renzi and A. Libera

423 CITTÀ   1933
    UNIVERSITARIA
    (University City)
    Via Dell'Universito *L5*
    M. Piacentini (chief architect)
    and others

    Physics Institute (1933–35) by
    G. Pagano; Institute of Botany
    (1934) by G. Capponi;
    Mathematics Faculty (1934) by
    G. Ponti.

424 PALAZZO DELLE   1933
    POSTE
    (post office)
    Piazza Bologna *K6*
    M. Ridolfi

425 APARTMENT   1934
    BUILDING
    Viale di Villa Massimo 39 *K6*
    M. Ridolfi

426 CASA DELLA 1934–36
 SCHERMA
 (fencing house)
 Foro Italico *H2*
 L. Moretti

427 CINECITTÀ CENTER 1938
 Via Tuscolana 1051 *N6*
 B. Peressutti

428 PONTE DUCA 1939
 D'AOSTA
 (bridge)
 Piazza Lauro de Bosis/Via
 Filippo Brunelleschi *H2*
 V. Fasolo

429 APARTMENT 1939
 BUILDING
 Via Nicotera 29 *J2*
 L. Piccinato

430 CONVENTION HALL 1940
 Piazzale dei Congressi, E.U.R.
 P3
 A. Libera

431 INSTITUTO 1940
 NAZIONALE DEI
 RESTAURO LIBRARY
 Piazza di San Francesco di
 Paola 9 *E7*
 S. Radiconcini

432 APARTMENT 1940
 BUILDING
 Lungotevere Flaminio 18 *J3*
 M. De Renzi

433 FOSSE ARDEATINE 1945–50
 MAUSOLEUM
 Via Ardeatina *P5*
 N. Aprile, G. Calcaprina, A.
 Cardelli, M. Fiorentino and
 G. Perugini

434 VILLINO ALATRI 1948
 (upper floor addition)
 Via Paisiello 38 *J4*
 M. Ridolfi and M. Fiorentino

435 STAZIONE 1948–50
 TERMINI
 (railway station)
 Piazza dei Cinquecento *C9*
 E. Montuori, A. Vitellozzi, and
 others

436 CASA DEL GIRASOLE 1950
 (apartments)
 Viale Bruno Buozzi 64 *J3*
 L. Moretti

437 APARTMENT 1951
 BUILDINGS
 Via Tripolitania 195 and 211/
 Via Galla Sidama *H6*
 M. Ridolfi

438 HOUSING 1953–56
 Via Selinunte 49 *N6*
 A. Libera

439 PALAZZETTO 1956–57
 DELLA SPORT
 (sports palace)
 Viale Tiziano *H3*
 P. L. Nervi and A. Vitellozzi

•The Flaminio stadium (1960)
adjacent is also by Nervi.

440 LA RINASCENTE 1957–61
 (department store)
 Piazza Fiume *A9*
 F. Albini and F. Helg

441 MAESTOSO CINEMA 1958
 Via Appia Nuova 416 *N6*
 R. Morandi

442 PALAZZO 1958–59
 DELLA SPORT
 (sports palace)
 Via Cristoforo Colombo 42,
 E.U.R. *P3*
 P. L. Nervi and M. Piacentini

443 LEONARDO DA 1960
 VINCI AIRPORT
 Fiumicino *P3*
 R. Morandi, V. Monaco, and A.
 Luccichenti

Alitalia hangars (1964) by
Morandi.

444   VIA OLIMPICO   1960
         BRIDGE
         over the Corso Francia, near
            Ponte Flaminio *H3*
         R. Morandi

445   NOTRE DAME   1960
         INTERNATIONAL
         SCHOOL
         Via Aurelia 796 *L1*
         V., F., and L. Passarelli

446   RESIDENTIAL AREA   1960
         Via di Torre Spaccata, Viale dei
            Romanisti *N6*
         V. Passarelli, E. Montuori, P.
         Marconi, and others

447   CASA BALDI   1961
         (house)
         Via Sirmione 19, Labaro (12
            km/7 mi from Rome) *H3*
         P. Portoghesi

448   APARTMENT   1961
         BUILDING
         Via Arbia 21 *J5*
         C. and M. Aymonino and A.
         and B. De Rossi

449   SAN TOMASO   1962
         D'AQUINO SCHOOL
         (extension)
         Via degli Ibernesi 20 *E7*
         V., F., and L. Passarelli

450   APARTMENTS   1962–64
         Via Anagni 97–101 *M6*
         C. Aymonino

451   MULTIUSE   1963–65
         BUILDING
         Viale Campania 59 *A7*
         V., F., and L. Passarelli

452   ESSO OFFICES   1966
         Piazzale dell'Industria, E.U.R.
            P3
         L. Moretti and V. B. Morpurgo

453   MEDICAL   1972
         ASSOCIATION BUILDING
         Via de Rossi/Via Bosio *K5*
         P. Sartogo, C. Fegiz, and D.
         Gimigliano

454   OFFICE BUILDING   1974
         Piazzale Flaminio *K3*
         L. Moretti and C. Zacutti

   CITTÀ DE VATICANO
   (Vatican City)

      Only St. Peter's and the
   Vatican Museums are open to
   the general public. Other
   sections may be visited after
   making a written application
   (three days in advance) to the
   Ufficio Informazioni e Turisti
   in the Piazza San Pietro or

with a guided tour. The Papal
audience hall (1971) is by P. L.
Nervi.

455   SAN PIETRO   1452–1612
         IN VATICANO
         (St. Peter's)
         Piazza San Pietro *C1*

Originally a basilica built by
Constantine in 319. Demolished when rebuilding began in
1452. The following architects
were involved in the project,
but the church's appearance is,
in the main, due to Michelangelo: Bramante (1506–13),
Raphael (1514–20), B. Peruzzi
(1520–36), A. da Sangallo the
Younger (1536–46), Michelangelo (1546–64). Side cupolas
(1564) by G. da Vignola. Dome
completed (1585–90) by G.
della Porta and D. Fontana.
From 1606–12, C. Maderna
lengthened the nave and added
the facade, which effectively
blocked the view of the dome
from the piazza. Inside, among
many works of art, are two
masterpieces: Michelangelo's
Pietà (1498, first chapel, right)
and Bernini's *Baldaquin* (1633,
above the high altar). Access to
the interesting grottos (tombs)
is limited. Bernini's magnificent *Scala Regia* is off the right
side of the church's entry
portico.

456   PIAZZA SAN   1656–57
         PIETRO
         G. L. Bernini *C1*

The central obelisk was brought
from Heliopolis by Caligula and
placed in its present position
in 1586.

457   PALAZZO   ca. 1450
         VATICANO   onward
         (museum)
         Entrance on Viale Vaticano. *B1*

      Pinacoteca Vaticano: Paint-
      ings by Giotto, Fra Angel-
      ico, Gentile da Fabriano,
      Raphael, da Vinci, Caravag-
      gio, da Cortona, and others.

      Museo Pio-Clementino:
      Antique Greek and Roman
      sculptures. (*Laocoon, Apollo*

Belvedere, and *Torso of the Belvedere*).

Museo Egiziano: Egyptian sarcophagi and relics.
Museo Chiaramonti: Greek and Roman antique works.

Biblioteca: This library is by D. Fontana (1587–89).

Cappella Sistina: The Sistine Chapel was decorated with frescoes by Michelangelo on the ceiling (1508–12) and end wall (*Last Judgment,* 1536–41).

Appartamenti Borgia: Frescoes (*Lives of the Saints*) by Pintoricchio.

Stanze di Raffaelo: Frescoes by Raphael and his school. •At the end (on the right is the chapel of Nicholas V with frescoes by Fra Angelico) is the Loggia of Raphael, with grotesque decorations derived from the remains of the decorations of Nero's Golden House (see entry 335). This overlooks Bramante's Cortile di San Damaso (1504). The Cortile di Belvedere (by Bramante, 1504) was divided into three sections; the upper part (Giardino della Pigna) was altered by P. Ligorio.

458 CASINO OF PIUS IV 1558–62
Vatican Gardens *BI*
P. Ligorio

Limited access, but well worth the effort.

Outskirts of Roma

The following entries (459–467) are listed here (alphabetically) because of their convenient proximity to Roma. They are indicated on the general map of Italy.

ARICCIA G5
25 km (15 mi) SE of Roma

459 SANTA MARIA DELL'ASSUNZIONE 1662–64
(church)
Piazza della Republica
G. L. Bernini

An interpretation of the Pantheon. •The Palazzo Chigi, opposite, was restored by Bernini. Also by Bernini is the church of San Tommaso di Villanova (1661) at Castel Gandolfo (4 km/2.5 mi NW of Ariccia).

CERVETERI G5
40 km (25 mi) NW of Roma

460 ETRUSCAN NECROPOLIS 8th–2nd C B.C.

Many tombs in excellent condition.

FRASCATI G5
22 km (14 mi) SE of Roma

461 VILLA ALDOBRANDINI 1598–1603
(Belvedere)
off the Piazza del Municipio
G. della Porta

Completed by C. Maderna and D. Fontana. Remarkable baroque gardens and fountains. •The neighboring Villa Torlonia (1563, enlarged in 1605) has equally splendid fountains by C. Maderna.

462 VILLA FALCONIERI 1548
Via Falconieri (10-minute walk)

Enlarged by F. Borromini in 1648. Further along the road is the Villa Mondragone (1573–75, enlarged in 1615–20), modeled after plans by G. da Vignola and M. Longhi.

OSTIA (ANTICA) G5
24 km (15 mi) SW of Roma

463 ROMAN RUINS 1st–3rd C A.D.

The former port of Rome. Many well-preserved ancient buildings.

PALESTRINA G5
38 km (24 mi) E of Roma

464 TEMPIO DELLA FORTUNA PRIMIGENIA 82 B.C.
(Temple of Fortune)
Piazza Margherita

Lower sanctuary: various remains, including the Cave of Destiny (original mosaic floor). Upper sanctuary: the 17th-c Palazzo Barberini is built on the site of the former temple. Now a museum (of antiquities from the site).

TIVOLI G5
31 km (19 mi) E of Roma

465 TEMPIO DI VESTA ca. 30 B.C
(Temple of Vesta)

On the grounds of Villa Gregoriana, Largo San Angelo Circular temple. Ten columns are original. •The rectangular Temple of the Sibyl of the same period is adjacent. The waterfalls of the Villa Gregoriana are renowned.

466 VILLA ADRIANA A.D. 125–35
(Hadrian's Villa)
6 km (4 mi) SW of Tivoli

The Emperor Hadrian's recreation of various places in the Roman Empire.

467 VILLA D'ESTE 1550–72
Piazza Trento
P. Ligorio

Former monastery. The water gardens and vistas down a steep site are unrivaled.

SABBIONETA D3

468 TEATRO OLIMPICO 1588
(Olympic Theater)
V. Scamozzi

Influenced by A. Palladio. (Scamozzi designed the stage set for the Teatro Olimpico, Vicenza). •The octagonal Church of the Incoronata nearby has an interesting interior.

SALERNO J7

469 DUOMO 1076–85
(cathedral)
Piazza Alfano

Restored in the 18th c. The atrium incorporates twenty-eight Roman columns taken from Paestum. 12th-c campanile. The museum (through sacristy, north transept) has a rare 12th-c carved ivory altar front.

SAN CLEMENTE A CASAURIA G6
abbey 20 km (12 mi) NE of Popoli

470 SAN CLEMENTE 12th c
A CASAURIA
(abbey)

Transitional Romanesque-Gothic. 9th-c crypt. Good sculpture in the portico.

SAN GIMIGNANO E4
Well-preserved medieval town with many residential towers.

471 COLLEGIATA 12th c
(Santa Maria Assunta, cathedral)
Piazza del Duomo

Romanesque. Facade rebuilt in 1818. Chapel of Santa Fina (1486, end of nave, right) by G. da Maiano, altar by B. da Maiano, frescoes by Ghirlandaio. Choir remodeling (1468) by G. da Maiano. •The Museo Civico in the adjacent Palazzo del Popolo (1288) has 13th- to 15th-c Sienese paintings and frescoes.

472 SANT'AGOSTINO 13th c
Piazza Sant'Agostino

Frescoes (1465) in the choir by B. Gozzoli.

SAN MARINO E5
(republic)

SAN MARINO

473 CHIESA DI 1966
BORGO-MAGGOIRE
(church)
G. Michelucci

SANTA MARINELLA G5

474 VILLA LA 1954
SARACENA
Via Mazzini, Capolinaro
L. Moretti

SANTO STEFANO D'AVETO D3
67 km (42 mi) NE of Chiavari

475 COLONIA PIAGGIO 1939
(health resort)
L. C. Daneri

SARNICO C3
30 km (19 mi) E of Bergamo

476 FACCANONI 1907
MAUSOLEUM
G. Sommaruga

•Also by Sommaruga is Villa Faccanoni (1907) at Via Predore 50.

SEGESTA M5

477 TEMPIO 430–420 B.C.
(Greek temple)

Isolated. Doric peristyle (unfinished columns and pediment) in excellent condition. •The theater (same

period), further on, is cut into the mountainside. Splendid view.

SELINUNTE M5
14 km (8.5 mi) S of Castel-vetrano

478 GREEK COLONY 630 B.C.
(ruined)

Two main sites. The temples have been damaged by earthquake or human plundering. Some columns have been re-erected.

Templi Orientale ("Oriental Temples," from north to south):

Temple G: (Apollo, 550–480 B.C.) Colossal. One of the largest Greek temples known.

Temple F: (560–540 B.C.) Plundered. Little remains.

Temple E: (Hera, 490 B.C.) Reconstructed. The metopes are in the Palermo museum.

Acropolis (from south to north):

Temple O: Stylobate only.

Temple A: 490–480 B.C.

Temple B: Small Helenistic structure.

Temple C: (Demeter) Built in 575 B.C.

SIENA E4

Museum: Pinoteca, Palazzo Buonsignori, Via San Pietro. 13th- to 16th-c Sienese paintings in a fine 15th-c Gothic palace.

479 DUOMO   1226–1382
(cathedral)
Piazza del Duomo

Gothic. Facade by G. Pisano, upper section by G. di Cecco. The campanile and interior columns are clad in alternate stripes of black and white limestone. Remarkable floor paving decoration. Pulpit (1265–68) by N. and G. Pisano. Statues by G. L. Bernini (*St. Jerome, Mary Magdalene*, south transept) and Donatello (*St. John*, tombstone of Bishop Peccio). Frescoes (1509) by Pintoricchio in the Piccolomini "Library" (off left aisle). •The baptistry (San Giovanni, Piazza San Giovanni) is behind and under the cathedral. Font by J. della Quercia, L. Ghiberti, and Donatello. In the Museo dell' Opera del Duomo (entry off the Piazza) is Duccio's *Maesta* altarpiece, also works by G. Pisano. This gigantic unfinished extension was to incorporate the present cathedral as the transept of the proposed cathedral.

480 PALAZZO   1296–1310
PUBLICO
(town hall)
Piazza del Campo

Gothic. Frescoes by S. Martini (*Maesta*) and Ambrogio (in the Sala della Pace). The soaring tower (1338–48) is by Muccio and F. di Rinaldo. The piazza is one of the finest urban spaces in Europe.

481 SAN FRANCESCO 1326–1475
(church)
Piazza San Francesco

Gothic. Facade rebuilt in 1913.
•Frescoes in the Oratory of St. Bernard (15th c) on the left.

SIRACUSA N8 (Syracuse)

Museum: Museo Archeologico Nazionale, Piazza Duomo. Archaic Greek and Roman artifacts, sculpture (*Venus Anadyome* or *Landolina*), and vases.

482 PARCO MONUMENTALE DELLA NEAPOLIS
(archeological site)
Viale P. Orsi

The Teatro Greco (Greek theater, 5th c B.C.) is rock cut, extremely large, and very well preserved. A quarry (Latomia del Paradiso) with attractive natural caves lies to the east of the Anfiteatro Romano (amphitheater, 2nd c A.D.)

483 CASTELLO   402–397 B.C.
EURIALO
(Castle of Euryalus)
8 km (5 mi) NW of Siracusa

Built by Dionysius. A uniquely well-preserved Greek fortification.

484 DUOMO   7th c onward
(cathedral)
Piazza del Duomo

Built on the site of an earlier Temple of Minerva (5th c B.C.) Twelve columns from this temple have been incorporated in the present nave. Rebuilt in 1693. Baroque facade (1757) by Don A. Palma.

SPOLETO F5

485 SAN SALVATORE   4th c
(church)   onward

From the Piazza della Vittoria: cross the river, turn right, take left fork under the highway. Much authentic Roman detail. Oval dome over chancel.

486 DUOMO   12th c
(cathedral)
Piazza del Duomo

Renaissance porch (1491). Interior (17th c) has frescoes by Fra Lippi (and his tomb, by his son, Fillipino Lippi).

487 PONTE DELLE   14th c
TORRI
(pedestrian bridge)
Via del Ponte

Built over a Roman aqueduct.

STRA C5
12 km (7 mi) E of Padova

488 VILLA NAZIONALE   1730
(Pisani)
G. Frigimelica

Completely remodeled by
F. M. Preti. Frescoes by G. B.
Tiepolo. •In the summer
excursions by boat run between
Venezia and Padova along the
Brenta Canal and stop at the
Villa Nazionale. The canal is
lined with many 17th-c
Venetian villas.

SYRACUSE
See Siracusa

TAORMINA M8

489 TEATRO   3rd c B.C.
    GRECO
(Greek theater)
Via Teatro Greco

Rock cut. Fine views.

TARANTO J9

Museum: Museo Nazionale,
Corso Umberto. Archeological
exhibits, especially Greek
pottery.

490 DUOMO   11th c
(San Cataldo, church)
Via del Duomo, Città Vecchia
(on an island)

Byzantine frescoes in crypt.
Baroque chapel of San Cataldo
(1657). •Also on Via del Dumo
is San Domenico Maggiore
(church, 11th c, rebuilt in the
14th c).

491 CONCATTEDRALE   1971
(new cathedral)
Viale Magna Grecia
G. Ponti

TARQUINIA G4

Museum: Museo Nazionale
Tarquiniese, in the Palazzo
Vitelleschi (1439, transitional
Gothic-Renaissance), Via di
Porta Castello. Etruscan
antiquities (reliefs of the
Winged Horses), tombs, etc.

492 ETRUSCAN   6th–1st c B.C.
    NECROPOLIS
4 km (2.5 mi) SE of Tarquinia

Thousands of tombs. Remarkable frescoes.

TERNI F5

493 NUOVO   1971–74
    VILLAGIO MATTEOTTI
(housing)
G. di Carlo and F. Colombo

TIVOLI
See entry 465

TODI F5
Triple ramparts: Etruscan,
Roman, and medieval.

494 DUOMO   12th–14th c
(cathedral)
Piazza del Popolo

•The piazza is a splendid
urban square surrounded by
medieval buildings.

495 SANTA MARIA   1508–1609
    DELLA CONSOLAZIONE
(church)
1 km (0.5 mi) W of Todi
C. da Caprarola

Greek cross plan and details
after Bramante.

TORINO C1
(Turin)

Museums: Galleria d'Arte
Moderna, Via Magenta. 19th-
and 20th-c paintings. Futurist
works.
Palazzo dell'Accademia della
Scienze (Collegio dei Nobili,
1678, by G. Guarini), Via
Accademia della Scienze. Three
sections: Egyptian (outstanding); Antiquities—Greek and
Etruscan artifacts; and the
Galleria Sabauda—Italian
paintings by Botticelli, Fra
Angelico, Mantegna, and
others. Flemish and Dutch
paintings.

496 DUOMO SAN   1498
    GIOVANNI
(cathedral)
Piazza San Giovanni

Romanesque campanile
completed (1720) by F. Iuvara.
Inside, behind the apse, is G.
Guarini's Capella della Santa
Sindone (1667–94, Chapel of
the Holy Shroud), with an
amazing dome.

497 SAN CARLO   1619
(church)
Piazza San Carlo
M. Valperga

•The second matching church
(Santa Cristina, 1639) is by A.
di Castellamonte; the facade
(1714) is by F. Iuvara.

498 PALAZZO REALE   1658
Piazza Reale
A. di Castellamonte

Enlarged and remodeled (1721)
by F. Iuvara, who was responsible for the "scissors" staircase. Drawings in the library
(Leonardo da Vinci's *Self-
Portrait*). •In the center of the
larger Piazza Castello (on the
south) is the Palazzo Madama
(13th c onward, facade by F.

Iuvara in 1718), with a splendid doubled symmetrical stair. In the NW corner of the Piazza Castello, by the iron railing, is the church of San Lorenzo (1666–87, by G. Guarini), with a powerfully modeled dome.

499 PALAZZO DI   1658–65
    CITTÀ
Via Garibaldi/Via Bellezio
F. Lanfranchi

500 SAN FILIPPO NERI   1675
(church)
Via Maria Vittoria/Via
    Accademia della Scienze
G. Guarini

Radically transformed (1716) by F. Iuvara.

501 SANTUARIO   1679
    DELLA CONSOLATA
(church)
Via Giulio/Via della Consolata
G. Guarini

502 PALAZZO   1680
    CARIGNANO
Piazza Carignano
G. Guarini

503 SANTE CROCE   1718
(church)
Via Sante Croce
F. Iuvara

504 MOLE   1863
    ANTONELLIANA
Via Montebello
A. Antonelli

165-m-high (550-ft) tower. Originally intended to be used as a synagogue.

505 FABBRICA FIAT   1919–26
    LINGOTTO
(Fiat factory at Lingotto)
G. M. Trucco

506 PALAZZO DI   1948–50
    TORINO ESPOSIZIONI
Salone B and C (exhibition
    halls B and C)
Parco del Valentino
P. L. Nervi

The underground exhibition hall (1959) is by R. Morandi.

507 APARTMENT   1953–63
    BUILDING
Via Galileo Ferraris/Via Riberi
R. Gabetti and A. d'Isola

508 PALAZZO DEL   1960
    LAVORO
(exhibition hall)
Corso Polonia
P. L. Nervi and A. Nervi

509 TRADE CENTER   1968–74
Via San Francesco da Paola 24
C. Mollino, C. Graffi, and A.
    Galardi

•Also by Mollino is the Nuova Teatro Regio (theater, 1968–74) in the Piazza Castello.

510 SCUOLA MATERNA   1980
(nursery school)
Via Cecchi/Corso Emilia
P. Derossi and G. Ceretti

Outskirts of Torino

511 HUNTING LODGE   1714–26
(actually, a palace)
Venoria Reale (6 km/4 mi NW
    of Torino)
F. Iuvara

The chapel is outstanding.

512 CASTELLO DI   1715–25
    RIVOLI
(castle)
Rivoli (18 km/11 mi NE of
    Torino)
F. Iuvara

Design not fully executed.

513 BASILICA   1715–31
    DI SUPERGA
(church)
8 km (5mi) E of Torino
F. Iuvara

A superb building that dominates its hilltop site.

514 PALAZZINA   1719–38
    DI CACCIA
(hunting lodge/palace)
Stupinigi (10 km/6m S of
    Torino, near Nichelino)
F. Iuvara

The palace is Iuvara's masterpiece.

515 SAN BERNARDINO   1740–44
(church)
Chieri (18 km/11 mi SE of
    Torino)
B. Vittone

•Also by Vittone is the chapel of the Madonna della Grazie (1757–59) in the cathedral.

TRANI H8

516 CATTEDRALE   1094
(San Nicola, cathedral)

Romanesque. The crypt dates from 670. Norman influence apparent, especially in the bell tower.

TREMEZZO B2

517 VILLA CARLOTTA   1747
between Tremezzo and Caden-
    abbia

Sculpture by A. Canova and B. Thorvaldsen.

TREVISO C5

518 SPORT COMPLEX   1972
Viale Europa
G. Davanzo

Outskirts of Treviso

519 GIPSOTECA   1957
    CANOVIANA
(museum extension)
Possagno (41 km/25 mi NW of
    Treviso) C5
C. Scarpa

A. Canova's home is adjacent. •The Brion tomb (1970–72), also by Scarpa is at San Vito di Altivole (30 km/19 mi NW of Treviso).

520 CASA BENETTON   1967
(house)
Paderno di Ponzano (5 km/3mi
   N of Treviso) C5
T. Scarpa and C. Maschietto

TRIESTE C6

521 VILLAGGIO   1953–56
      DEL FANCIULLO
(children's village)
Trieste Opicina
M. d'Olivo

522 APARTMENT   1955–57
      BUILDING
Via San Francesco 12–14
Gino and Nani Valle

TROIA H7
16 km (10 mi) SW of Foggia

523 DUOMO   1093–1127
(cathedral)   onward

Magnificent 13th-c Pisan
Romanesque facade with some
Arabic influence. Superb rose
window. Bronze doors (1119)
by O. da Benevento.

TURIN
See Torino

TUSCANIA G5
24 km (15 mi) W of Viterbo

524 SAN PIETRO   8th c onward
(church)

Restored since an earthquake
in 1971. Most of the church
dates from the 12th and 13th c.
Some carvings are from the
Etruscan necropolis surrounding the church. Interesting
crypt. •Santa Maria Maggiore,
nearby, a contemporary
Romanesque church, has a
notable 13th c doorway.

UDINE B6

525 DUOMO   1236 onward
(cathedral)
Via Vittorio Veneto/Via
   Calzolai

Rebuilt in the 18th c. Frescoes
by G. B. Tiepolo (also in the
Oratorio della Purità to the
right of the cathedral and in
the Palazzo Arcivescovile in
Via Lovara). •The Piazza della
Liberta, close by, is an attractive space surrounded by Gothic
and Renaissance buildings. The
Arco Bollani (archway) on the
piazza is by A. Palladio.

526 CASA VERITTI   1955–60
(house)
Viale Duodo
C. Scarpa

527 APARTMENT   1958–60
      BUILDING
Via d'Aronco 1
Gino Valle and F. Toso

528 HOUSING (PEEP)   1976–79
Via Di Giusto
Gino Valle, M. Tondolo, and G.
Macola

URBINO E5

529 PALAZZO   1444–82
      DUCALE
Piazza Duca Federico

Courtyard (1470) by L. da
Laurana. The Galleria Na-
zionale della Marche, inside the
palazzo, has an important collection: paintings by Botticelli,
Raphael, della Francesca
(*Flagellation*), and others. The
study has remarkable mar-
quetry work on the walls after
designs by Botticelli.

530 COLLEGI   1964
      UNIVERSITARI
(student housing)
1.5 km (1 mi) E of Urbino
G. de Carlo

An apt interpretation of an
Italian hill town formed the
basis of this building. •The
Faculty of Education, Free
University (1976), also by de
Carlo, is in a restored convent
on Via Santa Maria in the town
center.

VENEZIA C5
(Venice)

Museums: Galleria dell'Accademia, Campo della Carità.
14th- to 18th-c Venetian paintings by Bellini, Titian, Carpaccio, Veronese, etc.
   Museo Correr, Piazza San
Marco (W side). Art and
history of Venice. Tiepolo,
Carpaccio, and others.
   Fondazione Guggenheim,
Calle San Gregorio. Superb

collection of 20th-C painting and sculpture by Arp, Picasso, Kandinsky, Ernst, and others.

Palazzo Labia, Campo San Geremia. Tiepolo's *Anthony and Cleopatra* frescoes. Entry permission needed.

Palazzo Querini-Stampalia, Campiello Querini-Stampalia. 18th-C furniture and paintings. Courtyard and arrangement (1963) by C. Scarpa.

531 DUOMO   864–1008
(cathedral)
Torcello (by boat from the Fondamenta Nuova)

Venetian Byzantine. Good mosaics. •The octagonal church of Santa Fosca (11th C) is on the right.

532 PIAZZA   1063 onward
    SAN MARCO

Basilica San Marco (Basilica of St. Mark): built from 1063–94 onward. Internal and external decoration of astonishing richness and originality. The facade is in two tiers, each of five arches. The four horses on the terrace are Greek, ca. 3rd C B.C. The Greek cross plan with five domes is preceded by an atrium with six smaller domes (13th-C mosaics). The interior mosaics are best seen from the second-floor galleries. Pala d'Oro (1105, 1209, and 1345) behind and above altar.

The piazza is contained by the Procuratie Vecchie (16th C, north side), Procuratie Nuova (ca. 1640, south side, by V. Scamozzi and then B. Longhena), and Fabbrica Nuova (1810, west side). The campanile and logetta (1540, by A. Sansovino) in the piazza were rebuilt in 1912 after collapsing. The interlocking Piazzetta, a magical space, is framed by the Palazzo Ducale, Libreria Vecchia and view of the island of San Giorgio Maggiore.

Palazzo Ducale (Doge's Palace): 14th–17th C.

Brilliant exterior Gothic facade (1309–1424, by G. and B. Bon). Fine internal courtyard with the monumental Scala dei Giganti (stair, 1484–1501 by A. Rizzo, statues by J. Sansovino).

Libreria Vecchia: J. Sansovino (1536–54), completed in 1584 by V. Scamozzi.

The Zecca (mint, 1536 by Sansovino) is on the south side, facing the water.

533 SANTA MARIA   1250–1443
    GLORIOSA DEI FRARI
(church)
Corso dei Frari

Gothic. Paintings by Titian and Bellini. *St. John* (chapel, right of chancel) by Donatello. •Outside, around the apse, is the Scuola di San Rocco (1517–49, by B. Bon, then S. Lombardo, then A. Scarpagnino) with an outstanding series of fifty-six paintings by Tintoretto (more works in the adjacent church of San Rocco).

534 SANTI   1260–1430
    GIOVANNI E PAOLO
(church)
Corso Santi Giovanni e Paolo

Gothic. Brick. Tombs of the doges.

535 CA' D'ORO   1421–40
(palace)
Canale Grande (access from Via 28 Aprile)
G. and B. Bon

The zenith of the Venetian Gothic style. The Galleria Franchetti inside has works by Mantegna, Titian, Guardi, and others.

536 SAN ZACCARIA   1444–65
(church)
A. Gambello

Completed (1480–1500) by M. Coducci. Transitional Gothic-Renaissance. Bellini's *Madonna with Saints* (1505).

537 SANTA MARIA   1481–89
       DEI MIRACOLI
    (church)
    Ponte di Cristo, then Fonda-
    menta Sanudo, then Calle
    Castelli
    P. Lombardo

Early Renaissance. Outstanding multicolored marble decoration. Difficult access to the
interior. Check with tourist
office first.

538 SAN SEBASTIANO   1504–47
    (church)
    Fondamenta San Sebastiano

    Built after A. Scarpagnino's
    designs. Paintings by Veronese
    and Titian.

539 SAN SALVATORE   1506–34
    (church)
    Campo San Salvatore
    G. Spavento and T. Lombardo

    Completed by J. Sansovino.
    Facade built in 1663.

540 PALAZZO   1509
       VENDRAMIN-CALERGI
    Canal Grande (E side), E of the
    San Marcuola station
    P. Lombardo

541 PALAZZO CORNER   1532
       DELLA CA'GRANDE
    Canal Grande (E side), E of
    S.M. del Giglio station
    J. Sansovino

542 SAN FRANCESCO   1535
       DELLA VIGNA
    (church)
    Campo San Francesco
    J. Sansovino

    Completed (including facade)
    by A. Palladio from 1568–72.

543 SCUOLA DI SAN   16th c
       GIORGIO DEGLI
       SCHIAVONI
    Calle dei Furlani
    J. Sansovino

    Paintings by Carpaccio: *St.
    Jerome in his Study, St. George,*
    etc.

544 PALAZZO GRIMANI 1556–72
    Canal Grande (E side)/Rio di
       San Luca
    M. Sanmicheli

545 SAN GIORGIO   1566–80
       MAGGIORE   onward
    (church)
    Isola di San Giorgio
    A. Palladio

Completed by V. Scamozzi
(1610). Paintings by Tintoretto
in the presbytery.

546 IL REDENTORE   1577–92
    (church)
    Isola della Guidecca
    A. Palladio

547 SANTA MARIA   1631–87
       DELLA SALUTE
    Canal Grande/Zattera
    B. Longhena

Octagonal plan. Tintoretto's
Marriage at Cana is in the
sacristy.

548 PALAZZO PESARO   1660–79
    Canal Grande (W side)/Rio di
       San Polo
    B. Longhena

    Top floor (1710) by Gaspari.
    Now the Galleria d'Arte
    Moderne. 19th- and 20th-c
    paintings. Works from the
    Biennale. Separate museum of
    oriental art with Japanese and
    Chinese works.

549 PALAZZO   1667 onward
       REZZONICO
    Canal Grande (W side)/Rio di
       San Barnaba
    B. Longhena

    Top floor (1756) by G.
    Massari. 18th-c interiors,
    furniture, and paintings.

550 VENEZUELA   1954–55
       PAVILION
    Giardini Della Biennale
    C. Scarpa

551 APARTMENT   1957
       BUILDING
    Canal Giudecca
    I. Gardella

552 HOTEL AND 1978–81
    YACHT CLUB
Lungomare Marconi, at the
    Lido
I. Cappai and P. Mainardis

VERCELLI C2

553 SANT'ANDREA 1219–27
    (church)
Via Galileo Ferraris

Transitional Romanesque/
Gothic.

VERONA C4

554 ARENA 1st C A.D.
    (Roman amphitheater)
Piazza Bra

Large and very well preserved.
•The remains of a Roman
theater from the same period
are on the Regaste Redentore.
A church was built in the
11th C inside the theater.

555 SAN ZENO 1117–1225
    MAGGIORE
    (church)
Piazza San Zeno

Outstanding Romanesque
church. Campanile (1045–
1175). Apse rebuilt from
1389–96. Entry porch by
Niccolò, bas-reliefs on either
side by Niccolò and Guglielmo.
Superb bronze doors. Man-
tegna's *Madonna and Three
Saints* tryptich by the high altar
(some sections still in the
Louvre, Paris).

556 DUOMO 1139 onward
    (cathedral)
Piazza del Duomo

Romanesque choir, Gothic
nave. Entry porch (lower

section) sculpted by Niccolò.
Assumption (first altar, left) by
Titian. Mazzanti Chapel (1508,
end right aisle) by D. da Lugo.

557 SANT' 1290–1323, 1422–81
    ANASTASIA
    (church)
Piazza Sant'Anastasia

Gothic. Fine campanile.
Frescoes by Altichiero and A.
Pisanello (*St. George and the
Princess,* third chapel, right
transept).

558 SAN FERMO 13th–14th C
    MAGGIORE
    (church)
Stradone San Fermo

Built over an earlier church
(ca. 1065, now the crypt).
Romanesque. Remodeled in
the Gothic style. 14th-C
frescoes. *Annunciation* (1424,
left, Brenzoni mausoleum) by
A. Pisanello.

559 CASTELVECCHIO 1354
    (castle)
Corso Castelvecchio

Houses the Civic Museum,
magnificently arranged (1960–
70) by C. Scarpa. The picture
gallery has 14th- to 18th-C
works by Pisanello, Bellini,
Veronese, etc. •The connected
Ponte Scaliger (bridge, 1354)
across the river was completely
rebuilt after 1945. No. 44,
Corso Cavour (Palazzo Ca-
nossa, 1537, much restored
after 1945) is by M. San-
micheli, as is the rather
mannerist Palazzo Bevilacqua
(1530), further east, opposite
San Lorenzo.

560 ARCHE SCALIGERE 14th C
    (Tombs of the Scaligeri)
Off the E end of the Piazza dei
    Signori

Gothic open-air mausoleums.
The original equestrian statue
from Cangrande I's tomb is in
the Castelvecchio museum.
•Other tombs in the adjacent
church of Santa Maria Antica.

561 LOGGIA DEL 1476–93
    CONSIGLIO
Piazza dei Signori (N side)
Fra Giocondo

562 SAN GIORGIO 1477 onward
    MAGGIORE
    (in Braida, church)
Via San Alessio/Porta San
    Giorgio

Dome and (unfinished) campanile by M. Sanmicheli. Important paintings by Veronese
(*Martydom of St. George,* in the
apse), Tintoretto, and Moretto.

563 PALAZZO POMPEII 1529
Lungadige Porta Vittoria 9
M. Sanmicheli

564 PORTA PALIO 1557
    (gateway)
Stradone di Porta Palio
M. Sanmicheli
•Other gateways by Sanmicheli

are the Porta Nuova and Porta San Zeno. His facade for the church of Santa Maria in Organo, Via Santa Maria in Organo, Verona, also resembles these defensive structures.

565 GRAN GUARDIA   1610
        VECCHIA
    Piazza Bra
    D. Curtoni

VICENZA C4

566 DUOMO   12th c onward
    (cathedral)
    Piazza del Duomo

15th-c Gothic remodeling. Restored since 1945.

567 SANTA CORONA   13th c
    (church)
    Corso Andrea Palladio/Contra
        Santa Corona

Known for two paintings: Veronese's *Adoration of the Magi* (north transept) and Bellini's *Baptism of Christ* (fifth altar, right).

568 PALAZZO   1489 onward
        THIENE
    Contra Porti 12
    L. di Bologna

The east facade on Via San Gaetano da Thiene and the north and east courtyard facades are by A. Palladio.

569 PALAZZO   1549–1614
        DEL RAGIONE
    (Basilica)
    Piazza dei Signori
    A. Palladio

Two open, colonnaded galleries (Ionic upon Doric) built around a Gothic palazzo (1444). Restored after 1945 (new roof). Contains the Centro Internazionale di Studi di Architettura Andrea Palladio (the international center of studies on the architecture of Andrea Palladio). •At the west end is the 12th-c Torre di Piazza (belfry). The unfinished Loggia del Capitano (1571, by Palladio) is opposite.

570 PALAZZO   1550 onward
        CHIERICATI
    (Museo Civico)
    Piazza Matteotti
    A. Palladio

Paintings by Vandyke, Piazzetta, and other Venetian painters. •The entrance to the Teatro Olimpico (theater,

1580–83) is on the north side of the piazza. This was Palladio's last building and was completed by V. Scamozzi. The stage set (of the streets of Thebes) in fixed perspective is by Scamozzi.

571 VILLA ROTONDA 1550–1606
    (Villa Capra)
    Via dei Nani
    2 km (1 mi) S of Vicenza
    A. Palladio

Completed by V. Scamozzi. Access to grounds only on certain days. Check first. •The Villa Valmarana (1669, by A. Muttoni) lies to the northwest (off Via dei Nani), with frescoes (1757) by G. B. Tiepolo.

572 PALAZZO   1565 onward
        VALMARANA
    (now Braga)
    Corso Fogazzaro 16
    A. Palladio

Never completed. Mannerist facade.

573 PALAZZO DEL   1588
        COMMUNE
    (formerly Trissimo)
    Corso Andrea Palladio 98
    V. Scamozzi

•Further east are nos. 145, the Venetian Gothic Palazzo Da Schio (Ca' d'Oro) and 163, the Casa di Palladio (1566, facade attributed to A. Palladio).

VITERBO G5

A well-preserved medieval section of the old town has been preserved.

574 PALAZZO PAPALE   1266
Piazza San Lorenzo

Superb open Gothic loggia.
•The cathedral (1192) opposite has been restored since 1945.

575 VILLA LANTE   1566 onward
Bagnaia, 5 km (3 mi) NE of
    Viterbo
G. da Vignola

Splendid gardens and fountains.

VOLTERRA E4

576 PORTA   ca 3rd C B.C.
    ALL'ARCO
(Etruscan gateway)
Via Porta all'Arco

The medieval ramparts are well preserved.

577 PALAZZO   1208–54
    DEI PRIORI
Piazza dei Priori

Now the town hall. Austere.

578 DUOMO   13th C
(cathedral)
Piazza San Giovanni

Romanesque. Much restored.

The Netherlands

Onze Lieve Vrouwebasiliek; *see entry 128*

Netherlands

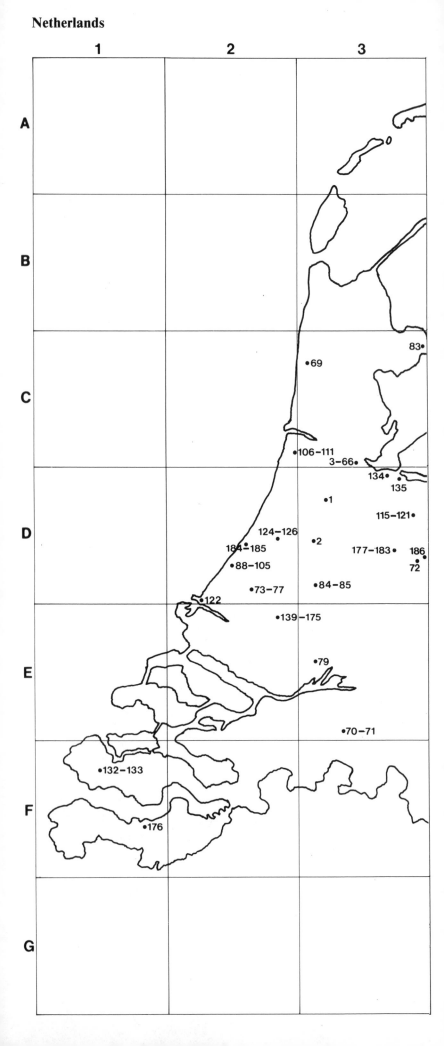

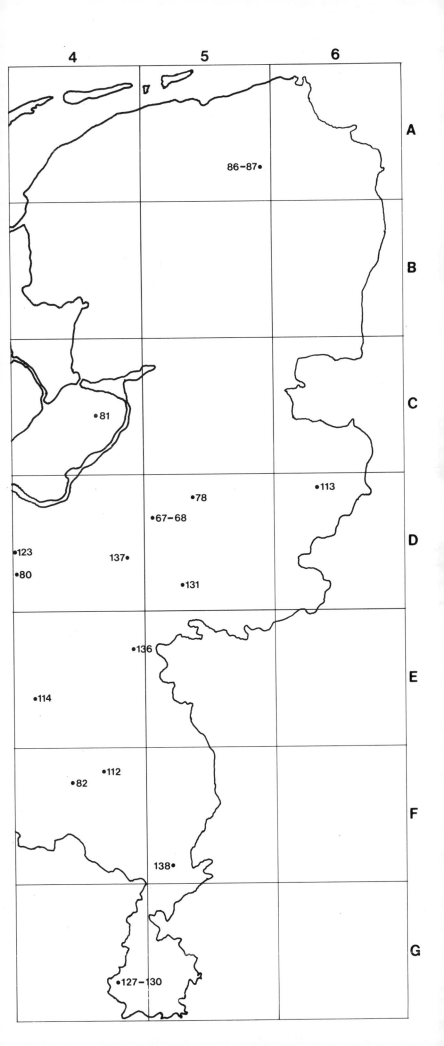

AALSMEER D3

1 HOUSE　　　　　　1924
Stommeerkade 64
J. Duiker and B. Bijvoet

Badly altered.

TER AAR D3

2 STADHUIS　　　　1970
(town hall)
J. van Stigt

AMSTERDAM C3

Tourist Information: VVV, Rokin 5 (tel. 266444).

Architect's Institute: Bond van Nederlandse Architekten, Keizersgracht 321 (tel. 228111).

Architectural Bookstores:
Architectura et Natura, Leliegracht 44
Van Gennep, Nieuwezijds Voorburgwal 330.

Museums: Architectuurmuseum (architecture), Droogbak 1a. Temporary exhibitions.
Amsterdams Historisch Museum, Kalverstraat 92. The history of Amsterdam from the 13th c until today. These buildings were the former municipal orphanage. Rebuilt in the 17th and 18th c. Restored (1975) by B. Van Kasteel and J. Schipper.
Amsterdam Urban Planning, Keizersgracht 440. History of urban development in the city, including the (fairly detailed) 20th c.
Van Loon Museum, Keizersgracht 672. Canal house (1672) by A. Dortsman. 18th-c interiors. •No. 674 (1672) is also by Dortsman.
Rembrandt Huis, Jodenbreestraat 4–6. Rembrandt's home (from 1639–60) contains three hundred of his etchings. The house was restored by K. P. C. de Bazel.
Rijksmuseum, Stadhouderskade 42. The greatest collection of 15th- to 19th-c Dutch paintings in Holland. Rembrandt's *Night Watch, The Jewish Bride*, etc. Also sculpture and applied arts sections. See entry 18.
Rijksmuseum Vincent van Gogh, Paulus Potterstraat 9 (see entry 64). Two hundred paintings by van Gogh. See the Kröller-Müller Museum near Otterloo (entry 137) for another exceptional collection of van Gogh paintings.
Stedelijk Museum (1895, by A. Weissman), Paulus Potterstraat 13. Paintings from 1850 onwards. Good representative collections of Mondrian and Malevich. Works by Dubuffet, de Kooning, Appel, etc.

3 OUDE KERK　　　1306 onward
(church)
Oudezijds Voorburgwal/
　Oudekerksplein *D6*

Brick construction. Tower (1565–66) by J. J. Bilhamer. Rebuilt in 1733.

4 BEGIJNHOF　　　1346 onward
(beguinage)
enter off the Spui, through a
　tiny door *D6*

The beguinage surrounds a beautiful green. In the center is the Presbyterian church (1607). House no. 31 is a Catholic chapel (1665). No. 34, built in wood ca. 1470, was restored in 1957.

5 NIEUWE KERK　　1408 onward
(church)
Dam/Nieuwezijds Voorburgwal
　D6

Rebuilt continuously after a series of fires. Recently restored.

6 ZUIDERKERK　　　1603–14
(church)
Zandstraat *D6*
H. de Keyser

7 WESTERKERK　　　1620
(church)
Prinsengracht, opposite the
　Rozengracht *D6*
H. de Keyser

Built by de Keyser's son Pieter. This church had considerable influence on later Protestant churches in Holland and Germany.

8 NOORDERKERK　　1620
(church)
Noordermarkt *C6*
H. de Keyser

Greek cross plan.

9 PAKHUIZEN　　　1624
(storehouses)
Prinseneiland *C6*

10 CANAL HOUSE　　1638
(now theater museum)
Herengracht 168 *D6*
P. Vingboons

Altered in 1730. •Nos. 170 and 172 (1618) are by H. de Keyser.

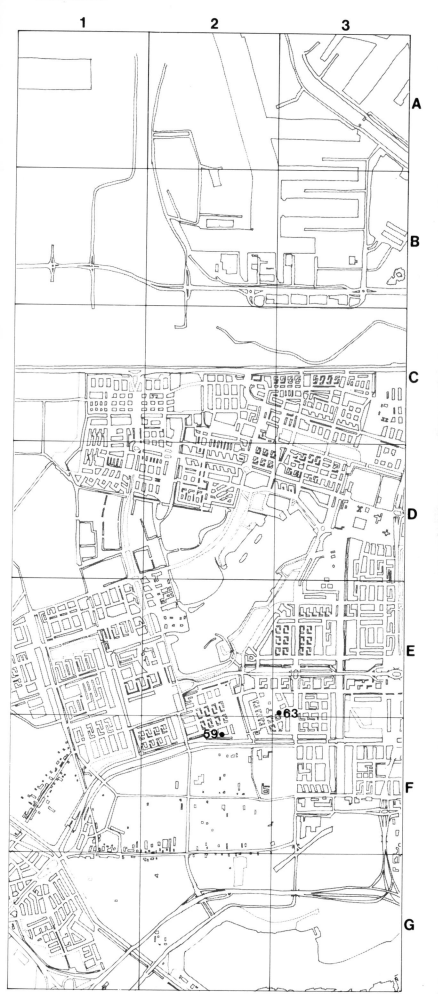

Amsterdam

Amsterdam

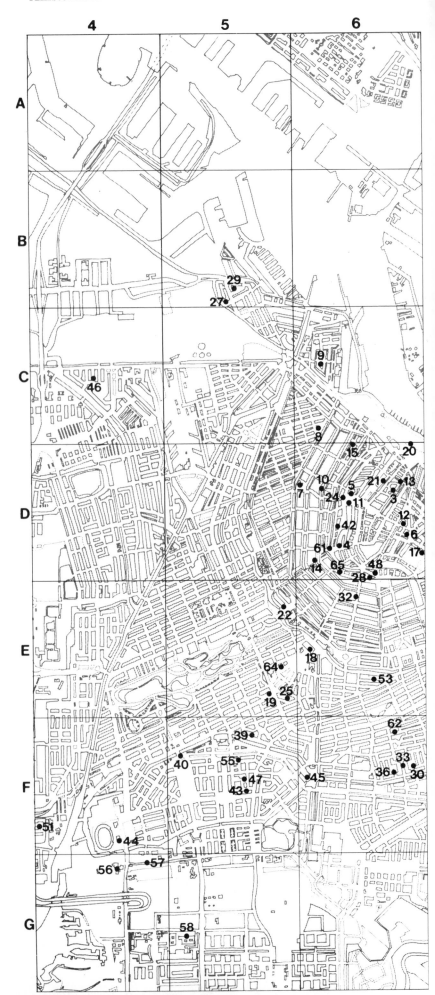

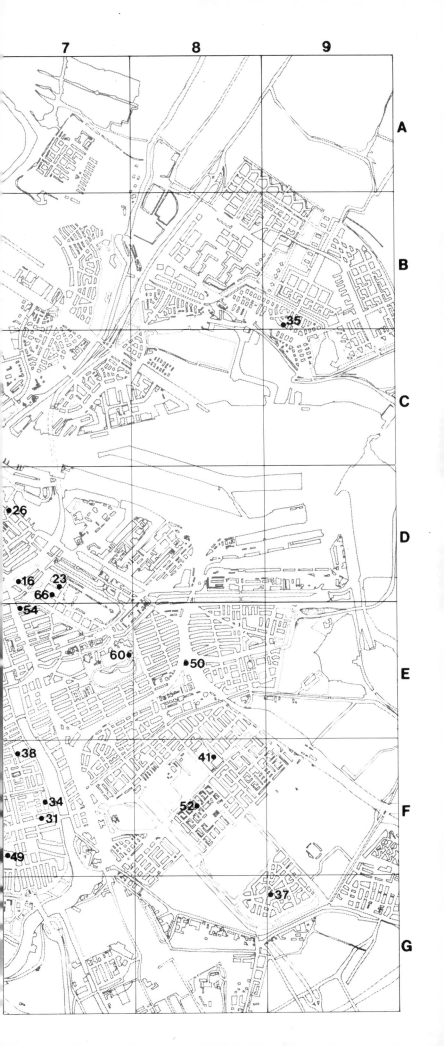

11 KONINKLIJK PALEIS 1648
(Royal Palace)
Dam (entry at rear) *D6*
J. van Campen

Former town hall. The
sculptures on the east
and west facades are
by A. Quellin the Elder.

12 TRIPPENHUIS 1660–64
(canal house)
Kloveniersburgwal 29 *D6*
P. Vingboons

Giant Corinthian order.

13 ONS' LIEVE 1661
HEER OP SOLDER
(Amstelkring Museum)
Oudezijds Voorburgwal 40 *D6*

Remarkable Catholic church
built on the top floor of a town
house to escape Protestant
restrictions.

14 CROMHOUT-HUIZEN 1662
(canal houses)
Herengracht 362–368 *D6*
P. Vingboons

15 RONDE 1668–71
LUTHERSE KERK
(former church)
Singel 11 *D6*
A. Dortsman

Rebuilt after a fire in 1823. Now
the auditorium of a hotel.

16 PORTUGEES– 1671
ISRAËLITISCHE
SYNAGOGE
(Portuguese Synagogue)
Jonas Daniël Meijerplein *D7*
D. Stalpaert and E. Bouman

17 MOZES EN 1839–41
AÄRONKERK
(church)
Waterlooplein 61a *D6*
T. F. Suys

Executed by J. van Straaten.
Now an exhibition center.

18 RIJKSMUSEUM 1885
Stadhouderskade 42 *E6*
P. J. H. Cuypers

19 CONCERTGEBOUW 1888
(concert hall)
Van Baerlestraat 98 *E5*
A. L. van Gendt

Unremarkable classical exterior.
Known, however, for its perfect
acoustics within.

20 CENTRAAL STATION 1889
(railway station)
Stationsplein *D6*
P. J. H. Cuypers with A. L.
van Gendt

21 BEURS 1897–1903
(stock exchange)
Damrak/Beursplein *D6*
H. P. Berlage

This building marks the
beginning of the rationalist
movement in Holland. Direct
expression of material and
structure.

22 HOTEL 1898–1902
AMÉRICAIN
Leidseplein 28 *E5*
W. Kromhout

Important precursor of the
Amsterdam School. Some well-
preserved interiors. •The city
theater, next door (no. 26, built
in 1894), is by J. Springer.

23 DIAMOND 1899
WORKERS' UNION
BUILDING (A.N.D.B)
Henri Polaklaan 9 *D7*
H. P. Berlage

Now offices. The stairway
inside clearly shows Berlage's
concern in treating each wall as
a flat, undisturbed, planar
surface.

24 HOOFDPOSTKANTOOR 1899
(post office)
Nieuwezijds Voorburgwal 182
D6
C. H. Peters

Neo-Gothic/Renaissance
hybrid.

25 HILLEHUIS HOUSING 1912
G. Metsustraat 22–34 *E5*
M. de Klerk

The very first appearance of the
Amsterdam School, just visible
in the roofline and some details.

26 SCHEEPVAARTHUIS 1913–16
(offices)
Prins Hendrikkade 113–114 *D7*
J. M. van der Mey

Amsterdam School. Many fine original interiors still intact. P. L. Kramer and M. de Klerk also worked on this building.

27 EIGEN HAARD   1913–19
    HOUSING *B5*
    Oostzaanstraat 2–6 (1913–15),
      1–21 (1918–19)
    Spaarndammerplantsoen 14–36
      (1913–15), 11–31 (1915–16)
    Zaanstraat 48–49 (1915–16),
      54–64 (1918–19)
    Wormerveerstraat 17–19
      (1915–16)
    Hembrugstraat 57–77 (1918–19)
    M. de Klerk

The later stages of this scheme mark the zenith of the Amsterdam School. Virtuoso brickwork.

28 TUSCHINSKI   1918–21
    CINEMA
    Reguliersbreestraat 26–28 *D6*
    H. de Jong

    Wonderful art deco interiors in perfect condition. Lobby design by J. Gidding.

29 HOUSING   1918–21
    Zaandammerplein 1–45 *B5*
    K. P. C. de Bazel

30 HOUSING   1920
    Henriette Ronnerplein 16–34 *F6*
    M. de Klerk

31 HOUSING   1920
    Vrijheidslaan 10–46, 50–52 *F7*
    M. de Klerk

    •Nos. 9–43 are by P. L. Kramer
    (1921–23).

32 ALGEMENE   1920–26
    BANK NEDERLAND
    (office building)
    Vijzelstraat 32 *E6*
    K. P. C. de Bazel

33 HOUSING   1921
    Burgemeester Tellegenstraat
      14–36, 38–60; P. L. Takstraat
      1–25, 2–26 *F6*
    P. L. Kramer

    •P. L. Takstraat 27–31, 28–32
    are by M. de Klerk (1922)

34 HOUSING   1921–22
    Holendrechtstraat 1–47 *F7*
    M. Staal-Kropholler

    The first female architect of note in Holland.

35 HOUSING AND   1921–25
    LANDSCAPING
    Purmerweg, Purmerplein *B9*
    B. T. Boeyinga, J. Boteren-
    brood, and others

36 HOUSING   1922
    Th. Schwartzeplein 15–33 *F6*
    M. de Klerk

    •Nos. 1–13 are by P. L. Kramer.

37 BETONDORP   1923–28
    GARDENCITY
    (Concrete Village) *G9*
    Planners:
    A. Keppler, P. Vorkink, and
    J. Wormser.
    Architects:
    J. B. van Loghem:
    Schovenstraat 3–25, 4–26,
    Graanstraat 20–66, 29–63
    D. Greiner: Veeteeltstraat,
    Landbouwstraat, Graanstraat,
    Huismanshof
    W. Greve: Oogststraat
    J. Gratama: Tuinbouwstraat.

38 THEOSOPHICAL   1925–26
    UNION MEETING HALL
    Tolstraat 154, 160 *F7*
    J. A. Brinkman and L. C. van
    der Vlugt

    Altered. Now a public library.

39 SYNAGOGUE   1928
    Heinzestraat 1–3 *F5*
    H. Elte

40 BOATHOUSE   1928
    AND BRIDGE
    Olympiaplein/Noorder
      Amstelkanaal *F5*
    P. L. Kramer

Curious anthropomorphic pavilions.

41 HOUSING   1928
    AND CHURCH
    Linnaeushof 7–30, 50–94 *F8*
    A. J. Kropholler

42 DE TELEGRAAF   1928–30
    (newspaper building)
    Nieuwezijds Voorburgwal 225
      D6
    J. F. Staal and G. J. Langhout

43 OPENLUCHTSCHOOL   1930
    VOOR HET GEZONDE
    KIND
    (open-air school)
    Cliostraat 40 *F5*
    J. Duiker

Key modern-movement building in Holland. Original windows replaced with heavier glazing sections but still in very good condition. The gatehouse on the street was added later.

44 CITROËN BUILDING 1931
Stadionplein 26-30 *F4*
J. Wils

•New Citroën building next door (22–24, built 1964) also by Wils. Both Citroën buildings create a symmetrical entry to the Olympic stadium (1924, also by Wils with C. van Eesteren and G. Jonkheid).

45 APOLLOHAL 1933–35
(apartments and sports hall)
Stadionweg 1–5 *F6*
A. Boeken

46 PLAN LANDLUST 1934
Gibraltarstraat *C4*
B. Merkelbach and C. J. F. Karsten

One of the first row housing layouts in Holland.

47 MONTESSORI SCHOOL 1934
Anth. van Dijkstraat 2 *F5*
W. van Tijen, M. Stam, and L. Beese

Similar to J. Duiker's open-air school (entry 43). •Next door (nos. 4–12) are five row houses in good condition by Stam (with van Tijen and Beese).

48 CINEAC 1934–35
(cinema)
Reguliersbreestraat 31 *D6*
J. Duiker

Early supergraphic neon signage has recently been removed. Ingenious planning makes full use of a very tight site.

49 SYNAGOGUE 1936
Lekstraat 61–63 *F6*
A. Elzas

50 MUIDERPOORTSTATION
(railway station) 1939
Oosterspoorplein *E8*
H. G. J. Schelling

Clinically pure architecture.
•Amstel station also by Schelling.

51 NATIONAAL 1939–46
LUCHTVAART-
LABORATORIUM
(aviation laboratory)
A. Fokkerweg 2 *F3*
H. A. Maaskant with W. van Tijen

52 GARDENCITY 1949–51
"FRANKENDAAL"
Lorenzlaan, Van 't Hofflaan, Maxwellstraat, and H. de Vrieslaan *F8*
Planners:
C. van Eesteren and J. H. Mulder
Architects:
B. Merkelbach and P. Elling, with C. J. F. Karsten and M. Stam

Landscape architect: M. Ruys

53 "GEILLUSTREERDE 1957–59
PERS" OFFICES
Stadhouderskade 85 *E6*
B. Merkelbach and M. Stam

Minimal glazed curtain wall.

54 STUDENTS' 1958–64
HOUSING AND MENSA
Weesperstraat 7–57 *E7*
H. Hertzberger, with T. Hazewinkel

55 PRIVATE HOUSE 1960
Apollolaan 141 *F5*
H. Salomonson

56 BURGERWEESHUIS 1960–62
(orphanage)
Ijsbaanpad 3 *G4*
A. van Eyck

A marvelous building made up of separate "houses" grouped along an interior street.

57 RIETVELD ACADEMY 1965
F. Roeskestraat 96 *G4*
G. Rietveld

58 VRIJE UNIVERSITEIT 1967
HOOFDGEBOUW
(Free University main building)
de Boelelaan 1105 *G5*
Architektengroep 69

59 PRIVATE HOUSE   1967
F. Küpperstraat 9 *F2*
A. Cahen with J. P. Girod and
R. Groenevelt

60 HIGH-RISE   1967
   APARTMENTS
Linnaeusstraat 2c *E7*
T. Dijkstra

61 ATHENEUM   1968
   BOEKHANDEL
(bookstore)
Spui 14 *D6*
J. P. Girod and W. Röling

The Jugendstil exteriors (1904)
are by L. G. Mohrmann.

62 DE HOEKSTEEN KERK 1968
(church)
Van Ostadestraat 270 *F6*
J. van Stigt

63 DE DRIE HOVEN   1973
   BEJAARDENCENTRUM
(center for the aged)
L. Chrispijnstraat 50 *E3*
H. Hertzberger

64 VAN GOGH MUSEUM   1973
Paulus Potterstraat *E5*
G. Rietveld, then J. J. van
Dillen, then J. van Tricht

65 APARTMENTS   1974
Singel 428 *D6*
A. Cahen, with J. P. Girod and
J. Koning

Fine, uncompromisingly
modern building, well
integrated into historical
surroundings.

66 HUBERTUS HOME   1975–79
(for single mothers)
Plantage Middenlaan 33 *D7*
A. van Eyck and T. Bosch

APELDOORN D5

67 PALAIS HET LOO   1685–92
NW of town center, just off the
   ring road
J. Roman and D. Marot

The palace was built for William
III of Orange. Marot was largely
responsible for the interiors and
fine gardens.

68 CENTRAAL BEHEER   1972
   OFFICE BUILDING
Prins Willem Alexanderlaan
H. Hertzberger

Megastructure of repetitive
cells joined by internal streets.
The feeling of being in a public
street is consciously evoked
throughout the building.

BERGEN-BINNEN C3

69 PARK MEERWIJK   1916–18
Meerweg/Studler van Surchlaan
J. F. Staal, M. Staal-
Kropholler, P. L. Kramer, G. F.
La Croix, and C. J. Blaauw

Country estate of Amsterdam
School houses, in good
condition.

BREDA E3

70 GROTE KERK 15th and 16th c
(cathedral)
Havermarkt

Brabantine Gothic. The tomb of
Count Engelbert II was designed
by T. V. da Bologna in the
Renaissance style, after Michelangelo.

71 KASTEEL   1536 onward
(castle)
Kasteelplein
T. V. da Bologna (remodeling)

Surrounded by water, protected
by the Spanjaardsgat defensive
works. Access is restricted to
certain days. Apply first at the
local VVV.

BUNNIK D3

72 HOUSE   1934
Prof. Grindweg
P. Elling

DELFT D2

73 NIEUWE KERK 1430 onward
(church)
Grote Markt

The tower dates from 1396.
Monument to William of
Orange (1610–21) by H. de
Keyser in the choir.

74 STADHUIS   1620
(town hall)
Grote Markt
H. de Keyser

Restored in 1965.

75 AUDITORIUM T. H.   1965
Prof. Mekelweg
J. H. van den Broek and J. B.
Bakema

76 SCHOOL   1967
    Prof. Mekelweg
    P. Elling

77 SCHOOL   1967
    J. van Beierenlaan
    H. Hertzberger

DEVENTER D5

78 GROTEKERK   1040 onward
    (church)
    Grotekerkhof

    Gothic. Romanesque crypt.

DORDRECHT E3

79 GROTEKERK   1460–1500
    (church)
    Lange Geldersekade

    Gothic. Richly carved Renais-
    sance choir stalls (1538–
    42, by J. T. Aertsz). Fine
    choir screen (1743).

DRIEBERGEN D4

80 DE BLAUWVOET   1930
    REST HOME
    J. B. van Loghem

DRONTEN C4

81 AGORA DE MEERPAAL 1967
    (community center)
    Town center
    F. van Klingeren

EINDHOVEN F4

Museum: Stedelijk Van
Abbemuseum, Bilderdijklaan
10. Major collection of modern
art including works by Picasso,
Braque, Mondriaan, Miró,
Appel, Vasarely, Stella, and
others.

82 STUDENT HOUSING   1959
    Boutenslaan
    J. W. H. C. Pot

ENKHUIZEN C3

83 STADHUIS   1686–88
    (town hall)
    Breestraat
    S. Vennecool

GOUDA D3

84 ST.-JANSKERK   13th c
    (church)   onward
    Markt

    Rebuilt after fires in 1438 and
    1552. The stained glass windows
    (1555–71) are by D. and W.
    Crabeth.

85 STADHUIS   1449–59
    (town hall)
    Markt

GRONINGEN A5

86 MARTINIKERK   13th–15th c
    (church)
    Grote Markt

87 TECHNICAL   1922
    SCHOOL
    P. Driessenstraat
    L. C. van der Vlugt and J. G.
    Wiebenga

DEN HAAG D2
(The Hague)

Museums: Museum Bredius,
Prinsegracht 6. 17th-c paintings
and decorative arts.
    Haags Gemeentemuseum,
Stadhouderslaan 41. 19th- and
20th-c works. Large Mondriaan
collection.
    Mauritshuis, Plein 29.
Important 17th-c Dutch
paintings: Rembrandt (*The
Anatomy Lesson of Dr. Tulp*),
Vermeer, Hals, Rubens,
Holbein, and others.

88 OUDE RAADHUIS   1564
    (old town hall)
    Riviervismarkt

    Restored in 1647, enlarged in
    1734. Restored and enlarged in
    1883.

89 MAURITSHUIS   1633
    (museum)
    Plein 29
    J. van Campen

• Inside the Binnenhof next door
is the medieval Ridderzaal
(Knights' Hall), built in 1280,
restored in 1904.

90 HUIS TEN BOSCH   1645–51
    off Leidsestraatweg, in the
      Haagse Bos
    P. Post

    Post's best work. The
    Palladian exterior has been
    badly disfigured by 18th-c
    additions. No visits allowed.

91 GERMAN EMBASSY   1715
    Lange Vijverberg 8
    D. Marot

92 KONINKLIJKE   1734–36
      BIBLIOTHEEK
    (Royal Library, former Hotel
    Huguetan)
    Lange Voorhout 34
    D. Marot

93 KURHAUS   1884–86
    Strandweg, Scheveningen
    Henkenhof and Ebert

Burnt down in 1886 and rebuilt immediately. Now a casino.

94 VILLA HENNY 1898
Oude Scheveningseweg 42
H. P. Berlage

95 VILLA LEURING 1903
Wagenaarweg 30, Scheveningen
H. van de Velde

96 HOUSING 1922
Papaverhof, off Klimopstraat
J. Wils

97 FIRST CHURCH OF 1925
CHRISTIAN SCIENCE
Banstraat (park)
H. P. Berlage

Heavy massing of blocklike elements.

98 OFFICE BUILDING 1925
(Nederlanden van 1845)
Groenhovenstraat 2
H. P. Berlage

99 NIRWANA 1927–30
APARTMENTS
Benoordenhoutseweg/Willem
Witsenplein
J. Duiker and J. G. Wiebenga

100 DE VOLHARDING 1928
(cooperative building)
Prinsegracht 39
J. W. E. Buys and J. B. Lürsen

De Stijl influence visible in the massing.

101 RUDOLF STEINER 1929
CLINIC
Nieuwe Parklaan 26
J. W. E. Buys and J. B. Lürsen

Utterly different from the above building. A modified small Goetheanum (see Dornach, Switzerland).

102 TECHNICAL SCHOOL 1930
Zwaardstraat 16, Scheveningen
J. Duiker and B. Bijvoet

•An early row house scheme (1916) by Bijvoet and Duiker is at 98–114. Joh. van Oldebarneveldlaan. This was followed by a luxurious

scheme of double villas (1920) at Scheveningselaan, Kijkduin, by Duiker in a style directly derived from that of Frank Lloyd Wright.

103 GEMEENTEMUSEUM 1934
(art museum)
Stadhouderslaan 41
H. P. Berlage

Wrightian massing with effective use of large reflecting pools.

104 HEAD OFFICE, 1938–42
SHELL NEDERLAND
Wassenaarseweg
J. J. P. Oud

105 CHURCH 1969
Laan van Meerdervoort/Aaltje
Noorderwierstraat
A. van Eyck

The blank facade conceals a rich and mystical interior. Beautiful control of daylight through circular roof lights.

HAARLEM C2

Museum: Frans Halsmuseum, Groot Heiligland 62. Outstanding collection of works by Hals. Also works by Scorel, van de Velde, and other Haarlem painters. The building (1608) was designed by L. de Key.

106 ST. BAVOKERK 1400–1490
(cathedral)
Grote Markt

107 WAAG   1598
    (weigh house)
    Damstraat/Donkere Spaarne
    L. de Key

108 VLEESHAL   1602
    (butchers' hall)
    Grote Markt
    L. de Key

Rich gables and strapwork.

109 NIEUWE KERK   1647
    (church)
    Kerkplein/Annastraat
    J. van Campen

    Greek cross plan. The tower
    (1613) is from an earlier church
    by L. de Key.

110 ROSENHAGHE   1920
    HOUSING
    Anslijnstraat, Brouwerskade,
      Hoosmanstraat,   Kotsstraat,
      and Nerkmanstraat
    J. B. van Loghem

111 TUINWIJK   1921
    ZUID HOUSING
    near Zonnelaan
    J. B. van Loghem

    •Tuinwijk Noord by van
    Loghem was built one year later.

THE HAGUE
See Den Haag

HELMOND F4

112 PAALWONINGEN   1978
    ("tree houses")
    P. Blom

    Cubic interlocking blocks built
    at a 45-degree angle to the
    ground. A Herculean effort to
    obtain these results.

HENGELO D6
(Overijssel)

113 KASBAH–   1972–73
    HOUSING
    Groot-Drienen Zwavertsweg
    P. Blom

    Housing on pilotis. Conceived
    as an urban infill scheme (and
    built in the countryside).

'S–HERTOGEN–
BOSCH E4

114 ST. JANS   1370–1529
    KATHEDRAAL
    (cathedral)
    Parade

    Nothing remains of the original
    11th-c Romanesque church.
    The Lady Chapel dates from
    1286. Although much restored,

the cathedral is an outstanding
example of the Brabantine
Gothic style; its rich decoration
is very rare in Holland.

HILVERSUM D3

115 SCHOOL   1921
    Bosdrift
    W. M. Dudok

116 STADHUIS   1924–30
    (town hall)
    W. M. Dudok

Brilliant Wrightian building.

117 ZONNESTRAAL   1926–28
    SANATORIUM
    Pampahoeve (S of Hilversum)
    J. Duiker and B. Bijvoet

A key modern-movement
building. Very badly altered,
inexplicably, by Bijvoet, but
what remains of the original
buildings (in terrible
condition) is most rewarding.

118 HOTEL GOOILAND 1934–36
    Emmastraat/Langestraat
    J. Duiker

Now a residential home for the
handicapped. •The theater next
door is by B. Bijvoet.

119 AVRO   1935–40
    BROADCASTING STUDIO
    's-Gravenlandseweg
    B. Merkelbach, C. J. F.
    Karsten, and A. Bodon

120 VARA   1958–69
    BROADCASTING STUDIO
    between Steynlaan and
      Heuvellaan
    B. Merkelbach and P. Elling

121 WERELDOMROEP 1960
Witte Kruislaan/Lage
Naarderweg
J. H. van den Broek

HOEK VAN HOLLAND D2
(Hook of Holland)

122 HOUSING 1924
2e Scheepvaartstraat 91a–113a
J. J. P. Oud

Two-story terrace housing in
excellent condition.

HUIS TER HEIDE D4
10 km (6 mi) E of Utrecht

123 VILLA HENNY 1915–16
on the road to Amersfoort
R. van 't Hoff

In good condition. One of the
first concrete-framed houses in
Holland. Closely modeled after
F. L. Wright's design of a
fireproof house for $5,000.
Van 't Hoff worked in Wright's
office in America briefly.
•Villa Verloop (1915–16), at
Ruysdaellaan 2, close by, also
by van 't Hoff, is again
influenced by Wright (this time
the Martin House, Buffalo).

LEIDEN D2

124 STADHUIS 1595–1603
(town hall)
Breestraat
L. de Key

The strapwork decoration is
derived from H. de Vries's
books on ornament.

125 STEDELIJK MUSEUM 1640
"DE LAKENHAL"
(former cloth hall)
Oude Singel 32
A. van 's-Gravensande

Painting collection includes
16th-c Leiden painters
C. Engebrechtsz, Lucas van
Leyden (*Last Judgment*), and
others. •The Mare Kerk (1640–
48), a domed octagonal church
on the Lange Mare close by, is
also by van 's-Gravensande.

126 WAAG 1657–59
(weigh house)
Aalmarkt
P. Post

MAASTRICHT G4

127 ST. SERVAASKERK 1000
(church) onward
St. Servaasklooster

The oldest church in the
country. The crypt dates from
the 6th c. The 11th-c towers
flanking the eastern apse show
the influence of the Rhineland
churches. The interior has been
considerably altered by P. J. H.
Cuyper's renovation in 1886.

128 ONZE LIEVE 1150 onward
VROUWEBASILIEK
(church)
Onze Lieve Vrouwplein

Massive westwork. Notable
13th-c choir.

129 ST. JANSKERK 1450
(church)
St. Servaasklooster

130 STADHUIS 1659
(town hall)
Markt
P. Post

Post's influence was
considerable. His Palladian
style was introduced to England
by H. May (see entry GB–272).

KASTEEL
MIDDACHTEN D5
castle just east of De Steeg

131 KASTEEL 1694–97
MIDDACHTEN
(castle)
S. Vennecool

MIDDELBURG F1

132 ABDIJ 1128–1560
(abbey)
Groenmarkt/Korte Burg

•In the Groenmarkt is the
Nieuwe Kerk, a flamboyant
Gothic structure, originally
the abbey church. The choir has
been closed off and is now
known as the Koor Kerk.

133 STADHUIS 1412–1599
(town hall)
Markt

Rebuilt after 1945. Compare
with Hôtel de Ville, Brussel.

MUIDEN D3

134 MUIDERSLOT 13th–15th c

Moated brick castle.

NAARDEN D3

135 NAARDEN- 1675–85
VESTING
(city walls)
A. Dortsman

NIJMEGEN E4

136 ST.-STEVENSKERK   1272
Grote Markt   onward

• The Waag (weigh house, 1612)
is opposite. The ruins of the
palace of the Carolingian
emperors can be seen nearby at
Valkhof on Voerweg. There are
two churches of interest on the
grounds: St.-Nicolaaskapel
(799, rebuilt many times, finally
in the Gothic style) and the
remains of the Romanesque
chapel of St. Maartens.

OTTERLO D4

137 KRÖLLER-   1937
MÜLLER MUSEUM
inside the park (National
Park de Hoge Veluwe)
H. van de Velde

A magnificent collection of
modern art (especially van
Gogh) and sculpture. The
building extension with
meticulous detailing (1972) is
by W. G. Quist. In the outdoor
sculpture garden is the re-
erected Sonsbeek Pavilion
(1955) by G. Rietveld.

• 4 km (2.5 mi) to the north at
Hoenderloo is Castle St.
Hubertus (1917), a palatial
hunting lodge, by H. P. Berlage.

ROERMOND F5

138 ONZE LIEVE VROUWE   1218
MUNSTERKERK
(church)
Munsterplein

Romanesque. Restored by
P. J. H. Cuypers.

ROTTERDAM E2

Tourist Information: VVV,
Stadhuisplein 19, (tel.
136-000).

Museums: Museum
Boymans-van Beuningen,
Mathenesserlaan 18. 15th- to
17th-c Dutch and Flemish
works. 20th-c surrealist and
abstract art (Kandinsky and
others). The building (1934),
by A. van den Steur, was
extended in 1972 by A. Bodon
and H. Salomonson.

139 ST. LAURENS-   1449–1525
KERK
(church)
St. Laurensplaats *C7*

Restored after 1945.

140 VREESWIJK   1918–50
GARDEN SUBURB
Lede *E7*
M. J. Granpré Molière,
Verhagen, and Kok

141 SPANGEN HOUSING   1919
Justus van Effenstraat *C4*
M. Brinkman

Influential early public-housing
project with raised-access
walkways.

142 HOUSING   1920
Spaansebocht *C4*
J. J. P. Oud

143 TUSSENDIJKEN   1920–22
HOUSING
Rösener Manz Straat/
Taanderstraat/
Gysingstraat *C4*
J. J. P. Oud

144 HET WITTE   1923
DORP HOUSING
Aakstraat/Baardsestraat/
Barkasstraat *C4*
J. J. P. Oud

145 ST. LUCIA SCHOOL   1925
Aert van Nesstraat 29b *C6*
P. C. Buskens and L. C. van der
Vlugt

146 VAN NELLE FACTORY   1928
Van Nelleweg 1 *C4*
J. A. Brinkman and L. C. van
der Vlugt

Design also attributed to
M. Stam, who was in Brinkman
and van der Vlugt's office at
the time. Eight-story metal and
glass curtain wall. Try to see
the roof pavilion.

147 KIEFHOEK   1928
HOUSING ESTATE
Kiefhoekstraat *E7*
J. J. P. Oud

Rotterdam

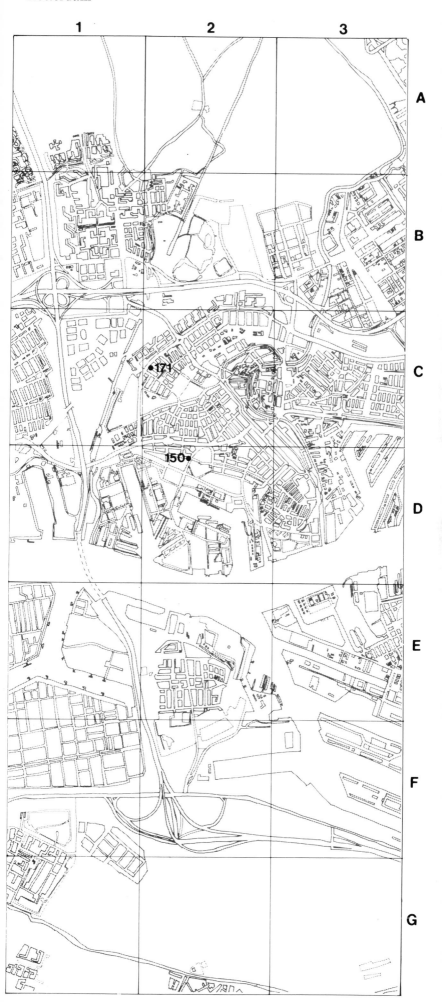

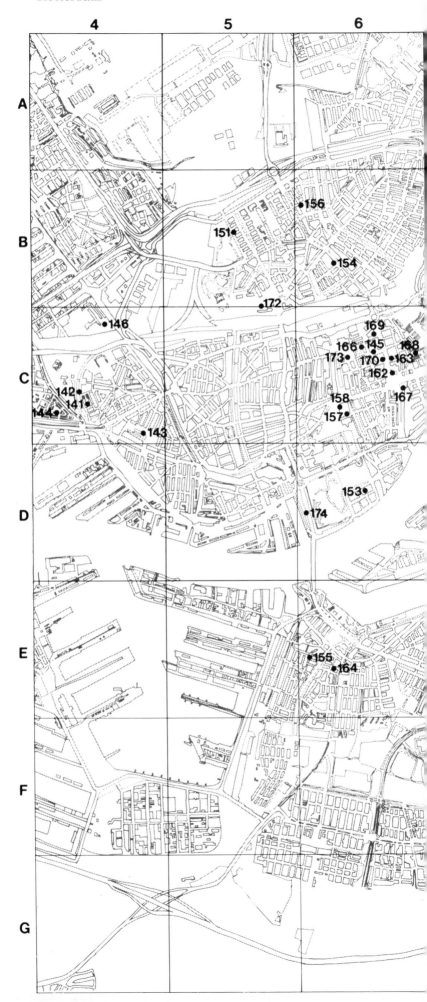

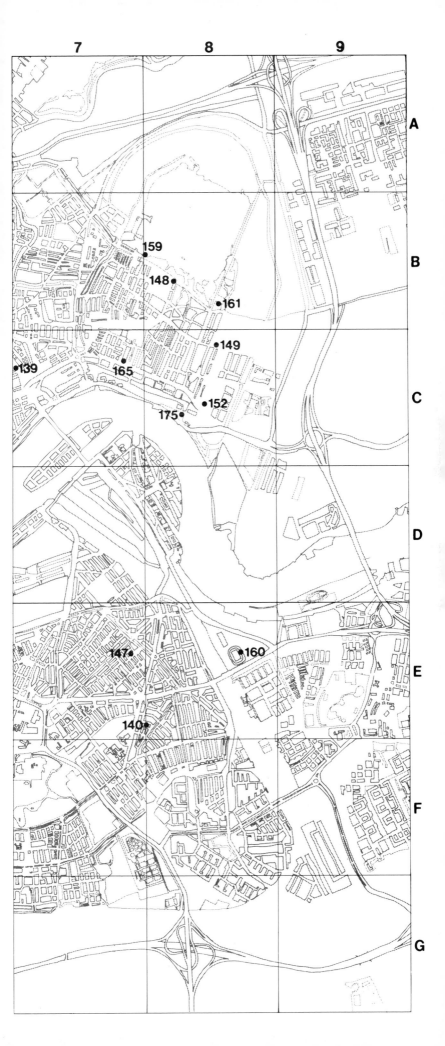

In its context, one realizes how truly revolutionary Oud's housing scheme was. In excellent condition. •The church at Eemstein 23 (1928) is also by Oud.

148 VAN DER 1930
   LEEUW HOUSE
   Kralingse Plaslaan 38 *B8*
   J. A. Brinkman and L. C. van der Vlugt

   Built for the director of Van Nelle.

149 HOUSE 1930
   's-Gravenweg 86 *C8*
   W. Kromhout

150 DE BRUYN HOUSE 1931
   Arij Prinslaan 14 *D2*
   J. A. Brinkman and L. C. van der Vlugt

151 APARTMENTS 1932
   Vroesenlaan/Navanderstraat
   B5
   J. H. van den Broek

152 HOUSE 1932
   Honingerdijk 64 *C8*
   J. B. van Loghem

153 PARKLAAN 1933
   APARTMENTS
   Parklaan *D6*
   W. van Tijen

   Luxury apartments.

154 SCHIEKADE 1934
   APARTMENTS
   Schiekade *B6*
   J. H. van den Broek

155 HOUSES 1934
   Frans Bekkerstraat 70–80 *E6*
   W. van Tijen

156 BERGPOLDER 1934
   APARTMENTS
   Dr. Abraham Kuyperlaan *B6*
   W. van Tijen, J. A. Brinkman, and L. C. van der Vlugt

157 BOEVÉ HOUSE 1935
   Mathenesserlaan 9 *C6*
   J. A. Brinkman and L. C. van der Vlugt

158 SONNEVELD HOUSE 1935
   Jongkindstraat 12 *C6*
   J. A. Brinkman and L. C. van der Vlugt

159 R. Z. V. JACHTCLUB 1935
   (yacht club)
   Kralingse Plaslaan 113 *B8*
   W. van Tijen and H. A. Maaskant

   The high-rise apartments (1938) are by van Tijen and Maaskant.

160 FEYENOORD 1937
   STADIUM
   Stadionweg *E8*
   J. A. Brinkman and L. C. van der Vlugt

161 VAES HOUSE 1937
   Plaszoom 1 *B8*
   J. A. Brinkman and L. C. van der Vlugt

   Altered.

162 ERASMUSHUIS 1939
   APARTMENTS
   Coolsingel *C6*
   W. M. Dudok

163 BEURS 1940
   (exchange)
   Coolsingel *C6*
   J. F. Staal

164 HOUSING 1946–49
   Pendrechtsestraat *E6*
   J. J. P. Oud, M. J. Granpré Molière, and W. van Tijen

165 APARTMENTS 1947
   Oostzeedijk 208–224 *C7*
   W. van Tijen and H. A. Maaskant

166 LIJNBAAN 1953
   SHOPPING CENTER
   Lijnbaan *C6*
   J. H. van den Broek and J. B. Bakema

The center of Rotterdam was destroyed in 1940. This pedestrian shopping mall had worldwide influence.

167 ZADKINE 1953
   SCULPTURE
   Blaak *C6*
   O. Zadkine

   Monument to the destruction of Rotterdam.

168 HUF SHOE STORE 1954
   Hoogstraat 183 *C6*
   J. H. van den Broek and J. B. Bakema

   •The Galeries Modernes department store (1956) at no. 177 is also by van den Broek and Bakema.

169 UTRECHT 1954–61
   BUILDING
   Coolsingel 75 *C6*
   J. J. P. Oud

170 DE BIJENKORF 1956
   DEPARTMENT STORE
   Coolsingel 1 *C6*
   M. Breuer and A. Elzas

171 PROTESTANT 1957
   CHURCH
   Burg. Honnerlage Gretelaan, Schiedam *C2*

J. H. van den Broek and J. B. Bakema

172 MONTESSORI SCHOOL 1959
Schimmelpenninckstraat 20 *B5*
J. H. van den Broek and J. B. Bakema

173 RIJN HOTEL 1959
Schouwburgplein 1 *C6*
B. Merkelbach and P. Elling

174 EUROMAST 1960
OBSERVATION TOWER
Parkhaven *D6*
H. A. Maaskant

175 ECUMENICAL 1968
CENTER
Maas Boulevard *C8*
G. Rietveld, J. J. van Dillen, and J. van Tricht

TERNEUZEN F1

176 STADHUIS 1960–68
(town hall)
J. H. van den Broek and J. B. Bakema

UTRECHT D3

Museums: Centraal Museum, Agnietenstraat 1. Utrecht School paintings: van Scorel, Terbrugghen, Savery, etc.
Rijksmuseum Het Catharijneconvent, Nieuwe Gracht. Outstanding collection of Dutch sacred art.

177 DOMKERK 1015 onward
(cathedral)
Domplein

The nave collapsed in 1674 and was not rebuilt.
Accordingly, the tower (1320–81) by J. ten Doem is separated from the Gothic choir. The cloisters (13th- to 15th-c) were restored by P. J. H. Cuypers in 1880.

178 PIETERSKERK 1039 onward
(church)
Pieterskerkhof

Romanesque, renovated in Gothic style.

179 SCHRÖDER HOUSE 1924
Prins Hendriklaan 50
G. Rietveld

This house for Mrs. Schröder (who collaborated with Rietveld on the design of the interiors) realized the architectural potential of the de Stijl movement more fully than any other building of its generation

would. The upper floor is divisible by sliding partitions.
•On the other side of the highway are four row houses at 5–11 Erasmuslaan (1930) by Rietveld.

180 ONE-FAMILY 1932
DWELLINGS
R. Schumannlaan 13–19
G. Rietveld

181 CINEMA VREEBURG 1935
Vredenburgplein
G. Rietveld

Completely altered.

182 DENTAL SCHOOL 1972
Kaap Hoorndreef 34
T. Koolhaas

183 MUSIC CENTER 1975–79
Vredenburgplein
H. Hertzberger

Visually exciting spaces manipulated in a similar fashion to Central Beheer, Apeldoorn.

WASSENAAR D2

184 GROOT 1928–30
HAESEBROEK
Groot Haesebroekseweg
H. van de Velde

185 RIJNLANDS LYCEUM 1937
(school)
Backershagenlaan
J. P. Kloos

ZEIST D3
10 km (6 mi) E of Utrecht

186 ZEISTER SLOT 1677–86
(castle)
J. Roman

Interiors by D. Marot. Much restored in 1960.

Spain

Burgos Cathedral; *see entry 114*

Spain

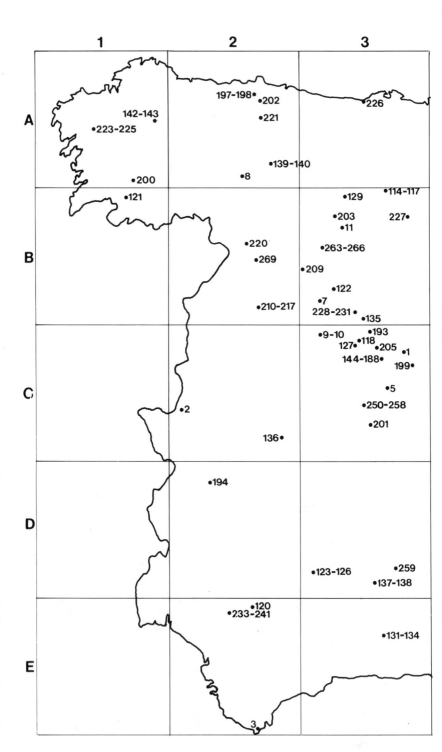

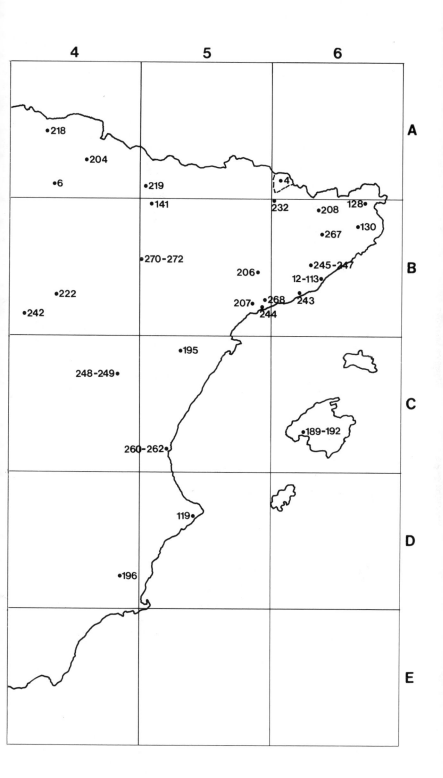

ALCALÁ DE HENARES C3

1 COLEGIO DE 1537–53
  SAN ILDEFONSO
  (old university)
  Plaza San Diego
  R. Gil de Hontañón

  Plateresque facade.

ALCÁNTARA C2

2 ROMAN BRIDGE A.D. 106
  2 km (1 mi) NW of Alcántara

  Built in granite without
  mortar. The temple and
  triumphal arch are original.

ALGECIRAS E2

3 MARKET HALL 1933
  E. Torroja and M. Sánchez
  Arcos

ANDORRA A6
(principality)

MERITXELL

4 MERITXELL 1973–78
  RELIGIOUS CENTER
  Taller de Arquitectura/R. Bofill

  This complex is a replacement of
  an ancient sanctuary that
  burned down in 1972.

ARANJUEZ C3

5 PALACIO REAL 1569 onward
  (Royal Palace)
  Plaza de Santiago Rusiñol
  J. de Herrera and J. B. de
  Toledo

Grand stair (1748) by G.
Bonavia. Rococo Porcelain
Salon (1763) decorated with tiles
from the Buen Retiro Factory in
Madrid. Formal garden (1746)
and the Jardin del Principe
(Prince's Garden, 1763) by
Boutelou. The "Labourer's
Cottage" is modeled after
the Trianon, Versailles.

LOS ARCOS A4
28 km (17.5 mi) NE of Logroño

6 CHURCH OF 15th c onward
  THE ASUNCIÓN
  (Assumption)

  Emotional baroque interior.
  15th-c Gothic cloisters. •7 km
  (4.5 mi) S is the Church of the
  Holy Sepulchre at Torres del
  Rio. Built ca. 1200. Octagonal
  plan with Mudejar cupola.

ARÉVALO B3

7 LA LUGAREJA 13th c
  CHURCH
  2 km (1 mi) S of Arévalo

  Mudejar work with fine blind
  brick arcades. Sited on an
  isolated hilltop.

ASTORGA A2

8 EPISCOPAL 1887–93
  PALACE (GRAU)
  A. Gaudí i Cornet

  Work stopped in 1893. Addition
  (1905–7) by L. de Guereta.

AVILA C3

9 TOWN WALLS 11th c
  Built by Raymond of Burgundy

Strengthened in the 14th c and
still complete today. The
fortified apse of Avila cathedral
(1160–1211 and later) forms one
of the ninety bastions in the
town defenses.

10 SAN 12th–14th c
  VINCENTE BASILICA

  Exceptional carvings on west
  portal. 12th-c martyr's tomb
  inside the eastern tower.

BAÑOS DE CERRATO B3
14 km (8.5 mi) S of Palencia

11 CHURCH OF SAN JUAN 661

The finest Visigoth basilica
surviving in Spain. The nave
arcades are of marble columns
supporting horseshoe-shaped
arches above.

BARCELONA B6

Tourist Information: Oficina de
Información de Turismo,
Avenida José Antonia, 658
(tel. 218–0570).

Architect's Institute: Colegio
Oficial de Arquitectos, Gran
Via de les Corts Catalanes, 563
(tel. 323–1407).

Barcelona

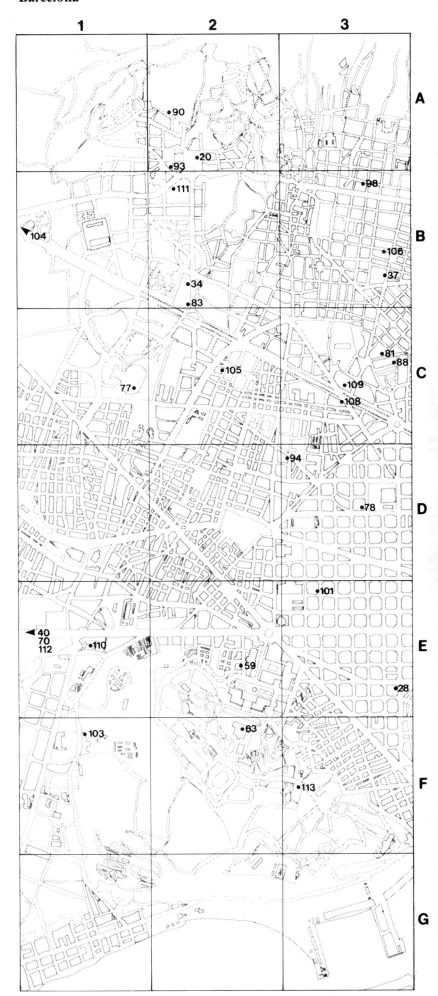

Barcelona

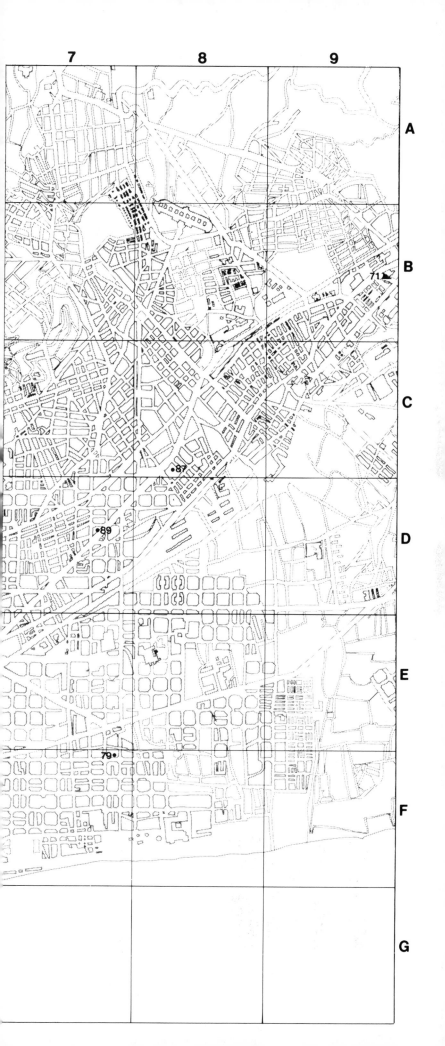

Museums: Museo de Arte de
Cataluña, Palacio Nacional,
Parque de Montjuich.
Important collection of
medieval paintings and
sculptures. Also Tintoretto, El
Greco, Velásquez, Ribera,
Viladomat, and others.

Museo de Arte Moderno,
Palacio de la Ciudadela.
Catalan 19th- and 20th-c
paintings. Fortuny, Dali, Miró,
Picasso, etc.

Colección Cambo, Palacio
de la Virreina, Ramblas, 99.
Small and excellent collection
of works by Raphael,
Botticelli, Titian, Tintoretto,
Fragonard, Rubens, Vandyke,
Goya, Murillo, Zurbarán, and
El Greco.

Fundación Miró, Avenida de
Miramar, Montjuich. Miró
paintings and sculptures. See
entry 113.

Museo Pablo Picasso, Calle
de Montcada, 15. Early
Picasso works and Picasso's
series of variations of *Las
Meninas* by Velázquez (in the
Prado, Madrid). See entry 22.

12 BARRIO   11th c onward
   GÓTICO *F4*
   (Gothic quarter)

a Episcopal   12th–15th
  Palace   and 18th c
  Calle Obispo Irurita, 5

•The towers on the Plaza
Nuova remain from the 4th-c
Roman defensive wall.

b San Severo   1699–1705
  (church)
  Calle San Severo, 9–11
  J. Arnaudies

c Diputación   15th c
  (Provincial Council)
  Plaza San Jaime

d Casa de la   14th–19th c
  Ciudad
  (City Hall)

Plaza San Jaime/Calle
  Ciudad

e Casa del   15th c
  Arcediano
  Calle Sante Lucia, 1

f Catedral   1298–1448
  (Barcelona Cathedral)
  Plaza de Cristo Rey

The rather cold west facade is
a 19th-c reconstruction of the
original design (1408).

g Lloctinent Palace 1549–57
  (Archivo de la Corona de
   Aragón)
  Plaza del Rey/Calle Condes
   de Barcelona, 2
  A. Carbonell

Now the archives of the
House of Aragón.

h Salon del Tinell 12th–15th c
  (Tinell Salon)
  Plaza del Rey

Former Hall of State. The
Santa Agueda Chapel (ca.
1350) is to the right of the
Salon.

13 SAN PABLO   1117
   DEL CAMPO
   (church)
   Calle San Pablo, 99 *F4*

14 SANTA ANA   1141–46
   (church)
   Calle Santa Ana, 27 *E4*

15 SANTA MARIA   ca. 1320
   DEL PINO
   (church)
   Plaza del Pino *F4*

16 SANTOS JUSTO   1342
   Y PASTOR
   (church)
   Plaza de San Justo *F4*

17 "LLOTJA"   14th c
   (mercantile exchange)
   Plaza Palacio *F5*

The Salón Contrataciones
(1380–92) is by P. Arbey.
Restored and enlarged
(1764–98) by J. S. Faneca.

18 ATARAZANAS   1381
   (naval dockyard)
   Puerta de la Paz *F4*
   A. Ferrer

19 SANTA MARIA   14th c
   DEL MAR
   (church)
   Plaza de Santa Maria *F5*

20 PEDRALBES   14th–15th c
   MONASTERY
   Plaza del Monasterio *A2*

Catalan Gothic church and
cloisters.

21 ANTIGUO   15th–18th c
   HOSPITAL DE LA
   SANTA CRUZ
   (former Hospital of Santa Cruz)
   Calle Hospital, 56 *F4*

•The Academy of Medicine
(1762–64) at Calle Carmen, 47,
is by P. Virgili. The courtyard
inside (Patio de la casa de
Convalecencia, 1629–80) is by
J. Juli.

22 CALLE DE MONTCADA *F5*

Lined with Gothic mansions.
Some are open to the public.
   No. 12: Palacio   14th–18th c
   del Marques de Llio
   No. 15: Casa   15th c
   Berenguer de Aguilar
   (Picasso Museum)
   No. 20: Palacio   17th c
   Dalmases
   No. 23: House   13th–14th c
   No. 25: Casa   16th c
   Cerveló o Giúdice

23 NUESTRA   1681–1730
   SEÑORA DE BELÉN
  (church)
  Calle Carmen, 2/Ramblas *E4*
  J. Juli

24 SAN FELIPE NERI   1721–52
  (church)
  Plaza de San Felipe Neri *F4*

25 SAN MIGUEL   1753
   DEL PORT
  (church)
  Plaza del Marques de Mina *G5*
  P. M. Cermeno

26 VIRREINA PALACE 1772–78
  Ramblas, 99 *F4*
  C. Grau

27 PLAZA REAL *F4*   1848–59
  (Royal Square)
  F. D. Molina

28 SAN ANTONIO   1876–82
   MARKET
  Calle Urgel/Calle Tamarit *E3*
  A. Rovira i Trias

29 CASA VICÉNS   1878–80
  Calle Carolinas, 24 *C4*
  A. Gaudí i Cornet

Gaudí's first important
building. Symmetrical plan.
The rubble facade is gradually
transformed into a brick and
tile surface, culminating in
elaborate corbeled corner turrets. Altered in 1926.

30 EDITORIAL   1881–86
   MONTANER I SIMÓ
  Calle Aragón, 255 *D4*
  L. Domènech i Montaner

Superb detailing and ironwork.

31 SALESAS CHURCH 1882–85
  Paseo de San Juan, 88 *D5*
  J. Martorell i Montells

32 EXPIATORY   1883 onward
   TEMPLE OF THE
   SAGRADA FAMILY
  Plaza de la Sagrada Familia *D6*
  A. Gaudí i Cornet

Gaudí directed the construction
of the temple until his death in

1926. Only one of the towers
of the Nativity facade was
completed by this time, the
other three shortly afterwards.
Construction continued in 1954
and is still in progress. Note
the small parochial school
(1909) by Gaudí in the corner
of the site (visible from the
bridge joining the two towers).

33 PALACIO GÜELL   1885–89
  Calle Conde del Asalto, 3 *F4*
  A. Gaudí i Cornet

Now the Museum of Stage
Design. The plan is generated
around a central skylit hall. The
back lighting of the dome above
this hall is similar to that of
St. Paul's, London.

34 PAVILIONS AND   1887–93
   ENTRY GATES, FINCA
   GÜELL ESTATE
  Avenida de la Victoria/Plaza
   Manuel Girona *B2*
  A. Gaudí i Cornet

35 CAFÉ-RESTAURANT   1888
  (1888 International Exhibition)
  Parque de la Ciudada *F5*
  L. Domènech i Montaner

Now the Zoological Museum.

36 TRIUMPHAL ARCH   1888
  (1888 International Exhibition)
  Calle Salón de Victor Pradera
  E5
  J. Vilaseca i Casanovas

37 COLEGIO DE   1889–94
   SANTA TERESA DE
   JESUS CONVENT
  Calle Ganduxer, 105 *B3*
  A. Gaudí i Cornet

38 CASA THOMAS   1895–98
  (apartments)
  Calle Mallorca, 291 *D5*
  L. Domènech i Montaner

39 COMPAÑÍA DE   1897–99
   FLUIDO ELECTRICO
  Calle Vilanova, 12 *E5*
  P. Falqués i Urpí

40 COLONIA   1898, 1908–15
   GÜELL CHAPEL
  Sante Coloma de Cervelló
  (20 km/12 mi W of Barcelona)
  E1
  A. Gaudí i Cornet

Only the crypt was built.
Extraordinary integration with
surrounding pine forest. The
structural resolution is a work of
genius. The model of the chapel
is behind the altar. The altar
(1943–48) is by J. M. Jujol i
Gibert.

41 CASA CALVET 1899
(apartments)
Calle Caspe, 48 *E5*
A. Gaudí i Cornet

42 CASA AMATLLER 1900
(apartments)
Paseo de Gracia, 41 *E4*
J. Puig i Cadafalch

43 "BELLESGUARD" 1900–1902
(Figueras Villa)
Calle Bellesguard, 16 *A4*
A. Gaudí i Cornet

The paper-thin brick vaulting
supporting the roof is a good
example of Gaudí's structural
genius.

44 PARQUE GÜELL 1900–1914
Calle Olot *B5*
A. Gaudí i Cornet

The park with its two gatehouses
is all that was built of Gaudí's
original design for a garden city
of sixty houses.

45 CASA ROMÁN 1901
MACAYA
Paseo General Mola, 8 *D5*
J. Puig i Cadafalch

46 CASA LAMADRID 1902
Calle Gerona, 113 *D5*
L. Domènech i Montaner

47 SAN PABLO 1902–12
HOSPITAL
Avenida San Antonio Maria
Calvet, 167 *D6*
L. Domènech i Montaner

48 CASA TERRADES 1905
("de les Punxes")
Diagonal, 416 *D5*
J. Puig i Cadafalch

49 CASA BATLLO 1905–7
(remodeling)
Paseo de Gracia, 43 *E4*
A. Gaudí i Cornet

Masklike balconies combine
with bone-shaped stone
columns to create a frenzied
yet totally controlled facade.

50 PALACIO DE 1905–8
LA MÚSICA CATALANA
Calle Alta de San Pedro, 13 *E5*
L. Domènech i Montaner

This concert hall is Domènech's
masterpiece, as well as the high
point of the Spanish
Modernisme movement.

51 CASA MILA 1905–10
("La Pedrada")
Paseo de Gracia, 92 *D5*
A. Gaudí i Cornet

Aptly nicknamed "The
Quarry," this fantastic
apartment building is freely
planned around two open
courtyards. The stone facade
undulates in every direction
and is punctuated with balcony
railings of wildly twisted
strands of wrought iron
resembling seaweed. The roof
is a surrealist landscape and
should be seen.

52 PALACIO QUADRAS 1906
Diagonal, 373 *D5*
J. Puig i Cadafalch

53 CASA FUSTER 1908–10
(now offices)
Paseo de Gracia, 132 *D5*
L. Domènech i Montaner

54 APARTMENTS 1909
Calle Oro, 44 *C5*
F. Berenguer i Mestres

55 TORRE SAN 1909
SALVADOR
(house)
Paseo de Nuestra Senora
del Coll *B5*
J. M. Jujol i Gibert

56 APARTMENTS 1910
Calle Gerona, 122 *D5*
J. F. Granell i Manresa

57 VALLDONCELLA 1910
CONVENT
Calle Císter, 41 *A4*
B. Martorell i Puig

58 IGLESIA 1910–14
DEL CARMEN
(church)
Calle Obispo Laguarda *E4*
J. M. Pericas i Morros

59 CASARRAMONA 1911
FACTORY
Calle Méjico *E2*
J. Puig i Cadafalch

Now police barracks.

60 CASA COMALAT 1911
Diagonal, 442/Calle Corcega,
316 *D5*
S. Valeri i Pupurull

61 TORRE ROVIRALTA 1913
Avenida Dr. Andreu, 31 *A4*
J. Rubió i Bellver

62 APARTMENTS 1922
Diagonal, 332 *D6*
J. M. Jujol i Gibert

63 NATIONAL 1926–29
PALACE OF MONTJUICH
Montjuich *F2*
P. Domènech i Montaner and
E. P. Candoya

64 CASA VILARÓ 1929–30
(house)
Calle de Porteli, 43 *B5*
S. Illescas Mirosa

65 CASAL DE 1929–31
SANT JORDI
(apartments)
Via Layetana, 81 *E5*
F. Folguera i Grassi

66 MYRURGIA FACTORY 1930
Calle Mallorca, 351 *D5*
A. Puig Gairalt

67 APARTMENTS 1930–31
Calle Muntaner, 342–348 *C4*
J. L. Sert

•No. 314, the Barraquer Clinic
(1936–39), is by J. Llovet.

68 APARTMENTS 1931
Via Augusta, 61 *C4*
G. Rodriguez Arias

69 "COLLASO I GIL" 1932
(college)
Calle San Pablo, 101 *F4*
J. Goday Casals

70 TORRE JUJOL 1932
(own house)
Calle Mossèn Cinto Verdaguer,
45, Sant Joan Despí (4 km/
2.5 mi W of Barcelona) *E1*
J. M. Jujol i Gibert

•Also by Jujol is the Casa
Negre (1915) at Torrent del
Negre, 37, Sant Joan Despí.

71 CASA BLOC 1932–36
Avenida Torras y Bages, 91–105
B9
G.A.T.C.P.A.C.

G.A.T.C.P.A.C. was a group
of architects affiliated with
CIAM. Experimental
minimum-standard housing.

72 ASTORIA BUILDING 1933–34
Calle París, 193–199 *D4*
G. Rodriguez Arias

73 APARTMENTS 1934–35
Calle Padua, 96 *B4*
S. Illescas Mirosa

74 APARTMENTS 1934–35
Calle Aribau, 243/Calle Campo
Vidal, 16 *C4*
R. Duràn Reynals

75 ANTITUBERCULAR 1934–38
DISPENSARY
Calle Torres Amat/Calle San
Bernardo, 10 *E4*
J. L. Sert, J. Torres Clave,
and J. B. Subirana

76 APARTMENTS 1952–54
FOR I.S.M. EMPLOYEES
Paseo Nacional, 43 *G5*
J. A. Coderch de Sentmenat and
M. Valls Vergés

77 BARCELONA 1954–57
FOOTBALL STADIUM
Traversa de las Corts/Avenida
de la División Azul *C1*
F. Mitjans Miró, J. Soteras
Mauri, and L. García-Barbón
Fernández

78 EDITORIAL GILI 1954–61
Calle Rosellón, 89 *D3*
F. Bassó Birulés and J. Gili
Moros

79 APARTMENTS 1955–59
Calle Pallars, 301–319 *F7*
O. Bohigas Guardiola and J. M.
Martorell Codina

80 "ESCORIAL" 1955–62
RESIDENTIAL AREA
Calle Escorial *C5*
J. Almenay Juve, O. Bohigas
Guardiola, J. M. Martorell
Codina, F. Mitjans Miró,
A. Perpina Sebria, J. M. Ribas
Casas, and M. Ribas Piera

81 APARTMENTS 1957–60
Calle Juan Sebastián Bach, 7 *C3*
J. A. Coderch de Sentmenat and
M. Valls Vergés

82 APARTMENTS 1957–64
Via Augusta, 168 *C4*
J. M. Martorell Codina,
O. Bohigas Guardiola, and
D. Mackay

83 FACULTAD DE 1958
DERECHO
(Law Faculty)
Zona Universitaria—Pedrables
B2
G. Giráldez Dávila, P. López
Iñigo, and X. Subias Fages

84 COLEGIO OFICIAL 1958–62
DE ARQUITECTOS
(School of Architecture)
Plaza Nueva, 5 *F4*
X. Busquets Sindreu

85 "MONES" 1959–62
FACTORY AND OFFICES
Calle Guillermo Tell, 51 *C4*
J. A. Ballesteros Figueras and
others

86 APARTMENTS 1959–62
Calle Padilla, 323–329 *D6*
A. de Moragas Gallissá and
F. de Riba de Salas

87 APARTMENTS 1959–65
Avenida Meridiana, 312–314 *C8*
J. M. Martorell Codina,
O. Bohigas Guardiola, and
D. Mackay

88 APARTMENTS   1960–62
Calle Juan Sebastián Bach, 28
C 3
Taller de Arquitectura/R. Bofill
•No. 4 (1964) is also by Bofill.

89 APARTMENTS   1960–62
Calle Navas de Tolosa, 296 *D7*
J. M. Martorell Codina,
O. Bohigas Guardiola, and
D. Mackay

90 BALLVÉ HOUSE   1960–62
Avenida Nuestra Senora de
   Lourdes, 21–23 *A2*
J. M. Fargas Falp and E. Tous
Carbó

91 HISPANO-   1960–65
   OLIVETTI BUILDING
Ronda de la Universidad, 18 *E4*
BBPR Architectural Studio with
J. Soteras Mauri

92 APARTMENTS   1961–64
Ronda del Guinardó/42–44
   Calle Lepanto *C6*
J. M. Martorell Codina,
O. Bohigas Guardiola,
and D. Mackay

93 CASA PANIKER   1962
Castellet, 9–11 *A2*
J. A. Ballesteros Figueras,
C. Cardenal, and others

94 SCHENKEL   1962–64
   APARTMENTS
Calle Nicaragua, 99 *D3*
Taller de Arquitectura/R. Bofill

95 CASA TAPIES   1962–63
(house and studio)
Zaragoza, 57 *C4*
J. A. Coderch de Sentmenat

96 APARTMENTS   1963
Ronda San Pablo, 42–44 *E4*
A. de Moragas Gallissá and
F. de Riba de Salas

97 "NOTICIERO   1963–65
   UNIVERSAL" BUILDING
Calle Lauria, 35 *E5*
J. M. Sostres Maluquer

98 MADRE GÜELL   1963–67
   CONVENT
Calle Esperanza, 5–7 *B3*
L. Cantallops Valeri and
J. Rodrigo Dalmau

99 COOPERATIVE   1963–68
   HOUSING
Polígono de Montbau *A6*
J. Bosch Agustí and P. López
Iñigo

100 APARTMENTS   1964
Calle Muntaner, 370 *C4*
J. M. Martorell Codina,
O. Bohigas Guardiola, and
D. Mackay

101 APARTMENTS   1964–66
Calle Entenza, 99 *E3*
J. M. Martorell Codina,
O. Bohigas Guardiola, and
D. Mackay

102 APARTMENTS   1964–67
Calle Muntaner, 271/Calle
   Porvenir, 35–37 *D4*
M. de Solá-Morales de
Rosselló and M. de Solá-
Morales Rubió

103 LA VIÑA   1964–69
   APARTMENTS
Calle Altos Hornos/Nuestra
   Señora del Port *F1*
V. Bonet Ferrer and others

104 GARBI SCHOOL   1965–68
Diagonal, 18 *B1*
J. M. Martorell Codina,
O. Bohigas Guardiola, and
D. Mackay

105 TRADE OFFICE   1966–69
   BUILDING
Avenida Carlos III, 84 *C2*
J. A. Coderch de Sentmenat and
M. Valls Vergés

106 APARTMENTS   1967
Calle Dr. Carulla, 53 *B3*
J. M. Martorell Codina,
O. Bohigas Guardiola, and
D. Mackay

107 APARTMENTS   1967–69
Calle Génova, 27 *C6*
L. Clotet Ballús and
O. Tusquets Guillén

108 ATALAYA DE   1967–71
   BARCELONA
Diagonal, 523 *C3*
F. Correa Ruiz, A. Mila
Sagnier, and J. Sanz Magallón
•No. 670 (1968) is by Ruiz and
Sagnier.

109 APARTMENTS   1968
Diagonal, 628–630 *C3*
G. Giráldez Dávila, P. López
Iñigo, and X. Subias Fages

110 APARTMENTS   1968
Gran Via, 152–158 *E1*
G. Giráldez Dávila, P. López
Iñigo, and X. Subias Fages

111 THAU SCHOOL   1972–74
Carretera de Esplugues, 49–53
   B2
J. M. Martorell Codina,
O. Bohigas Guardiola, and
D. Mackay

112 WALDEN 7   1970–75
(high-rise apartments)
Sant Just Desvern (4 km/2.5 mi
   W of Barcelona) *E1*
Taller de Arquitectura/R. Bofill

A radical interpretation of a
high-rise apartment building.
Vertiginous open galleries give
access to minuscule apartments.
•The offices of Taller de
Arquitectura (1973–76), a
converted cement factory, are
close by.

113 MIRÓ   1972–75
   FOUNDATION
(museum)
Avenida de Miramar,
   Montjuich Park *F3*
J. L. Sert

•It is intended to reconstruct a
replica of the German Pavilion
(1929) by L. Mies van der Rohe
on Avenida del Marqués de
Comillas nearby.

BURGOS B3

114 BURGOS   1221 onward
     CATHEDRAL
Plaza del Rey San Fernando

West front by J. de Colonia
(Johan of Cologne). Los
Condestables (Constable's
Chapel, 1482) by S. de
Colonia; octagonal chapel
with superlative carving.
Painting of *Mary Magdalene,*
by da Vinci, in the adjacent
sacristy. The Coronería
(Dorada) Stair (1519–23), by
D. de Siloé (sculptor and
architect), is derived from
Bramante's Belvedere Court.
The central lantern (1539–67)
was rebuilt by J. de Vallejo
and F. de Colonia after the
piers collapsed in 1539. The
ambulatory chapel and cloisters
all contain an abundance of
Gothic and plateresque art.
The Chapel of Santa Ana
contains an altarpiece by
G. de Siloé and D. de la
Cruz.

115 CASA DE MIRANDA   1545
Calle Miranda

Now an archeological museum.
Noted courtyard inside.

Outskirts of Burgos

116 LAS HUELGAS   12th–13th C
     REALES CONVENT
1.5 km (1 mi) W of Burgos

Originally the summer residence
of the kings of Castile.
Converted into a monastery in
1187. Cistercian construction
overlaid with some Mudejar
decoration.

117 CARTUJA DE   1442–98
     MIRAFLORES
     MONASTERY
4 km (2.5 mi) E of Burgos
J. and S. de Colonia

The plain exterior contrasts
with the extremely rich interiors.
The altarpiece, sculpted in
polychrome wood, is by G. de
Siloé and D. de la Cruz. The
royal mausoleum is in the
flamboyant Gothic style.

VALLE DE LOS CAIDOS C3 (Valley of the Fallen)

11 km (7 mi) SW of Guadarrama

118 BASILICA AND   1941–59
     MONUMENT

The Monument to the Dead of
the Civil War consists of a

basilica cut out of the granite
rock and a gigantic cross above.

CALPE D5

29 km (18 mi) NE of Villajoyosa

119 LA MANZANERA   1963–73
     RESORT
Taller de Arquitectura/R. Bofill

Apartment buildings: 1965,
1968, and 1971. Xanadu
apartment house: 1966–67.
La Muralla Roja (The Red
Wall) apartments: 1968–73.

CARMONA E2

120 ROMAN   ca. 2nd C B.C.
     NECROPOLIS
just outside the town, on the
     road to Sevilla

Approximately three hundred
of the nine hundred tombs have
been excavated. Many tombs
are carved out of solid rock.

CELANOVA B1

27 km (17 mi) S of Orense

121 MONASTERY   10th C
     onward

Marvelous baroque cloisters
(1550–1720). The church (1681)
is neoclassic. •Behind, is the
Mozarabic chapel of San
Miguel (937), in good repair.

COCA B3

122 MUDEJAR FORTRESS 15th C

Three concentric battlements
surround a huge keep. Built
by Moorish craftsmen.

CÓRDOBA D3

123 MEZQUITA   785 onward
     (mosque)
Cardenal Herrera

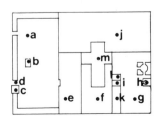

Unique fusion of two religions
in one building.

a Court of the Orange Trees.

b Al Mansur basin (987). For ritual Muslim ablutions.

c Minaret. Surrounded by a baroque tower in the 17th C.

d Pardon Door. 14th-C Mudejar addition (present entrance).

e Original mosque. Built by Abd-er-Rahman I (785).

f First extension by Abd-er-Rahman II (848).

g Second extension by Hakam II (961).

h Mihrab (961).

i Lucernario (Villaviciosa Chapel). Built in 961.

j Third extension by al-Mansur (987).

k First cathedral. 13th C.

l Royal chapel—14th-C Mudejar.

m Second cathedral (1523–1600). Largely Gothic and Renaissance. Baroque choir stalls and twin pulpits by P. Cornejo (1750).

124 ALCÁZAR   14th C
    Avenida del Alcázar

The present buildings were built by Alfonso XI. The gardens are in the Arabic style.

125 SYNAGOGUE   14th C
    Calle Maimonides

Outskirts of Córdoba

126 MEDINA   936–1013
    AZAHARA PALACE
    6 km (4 mi) W of Córdoba

Begun by Abd-er-Rahman III. Built on three levels, with the alcázar above. Much restored.

EL ESCORIAL C3
46 km (28 mi) NW of Madrid

127 EL ESCORIAL   1563–84
    J. B. de Toledo and J. de Herrera

Commissioned by Philip II as a monastery, palace, and pantheon. Austere design and enormous size. The Nuevos Museos (New Museums) have important works by Tintoretto, Titian, El Greco (*Martyrdom of St. Maurice*), and Velásquez. •Further along the road (NE) is the Casita del Principe (Prince's Palace), built by J. de Villaneuva in 1784. 3 km (2 mi) SW lies the Casita de Arriba (1773), a hunting lodge, also by de Villaneuva.

FIGUERAS B6
38 km (23 mi) N of Gerona

Museum: Museo Dali. Works by Salvador Dali, who was born in Figueras in 1904.

128 IGLESIA DE   14th C
    SAN PEDRO
    (church)

FRÓMISTA B3
31 km (19 mi) N of Palencia

129 SAN MARTIN   1066
    (church)

Of the original monastery, only the church remains. An outstanding, completely resolved Romanesque building.

GERONA B6

130 CATHEDRAL 1312–1598

The chancel was begun in 1312. Upon completion, a single-aisled nave was added (1417–1598), resulting in a vault spanning 22.2 m (74 ft). This is braced by massive buttresses containing chapels between them. The baroque facade (1730–33) dominating the approach up a 17th-c stairway is by P. Costa.

GRANADA E3

131 THE ALHAMBRA 1248 onward
entry through Puerta de las Granadas on Cuesta de Gomérez

Built around open courtyards, the Alcázar or Casa Real (1338–90) is a miracle of sublime decoration. The Emperor Charles V's Palace (1526–68) by P. Machuga abuts the Alcázar. (Enter through the Partal Gardens.) This is the most convincing Renaissance building in Spain. Graceful circular courtyard inside a square plan.

132 THE GENERALIFE 14th c
Paseo de los Cipreses, to the Paseo de los Adelfas

The summer palace of the king. Enchanting gardens.

133 GRANADA 1523–63
CATHEDRAL onward
Calle de la Carcel
D. de Siloé

The west facade (1667–1703) is by A. Cano. The Sagrario

(Sacrament Chapel) by F. Hurtado was built from 1704–5. The Capilla Real (Royal Chapel, 1506–21) next door is by E. Egas. Enter through the courtyard of the Lonja (also by Egas). This contains the tombs of Ferdinand and Isabella (by Fanicelli, 1517) and Philip the Fair and Joan the Mad (by B. Ordoñez, 1519–20). Queen Isabella's painting collection is in the sacristy.

134 CARTUJA ca. 1700 onward
(Carthusian monastery)
Real de la Cartuja (just N of the town)
F. Hurtado

The Sacrament Chapel in the chapel in the church (1702–20) is by Hurtado. The Sacristy (1727–64), by de Arevalo and F. M. Vasquez, takes the churrigueresque style to the limit.

LA GRANJA DE SAN ILDEFONSO B3
11 km (7 mi) SE of Segovia

135 PALACE OF 1721–42
PHILIP V
G. B. Sacchetti

A smaller version of Versailles. The garden facade is after a design by F. Iuvara. The gardens and fountains (1727–43) are in the French style.

GUADALUPE C2

136 MONASTERY 14th c onward

Flamboyant Gothic facade facing the square. The 14th-c church has suffered from 18th-c alterations. Two-story Mudejar cloisters (15th c), also Gothic cloisters (16th c). The sacristy, a magnificent space, contains Zurbarán's masterpiece, *The Life of St. Jerome* (1638–47). Other works by Zurbarán in the 15th-c chapter house. The statue of the Virgin of Guadalupe is in the "Camarin."

JAÉN D3

137 CATHEDRAL 1525 onward
A. de Vandelvira

Baroque west front added from 1667–88.

138 CAPILLA SAN   16th c
    ANDRÉS
(Chapel of the Immaculate
Conception)

Good plateresque decoration.

LEÓN A2

139 SAN ISIDORO   1054–67
    BASILICA
Calle Ramon y Cajal

Built into the town's defensive
walls. South facade remodeled
in the Gothic and (later)
Renaissance styles. The
Pantheon (entry on left of
church) has well-preserved
painted frescoes (1175) executed
in the Burgundian style.

140 CATHEDRAL   1255 onward
Puerta Obispo

Gothic throughout. Enormous
stained glass windows (13th to
15th c). The remaining
medieval defensive walls run
from the cathedral to the
Church of San Isidoro.

LOARRE CASTLE B5
5 km (3 mi) NE of Ayerbe.

141 LOARRE CASTLE   1070–96

Beautiful and isolated site.
Romanesque castle built by
Sancho Ramírez, King of
Aragón. The Augustinian
church within the castle is in
good condition.

LUGO A1

142 CATHEDRAL   12th c
Plaza de Pio XII

Romanesque structure with
French appearance. Remodeled
in the Gothic style. Remodeled
again in the 18th c. Baroque
Chapel of the Virgin. •The
town walls, continuously rebuilt
since Roman times, still enclose
the old section of the town.

143 SANTO DOMINGO   14th c
(church)
Plaza de Santo Domingo

MADRID C3

Tourist Information: Officina
de Informacion de Turismo,
Plaza Mayor, 3 (tel. 266–
4874).
    Centro de Iniciativas
Turisticas, Estacion del Metro
"Sevilla" (tel. 233–0033).

Architect's Institute: Colegio
Oficial de Arquitectos, Calle
T. Tucuman, 20 (tel. 250–3543).

Museums: Museo de la Real
Academia de Bellas Artes de
San Fernando, Paseo de
Recoletos, 20. Paintings by
Zurbarán, Pereda, Goya, and
Meng.
    Museo Cerralbo, Calle
Ventura Rodriguez, 17. El
Greco, Ribera (*Jacob with the
Flocks*), Ribalta, Tintoretto,
Titian, and Vandyke.
    Museo Lazaro Galdiano,
Calle Serrano, 122.
Outstanding collection of
decorative arts (especially
ivories and enamels). Also
paintings by Berruguete, El
Greco, Ribalta, Gainsborough,
Reynolds, Constable, Guardi,
and Tiepolo.
    Museo del Prado, Paseo de
Prado. One of the world's
greatest art collections. Bosch
(*The Garden of Earthly
Delights*), Brueghel, Dürer,
Fra Angelica, Mantegna,
Raphael, Titian, Tintoretto,
El Greco, Ribalta, Ribera,
Velásquez (*Las Hilanderas* and
Las Meninas), Goya, Rubens,
Rembrandt, Lorrain, Watteau,
Tiepolo and others. See entry
158.
    Palacio Real, Calle Bailen.
Most of the original furnishings
and character of the palace
have been retained. The
Museum of Painting has works
by Bosch, Rubens, Goya, El
Greco, Zurbarán, and
Velásquez.
    Museo Sorolla, General
Martinez Campos, 37. Works
by J. Sorollay Bastida.

144 LAS DESCALZAS   1559
    REALES MONASTERY
Plaza de las Descalzas Reales *E3*
J. B. de Toledo and A. Sillero

Rich interiors. See the twelve
17th-c tapestries after Rubens's
cartoons (*Apotheosis of the
Eucharist*). Paintings by
Brueghel, Titian (*Caesar's
Pence*), etc. Guided tours.

145 LA ENCARNACIÓN   1611–16
    CONVENT
Plaza de la Encarnación *E3*
J. Gómez de Mora

146 PLAZA MAYOR   1617–19
(Main Square) *E3*
J. Gómez de Mora

147 SAN ISIDRO EL REAL 1629
(church)
Calle de Toledo/Calle
    Estudios *F3*
F. Bautista

Influential church based on the
Gesù in Roma (entry I–373).

148 LA VIRGEN   1718
    DEL PUERTO
    (church)
    Paseo de la Virgen del
      Puerto *E2*
    P. Ribera

149 PUENTE DE   1719-24
    TOLEDO
    (Toledo Bridge)
    Calle de Toledo *G3*
    P. Ribera

150 CUARTEL DEL   1720
    CONDE DUQUE
    (military barracks)
    Calle de Conde Duque, 9 *D3*
    P. Ribera

151 MUNICIPAL   1722-99
    MUSEUM
    Calle de Fuencarral, 98 *D4*
    P. Ribera

Former Hospicio San
Fernando. The doorway
displays Ribera's most frenzied
use of ornament in this ultimate
development of the
churrigueresque style.

152 PALACIO REAL   1738-64
    (Royal Palace)
    Calle de Bailén *E3*
    F. Iuvara

Completed by G. B. Sacchetti,
who enlarged the original
design. The new scheme shows
the influence of G. L. Bernini's
Louvre project.

153 SAN MIGUEL   1739-46
    (church)
    Calle de San Justo *E3*
    G. Bonavia

Unusual "Italian" baroque
church.

154 SAN MARCOS   1749-53
    (church)
    Calle de San Leonardo *D3*
    V. Rodriguez

Oval plan derived from G. L.
Bernini's San Andrea al
Quirinale, Roma (entry I-398).

155 SAN FRANCISCO   1761-84
    EL GRANDE
    (church)
    Plaza de San Francisco *F3*
    F. de las Cabezas

Modeled after the Pantheon,
Roma (entry I-338).

156 PUERTA DE ALCALÁ   1778
    (traffic circle)
    Plaza de la Independencia *E5*
    F. Sabatini

157 ASTRONOMICAL   1785
    OBSERVATORY
    Parque del Retiro *F5*
    J. Villanueva

Madrid

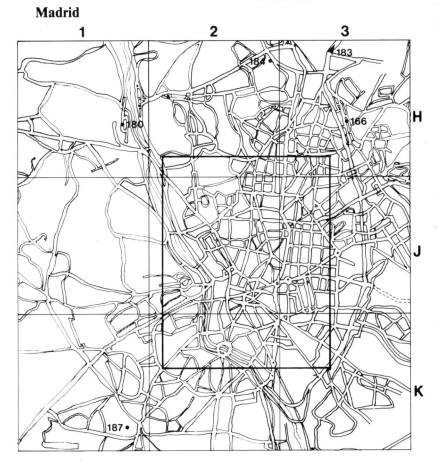

Madrid detail

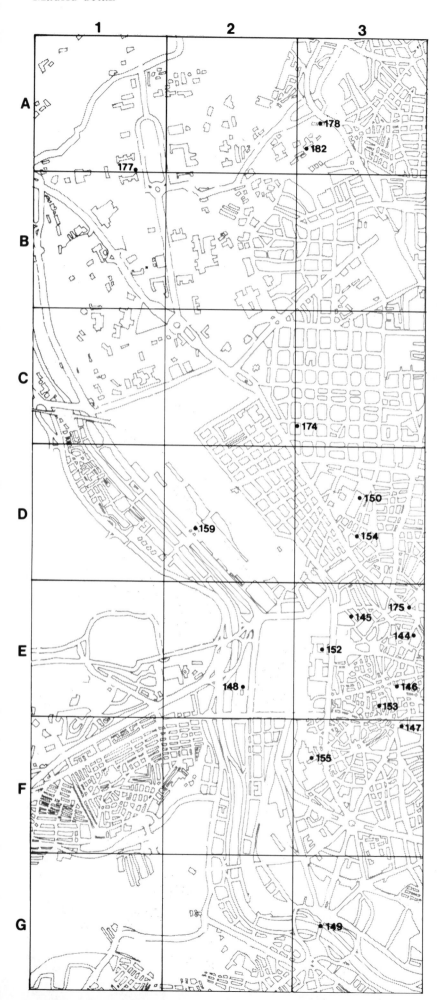

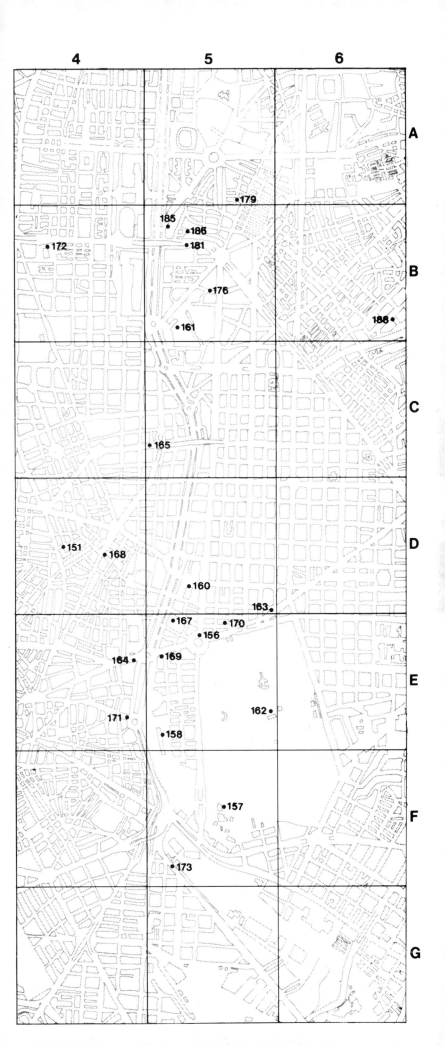

158 MUSEO DEL   1785–1811
    PRADO
    (Prado Museum)
    Paseo del Prado *E5*
    J. Villanueva

Neoclassic reaction to the
rococo style (Villanueva studied
in Roma, 1759–65).

159 CHAPEL OF SAN   1798
    ANTONIO DE LA
    FLORIDA
    Paseo de la Florida *D2*
    F. Fontana

Cupola fresco *St. Anthony of
Padua* by Goya, who is buried
here. There are two identical
chapels: the original and a copy
built for uninterrupted worship.

160 NATIONAL   1866–96
    LIBRARY
    Paseo de Recoletos, 20 *D5*
    F. Jareño

161 NATURAL   1881–87
    SCIENCE MUSEUM
    Paseo de la Castellana *B5*
    F. de la Torriente

162 EXHIBITION   1883
    BUILDINGS
    Parque del Retiro *E5*
    R. V. Bosco

163 AGUIRRE SCHOOL   1884
    Calle de Alcalá, 64 *D5*
    E. Rodriguez Ayuso

164 BANK OF SPAIN   1884–91
    Calle de Alcalá, 48 *E4*
    E. Adaro and S. Sainz de la
    Lastra

165 SAN FERMÍN   1885–91
    DE LOS NAVARROS
    (church)
    Paseo de Eduardo Dato, 10 *C5*
    C. Velasco and E. Jimenez
    Corera

166 CIUDAD   1895–1920
    LINEAL
    (linear city)
    Calle de Arturo Soria *H3*
    A. Soria

Far in advance of its time, this
was the first linear megastructure to be (partially) built.

167 HEREDIA   1898
    ESPÍNOLA PALACE
    Calle del Marqués del Duero *E5*
    L. Landecho

168 LONGORIA   1900–1902
    PALACE
    Calle de Fernando VI, 4 *D4*
    J. Grases Rivera

169 COMMUNICATION   1903–18
    BUILDING
    Plaza de la Cibeles *E5*
    A. Palacios

170 SAN MANUEL Y   1910
    SAN BENITO
    (church)
    Calle de Alcalá, 83 *E5*
    F. Arbós

171 PALACE HOTEL   1911–12
    Plaza de las Cortes, 7 *E4*
    M. Alvarez Naya

172 WORKERS'   1916
    HOSPITAL
    Calle de Maudes, 17 *B4*
    A. Palacios

173 MENÉNDEZ Y   1923–29
    PELAYO SCHOOL
    Calle de Méndez Alvaro, 14 *F5*
    A. Flórez

174 LAS FLORES   1930–32
    HOUSE
    Calle de Rodriguez San Pedro/
    Calle de Gaztambide *C3*
    S. de Zuazo

175 CAPITOL BUILDING   1931
    Avenida de Gran Vía, 41 *E3*
    L. Martinez-Feduchi and
    V. Eced

176 INSTITUTO   1932–33
    ESCUELA BUILDING
    Calle de Serrano, 129 *B5*
    C. Arniches, M. Dominguez,
    and E. Torroja

177 FACULTY OF   1932–35
    PHILOSOPHY
    Ciudad Universitaria *A1*
    A. Aguirre

Rebuilt in 1942. •The Science
Faculty (1934) by M. de los
Santos was rebuilt in 1941.

178 TÉRMICA CENTER   1933
    Cuidad Universitaria *A3*
    M. Sánchez Arcas

179 EL VISO COMPLEX   1933–36
    Calle de Guadiana/Calle de
    Serrano *A5*
    R. Bergamín

180 LA ZARZUELA   1935
    RACECOURSE STAND
    Avenida del Padre Huidobro
    H1
    C. Arniches, M. Dominguez,
    and E. Torroja

Torroja's masterpiece. The
roof shell, which is 5–12 cm
(2–5 in) thick, cantilevers 12.5 m
(42 ft) in a continuous series of
sectional hyperbolic
paraboloids.

181 SAN AGUSTÍN   1946–50
    (church)
    Calle de Joaquín Costa, 10 *B5*
    L. Moya

182 AQUINAS   1953–57
    COLLEGE
    Ciudad Universitaria *A3*
    J. M. García de Paredes and
    R. de la Hoz

183 LOS DOMINICOS   1959–60
    (church)
    8 km (5 mi) N along the
    Carretera de Alcobendas
    road *H3*
    M. Fisac

184 LECHERA   1959–63
    CLESA CENTER
Carretera del poblado de
"Fuencarral" *H2*
A. de la Sota

185 HUARTE   1961
    EXHIBITION HALL
Paseo de la Castellana, 8 *B5*
F. J. Sáenz de Oiza

186 COLEGIO   1961–62
    MARAVILLAS
    GYMNASIUM
Calle de Joaquín Costa, 21 *B5*
A. de la Sota

187 LOYOLA   1961–63
    SETTLEMENT
Carabanchel Alto *K1*
C. Férran, E. Mangade, J. L.
Romany, and F. J. Sáenz de
Oiza

188 "TORRES   1962–68
    BLANCAS" SETTLEMENT
Autopista de Barajas *B6*
F. J. Sáenz de Oiza

MALLORCA C6
on the island of Majorca

PALMA DE MALLORCA

189 CATHEDRAL   13th–16th C
Plaza Almoina

Gothic. Richly decorated
Puerta del Mirador (south door,
14th C). Renaissance portal
(1594, by M. Verger)
surrounded by a facade rebuilt
in the Gothic style in 1852.
•The Moorish fortress opposite
dates from the 14th C.

190 SAN FRANCISCO   13th C
    (church)   onward
Plaza San Francisco

Gothic nave. Baroque facade
added in the 17th C.

191 BELLVER CASTLE   14th C
3 km (2 mi) W of Palma de
    Mallorca

Intriguing circular geometry.

192 LONJA   15th C
    (exchange)
Paseo de Sagrera
G. Sagrera

MANZANARES EL REAL C3

193 CASTLE   15th C

Well-preserved fortress.

MÉRIDA D2

194 TEATRO ROMANO   24 B.C.
    (Roman theater)
at the end of Calle Ramon
    Melida

Built by Agrippa. Stage wall
much restored. •The adjacent
1st-C amphitheater could hold
14,000 spectators. The Roman
villa below the amphitheater has
some mosaics in good
condition. Two Roman bridges
in the town remain in good condition (the Guardiana bridge is
still the main entry into the
town).

MORELLA C5

195 FORTIFIED   14th C onward
    HILL TOWN

The walls are in good condition.
Ruined medieval castle on the
summit. 14th-C Gothic
St. Mary Mayor Basilica.
Successful later additions
include a Renaissance *coro* and
baroque sacristy.

MURCIA D4

196 CATHEDRAL   14th C onward
Plaza Cardenal Belluga

Baroque facade and belfry
(1730–49) by J. Milia. Gothic
interior contains Capilla de
los Junterones (16th-C
Renaissance) and Capilla de
los Véles. The sacristy makes
use of both baroque and
plateresque styles in a most
satisfying manner.

NARANCO A2
4 km (2.5 mi) NW of Orviedo

197 SANTA MARIA   848
    DE NARANCO
    (church)

Built by Ramiro I. Two stories
high, with an audience hall and
two open antechambers above.
Converted into a church.

198 SAN MIGUEL   9th c
    DE LILLO
    (church)

Fine interior carving. East end
altered in the 17th c.

NUEVO BAZTÁN C3
40 km (25 mi) E of Madrid

199 TOWN PLAN   1709 onward

"New town" laid out by José
Churriguera.

ORENSE A1

200 CATHEDRAL   12th c onward
    Calle Ceano

Continuously rebuilt. Chapel
of Santismo Cristo off north
transept. The Romanesque
Pórtico del Paraíso (Door of
Paradise) has retained its
original coloring. The theme
of these carvings is identical to
the Door of Glory in Santiago
de Compostela cathedral.

ORGAZ C3
34 km (21 mi) S of Toledo

201 PARISH CHURCH   1738
    A. Churriguera

ORVIEDO A2

202 CATHEDRAL   14th–16th c
    Plaza Alfonso II

Flamboyant Gothic. The
entrance of the Camara Santa
crypt (enter through south
transept), rebuilt after being
damaged in 1934, has
outstanding 12th-c carvings of
the apostles.

PALENCIA B3

203 CATHEDRAL   14th–16th c

Many architects. The interior
is magnificent. The *trascoro*
sculptures are by S. de Colonia
and G. de Siloé. The Sagrario
(Chapel of the Holy Sacrament)
behind the 16th-c high altar
has an altarpiece (1529) by
Valmaseda. 15th-c tapestries
in the museum in the cloisters.
Also works by El Greco and
Berruguete.

PAMPLONA A4

204 CATHEDRAL   14th–15th c

The Gothic structure was built
over an earlier Romanesque
church. The west front (1783)
is by V. Rodriguez in a baroque
interpretation of the
neoclassical style then
fashionable. Barbazán Chapel
in the elegant Gothic cloisters.

EL PARDO C3

205 CASÍTA DEL   1772
    PRÍNCIPE
    (Prince's Pavilion)
    J. de Villanueva

Although small, the decorations
are extremely rich and very
sophisticated.

POBLET MONASTERY B5
93 km (58 mi) N of Tarragona

206 POBLET   1150 onward
    MONASTERY

Medieval Cistercian monastery.
Restored from 1935–40. The
church, unadorned within,
became the Royal Pantheon
in 1350. High altar (1527) by
D. Forment. Fine cloisters.

REUS B5

207 BARRIO GAUDÍ   1964–72
    RESIDENTIAL AREA
    Taller de Arquitectura/R. Bofill

RIPOLL B6

208 CHURCH OF   1020–32
    SANTA MARIA
    (former monastery)

Important example of early
Catalan Romanesque planning.
Only the portal (an explanation
of the Bible carved in stone)
survived an earthquake in 1428
and a later fire. A new church
has been built around the portal.

RUEDA B3

10 km (6 mi) S of Tordesillas

209 CHURCH OF   1738–47
    THE ASSUMPTION
    A. Churriguera

SALAMANCA B2

210 CATEDRAL   1513–60, 1734
    NUEVA
    (New Cathedral)
    Plaza de Anaya
    J. Gil de Hontañón

Late Gothic with plateresque
details (resulting from lengthy
construction). The 18th-c
choir stalls, retrochoir, and
organ loft are by the
Churrigueras; the tower (1734)
is by P. Ribera.

CATEDRAL VIEJA   1160
(Old Cathedral)
entry through New Cathedral—
    first bay, south aisle

Well-preserved Romanesque
building dominated by the
adjacent New Cathedral.
Altarpiece (1445) by Nicholas
of Florence. Cloisters rebuilt
in 18th c.

211 CASA DE LAS   1514
    CONCHAS
    (House of Shells)
    Rúa Mayor

The facade is covered with
hundreds of carved shells.

212 SAN ESTEBAN   1524–1610
    MONASTERY
    Arroyo de Santo Domingo
    J. de Alava

Gothic with later plateresque
west facade. The church's
altarpiece (1693) is by José
Churriguera.

213 PATIO DE   16th c
    LAS ESCUELAS
    (The School's Square)
    Calle Libreros

The University entrance (1514–
34) is a masterpiece of the
plateresque style. The Escuelas
Menores' (Minorite School's)
entrance is similarly decorated.
See the patio (1428) inside.
The Calderon gallery in the
library houses the "Salamanca
ceiling," originally in the
University library.

214 CLERECIA   1617–1755
    Rúa Antigua

Jesuit college. Baroque towers
(1755) by A. García de
Quiñones. Baroque cloister
on Calle Companía.

215 PALACIO DE   1710–20
    ANAYA
    (Old College of San
    Bartolomeo)
    Plaza de Anaya
    Joaquín Churriguera

216 COLEGIO DE   1717–19
    CALATRAVA
    Calle del Escobo/Plaza F.
    Montejo
    Joaquín Churriguera

Altered in 1790.

217 PLAZA MAYOR   1729
    (Main Square)   onward
    A. Churriguera

The town hall is by A. García
de Quiñones.

SAN IGNACIO DE LOYALA A4

monastery 3 km (2 mi) W of
Azpeitia

218 BASILICA   1689 onward
    C. Fontana

The circular basilica is covered
by a cupola by Joaquín
Churriguera.

SAN JUAN DE LA PEÑA A5

monastery 28 km (17 mi) SW of Jaca

The upper monastery is reconstructed. Take the road down to the lower monastery on a spectacular site.

219 LOWER   10th c onward
     MONASTERY

The lower church (922), now the crypt, is Mozarabic in style. Twin aisles. The twin apses are cut out of the cliffside. Upper Church (11th c): partly roofed by the rock cliff, 18th-c renovations. The Pantheon (11th to 14th c) is adjacent. The carved capitals of the 12th-c cloisters, sheltered by the cliff overhang, tell the story of mankind from creation.

SAN PEDRO DE LA NAVE B2

church 19 km (12 mi) NW of Zamora

220 CHURCH OF SAN   7th c
    PEDRO DE LA NAVE

The church has been moved and rebuilt at El Campillo, which is 19 km (12 mi) NW of Zamora.

SANTA CRISTINA DE LENA A2

church near Vega del Ciego

221 SANTA CRISTINA   905
    DE LENA
    (church)

Sited on a mountaintop near the viaduct. Traditional barrel vaulting used in this Greek cross plan.

SANTA MARIA DE HUERTA B4

monastery 56 km (35 mi) W of Calatayud

222 SANTA   12th c onward
    MARIA DE HUERTA
    MONASTERY

Gothic refectory (13th c). The Knights' Cloister displays an elaborate plateresque gallery added in the 16th c. Churrigueresque decoration has been added to the church.

SANTIAGO DE COMPOSTELA A1

223 CATHEDRAL   11th–13th c
    Plaza de España

The only original facade to survive is that of the south transept (1103, rebuilt in 1116 after a fire), known as the "Puerta de las Platerias". The Door of Glory (1168–88), a medieval masterpiece by Mateo, is behind the baroque Obradoiro facade (1738–49, facing the Plaza de España) by F. Casas y Novoa. Tapestry museum on the second floor.

224 HOSPITAL DE   1501–11
    LOS REYES CATOLICOS
    Plaza de España, 1
    E. Egas

Carefully restored. Now a hotel.

Outskirts of Santiago de Compostela

225 PAZO DE OCA   18th c
    (palace)
    San Esteban de Oca (25 km/15.5 mi) SE of Santiago de Compostela

18th-c Galician palace with remarkable baroque gardens.

SANTILLANA A3

30 km (18.5 mi) W of Santander

226 VILLAGE   15th c

Well-preserved. Exceptional Romanesque Collegiate Church (12th c). •20 km (12.5 mi) E is Comillas, where the Marqués de Comillas built a colony of houses by J. Martorell Domènech, A. Gaudí i Cornet, and other architects.

SANTO DOMINGO DE SILOS B3

30 km (18.5 mi) E of Lerma

227 BENEDICTINE   11th c
    MONASTERY

Early and superb Romanesque cloisters with superlative carving. The church was built from 1756–1816.

SEGOVIA B3

228 ACUEDUCTO   A.D. 10
    ROMANO
    (Roman aqueduct)
    Plaza del Azoguejo

730 m (2,400 ft) long, this aqueduct still carries water to the city.

229 LA VERA   13th c
      CRUZ CHAPEL
Across the Eresma River,
     opposite the Alcázar (not in
     the Convento de Santa Cruz)

Built by the Templars.
Octagonal centralized plan.

230 ALCÁZAR   1410–55, 19th c

Advantageously sited on a cliff
edge overlooking the Eresma
River. Romantic profile.

231 CATHEDRAL   1525 onward
Marqués de Arco
J. Gil de Hontañón

Gothic design even at this late
date. The cloisters were moved
and rebuilt next to the cathedral
in the 16th c.

SEO DE URGEL B6

232 SANTA MARIA   12th c
      CATHEDRAL

Plain and well-proportioned.
The cloisters are 13th-c (enter
through the diocesan museum).
•The church of San Miguel
(11th c) is off the cloisters.

SEVILLA E2
(Seville)

Museum: Museo de Bellas
Artes, Plaza del Museo.
Paintings by El Greco,
Velázquez, Zurbarán, Murillo,
and others.

233 GIRALDA   1185–96
Plaza de Triunfo

Former minaret. Upper
section added in 1568.

234 TORRE DE ORO   1220
Paseo de Cristobel Colon,
     near the Puenta San Telmo

Defensive tower guarding the
old port.

235 REALES   1350–69
      ALCÁZARES
(Royal Palace)
Plaza de Triunfo

Built by Peter I. The decoration
is based on the Alhambra. See
the *Virgin of the Navigators*
(1531–36) by A. Fernández.

236 CATHEDRAL   1401–1520
Plaza de Triunfo

The third-largest medieval
cathedral in Europe (only St.
Peter's, Roma, and St. Paul's,
London, are larger). The plan
is derived from the previous
mosque's foundations. The
Sanctuary is sumptuously
decorated with plateresque
grilles (1518–33) surrounding
the Flemish altar (1482–1525).
Magnificent choir stalls. Works
by Murillo and Goya in the
Baptistry. •The Archivo
General de Indias (1582,
Indies Archives, formerly
an exchange) by J. de Herrera
is adjacent.

237 CASA DE PILATOS   1540
(Pilate's House)
Plaza del Pilatos

Modeled on the original in
Jerusalem. Remarkable
interiors.

238 HOSPITAL DE   1687–97
      VENERABLES
      SACERDOTES
Calle Villa Jamerdana
L. de Figueroa

239 IGLESIA DEL   1696–1711
      SALVADOR
(church)
Plaza del Salvador
L. de Figueroa

240 SAN LUIS   1699–1731
(church)
Calle de San Luis/
     Calle Duque Cornejo
L. de Figueroa

241 SAN TELMO PALACE   18th c
Avenida de Roma
L. de Figueroa

Now a seminary. Grandiose
baroque entrance (1724–34)
three stories high.

SIGÜENZA B4

242 CATHEDRAL   12th–15th c

Fortresslike exterior. The
transept has marvelous 16th-c
sculptures. The Doncel Chapel
(off S end of transept) contains
the tomb of Don Martín
Vásquez de Arca, an amazingly
lifelike sculpture. The Sacristy
has a remarkable carved ceiling
and plateresque wood paneling.
The 16th-c cloisters are largely
Gothic in style, with some
plateresque detail.

SITGES B6

243 EL CASTELL   1965–68
    APARTMENTS
    Vallpineda
    Taller de Arquitectura/R. Bofill

TARRAGONA B5

244 ROMAN RUINS   ca. 3rd C B.C.

The Archeological Museum
(on the Plaza del Rey) has
mostly Roman artifacts. Other
Roman remains in the city are
the Arena (Plaza del Cardinal
Arce Ochotorena), (partial)
Forum on Plaza Pallol, and
town walls (3rd C B.C.), which
have been incorporated into
later defensive works. These
can be seen on a walk known
as the Paseo Arqueológico.
•4 km (2.5 mi) NW of the city
on route N240 is Las Ferreras,
a fairly well-preserved Roman
aqueduct (2nd C A.D.).

TARRASA B6

245 CHURCH OF   9th C
    SAN MIGUEL

Dome supported on eight
different marble columns.
Compare to A. Gaudí i Cornet's
Colonia Güell Chapel,
Barcelona (entry 40).

246 CHURCH OF   10th C
    SAN PEDRO

247 CHURCH OF   12th C
    SANTA MARIA

Romanesque. 15th-C altarpiece
in the north transept by
J. Huguet.

TERUEL C4

248 TORRE SAN MARTIN   13th C
    Plaza de Pérez Prado

Authentic Mudejar tower.
Other Mudejar towers are del
Salvador (see next entry), San
Pedro and that on the Plaza
de Aranda.

249 CATHEDRAL,   13th C onward
    TORRE DEL SALVADOR
    Calle Salvador

Enlarged in the 15th and 17th C.
Original 14th-C *artesonado*
ceiling.

TOLEDO C3

250 CRISTO DE LA LUZ   1000
    (church)   onward
    Cuesto del Cristo de la Luz

An Arab mosque built over
an earlier Visigoth church
was converted into a Mudejar
church in 1200. Visigoth pillars
support nine different domes
that are modeled on those of
the mosque in Córdoba.

251 TOLEDO   1227 onward
    CATHEDRAL
    Arco de Palacio

Stained glass windows (1420–
1560). Magnificent 15th- and
16th-C choir stalls in the
Coro by Aleman, A.
Berruguete, and de Borgona.
Behind the sanctuary is the
Transparente by N. Tome, a
supreme work of architectural
illusion and unrestrained
emotion. In the sacristy are
works by El Greco (*El Espolio*),
Goya (*Betrayal*), de Mena
(*St. Francis of Assisi*), etc.
The sacristy's ceiling fresco
(*The Miracle of St. Ildefonso*)
is by L. Giordano. The Capilla
de los Reyes Nuevos (Chapel
of the New Kings, 1531–34) is
by A. de Covarrubias and has
survived intact.

252 PUENTE DE   1258
    ALCÁNTARA
    (Veija)
    NE of the city, off the N400

The Alcántara bridge over the
Tagus is protected by a Mudejar
tower on the western side. •The
Castle of San Servando is
adjacent.

253 SANTO TOMÉ   13th C
    (church)
    Travesia Santo Tomé

Inside is El Greco's *The Burial
of the Count of Orgaz.* •The
church of the La Caridad
Convent at Illescas (33 km/20.5
mi N of Toledo) has five
outstanding El Greco paintings.

254 ALCÁZAR   13th C onward
    (fort)
    Calle de Capuchinos

Converted into a residence for
Charles V by A. de Covarrubias
(1538–51). Destroyed in 1936.

Rebuilt since. Severe yet
graceful courtyard inside.

255 EL TRANSITO   1366
     SYNAGOGUE
Reyes Catolicos

Transformed into a church in
1492. The simple exterior
disguises a marvelously complex
Mudejar interior. The original
Hebrew inscriptions remain.

256 SAN JUAN DE LOS   1476–92
     REYES MONASTERY
Plaza de San Martin

Late Gothic with both
Mudejar and Renaissance
influence. The raised galleries
in the church were for the use of
the nobility. The church (1476–
92) is by J. Gras. Beautiful two-
story Gothic cloisters.

257 MUSEO   1504–15 onward
     DE SANTA CRUZ
Calle de Cervantes
E. Egas

Exterior facade and staircase
in courtyard by A. de
Covarrubias. Now a museum.

258 HOSPITAL   1542–79
     DE TAVERA
Carretera a Madrid
B. de Bustamante

Severe facade. Renaissance
courtyards by A. de
Covarrubias. The interiors
include works by Titian, El
Greco (*The Baptism of Christ*),
Tintoretto, Ribera (*Bearded
Woman*), etc.

UBEDA D3

259 CHURCH OF   1536
     EL SALVADOR
Plaza Vásquez de Molina
D. de Siloé

Renaissance. Grandiose
interior. Sacristy by A. de
Vandelvira. •Also on the plaza
is the town hall (1562, Casa de
las Cadenas) by de Vandelvira.
Two other churches worth
seeing are San Pablo, Plaza
del Generalisimo, and San
Isidore, off Alférez Rojas
Navarrete.

VALENCIA C5

260 CATHEDRAL   1262 onward
Plaza de la Virgen

Built mostly during the 14th and
15th C. The neoclassic baroque
renovation is now being
removed.

261 LA LONJA   15th C
     (exchange)
Plaza del Collado

Flamboyant Gothic. Notable
ceiling in the Maritime Court
within.

262 DOS AGUAS   1740–44
     PALACE
Calle Maria de Molina

The churrigueresque facade is
dominated by the doorway,
carved in alabaster by I.
Vergara, from the designs of
H. Rovera. Now the Museo
Nacional de Ceramica.

VALLADOLID B3

263 SAN PABLO   1276
     (church)
Cadenas de San Gregorio
S. de Colonia

Wildly exuberant late Gothic.
The upper half of the facade was
built later and is subdivided
in the plateresque manner.

264 SAN GREGORIO   1488–96
     COLLEGE
Cadenas de San Gregorio

The highly ornate facade by
G. de Siloé is an outstanding
example of the Isabelline style.
Now the Museum of
Polychrome Sculpture, with
works by de Juni, de Mena,
Berruguete (*Retablo,* 1527–32),
Martínez, etc. The chapel is
by J. Gras.

265 CATHEDRAL   1580 onward
Cardenal Cos
J. de Herrera

Built over a lengthy period,
Herrera's design was reduced
and altered. The west facade
was completed by A.
Churriguera in the baroque
style. Altarpiece (1551) by
J. de Juni.

266 UNIVERSITY   1715 onward
Calle de Lopez Gomez
N. Tome

Churrigueresque entrance.

VICH B6

267 CATHEDRAL   1781–1803

Murals (1939–44) by J. M.
Sert. The original murals (1930,
also by Sert) were destroyed in
1936.

VISTABELLA B5

8 km (5mi) N of Tarragona,
between Garidells and la Secuita

268 PARISH CHURCH   1918–23
J. M. Jujol i Gibert

ZAMORA B2

269 CATHEDRAL   1152–74
Plaza Antonio del Aguila.

The Romanesque south facade
is original. The lantern tower
is crowned by a ribbed dome
covered with stone tiles,
resembling fish scales.

ZARAGOZA B5
(Saragossa)

270 ALJAFERIA   11th c onward
    PALACE
    Calle Castillo

Much changed and mostly
restored, the ground floor is
Moorish; the upper, flamboyant
Gothic.

271 SEO   14th–17th c
    (cathedral)
    Plaza de Seo

An amalgam of styles from
Gothic through churrigue-
resque. Outstanding Tapestry
Museum inside.

272 NUESTRA   1677 onward
    SEÑORA DEL PILAR
    (basilica)
    Plaza del Pilar
    F. Herrera the Younger

Square plan with central dome.
Altered 1753–66. Retable
above high altar by D. Forment.
Lady Chapel (18th c) by
V. Rodríguez. Frescoes by Goya
on the ceiling of the *coreto*
(*Adoration of the Name of
God*) and the main cupola
(*Queen of the Martyrs*).

Sweden

Riddarholmskyrkan; *see entry 33*

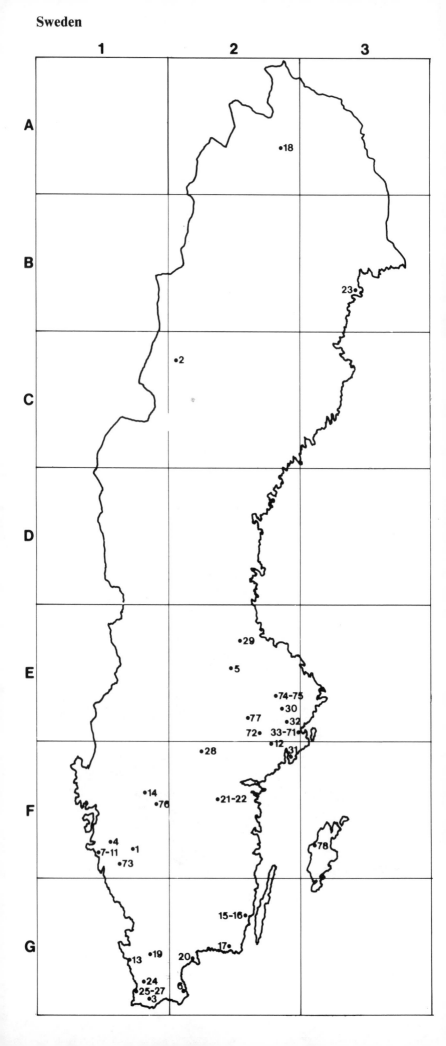

Sweden

BORÅS F1

1 RÅDHUS   1907–10
(town hall)
Torvplads
I. Tengbom

BORGAFJÄLL C2
40 km (25 mi) NW of Risbäck

2 SKI HOTEL   1948–50
R. Erskine

DALBY G1
13 km (8 mi) SE of Lund

3 DOMKYRKA   ca. 1016 onward
(cathedral)

FLODA F1
26 km (16 mi) NE of Göteborg

4 KRYRKA   12th C
(church)

Lars Kagg Mausoleum (1661) by
E. Dahlberg.

FORS E2
20 km (12 mi) N of Avesta

5 CARDBOARD   1950–53
   FACTORY
R. Erskine

GLIMMINGEHUS SLOTT G2
castle SW of Simrishamn (on
Skåne)

6 GLIMMINGEHUS   1499
   SLOTT
(castle)
A. van Düren

GÖTEBORG F1 (Gothenburg)

Museum: Göteborgs
Konstmuseum, Götaplatsen.
17th- to 20th-c Scandinavian
art. Venetian, Flemish, and
Dutch old masters and a good
range of French impressionist
works.

7 RÅDHUS   1670
(town hall)
Hamngatan
N. Tessin the Elder

Much altered. The north wing
extension (1937) is by G.
Asplund.

8 EAST INDIA   1700–1753
   COMPANY BUILDING
12 Norra Hamngatan
C. Hårleman

9 MASTHUGGSKYRKAN
(church)   1910–14
Bangatan
S. Ericsson

10 KONSERTHUSET   1931–35
(concert hall)
Götaplats
N. E. Erikson

11 CREMATORIUM   1936–40
Kviberg Cemetery
G. Asplund

GRIPSHOLM SLOTT F2
castle 25 km (15 mi) W of
Södertälje

12 GRIPSHOLM   ca. 1537–72
    SLOTT
(castle)

Neoclassic theater (1782) inside
by E. Palmstädt. Part of a chain
of Vasa castles. •Others at
Västerås, Uppsala, Vadstena,
and Kalmar.

HÄLSINGBORG G1 (Helsingborg)

13 KONSERTHUSET   1932–34
(concert hall)
S. Markelius

•The adjacent city theater
(1974–75) is by Arton Arkitekter.

HUSABY F1
church 10 km (6 mi) W of Götene

14 HUSABY KYRKA   ca. 1150
(church)

Notable western tower flanked
by two smaller, rounded towers.

KALMAR G2

15 KALMAR SLOTT   14th–16th C
(castle)

16 DOMKYRKA   1660–1703
(cathedral)
Stortorg
N. Tessin the Elder

Baroque. Fine interior. •The
town hall opposite is also by
Tessin.

KARLSKRONA G2

17 TREFALDIGHETS   1709
    KYRKA
(Trinity church)
Stortorg
N. Tessin the Younger

•The baroque Frederiks Kyrka
(church) is attributed to Tessin.

KIRUNA A2

18 KV ORTDRIVAREN   1961–62
    HOUSING AND CHAPEL
R. Erskine

KLIPPAN G1
6 km (4 mi) E of Åstorp

19 ST. PETRI KYRKA   1966
(church)
S. Lewerentz

KRISTIANSTAD G2

20 TREFALDIGHETS   1617–28
    KYRKA
(Trinity church)
H. and L. Steenwinkel
(attributed)

LINKÖPING F2

21 DOMKYRKA   1150–ca. 1490
(cathedral)

Transitional Romanesque-
Gothic. Restored (and west
tower completed) from 1871–86.

22 FOLKETSHUS   1954
(syndicate headquarters)
S. Markelius

LULEÅ B3

23 SHOPPING CENTER   1954
Storgatan
R. Erskine

LUND G1

24 DOMKYRKA   1080–1146
(cathedral)   onward

Construction directed by
Donatus after 1103. Twin west
towers (ca. 1150). Strong
Lombardian influence visible
(after Speyer cathedral,
Germany; see entry G–467).
Nave vaulting rebuilt after
1234 and again in the 19th c.
Fine crypt.

MALMÖ G1

25 ST. PETRI KYRKA   1319
(St. Peter's church)
Rundelsgatan

Brick. Modeled after St. Mary's,
Lübeck, Germany. Restored
ca. 1890.

26 MALMÖHUS   1536–42
(castle)
Malmöhusvägen
M. Bussaert

Now a museum.

27 CREMATORIUM   1943
Eastern Cemetery
S. Lewerentz

ÖREBRO F2

28 MOSJÖ KYRKA   12th c
(church)
17 km (10.5 mi) S of town

Medieval church in good
condition.

SANDVIKEN E2

29 BABERAREN   1962–70
HOUSING ESTATE
Hyttgatan
R. Erskine

•Bruket, another housing estate
in Sandviken, is also by Erskine.

SIGTUNA E2
30 km (20 mi) S of Uppsala

30 ST. PETRI KYRKA   1080–1100
(St. Peter's church, ruined)

•The more substantial remains
of the church of St. Olof (1100–
1135) are more interesting.

SORUNDA F2
on Lisön, near Nynäshamn

31 VILLA   1956
R. Erskine

Steel dome on a sculpted
concrete base.

STEININGE E2
country house 8 km (5 mi) SE of
Sigtuna, on the lake shore

32 STEININGE   1694–98
(counry house)
N. Tessin the Younger

Modeled after Vaux-le-Vicomte,
France. •10 km (6 mi) NW of
Sigtuna (access off the E18 only)
is Skokloster Castle (1654–57)
by J. de la Vallée, succeeded by
N. Tessin the Elder.

STOCKHOLM E2

Tourist Information:
Turisttrafikforbund, at Sweden
House (1969, by S. Markelius),
Hamngatan 27 (tel. 223–280).

Architect's Institute: Svenska
Arkitekters Riksförbund (SAR),
Odengatan 3 (tel. 240–230).

Museums: Arkitekturmuseet,
Skeppsholmen. Museum of
architecture.
    Millesgarden, at Lidingo.
Sculpture by C. Milles.
    Moderna Museet,
Skeppsholmen. An international
collection of 20th-c art. Braque,
Picasso, Oldenburg,
Rauschenburg, and others.
    Nationalmuseum (1865, by
A. Stüler), Södra Blasieholmen.
A good collection of paintings.
Rembrandt, Rubens, de la Tour,
Watteau, Courbet, Manet,
Cranach, and important Swedish
works.
    Waldemarsudde, Djurgarden.
Period residence (of Prince
Eugen). Swedish and 19th-c
French paintings.

33 RIDDARHOLMS-   13th c
    KYRKAN
(church)
Centralbron *D9*

Cast-iron spire. Greek cross
plan, dome added in 1740. The
Karolinska Grafkoret (1671,
Caroline Mausoleum) by N.
Tessin the Elder is on the north
side.

34 DE GEER HOUSE   1646
(now Brahe)
Götgatan 16, Södermalm *D9*

35 BONDESKA PALATSET   1650
Myntgatan *D9*

Restored (1945–51) by I.
Tengbom. Now law courts.

36 OXENSTJERNA   1650
    PALACE
Storkyrkobrinken 2 *D9*
J. de la Vallée

37 RIDDARHUSET   1652–65
(house of the nobility)
Riddarhusetorget *C9*
S. and J. de la Vallée, with
J. Vingboons

Dutch Palladian.

38 ST. KATARINA KYRKA   1656
(church)
Högbergsgatan/Västra
  Kyrkogatan *E9*
J. de la Vallée

Greek cross plan.

39 DROTTNINGHOLM   1660
  SLOTT   onward
(palace)
Drottningholmsvägen *D1*
N. Tessin the Elder

Completed by N. Tessin the
Younger. Modeled after
Versailles. Court Theater (1766)
and Kina Slott (Chinese
Pavilion, 1770, by Cronstedt
and Adelkrantz) on the grounds.

40 KUNGLIGA   1690–1753
  SLOTTET
(royal palace)
Slottsbacken *C9*
N. Tessin the Younger

Parti owes much to Bernini's
Louvre project.

41 BÖRSEN   1767–76
(exchange)
Stortorget *D9*
E. Palmstädt

42 GUSTAV III'S   1790
  PAVILION
Haga *A7*

Restored (1937–46) by R. Hjorth.

43 ROSENDALS   1823–25
  SLOTT
(manor)
Djurgården *C11*
F. Blom

44 SKEPPSHOLM   1824–42
  KYRKA
(church)
Skeppsholmsbron *C10*
F. Blom

45 SKANDIUS   1841–90
  BUILDING
Mynttorget *C9*
P. M. R. Isaeus

46 NORDISKA   1890–1907
  MUSEUM
Djurgården *C10*
I. G. Clason

47 RIKSTAGHUSET   1897–1905
(Parliament)
Helgeandsholmen *C9*
A. Johansson

48 ENGELBRECHT   1906–14
  KYRKA
(church)
Karlavägen/Rådmansgatan *B9*
L. I. Wahlman

Renaissance exterior. Parabolic
arches within.

49 STADSHUSET   1911–23
(city hall)
Ragner Östberg plan *C8*
R. Östberg

A superb civic building on a
waterside site. Richly decorated
council hall.

50 HÖGALID KYRKA   1912–23
(church)
Högalidsparken *D7*
I. Tengbom

51 ENSKILDA BANK   1913
Kungsträdgårdsgatan 8 *C9*
I. Tengbom

52 SKOGSKYRKOGÅRDEN 1914
(south cemetery, layout)
Sockenvägen, Enskede *G10*
G. Asplund with S. Lewerentz

•In the cemetery, also by
Asplund, are the Woodland
Chapel (1918–20), office
buildings (1922–24), and
timeless Woodland Crematorium
(1935–40). The Chapel of the
Resurrection (1927) is by
Lewerentz.

53 KONSERTHUSET   1920–26
(concert hall)
Oxtorgsgatan/Sveavägan *B8*
I. Tengbom

54 STADS BIBLIOTEK   1921–28
(city library)
Odengatan/Sveavägan *B8*
G. Asplund

55 SKANDIA CINEMA   1923
(interior)
Drottninggatan 82 *B8*
G. Asplund

56 EDEN HOTEL   1929
(and offices)
Sturegatan 10 *B9*
B. Hedvall

Stockholm

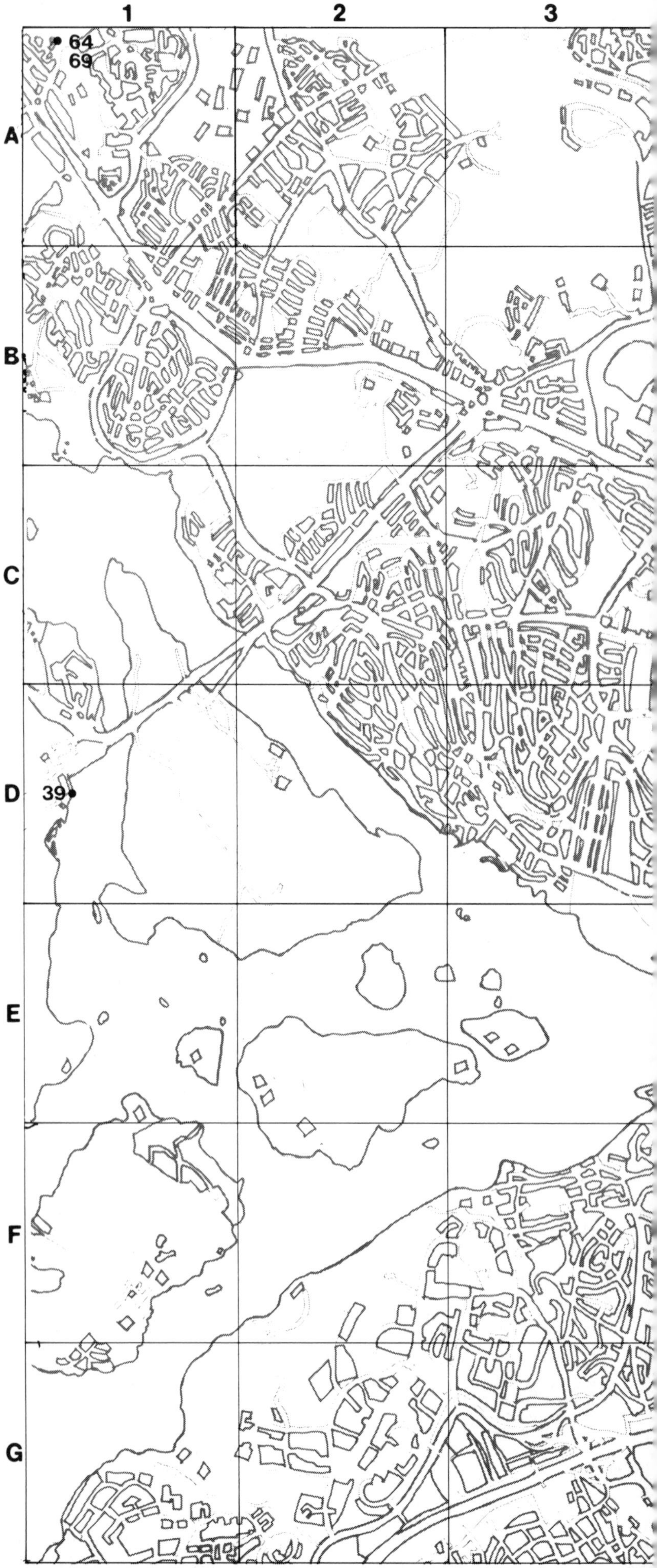

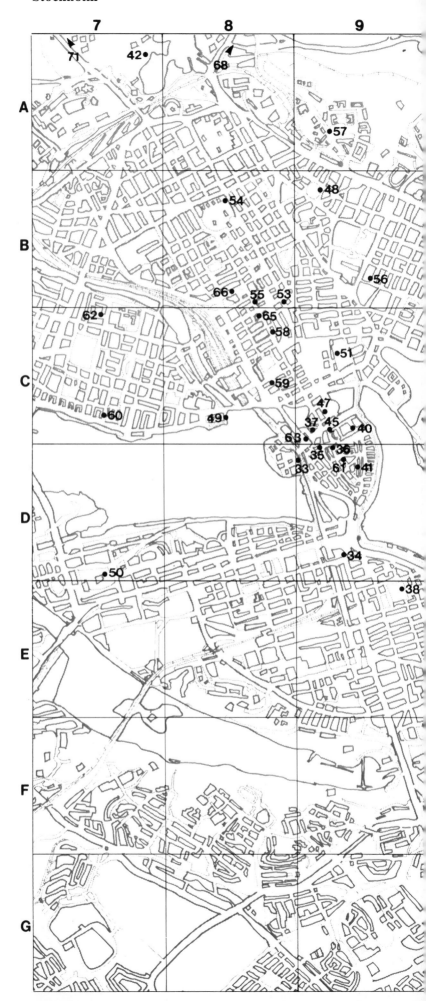

57 KTH KARHUS   1930–52
(student club)
Drottning Kristinas väg 15 *A9*
S. Markelius and U. Åhren

58 BREDENBERG   1933–35
DEPARTMENT STORE
Drottninggatan 54 *C8*
G. Asplund

59 ESSELTE OFFICES   1934
AND PRINTING WORKS
Vasagatan 16 *C8*
I. Tengbom

60 APARTMENT   1935
BUILDING
John Ericsonsgatan 6 *C7*
S. Markelius

Collective housing. Apartments
connected to a central kitchen by
food-lifts. Communal nursery
school.

61 KV CEPHEUS   1937
Köpmangatan 5–15 *D9*
A. Stark

Restoration of a medieval city
block.

62 YRKESSKOLA   1938
(school)
Polhemsgatan 35 *C7*
P. Hedqvist

63 KANSLIHUSANNEXET
(office building)   1945–50
Riddarhustorget *C9*
A. von Schmalensee

64 VÄLLINGBY   1953 onward
(new town) *A1*
Planned by S. Markelius

Satellite town of Stockholm.
The town center is by S.
Backström and L. Reinius.

65 PUB DEPARTMENT   1955–59
STORE
Drottninggatan 63 *C8*
E. and T. Ahlsén

66 THEATER AND   1960
SYNDICATE OFFICES
Barnhusgatan 12–14 *B8*
S. Markelius

67 SÖDERLEDSKYRKAN   1960
(church)
Lingvägen 145, Farsta *G10*
H. Borgström and B. Lindroos

68 VILLA STRÖM   1961
Granhällsvägen 31, Stockslund
A8
R. Erskine

69 RÅCKSTRA   1963
CREMATORIUM
Silversmedsgränd, Vällingby *A1*
K. Fähraeus

70 UNDERGROUND   1973–78
METRO STATIONS
Järva, Täby, and Botkyrka lines
M. Granit and and P. Reimers
(SL Arkitektkontor)

Built to resemble an underground
cave. Decoration by Swedish
artists.

71 UNIVERSITY   1975–79
LIBRARY AND STUDENT
UNION
Universitetswegen, Frescati *A7*
R. Erskine

STRÄNGNÄS E2

72 DOMKYRKA   1291
(cathedral)

Brick. Repeatedly burned and
restored. Height lowered in 1551.

TORPA SLOTT F1
castle 25 km (15 mi) SE of Borås

73 TORPA SLOTT   14th C onward
(castle)
on Lake Åsund

Renaissance hall. Baroque chapel
(1699).

UPPSALA E2

74 FORMER   1134–50
CATHEDRAL
Gamla Uppsala (5 km/3 mi N of
Uppsala)

Built on the site of a pagan
temple. Rebuilt ca. 1245. •The
royal burial mounds are
adjacent.

75 DOMKYRKA   1260–1435
(cathedral)

Construction directed by E. de
Bonneuil from 1287. French plan
with chapels off an ambulatory.
Restored in 1890 and 1976.
•On the south side is the 12th-C
Trefaldighets kyrka (Trinity
church).

VARNHEM F1
14 km (9 mi) E of Skara

76 KYRKA   1235–60
(church)

Restored from 1654–73.

VÄSTERÅS E2

77 DOMKYRKA   1271 onward
(cathedral)
Biskopsgatan

Brick. Tower (1694) added by
N. Tessin the Younger.

VISBY F3
on the island of Gotland

78 ST. MARIEN   1225
(cathedral)

•Of the other ninety-two
medieval churches on the island,
the following are recommended:
Lärbro (14th C; the centering
in the tower is still in position),
Dalhem (1250, restored ca. 1900),
Oja, and Roma.

Switzerland

Reformierte Kirche; *see entry 64*

Switzerland

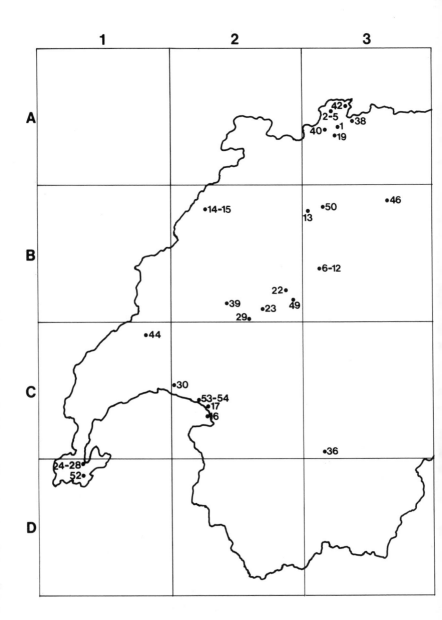

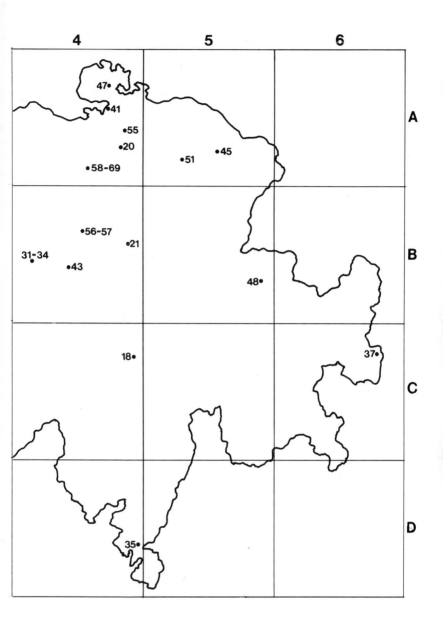

ARLESHEIM A3
7 km (4 mi) S of Basel

1 DOMKIRCHE   1680
(collegiate church)

Baroque. Remodeled in the
rococo style in 1771.

BASEL A3
(Basle/Bâle)

Museum: Öffentliche
Kunstsammlung, St.
Albangraben 16. Paintings by
Witz, Grünewald (*Dead
Christ*), Baldung, Holbein
(the Elder, the Younger, and
Ambrose), Rembrandt (*David
before Saul*), Caravaggio, and
others. Good representative
collection of 19th-c French
painters (Monet, Gauguin, etc.).
Also Picasso, Kandinsky, Klee,
and others.

2 MÜNSTER   12th c onward
(cathedral)
Münsterplatz

Rebuilt in the 15th c. Much
restored. Romanesque portal
(St. Gall) on the north side.

3 BADISCHER   1912–13
   BAHNHOF
(railway station)
H. Curjel and K. Moser

4 ANTONIUSKIRCHE   1926
(church)
Kannenfeldstrasse
K. Moser

Off shutter concrete throughout.
Traditional plan.

5 JOHANNESKIRCHE   1936
(church)
Metzerstrasse/Mülhauserstrasse
K. Egender and E. F. Burckhardt

BERN B3
(Berne)

Museum: Kunstmuseum,
Hodlerstrasse 12. 15th- to 20th-c
Swiss paintings, including the
Klee Foundation's collection
of works by Paul Klee. Also
works by Cézanne, Braque,
Picasso, etc.

6 MÜNSTER   1421–1573
(cathedral)
Münsterplatz

Gothic. The tower was completed
in 1893.

7 KANTONALES   1929–30
   SÄUGLINGSHEIM
(maternity home)
Freiburgstrasse 23
O. R. Salvisberg and
O. Brechbühl

8 SUVA HOUSE   1930–31
Laupenstrasse
O. R. Salvisberg and
O. Brechbühl

9 GEWERBESCHULE   1937–39
(trade school)
Lorrainestrasse 11
H. Brechbühler

Skillful massing and precise
detailing.

10 SIEDLUNG HALEN   1959–61
(housing estate)
Länggasse/Halenbrücke
5 km/3 mi N of the town center
Atelier 5

Well screened. An enormously
influential terraced row
housing scheme that makes full
use of a beautiful sloping site
overlooking the river.

11 ROW HOUSING   1970–72
Brunnadernstrasse 62–68
Atelier 5

12 SIEDLUNG THALMATT   1974
(housing estate)
Herrenschwanden, near Bern
Atelier 5

A further development on
Siedlung Halen (entry 10).

BETTLACH B3
8 km (5 mi) W of Solothurn

13 KATHOLISCHE   1965–68
   KIRCHE ST. KLEMENS
(church)
W. Foerderer

LA CHAUX-DE-
FONDS B2

14 FALLET HOUSE   1907
1 Chemin de Pouillerel
Le Corbusier

Le Corbusier's first building.
•Other houses by Le Corbusier
on this street are nos. 6, Stotzer
(1908); 8, Jaquemet (1908); 12,
Jeanneret (1912). The Schwob
house (1916) is at 167, rue du
Doubs.

15 CREMATORIUM   1908
   R. Belli and H. Robert

Splendid interior.

CHILLON C2
an island in Lac Lemán/Lake
Geneva

16 CHILLON   13th c onward
    CASTLE

CLARENS C2

17 VILLA KARMA   1904–6
   on the N shore of Lac Léman
   (Lake Geneva)
   A. Loos

Top floor added later.

DISENTIS C4

18 KLOSTERKIRCHE   1696–1712
   (abbey church)
   C. Moosbrugger

Extension of an 8th-c church.
Restored after 1799 (fire).

DORNACH A3
9 km (6 mi) S of Basel

19 GOETHEANUM II   1925–28
   R. Steiner

The center and architectural
statement of Steiner's
Anthroposophical Society. A
remarkable technical and
aesthetic achievement in off
shutter concrete. This replaced
the previous Goetheanum I
built in timber (burned in 1923).
On the grounds are other
expressionist houses, studios,
and an explicitly phallic boiler
house, all by O. F. Ebbell, the
chief structural engineer for
Goetheanum I and II.

EFFRETIKON A4

20 REFORMIERTE   1959–61
    KIRCHE
   (church)
   on the hilltop above the village
   E. Gisel

EINSIEDELN B4

21 KLOSTER   18th c
   (abbey)

Imposing semicircular entrance
court. The magnificent baroque
church (1719–35) is by C.
Moosbrugger, with decorations
by the Asam brothers and
others. Fürstensaal (great hall,
18th c) on second floor;
decoration by M. Roncati and J.
Brandenberg.

FLAMATT B2
12 km (7.5 mi) SE of Bern

22 APARTMENT   1957, 1960
    BUILDINGS
   on the road to Laupen
   Atelier 5

Breton brut after Le Corbusier.

FRIBOURG B2
(Freiburg)

23 ST. NICHOLAS   1283–17th c
   (cathedral)

15th-c tower. •North of the
cathedral is the Eglise des
Cordeliers (Franciscan church,
13th c onward) with an altarpiece
by the Masters of the Carnation.

GENÈVE D1
(Geneva/Genf/
Ginevra)

Museusm: Musée d'Art et
d'Histoire, 2, rue Charles
Galland. Paintings by Witz
(*Miraculous Draught of Fishes*),
Perroneau, Q. de la Tour,
Liotard, and others.
   Petit Palais (Musée d'Art
Moderne), 2, terasse St.-Victor.
Works by French painters and
foreign artists who worked in
Paris from 1880–1930.

24 CATHÉDRALE   10th–13th c
   ST.-PIERRE
   (cathedral)
   rue St.-Pierre

Neoclassic west doorway (1756)
by Alfieri.

25 MAISON CLARTÉ   1930–32
   (apartment building)
   2, rue St.-Laurent
   Le Corbusier

Duplex apartments. In poor
condition.

26 GROUPE SCOLAIRE   1952
    DU PARC GEISENDORF
   (school)
   rue de Lyon
   G. Brera and P. Waltenspuhl

Extended in 1956 and 1963.

27 APARTMENT   1956
    BUILDING
   8, avenue Miremont
   M. J. Saugey

28 STATION   1965–67
    D'ÉPURATION DES
    EAUX USÉES D'AIRE
   (sewage treatment plant)
   on the Rhone River
   G. Brera

HAUTERIVE ABBEY B2
7 km (4 mi) SW of Fribourg

29 HAUTERIVE   12th c onward
   ABBEY

Cistercian church (1160) with
14th-c stained glass windows.
The monastery buildings were
rebuilt in the 18th c. Baroque
facade.

LAUSANNE C2

Museum: Musée Cantonal des
Beaux-Arts, Palais de Rumine,
place de la Riponne 6. Many
Swiss works. Also Rembrandt,
Cézanne, Degas, and other
French impressionists.

30 CATHÉDRALE   1175–1232
   (cathedral)
   place de la Cathédrale

Gothic. Restored by E. E.
Viollet-le-Duc.

LUCERNE B4 (Luzern)

31 JESUITENKIRCHE   1667–77
   (church)
   Reuss-steg

32 PFARRKIRCHE   1694–98
   (parish church)
   Muri (on the outskirts of
   Lucerne)
   C. Moosbrugger

33 ST. KARL-KIRCHE   1930–31
   (church)
   St. Karlistrasse/St. Karlibrücke
   F. Metzger

34 WOHNHOCHHAUS   1965–68
   SCHÖNBÜHL
   (high-rise apartments)
   Langensandstrasse
   A. Aalto

LUGANO D4 (Lauis)

Museum: Villa Favorita,
Castagnola (just E of Lugano).
The Thyssen-Bornemisza
collection: 15th- to 19th-c
paintings by Dürer, Holbein,
Memling, Baldung, Raphael,
Titian, Fragonard, Boucher,
Rubens, etc.

35 BIBLIOTECA   1940
   CANTONALE
   (library)
   Parco Ciani
   R. Tami

MONTANA C3

36 BELLA LUI HOTEL   1931
   (former sanatorium)
   J. Itten and R. Steiger

MUSTAIR C2
3 km (2 mi) NE of Santa Maria

37 KIRCHE   8th c onward
   (church)

Basilican plan enlarged in the
15th c with Gothic side aisles.
9th- and 12th-c frescoes.

MUTTENZ A3
7 km (4 mi) E of Basel

38 SIEDLUNG   1919–21
   FREIDORF
   (housing)
   H. Meyer

PAYERNE B2 (Peterlingen)

39 KLOSTERKIRCHE   12th c
   (abbey church)

Romanesque. Recently restored.

REINACH A3
7 km (4 mi) S of Basel

40 EVANGELISCH-   1961–63
   REFORMIERTE KIRCHE
   (church)
   E. Gisel

RHEINAU A4

41 KLOSTERKIRCHE   1704–11
   (abbey church)
   Franz Beer

Baroque remodeling. The
abbey buildings are now a mental
hospital. Access to church only.

RIEHEN A3
5 km (3 mi) NE of Basel

42 KORNFELDKIRCHE   1964
   (church)
   W. Moser

RIGI KALTBAD B4

43 EVANGELISCH-   1963
   REFORMIERTE
   BERGKIRCHE
   (church)
   E. Gisel

ROMAINMÔTIER C1
8 km (5 mi) SW of Orbe

44 KIRCHE   12th–15th c
   (church)

After St. Pierre-le-Vieux (the
second abbey at Cluny, France).

ST. GALL A5 (Sankt Gallen)

45 KLOSTER   17th–18th c
   (former abbey)
   Gallusstrasse/Klosterhof

The last great baroque complex
to be built in Europe. Domkirche
(cathedral, 1755–68) by J. M.
Beer and P. Thumb. Superb
chancel. The Stiftsbibliothek
(abbey library, 1755–68), a
magnificent space, is by
Ferdinand Beer.

ST. URBAN B3
5 km (3 mi) NE of Langenthal

46 KLOSTERKIRCHE   1711–15
   (abbey church)
   Franz Beer

The abbey buildings are now
used as a clinic.

SCHAFFHAUSEN A4

47 MÜNSTER   12th c
(cathedral)
Münsterplatz

Romanesque. Plan derived from
Hirsau, Germany.

SCHIERS B5

48 SALGINATOBELBRÜCKE
(bridge)   1929–30
R. Maillart

SCHWARZENBURG B2

11 km (7 mi) E of Fribourg

49 SCHWANDBACHBRÜCKE
(bridge)   1933
R. Maillart

SOLOTHURN B3

Museum: Städtiches Museum,
Nordringstrasse. Noted for
The Virgin with Strawberries
(ca. 1410) and Holbein's
Solothurn *Madonna*.

50 KATHEDRALE   18th c
(St. Urs, cathedral)
Hauptgasse

Italianate baroque.

UZWIL A5

8 km (5 mi) SE of Wil

51 WALDBÜHL HOUSE   1903
M. H. Baillie Scott

Perfectly preserved. Original
furnishings.

VESSEY D1

S of Genève

52 PONT SUR L'ARVE   1936
(bridge)
R. Maillart

VEVEY C2 (Vivis)

53 VILLA JEANNERET   1923–25
(house)
route 21 to Lavaux, on Lac
   Léman (Lake Geneva)
Le Corbusier

Built for his parents.

54 BÂTIMENT   1960
ADMINISTRATIF NESTLÉ
(headquarters)
on the shore of Lac Léman
   (Lake Geneva), W of Vevey
J. Tschumi

Triple-spoked radial plan.
Aluminum cladding.

WINTERTHUR A4

Museums: Kunstmuseum,
Museumstrasse 52. Paintings by
Bonnard, van Gogh, Vuillard,
and others.
   Oskar Reinhart Collection
"Am Römerholz," Halden-
strasse 95. An unparalleled
private collection. Paintings by
Brueghel, Cranach, Rembrandt,
Rubens, Goya, El Greco,
Géricault, Manet, Cézanne, and
others.
   Stiftung Oskar Reinhart
Winterthur, Stadthausstrasse 6.
Swiss, German, and Austrian
paintings from the 18th c
onward.

55 SCHOOL   1965–67
Scheideggstrasse
U. J. Baumgartner

ZUG B4

56 ST. OSWALD   1478–ca. 1580
   KIRCHE
(church)
Oswaldsgasse

Late Gothic.

57 TERRASSENHÄUSER 1958–61
(terraced housing)
Terrassenweg
F. Stucky and R. Meuli

ZÜRICH A4

Tourist Information:
Verkehrsbüro, Bahnhofbrücke 1.
(tel. 211–1256).

Architect's Institute:
Schweizerischer Eingenieur und
Architekten-Verein,
Selnaustrasse 16 (tel. 201–1570).

Bookstore: Robert
Krauthammer, Predigerplatz 26.

Museums: Kunsthaus,
Heimplatz. Good collection of
18th- to 20th-c Swiss and
French paintings. Many works
by Munch and Giacometti.
   Rietberg Museum,
Gablerstrasse 15. Asiatic,
oriental, African, and pre-
Columbian works of art and
sculpture.
   Stiftung Sammlung E. G.
Bührle, Zollikerstrasse 172.
A superb collection of French
paintings by Corot, Monet,
Renoir, Sisley, and others. Also
17th- and 18th-c works.

58 GROSSMÜNSTER   11th–13th c
(cathedral)
Grossmünsterplatz *D3*

• Across the Münsterbrücke
(bridge) is the Fraumünster
(12th to 15th c) on
Münsterplatz.

Zürich

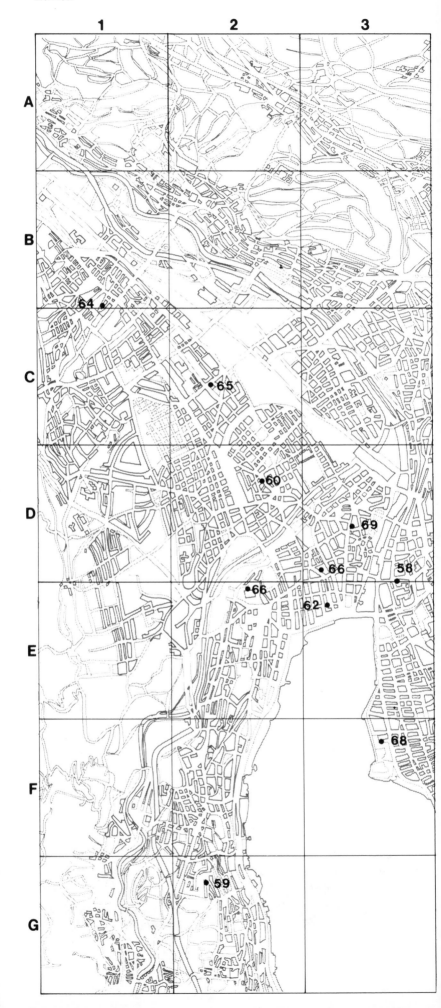

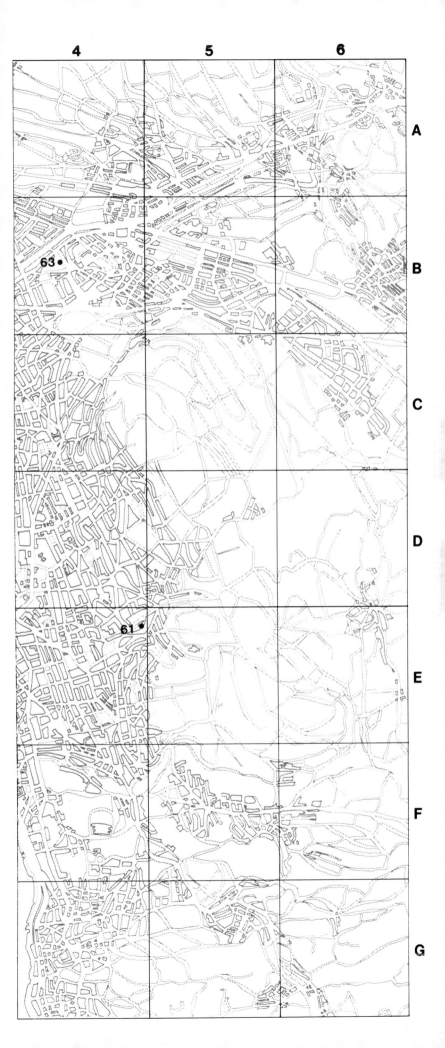

59 SIEDLUNG   1930–32
    NEUBÜHL
(housing estate)
Nidelbadstrasse, Zürich-
    Wollishofen *G2*
M. Haefeli, W. Moser,
E. Roth, R. Steiger,
C. Hubacher, P. Artaria,
and H. Schmidt

The Swiss modern movement
comes of age in this estate.

60 ZETTHAUS   1930
(multipurpose building)
Badénerstrasse 16 *D2*
R. Steiger and C. Hubacher

Offices, stores, cinema,
apartments, and a swimming
pool on the roof. This was one
of the first modern office
buildings in Switzerland
(financed by the architects).

61 APARTMENT   1935–36
    BUILDINGS
Doldertal 17–19 *E4*
A. and E. Roth and M. Breuer

Two luxurious apartment
buildings. Sophisticated planning and details.

62 KONGRESSHAUS   1937–39
(congress center)
General Guisan-Quai 18 *E3*
M. Haefeli, W. Moser, and
R. Steiger

•The IBM building next door is
by J. Schader (1973).

63 FREIBAD   1938–39
    ALLENMOOS
(swimming baths)
Ringstrasse *B4*
M. Haefeli and W. Moser

Open-air baths and pavilions.

64 REFORMIERTE   1941
    KIRCHE
(church)
Pfarrhausstrasse, Zürich-
    Altstetten *B1*
W. Moser

65 FELIX–UND–   1948–49
    REGULA-KIRCHE
(church)
Hardstrasse/Hirzelstrasse *C2*
F. Metzger

66 KANTONSCHULE   1959
    FREUDENBERG
(school)
Brandschenkestrasse *E2*
J. Schader

67 HOCHHAUS   1960–64
    "ZUR PALME"
(office building)
Bleicherweg 33 *D3*
M. Haefeli, W. Moser,
R. Steiger, and A. Studer

High-rise offices. Cruciform
plan.

68 CENTRE LE   1966–67
    CORBUSIER
in Zürichhorn park, off
    Höschgasse/Bellerivestrasse
    F3
Le Corbusier

An exhibition gallery commissioned by Heidi Weber.
Completed after Le Corbusier's
death.

69 OMEGA STORE   1975
Bahnhofstrasse 64 *D3*
A. Steger

Photograph
Acknowledgments

The following organizations and individuals provided the photographs listed (by entry number). All other photographs were taken by the author.

Architect's Co-Partnership: *Great Britain*: 147

Architectural Color Slides: *Austria*: Austria chapter opener, 1, 66, 100, 109, 110, 119b, 119j, 119l, 206. *Belgium*: 10a, 14, 20. *Denmark*: Denmark chapter opener, 25, 28, 33, 36, 68, 69, 94, 102, 104. *Finland*: Finland chapter opener, 12, 13, 41, 51, 55, 72. *France*: 3, 9, 15, 19, 30, 73, 77, 78, 104, 147, 158, Nîmes museum, 171, 172, 194, 196, 211, 220, 262, 297, 339, 344, 345, 377c, 377d, 394, 402, 405, 430, 432, 439, 463, 480. *Germany*: Germany chapter opener, 89, 197, 241, 246, 363. *Great Britain*: Great Britain chapter opener, 54, 55, 61, 62, 64, 111, 136, 150, 151, 176, 248, 249, 257, 259, 323, 374, 421, 470, 474, 477, 478, 502, 561, 638. *Italy*: 1, 21, 36, 56, 73, 81, Firenze museums, 84, 90, 92, 97, 119, 135, 145, 154, 162, 170, 229, 243, 255, 263, 284, 288, 300, 318, 319, 323, 325, 326, 329, 331, 334, 336, 338, 339, 344, 347, 348, 350, 351, 355, 358, 361, 391, 392, 393, 406, 430, 435, 439, 442, 455, 456, 467, 477, 478, 482, 489, 529, Venezia museums, 531, 531a, 531b, 537, 545, 547, 548, 554, 555, 556, 569, 570. *The Netherlands*: Netherlands chapter opener, 5, 89, 106, 108, 166. *Spain*: 118, 123g, 123m, 131, 133, 151, 236, 244. *Sweden*: Sweden chapter opener, 40, 41, 47, 49, 64. *Switzerland*: Switzerland chapter opener, 9, 16, 25, 52, 58, 59, 62, 63.

Atelier 5: *Switzerland*: 10, 12.

Austrian National Tourist Office: *Austria*: 2, 7, 14, 15, 41, 50, 56, 94a, 123, 127, 186, 208.

BBPR Architectural Studio: *Italy*: 198, 209.

P. Baumgarten: *Germany*: 501.

Jeff Bianco: *France*: France chapter opener, 377a. *Spain*: Spain chapter opener, 44, 228.

Belgium National Tourist Office: *Belgium*: 9, 25, 89, 92, 96, 100.

Jorgen Bo: *Denmark*: 20.

Jorgen Bo and V. Wohlert: *Denmark*: 124.

Lyons Israel Ellis: *Great Britain*: 491.

Figini and Pollini: *Italy*: 190.

Finnish National Tourist Office: *Finland*: 3, 27, 35, 47, 56, 75, 84, 143.

Norman Foster: *Great Britain*: 509, 548a, 622.

Revel Fox: *Denmark*: 78, 81. *Finland*: 94, 95. *France*: 18, 32, 62, 96, 358. *Germany*: 93, 96, 404. *Great Britain*: 58, 495, 562, 580, 616. *Italy*: Italy chapter opener, 215, 320, 337, 349, 398, 415. *The Netherlands*: 75. *Spain*: 123e, 217.

Maxwell Fry: *Great Britain*: 109, 468, 473.

Erno Goldfinger: *Great Britain*: 476.

Patrick Gwynne: *Great Britain*: 168.

Herman Hertzberger: *The Netherlands*: 54, 183.

Herman Hertzberger: *The Netherlands*: 54, 183.

Wilhelm Holzbauer: *Austria*: 74.

Howell, Killick, Partridge and Amis: *Great Britain*: 101.

Lucien Kroll: *Belgium*: 81.

Denys Lasdun: *Great Britain*: 106, 490, 507, 516, 548.

A. Mangiarotti: *Italy*: 125, 237.

R. Morandi: *Italy*: 443.

Gustave Peichl: *Austria*: 23, 71, 197.

P. Portughesi: *Italy*: 447.

Roland Rainer: *Austria*: 57. *Germany*: 340.

John Rennie: *Great Britain*: 164, 165, 494, 590, 650.

Alfred Roth: *Switzerland*: 61.

A. Ruusuvuori: *Finland*: 2, 14, 67, 85, 86, 162.

Kaija and Heikki Siren: *Austria*: 43. *Finland*, 53, 76.

Spanish National Tourist Office: *Spain*: 5, 9, 11, 50, 122, 126, 127, 129, 134, 140, 142, 193, 194, 195, 196, 197, 198, 203, 206, 208, 210, 218, 220, 231, 247, 251, 256, 269, 271.

James Stirling: *Great Britain*: 102, 201, 229, 486, 577, 595, 597.

O. M. Ungers: *Germany*: 318.

Pierre Vago: *France*: 136.

Henry Villet: *Finland*: 6, 46, 63, 121, 128.

Bernard Zehrfuss: *France*: 142, 356.

Bibliography

Ackerman, James S. *The Architecture of Michelangelo.* Harmondsworth and Baltimore: Penguin Books, 1970.

Adams, Henry. *Mont-Saint-Michel and Chartres.* New York: Doubleday, Anchor Books, 1959.

Anderson, William J., and Spiers, R. Phené. *The Architecture of Greece and Rome.* London: B. T. Batsford, 1907.

Arndt, Hervor van, et al. *The SAR Guide to Contemporary Swedish Architecture 1968–78.* Stockholm: National Association of Swedish Architects, 1978.

Bakema, J. B. *L. C. van der Vlugt.* Amsterdam: Meulenhoff, 1968.

Banham, Reyner. *Theory and Design in the First Machine Age.* London: Architectural Press, 1960.

———. *Age of the Masters.* London: Architectural Press, 1975.

Baroero, Claudio, et al. *Florence, Guide to the City.* Turin: Univis, 1979.

Baudon, Jaques Henry, et al. *Bruxelles Guide d'Architecture 1890–1972.* Brussels: Laconti, 1972.

Bazin, Germain. *Baroque and Rococo.* New York: Oxford University Press, 1964.

Benevolo, Leonardo. *The Origins of Modern Town Planning.* Cambridge, MA: M.I.T. Press, 1971.

———. *History of Modern Architecture.* 2 vols., rev. ed. Cambridge, MA: M.I.T. Press, 1971.

Blaser, Werner. *Mies van der Rohe.* London: Thames and Hudson, 1972.

Blijstra, R. *Dutch Architecture after 1900.* Amsterdam: P. N. van Kampen, 1966.

Blunt, Anthony. *Art and Architecture in France 1500–1700.* 2nd ed. Harmondsworth and Baltimore: Penguin Books, 1970.

Bock, Manfred; Singelenberg, Pieter. *Berlage.* Exhibition Catalog. The Hague: Haags Gemeentemuseum, 1975.

Boesiger, W., ed. *Le Corbusier Oeuvre complète.* 7 vols. Zurich: Verlag für Architektur Artemis, 1937–57.

Boëthius, Axel. *Etruscan and Early Roman Architecture.* Harmondsworth and Baltimore: Penguin Books, 1979.

Borsi, Franco; Portoghesi, Paolo. *Victor Horta.* Brussels: Vokaer, 1970.

Bremer, Jaap; Reedijk, Hein. *Bauen 20/40 Der Niederländische Beitrag zum Neuen Bauen.* Exhibition Catalog. Eindhoven: Van Abbemuseum, 1971.

Briggs, Martin S. *Everyman's Concise Encyclopedia of Architecture.* London: J. M. Dent and Sons, 1959.

Brown, Theodore M. *The Work of G. Rietveld, Architect.* Cambridge, MA: M.I.T. Press, 1958.

Burkom, Frans van, and Wit, Wim de. *Amsterdamse School.* Exhibition Catalog. Amsterdam: Stedelijk Museum, 1975.

Camesasca, Ettore. *History of the House.* New York: G. P. Putnam's Sons, 1971.

Casciato, Maristella, et al. *Architektuur en volkshuisvesting, Nederland 1879–1940.* Nijmegen: Socialisties Uitgeverij Nijmegen, 1980.

Chase, Post, and Pope. *European Architecture.* vols 1–3. Cambridge, MA: The University Prints.

Cirlot, Juan-Eduardo. *Guadi.* Barcelona: Editorial RM, 1966.

Collins, George R.; Elfers, Joost; and Schuyt, Michael. *Fantastic Architecture.* New York: Harry N. Abrams, 1980.

Connant, Kenneth John. *Carolingian and Romanesque Architecture 800–1200.* 4th ed. rev. Harmondsworth and Baltimore: Penguin Books, 1979.

Coombs, Robert, ed. *Perspecta Thirteen and Fourteen.* New Haven: Perspecta; The Yale Architectural Journal, 1971.

Delevoy, Robert-L., et al. *Bruxelles 1900, Capitale de l'Art Nouveau.* Exhibition Catalog. Brussels: Hôtel van de Velde, 1972.

Dixon, Roger; Muthesius, Stefan. *Victorian Architecture.* New York: Oxford University Press, 1978.

Dogo, Giuliano. *Guide to Artistic Italy.* Milan: Electa, 1981.

Egelius, Mats. *Ralph Erskine.* AD Profiles 9. London: Architectural Design, 1977.

Emanuel, Muriel, ed. *Contemporary Architects.* New York: St. Martin's Press, 1980.

Fawcett, Jane, ed. *Seven Victorian Architects.* London: Thames and Hudson, 1976.

Finnish Architecture. Exhibition Catalog. The Hague: Museum of Finnish Architecture and the Netherlands Congress Center, 1975.

Fleig, Karl, ed. *Alvar Aalto.* vols 1–2. Zurich: Verlag für Architektur Artemis, 1963 and 1971.

Fleming, John; Honour, Hugh; and Pevsner, Nikolaus. *The Penguin Dictionary of Architecture.* 2nd ed. Harmondsworth and Baltimore: Penguin Books, 1972.

Fletcher, Banister F. *A History of Architecture.* 18th ed. New York: Charles Scribner's Sons, 1975.

Frampton, Kenneth. *Modern Architecture, A Critical History.* New York: Oxford University Press, 1980.

Frankl, Paul. *Gothic Architecture.* Harmondsworth and Baltimore: Penguin Books, 1962.

Gardner, Helen. *Art Through the Ages.* 5th ed. Revised by Horst de la Croix and Richard G. Tansey. New York: Harcourt, Brace & World, 1970.

Gerson, H.; Kuile, E. H. ter. *Art and Architecture in Belgium 1600–1800.* Harmondsworth and Baltimore: Penguin Books, 1960.

Giedion, Sigfried. *Space, Time and Architecture.* 5th ed. Cambridge, MA: Harvard University Press, 1967.

Girsberger, Hans; Adler, Florian, eds. *Architekturführer Schweiz.* Zurich: Verlag für Architektur Artemis, 1969.

Graham, F. Lanier. *Hector Guimard.* Exhibition Catalog. New York: Museum of Modern Art, 1970.

Haagsma, Ids, et al. *Amsterdamse Gebouwen 1880–1980.* Utrecht: Het Spectrum, 1981.

Hefting, Paul; Leeuwen, Tom van; and Woud, Auke van der. *Americana.* Exhibition Catalog. Otterlo: Rijksmuseum Kröller-Muller, 1975.

Hempel, Eberhard. *Baroque Art and Architecture in Central Europe.* Harmondsworth and Baltimore: Penguin Books, 1965.

Herbst, René. *Pierre Chareau.* Paris: Editions du Salon des Art Ménagers, 1954.

Heydenreich, Ludwig H.; Lotz, Wolfgang. *Architecture in Italy 1400–1600.* Harmondsworth and Baltimore: Penguin Books, 1974.

Hibbard, Howard. *Bernini.* Harmondsworth and Baltimore: Penguin Books, 1965.

Hitchcock, Henry-Russell. *Rococo Architecture in Southern Germany.* London: Phaidon, 1968.

———. *Architecture, Nineteenth and Twentieth Centuries.* 3rd ed. rev. Harmondsworth and Baltimore: Penguin Books, 1971.

Hitchcock, Henry-Russell; Johnson, Philip. *The International Style.* New York: Norton, 1966.

Hoffmann, Gretl. *Reiseführer zur Modernen Architektur.* Stuttgart: Julius Hoffmann Verlag, 1968.

Honour, Hugh. *Neo-classicism.* Harmondsworth and Baltimore: Penguin Books, 1968.

Hoskins, W. G. *The Making of the English Landscape.* Harmondsworth and Baltimore: Penguin Books, 1970.

Jaffe, Hans L. C. *De Stijl.* London: Thames and Hudson, 1970.

Jencks, Charles. *Modern Movements in Architecture.* New York: Doubleday, Anchor Press, 1973.

Kalnein, Wend Graf; Levey, Michael. *Art and Architecture of the Eighteenth Century in France.* Harmondsworth and Baltimore: Penguin Books, 1972.

Kightly, Charles. *Strongholds of the Realm*. London: Thames and Hudson, 1979.

Kinder, Herman; Hilgemann, Werner. *The Anchor Atlas of World History*. vols 1–2. New York: Doubleday, Anchor Press, 1974.

Kubler, George; Soria, Martin. *Art and Architecture in Spain and Portugal and their American Dominions 1500–1800*. Harmondsworth and Baltimore: Penguin Books, 1959.

Lavedan, Pierre. *French Architecture*. Harmondsworth and Baltimore: Penguin Books, 1956.

Linn, Björn, et al. *SAR Guide to Stockholm*. Stockholm: Byggmästarens Förlag, 1966.

McKean, Charles; Jestico, Tom. *Guide to Modern Buildings in London*. London: Academy Editions, 1976.

Meeks, Carroll, L. V. *Italian Architecture 1750–1914*. New Haven: Yale University Press, 1966.

Mulder, Bertus; Rook, Gerrit Jan de. *Rietveld Schröder Huis 1925–1975*. Exhibition Catalog. Utrecht: 1975.

Murray, Linda and Peter. *The Penguin Dictionary of Art and Artists*. 4th ed. Harmondsworth and Baltimore: Penguin Books, 1976.

Muschenheim, William. *Elements of the Art of Architecture*. London: Thames and Hudson, 1965.

Norberg-Schulz, Christian. *Existence, Space and Architecture*. London: Studio Vista, 1971.

———. *Late Baroque and Rococo Architecture*. New York: Harry N. Abrams, 1974.

———. *Meaning in Western Architecture*. London: Studio Vista, 1975.

Pevsner, Nikolaus. *An Outline of European Architecture*. 7th ed. rev. Harmondsworth and Baltimore: Penguin Books, 1963.

Portoghesi, Paolo. *Roma Barocca: The History of an Architectonic Culture*. Cambridge, MA: M.I.T. Press, 1970.

Puttemans, Pierre. *Modern Architecture in Belgium*. Brussels: Vokaer, 1976.

Rasmussen, Steen Eiler. *Experiencing Architecture*. Cambridge: MA: M.I.T. Press, 1962.

———. *Towns and Buildings*. Cambridge, MA: M.I.T. Press, 1969.

———. *London: The Unique City*. Cambridge, MA: M.I.T. Press, 1974.

Robertson, Charles. *Bath: An Architectural Guide*. London: Faber and Faber, 1975.

Rosenberg, Jakob; Slive, Seymour; and Kuile, E. H. ter. *Dutch Art and Architecture 1600–1800*. 3rd ed. Harmondsworth and Baltimore: Penguin Books, 1977.

Russel, Frank, ed. *Art Nouveau Architecture*. New York: Rizzoli, 1979.

Salokorpi, Asko. *Modern Architecture in Finland*. New York: Praeger, 1970.

Schein I. *Paris construit*. 2nd ed. Paris: Editions Vincent, Fréal et Co., 1970.

Service, Alastair. *Edwardian Architecture*. New York: Oxford University Press, 1977.

Service, Alastair; Bradbery, Jean. *Megaliths and Their Mysteries*. New York: Macmillan Publishing Co., 1979.

Sharp, Dennis. *Modern Architecture and Expressionism*. New York: George Braziller, 1966.

———. *A Visual History of Twentieth-Century Architecture*. London: Heinemann/Secker & Warburg, 1972.

———. ed. *The Rationalists*. London: Architectural Press, 1978.

Skriver, Poul Erik, ed. *Guide to Modern Danish Architecture*. Copenhagen: Arkitektens Forlag, 1973.

Smithson, Alison, ed. *Team 10 Primer*. Cambridge, MA: M.I.T. Press, 1974.

Summerson, John. *Inigo Jones*. Harmondsworth and Baltimore: Penguin Books, 1966.

———. *Architecture in Britain 1530–1830*. 6th ed. Harmondsworth and Baltimore: Penguin Books, 1977.

———. *The Classical Language of Architecture*. London: Thames and Hudson, 1980.

Tempel, Egon. *New Finnish Architecture*. London: Architectural Press, 1968.

Venturi, Robert. *Complexity and Contradiction in Architecture*. New York: Museum of Modern Art, 1966.

Ward-Perkins, J. B. *Roman Imperial Architecture.* Harmondsworth and Baltimore: Penguin Books, 1981.

Watkin, David. *English Architecture: A Concise History.* New York: Oxford University Press, 1979.

Webb, Geoffrey. *Architecture in Britain, The Middle Ages.* 2nd ed. Harmondsworth and Baltimore: Penguin Books, 1965.

White, John. *Art and Architecture in Italy 1250–1400.* Harmondsworth and Baltimore: Penguin Books, 1966.

Wickberg, Nils Erik. *Finnish Architecture.* Helsinki: Otava, 1962.

Wittkower, Rudolf. *Art and Architecture in Italy 1600–1750.* 2nd ed. rev. Harmondsworth and Baltimore: Penguin Books, 1965.

——. *Gothic vs. Classic.* New York: George Braziller, 1974.

——. *Idea and Image.* London: Thames and Hudson, 1978.

Wodehouse, Lawrence. *British Architects, 1840–1976.* Detroit: Gale, 1978.

Wrede, Stuart. *The Architecture of Erik Gunnar Asplund.* Cambridge, MA: M.I.T. Press, 1980.

Yorke, Francis Reginald Stevens. *The Modern House in England.* London: Architectural Press, 1947.

Index of Architects and Artists

This index lists the architects and artists in this book by *entry number*. The following abbreviations are used:

A: Austria
B: Belguim
D: Denmark
F: Finland
Fr: France
G: Germany

GB: Great Britain
I: Italy
N: The Netherlands
Sp: Spain
Sw: Sweden
S: Switzerland

Index of Cities
and Towns

This index lists the cities and towns in this book by *page number.*

Notes

Notes

Notes

Notes

Notes